The Ohio Politics Almanac

THE
Ohio Politics
ALMANAC
SECOND EDITION

BY MICHAEL F. CURTIN

IN COLLABORATION
WITH JULIA BARRY BELL

The Kent State University Press
Kent, Ohio

© 2006 by The Kent State University Press, Kent, Ohio 44242
Library of Congress Catalog Card Number 95-37710
ISBN-10   0-87338-889-5
ISBN-131978-0-87338-889-4
Manufactured in the United States of America
10 09 08 07 06   5 4 3 2

Second Edition

The Library of Congress has cataloged the earlier edition as follows:

Curtin, Michael F., 1951–
    The Ohio politics almanac / by Michael F. Curtin in collaboration
with Julia Barry Bell.
        p.   cm.
    Includes bibliographical references and index.
    ISBN 0-87338-540-3 (pbk. : alk.) ∞
    1. Ohio—Politics and government—Handbooks, manuals, etc.
2. Politicians—Ohio—Biography.   I. Bell, Julia Barry, 1965–.
II. Title.
JK5531.C87 1996
320.9771—dc20
                                                            95-37710
                                                            CIP

British Library Cataloging-in-Publication data are available.

Contents

Preface   vii

1.	Ohio's Political Heritage	1
2.	Presidential Elections	7
3.	The Ohio Presidents	15
4.	Governors of Ohio	25
5.	The Ohio General Assembly	65
6.	The Ohio Judiciary	71
7.	The Ohio Constitution	79
8.	Democrats and Republicans	85
9.	Ohio's Political Demographics	97
10.	Ohio's Counties	115
11.	Ohio's Cities	163
12.	Ohio by the Numbers	183

Appendix A: An Ohio Politics Timeline   197

Appendix B: Major Officeholders   199

Appendix C: Ohio Representation in the
U.S. House of Representatives   207

Appendix D: Campaign Expenditures for
State Executive Offices   208

Bibliography   211

Index of Names   213

Preface

The original edition of *The Ohio Politics Almanac* was published in 1996. It was a product of a political reporter's frustration. During many years of covering local and state government and politics for the *Columbus Dispatch*, I frequently found myself searching for just the right piece of information under deadline: What was the political division of the Ohio legislature in a given year? When were Ohio's constitutional conventions held? How have the various regions of Ohio differed in presidential elections? The goal was to create a helpful, single-source guide to Ohio government and politics that would answer these and many other questions.

Graphic designer Julia Barry Bell and I hoped to produce an attractive, easy-to-use reference that would appeal to journalists, elected officials, lobbyists, students and teachers of Ohio government and politics, and anyone with a passing interest in the state's political heritage.

Encouraged by the reception given the first edition, we have updated the text in this new edition to reflect the events of another decade in Ohio's political life. We hope it will be an invaluable addition to the state's newsrooms, schools, and libraries. We also hope it will encourage more Ohioans to take an active interest in the rich civic and political life of their state.

Michael F. Curtin

CHAPTER 1

Ohio's Political Heritage

THEY WERE FARMERS AND FRONTIERSMEN
WHO DISTRUSTED STRONG CENTRAL GOVERNMENT,
WHICH THEY SAW AS REMOVED, ELITIST, AND
CONTROLLED BY POWERFUL FINANCIAL INTERESTS.

For most of its history, Ohio has held a pivotal place in the national political landscape.

At the nation's founding, the 981-mile Ohio River was the primary route westward into the vast interior and the promise of America. The river ensured that pioneers who ventured into the Northwest Territory would come into the lands that would become Ohio. It also ensured that, with the river as its southern boundary, Ohio essentially would be settled from the south up. It explains why a southern community, Chillicothe, would become Ohio's first capital.

The first permanent white settlement in Ohio was along the river, at Marietta in April of 1788. The settlers were members of the Ohio Company of Associates and the first of many to claim land bounties in Ohio in exchange for their service in the Revolutionary War.

This first settlement occurred just seven months after adoption of the federal Constitution in Philadelphia, and while the original 13 states were in the process of ratification. The early pioneers largely were from the New England states and were descendants of English Protestants. Those who had made their way into the rich Ohio lands knew that the territory would attract many. In 1790, an estimated 4,200 people lived between the western boundary of Pennsylvania and the Mississippi River. By 1800, at the taking of the second national census, Ohio's population already had grown to 45,365.

DEMOCRATIC-REPUBLICANS TAKE POWER

A majority of the men who took part in public affairs in Ohio's earliest days identified with the Democratic-Republican Party of Thomas Jefferson. They were farmers and frontiersmen

Major Political Parties in the U.S.

Year	
1789	
1792	Federalists
1796	Democratic-Republican
1800	
1804	
1808	
1812	
1816	
1820	
1824	
1828	National Republicans
1832	Democrats
1836	Whigs
1840	
1844	
1848	
1852	
1856	Republicans
1860	
1864	
1868	
1872	
1876	
1880	
1884	
1888	
1892	
1896	
1900	
1904	
1908	
1912	
1916	
1920	
1924	
1928	
1932	
1936	
1940	
1944	
1948	
1952	
1956	
1960	
1964	
1968	
1972	
1976	
1980	
1984	
1988	
1992	
1996	
2000	
2004	

Source: Adapted from Congressional Quarterly, Guide to U.S. Elections (1975), p. 176.

who distrusted strong central government, which they saw as removed, elitist, and controlled by powerful financial interests. The early Ohioans favored statehood to ensure close-to-home representation.

The Federalists, members of the party of George Washington and Alexander Hamilton, opposed statehood for Ohio. One of them, Gen. Arthur St. Clair, had been appointed in 1788 by Congress as governor of the Territory of Ohio. St. Clair vetoed many bills of the territorial legislature, controlled by members of the Democratic-Republican Party, and otherwise frustrated the aims of the majority. Growing opposition to his rule soon would result in his ouster. Thomas Worthington, a leader of the Democratic-Republicans, accomplished that by filing charges against St. Clair with President Jefferson in 1802 at about the time Congress was passing an act to enable the people of Ohio to form a constitution and state government.

On November 1, 1802, an Ohio Constitutional Convention began meeting in Chillicothe. Of the 35 delegates there, 26 were members of the Democratic-Republican Party. Seven were Federalists. The affiliations of the two others are unknown. The dominance of the Democratic-Republican Party at Ohio's founding also is underscored by the fact that the state's first seven governors were members of it.

The experience under St. Clair was the major reason the drafters of Ohio's first constitution made sure that the document severely limited the governor's powers. For example, it gave the governor no veto authority. This initial distrust of strong, centralized authority would become engrained in the state's political culture. For decades to come, analysts would describe Ohio politics in terms of a suspicion toward government, an antitax sentiment, and a conservative outlook.

On February 19, 1803, Ohio was admitted into the

Union as the 17th state, after Tennessee and before Louisiana. Ohio's admission came one month after Edward Tiffin of Chillicothe was elected Ohio's first governor.

The members of the Democratic-Republican Party often referred to themselves as Republicans. Their opponents, though, frequently referred to them as Democrats, because the word democrat at the time carried negative connotations of mob rule identified with the French Revolution. Even today, some references to Ohio politics refer to the early governors as Democrats while others refer to them as Republicans. In fact, they were Democratic-Republicans.

RISE OF THE WHIGS

In the 1820s, the party shortened its name to the Democratic Party under the leadership of Andrew Jackson, who emphasized the rule of the common man. The Federalist Party had ceased to be a factor in national and state elections. Jackson was elected president in 1828 and reelected in 1832, and carried Ohio in both elections. Jacksonian democracy blossomed in the 1830s and 1840s.

In the 1830s, the Whig Party—the party of Henry Clay—arose to challenge the Jacksonian Democrats in Ohio and nationally. The Whigs were named after the English political party that opposed a monarchy and supported parliamentary power. Although derided by the Jacksonians as the party of wealth, the Whigs attracted a diverse following.

In Ohio, Whigs soon outnumbered Democrats in most parts of the state. Three of the first four mayors of Cleveland were Whigs, as were five of the first seven mayors of Cincinnati. In 1836, Joseph Vance of Champaign County became the first Whig governor of Ohio. And from 1844 to 1850, the state had three successive Whigs as governors. The Whigs won the presidency in 1840 and 1848. In 1844, Ohio went for Henry Clay in the presidential election, although he lost to Democrat James K. Polk.

Nationally, the Whig Party disintegrated between 1852 and 1854, while 1853 marked the end for it in Ohio, when Nelson Barrere was the party's final challenger for governor. The Whigs'

decline coincided with the emergence of slavery as the dominant issue of national politics. Proslavery Whigs found more comfort in the Democratic Party; antislavery Whigs were instrumental in founding the modern Republican Party.

Until the 1850s, the majority of those moving into Ohio settled in the southern half of the state, especially on the Ohio Company lands in the southeast and the Virginia Military District in the southwest. Cincinnati, on the Ohio River, was by far the state's largest city. In the 1850 census, Cincinnati's population was recorded at 115,436, compared to 17,882 for Columbus and 17,034 for Cleveland.

Between 1800 and 1830, the English, Scots, and Irish dominated the ethnic groups moving into Ohio. The Welsh were especially noticeable in the southern counties of Jackson, Scioto, Gallia, Lawrence, and Meigs. The movement had been so great that by 1840 Ohio was the third-largest state in the Union, behind New York and Pennsylvania. The state was entitled to 19 congressmen and 21 presidential electors, making it a force in national politics.

By midcentury, the Germans had come in droves to Ohio and the Midwest. They made up the largest ethnic group in the state, followed by the Irish. Cincinnati virtually became a German city. In the 1850 census, about as many Cincinnatians listed Germany as their place of birth as listed Ohio.

From the mid-1800s until today, Germans have remained the largest single nationality group in Ohio. Besides building Cincinnati, Germans for the most part established Alliance, Canton, Columbus, Lancaster, Massillon, and Steubenville.

THE NATIONAL ROAD

As people poured into Ohio and on to other western destinations, the need for improved roads became more evident. In 1806, Congress gave final approval to legislation authorizing construction of the nation's first federal highway—a National Road from Cumberland, Md., to Ohio. Money had been set aside from the sale of public lands. Construction had begun in 1811 but was

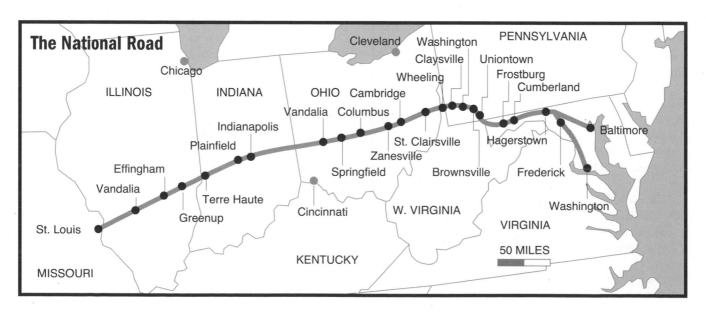

The National Road

2

largely interrupted until 1815 because of the War of 1812.

The National Road, later called the Cumberland Road and eventually U.S. Route 40, reached Wheeling, W.Va., in 1818 and was extended to Columbus by 1833. By 1840, the road had been completed through Ohio. A large share of the nation's westward travelers had to come to, or at least through, Ohio. The road, completed in 1856, eventually stretched to St. Louis.

In time, U.S. Route 40 would come to signify Ohio's political dividing line, separating a more highly urbanized, more ethnic, Democratic north from a more traditional, more conservative, Republican south. When the interstate highway system was developed, I-70 was laid out alongside Route 40 and inherited the role of demarcation line.

THE CANAL ERA

Although the National Road was extremely important to the development of Ohio, the state's early leaders recognized that much of the state's interior—especially the north—would not develop and prosper without better ways to cheaply move products to markets.

Taking notice of the success of New York's Erie Canal, begun in 1817 and opened in 1825, Ohio's political and business leaders made plans for a system of canals to link Lake Erie with the Ohio River. Canal construction began in July 1825. The Ohio & Erie Canal was completed from Portsmouth to Cleveland in 1833; the Miami & Erie Canal was completed from Cincinnati to Toledo in 1845.

The birth of the canal system brought more waves of immigrants and triggered the development of cities along their routes. In 1825, for example, Cleveland had fewer than 1,000 residents, mostly native-born. By 1850, after Ohio's canal system was completed and in full operation, Cleveland's population exceeded 17,000 and would continue to boom for decades as the city became a major port.

The selection of Cleveland as the northern terminus for the Ohio & Erie Canal is a major reason—perhaps the primary reason—that it eventually developed into Ohio's largest and most ethnically diverse metropolitan area. Some argue that Sandusky, Port Clinton, or any number of other lakefront cities could have developed into the state's largest if chosen as a canal terminus.

Ohio's location as gateway to the West also ensured that the state would attract many railroads, which replaced canals as the favored means of transport in the second half of the 19th century. In 1860, Ohio ranked first in the nation in length of rail lines. The rails especially speeded the development of Cleveland, Toledo, and the rest of northern Ohio.

The Canals of Ohio

Toledo
Cleveland
Defiance
PENNSYLVANIA OHIO CANAL
Akron
Youngstown
Canton
SANDY BEAVER CANAL
MIAMI & ERIE CANAL
OHIO & ERIE CANAL
Columbus
Canal Winchester
Dayton
Lancaster
HOCKING CANAL
Chillicothe
Cincinnati
Portsmouth

THE REPUBLICAN PARTY IS BORN

In the early 1850s, as Ohio's population surpassed two million, the Whig Party was disintegrating and proslavery elements controlled the Democratic Party. This prompted groups opposed to the extension of slavery, including many Whigs and antislavery Democrats, to begin efforts to organize another party.

On July 13, 1854, the 67th anniversary of passage of the Northwest Ordinance, state Republican nominating conventions were held in Ohio, Indiana, Wisconsin, and Vermont. Although those at the Ohio convention did not adopt the name *Republican* at that meeting, the *Ohio State Journal* referred to them as Republicans. The following year, during a convention on July 13, 1855, the name "Republican Party of Ohio" was officially adopted. The party's chief issues were opposition to the extension of slavery and economic conservatism.

In its first year, the Republican Party took control of the state legislature; by 1860, it controlled all statewide offices.

The 1856 presidential election had been won by Democrat James Buchanan, but Ohio went for Republican John C. Frèmont, who received 48.5 percent of the vote to Buchanan's 44 percent. The 1856 vote marked the first of 14 consecutive presidential elections in which Ohio voted Republican. The string would not be broken until 1912, when Ohio joined the nation in electing Democrat Woodrow Wilson. In the presidential elections from 1856 to 1992, the nation went Democratic three times without Ohio's help: 1856 (Buchanan); 1884 (Grover Cleveland); 1892 (Cleveland).

During the Civil War, Ohio's Republican Party went out of operation and the Union Party controlled state politics. The Union Party, which emphasized the paramount importance of saving the Union, was made up mostly of the Republican Party and one wing of the Democratic Party. In contrast, the Democratic state convention, held in Columbus on January 23, 1861, approved a resolution stating that war "should not be waged for the purpose of overthrowing the established institutions of the states."

Following the war, Ohio Republicans supported and Ohio Democrats opposed ratification of the 15th Amendment—to grant Negro suffrage. In 1867, the Ohio Democratic platform stated: "We are opposed to Negro suffrage believing that it would be productive of evil to both whites and blacks and tend to produce a disastrous conflict of races." The amendment was ratified on February 3, 1870.

Republicans continued to be the majority party in Ohio into the 1870s, but in 1873 Democrats elected their first governor in 20 years, William Allen. Despite that victory and some others, Democrats were not truly competitive with Republicans in Ohio until after the turn of the century, a time of massive immigration of the foreign-born into the state.

In the final third of the 19th century, five of the six presidents elected by the people were Ohio-born. All five were Republicans: Ulysses S. Grant, Rutherford B. Hayes, James A. Garfield, Benjamin Harrison, and William McKinley.

NORTHEASTERN OHIO BOOMS

The development of Cleveland and northeastern Ohio in the late 1800s and early 1900s dramatically changed the political complexion of the state. Until the 20th century, the 14 counties that made up the Connecticut Western Reserve were populated mostly by descendants of New Englanders who identified with the Whigs and Republicans.

But Ohio was becoming an industrial dynamo, and the factories

The Building of Ohio

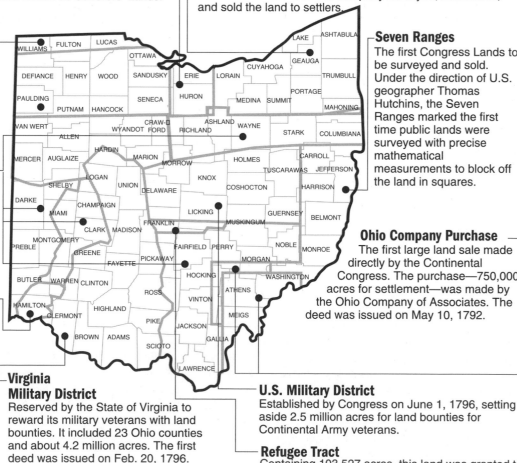

The Fire Lands
On May 10, 1792, the Connecticut legislature set aside 500,000 acres of the Western Reserve to compensate people whose property was destroyed by fire from British raids on Connecticut towns. This section of Ohio also was known as Sufferers' Lands.

Connecticut Western Reserve
Like Virginia, Connecticut had been given a great stretch of western land by a British monarch. When Connecticut ceded its land claim to the United States in 1786, it reserved about 3.3 million acres and later sold them to the Connecticut Land Co. The company surveyed, subdivided, and sold the land to settlers.

The Michigan Survey
The land claimed by both Ohio and the Territory of Michigan in a dispute that nearly triggered a war in 1835. Congress settled the conflict in Ohio's favor.

Seven Ranges
The first Congress Lands to be surveyed and sold. Under the direction of U.S. geographer Thomas Hutchins, the Seven Ranges marked the first time public lands were surveyed with precise mathematical measurements to block off the land in squares.

Congress Lands
Lands acquired by the federal government from the states and from Indians, surveyed into townships, and sold to raise money for the government.

Ohio Company Purchase
The first large land sale made directly by the Continental Congress. The purchase—750,000 acres for settlement—was made by the Ohio Company of Associates. The deed was issued on May 10, 1792.

The Symmes Purchase
Sometimes called the Miami Purchase, this land buy of 311,682 acres was made by Judge John Cleves Symmes and his associates. The deed was issued Sept. 30, 1794.

Virginia Military District
Reserved by the State of Virginia to reward its military veterans with land bounties. It included 23 Ohio counties and about 4.2 million acres. The first deed was issued on Feb. 20, 1796.

U.S. Military District
Established by Congress on June 1, 1796, setting aside 2.5 million acres for land bounties for Continental Army veterans.

Refugee Tract
Containing 103,527 acres, this land was granted to refugees from Canada and Nova Scotia who helped the American cause in the Revolutionary War.

4

of Cleveland, Akron, and Youngstown in northeastern Ohio were attracting an ethnic work force of Slavs, Italians, Greeks, and Scandinavians as well as more Germans and Irish. Similar immigration patterns were transforming cities outside northeastern Ohio, especially Toledo and Dayton.

By 1910, Ohio's population was nearing five million and, for the first time, more than half its population lived in cities rather than in rural areas. The combination of industrialization, immigration, and urbanization created a competitive marketplace for the Democratic Party in statewide elections and enabled the party to eventually dominate the large cities of the north.

In no small way, the Democratic upsurge in Ohio also benefited from the realignment of political affiliations—especially among blacks—triggered by the Great Depression. From 1870, when blacks cast their first votes in Ohio, until the 1930s, most black Ohioans were firmly aligned with the Republican Party, which had been the party of emancipation.

But the Depression cast the Republican Party as the party of economic calamity, and President Franklin D. Roosevelt cast the Democratic Party as the party of jobs and economic survival. Ever since, a sizable majority of black voters in Ohio has been firmly aligned with the Democratic Party.

This realignment coincided with a marked growth of Ohio's black population. Until 1920, blacks had not accounted for more than 3 percent of the state's residents. However, the period between World War I and World War II witnessed large-scale migration of blacks from the South to northern cities, including some in Ohio. By 1950, blacks made up 6.5 percent of the state's population. By 1980, the black share had grown to 10 percent. It was 11.5 percent in 2000.

The evolution of the Democratic Party's competitiveness after 1900 can be shown best, perhaps, by comparing the results of gubernatorial elections before and after the turn of the century. In the period from 1855 (the first gubernatorial election following the birth of the modern Republican Party) to 1899, Republicans won 18 of 23 Ohio gubernatorial elections. In gubernatorial elections from 1900 through 2002, Democrats have won 22 to Republicans' 18.

POLITICAL BALANCE OF POWER

Besides providing political balance in statewide elections, the diversification of Ohio's population in the 20th century enabled the state to become something of a political barometer for the entire nation. By the mid-1900s, political scientists had come to identify Ohio as a national microcosm. For most of the 20th century, Ohio

THE COMBINATION OF INDUSTRIALIZATION, IMMIGRATION, AND URBANIZATION CREATED A COMPETITIVE MARKETPLACE FOR THE DEMOCRATIC PARTY IN STATEWIDE ELECTIONS AND ENABLED THE PARTY TO EVENTUALLY DOMINATE THE LARGE CITIES OF THE NORTH

indeed mirrored the nation as closely as any state. On most demographic counts, Ohio did not differ from national averages by more than a percentage point or two.

Ohio's reputation as a barometer was enhanced by the state's performance in presidential elections. In the 20th century, Ohioans voted for the national winner 23 times in 25 presidential elections. In the 19th century, Ohioans voted for the national winner 18 times in 25 elections.

Ohio's status as a political laboratory also stemmed from the state's multiplicity of large and medium-sized cities. Ohio has never had a dominant city, like Michigan's Detroit or Illinois's Chicago. In 1870, Cincinnati accounted for 8 percent of the state's population, and by 1920 Cleveland had grown rapidly enough to represent nearly 14 percent of Ohio's residents. That's as dominant as any Ohio city has become in the state's history. Columbus, Ohio's largest city in 2000, accounted for just over 6 percent of the state's population.

By 1930, Ohio had six cities of more than 200,000 population, another two cities of more than 100,000 population, and 49 others of at least 10,000 population. With no large urban area able to dominate the state's politics, Ohio long has required candidates to appeal to a cross-section of voters from border to border. In the 2000 census, Ohio's ten largest counties accounted for about 54 percent of the state's population.

CHALLENGE OF READJUSTMENT

In recent decades, Ohio, like the rest of the industrial Midwest, has struggled with the decline of its aging manufacturing base, the loss of manufacturing jobs, and the lack of population growth. Manufacturing's share of employment in Ohio peaked at 53 percent during World War II and has been declining since. Total employment in goods-producing, blue-collar jobs reached its zenith in 1969.

By the 1970s, it was clear that Ohio no longer could claim bragging rights as the center of national economic and political activity. As jobs and population moved south and west, Ohio and its midwestern neighbors sought ways to readjust their economies to counter the Rust Belt label they had acquired. Reflecting this change in fortune, the major themes of state politics changed as well. In the 1950s and 1960s, the predominant theme was meeting the problems of growth through building projects. Beginning in the 1970s, the overriding emphasis became stabilizing the ship and trying to position the state to take advantage of new technologies.

As its population stagnated in the 1970s and 1980s, Ohio saw its congressional delegation shrink. After the 1990 census, Ohio was entitled to 19 members, its fewest in more than a century. After the 2000 census, Ohio lost another seat; it now has 18 congressional representatives. Some Ohioans, especially Democrats, thought the state might reclaim some of its political glory in 1984 when Sen. John Glenn, amid great hopes, launched a presidential bid. But unlike his world-famous space flight in 1962, Glenn's presidential campaign never got off the ground.

At the end of the 20th century, Ohio remained sufficiently large and diverse to be considered a political test market for the nation. But population and economic trends have been making the state less reflective of the nation than in previous decades. For example, the nation's newest immigrants, particularly Hispanics and Asians, have not flocked to Ohio as did their European predecessors. Nor did Ohio's prosperity in the last quarter-century, as measured in per capita income, keep up with the national average.

At the start of the 21st century, Ohio celebrated its bicentennial. It did so looking back on a political heritage as rich as that of any state in the nation while at the same time looking forward to a future as uncertain as that faced by the pioneers who settled it.

CHAPTER 2

Presidential Elections

ALTHOUGH OHIO'S REPUTATION AS A BAROMETER
HAS VALIDITY, THE STATE VOTES
A BIT MORE REPUBLICAN IN PRESIDENTIAL ELECTIONS
THAN THE NATION AS A WHOLE

Throughout the 20th century, Ohio was as reliable a barometer as any state in reflecting national preferences in presidential elections. From 1904 through 2000, the presidential candidate who carried Ohio won the presidency 23 of 25 times.

In 2004, the first presidential election of the 21st century, Ohio stayed true to its bellwether reputation, providing George W. Bush a 51-48 victory in the state, the same as Bush's winning margin nationally.

The state's ability to mirror the nation stems from a political and demographic balance that dates from the dawning of the 20th century, which marked Ohio's emergence as an industrial power. The new and quickly growing industries created a multitude of jobs, attracting a diverse population to the state. Urbanization followed, superimposing several major metropolitan areas over the state's traditional, rural-agricultural base.

Rather quickly, Ohio had hundreds of thousands of new residents whose natural sentiments were more in tune with the Democratic appeals to labor and the common man. The previously secure Republican domination of state politics came under assault. Ever since, Ohio has been a politically balanced state that reflects national party divisions.

In the 19th century, Ohio could not as easily claim to be a national mirror. In presidential elections from 1804 through 1900, the candidate who carried Ohio won the presidency 18 of 25 times. In two of those misses, however, Ohio was voting for favorite sons (William Henry Harrison in 1836; Benjamin Harrison in 1892). Overall, from the state's founding through 2004, Ohio compiled a 42-9 record in calling presidential elections.

A NATIONAL BAROMETER

Although Ohio's reputation as a barometer has validity, the state votes a bit more Republican in presidential elections than the nation as a whole. In 12 of the 15 presidential elections since World War II, Republican candidates did slightly better in Ohio than nationally.

On average in those elections, the Ohio presidential result has differed from the national result by about 1.5 percentage points, usually in the Republican direction. In 2004, however, Ohioans mirrored the nation almost exactly, giving Republican George W. Bush 51 percent of their votes, with 48 percent going to Democrat John F. Kerry. The last time a Republican presidential candidate did worse in Ohio than nationally was 1972, when Richard M. Nixon's showing in this state was about 1 percentage point below his national re-election result.

Of the 60.8 million votes cast by Ohioans for the major-party candidates in presidential elections from 1948 through 2004, almost 53 percent went to Republican candidates. Nationally, 51.5 percent of the major-party votes in those elections were cast for Republicans.

The Republican advantage in Ohio is broad-based geographically. In those 15 postwar elections, on average, Republicans won 68 of Ohio's 88 counties. To overcome that, Democrats must win their counties big—especially in the heavily populated urban northeast—and cut the size of Republican victory margins in other parts of the state. Winning Democrats also usually fare well in the Appalachian counties of southeast Ohio.

In 1992 and 1996, Democrat Bill Clinton won Ohio with this formula. In 1992, Clinton won 31 of Ohio's counties, defeated George Bush nearly 2-to-1 in much of northeastern Ohio, and kept Bush's winning margins in other parts of the state well below the level normally achieved by Republican presidential candidates. Clinton improved upon this formula in 1996, when he won 39 counties and easily outdistancing Republican Bob Dole statewide.

In 2000, Democrat Al Gore pulled out of Ohio with about three weeks remaining in the campaign and lost 23 of the counties that Bill Clinton had carried four years earlier, and lost the state by 3.5 percentage points.

In 2004, George W. Bush carried 72 of the 88 counties—the same number of counties he won four years earlier.

Democratic presidential candidates almost never win a majority of Ohio's counties. Since World War II, only Lyndon Baines Johnson has done so. In his 1964 landslide victory over Barry Goldwater, Johnson captured 83 of Ohio's counties. Clinton's 39 counties in 1996 ranks second among Democratic presidential candidates since World War II. Jimmy Carter won 27 counties in 1976; Harry Truman won Ohio in 1948 while taking only 22 counties.

AS OHIO GOES . . .

Since 1860, when Abraham Lincoln was elected, no Republican has won the presidency without Ohio in his column. However, five GOP presidential candidates—including the first one, John C. Frémont in 1856—carried Ohio yet lost the election. The other four were James G. Blaine in 1884, Benjamin Harrison in 1892, Thomas E. Dewey in 1944, and Richard M. Nixon in 1960.

Although Ohio's population and resulting electoral clout make it a prize in every presidential election, the state's votes have proved decisive in only four elections. In all other presidential elections through 2004, the winner would have taken the White House regardless of his showing in Ohio.

The four elections in which Ohio's votes proved crucial were in 1876, when Ohioan Rutherford B. Hayes was elected; in 1916, when Democrat Woodrow Wilson won re-election; and in 2000 and 2004, both won by Republican George W. Bush. In 1876, Hayes defeated Democrat Samuel J. Tilden in Ohio by 7,516 votes to win the state's 22 electoral votes. Nationally, Tilden had a 254,235-vote advantage. But Republicans disputed the election results, contending that thousands of blacks who would have supported Hayes were prevented from getting to polling places in South Carolina, Louisiana, and Florida, where Republican carpetbaggers controlled the election boards. The results also were disputed in Oregon. Hayes was awarded enough votes to carry those states. Amid the uproar that followed, a special electoral commission appointed by Congress voted 8–7, strictly along party lines, to award the election to Hayes. The decision gave Hayes the election by an electoral vote of 185 to 184.

In 1916, Woodrow Wilson was re-elected over Charles Evans Hughes. Wilson carried Ohio by 89,408 votes to take the state's 24 electoral votes. Nationally, Wilson won by only 23 electoral votes, 277 to 254. Ohio was the most populous state carried by Wilson and the only industrial state east of the Mississippi River.

In 2000, in one of the closest elections in U.S. history, George W. Bush won the electoral vote count, 271 to 266, although he lost the popular vote to Democrat Al Gore by more than a half-million votes. Ohio's 21 electoral votes, along with the electoral votes of two dozen other states, proved crucial to Bush.

In 2004, Bush was re-elected with the smallest margin of victory for a sitting president in U.S. history as he captured 51 percent of the vote. Once more, Ohio was crucial to the outcome; the state's 21 electoral votes pushed Bush over the top. With 270 electoral votes needed for victory, Bush captured 286 to Kerry's 251.

For more than a half-century—from the election of Ulysses S. Grant in 1868 to the end of Warren G. Harding's term in 1924—Ohio played a dominant role in presidential politics: seven of the ten presidents who served during that span were Ohioans. Grant was the first of three consecutive presidents born in Ohio, followed by Rutherford B. Hayes in 1876 and James Garfield in 1880. Even without Ohio, Garfield would have won the electoral vote in 1880 over Democrat Winfield S. Hancock. However, Garfield's 34,000-vote margin in Ohio was crucial to his razor-thin national plurality of 16,898 votes. Eight years later, Ohioan Benjamin Harrison carried his home state by 20,598 votes and won election over incumbent Democrat Grover Cleveland. Even though Cleveland had a 90,596 popular-vote margin nationally, Harrison won the electoral vote, 233 to 168.

The other three Ohio presidents were William McKinley (1896); William Howard Taft (1908); and Warren G. Harding (1920). All carried their native state, although Taft failed to win Ohio in his re-election bid in 1912 against Democrat Woodrow Wilson and Progressive Theodore Roosevelt.

The 1920 election was a distinctive indicator of Ohio's political clout. Both candidates were Ohio newspaper publishers: Harding, a Republican then serving as a U.S. senator, was publisher of the *Marion Star*; James M. Cox, a Democrat then serving as Ohio governor, was publisher of the *Dayton Daily News*. Harding carried the state by 401,985 votes.

In the 20th century, Ohioans voted for the national winner with two exceptions: Republican Thomas E. Dewey carried Ohio by 11,530 votes in 1944, when Franklin Delano Roosevelt won his fourth term; in 1960, Republican Richard M. Nixon carried Ohio handily—by 273,363 votes—against the winning Democratic candidate, John F. Kennedy.

Ohio Counties in Presidential Elections

DATE	DEMOCRATIC	REPUBLICAN
1948	22	66
1952	6	82
1956	1	87
1960	10	78
1964	83	5
1968	16	72
1972	2	86
1976	27	61
1980	10	78
1984	6	82
1988	13	75
1992	31	57
1996	39	49
2000	16	72
2004	16	72

How Ohioans Voted

1948

- ■ Democrat: Harry S. Truman   1,452,791   (49.48%)
- □ Republican: Thomas E. Dewey   1,445,684   (49.24%)
- Progressive: Henry A. Wallace   37,487   (1.28%)

2,935,962

1952

- ■ Democrat: Adlai E. Stevenson   1,600,367   (43.24%)
- □ Republican: Dwight D. Eisenhower 2,100,391   (56.76%)

3,700,758

1956

- ■ Democrat: Adlai E. Stevenson   1,439,655   (38.89%)
- □ Republican: Dwight D. Eisenhower 2,262,610   (61.11%)

3,702,265

1960

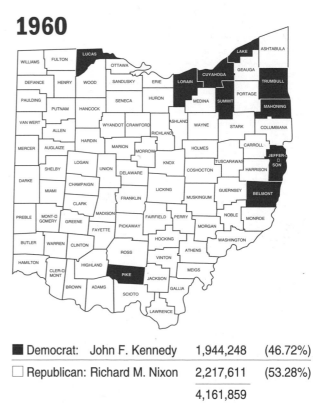

- ■ Democrat: John F. Kennedy   1,944,248   (46.72%)
- □ Republican: Richard M. Nixon   2,217,611   (53.28%)

4,161,859

1964

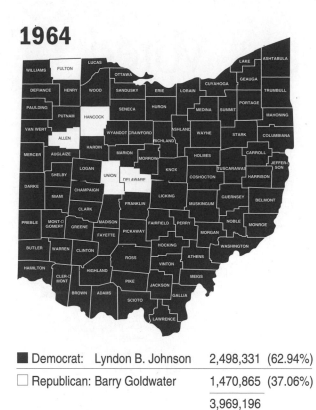

■ Democrat:	Lyndon B. Johnson	2,498,331	(62.94%)
□ Republican:	Barry Goldwater	1,470,865	(37.06%)
		3,969,196	

1968

■ Democrat:	Hubert H. Humphrey	1,700,586	(42.95%)
□ Republican:	Richard M. Nixon	1,791,014	(45.23%)
American Independent:	George C. Wallace	467,495	(11.81%)
Others:		603	
		3,959,698	

1972

■ Democrat:	George S. McGovern	1,558,889	(38.07%)
□ Republican:	Richard M. Nixon	2,441,827	(59.63%)
American Independent:	John G. Schmitz	80,067	(1.96%)
Others:		14,004	(0.34%)
		4,094,787	

1976

■ Democrat:	Jimmy Carter	2,011,621	(48.92%)
□ Republican:	Gerald Ford	2,000,505	(48.65%)
American Party:	Lester G. Maddox	15,529	(0.38%)
Independent:	Eugene J. McCarthy	58,258	(1.42%)
Others:		25,960	(0.63%)
		4,111,873	

1980

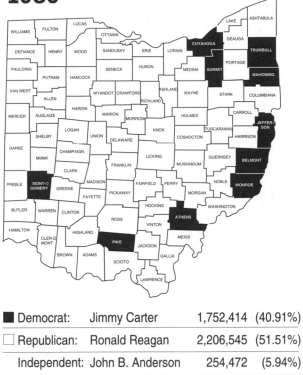

■ Democrat:	Jimmy Carter	1,752,414	(40.91%)
□ Republican:	Ronald Reagan	2,206,545	(51.51%)
Independent:	John B. Anderson	254,472	(5.94%)
	Others:	70,172	(1.64%)
		4,283,603	

1984

■ Democrat:	Walter F. Mondale	1,825,440	(40.14%)
□ Republican:	Ronald Reagan	2,678,560	(58.90%)
	Others:	43,619	(0.96%)
		4,547,619	

1988

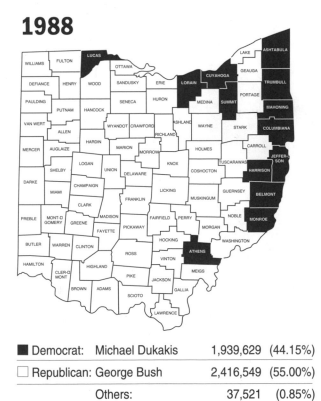

■ Democrat:	Michael Dukakis	1,939,629	(44.15%)
□ Republican:	George Bush	2,416,549	(55.00%)
	Others:	37,521	(0.85%)
		4,393,699	

1992

■ Democrat:	Bill Clinton	1,984,942	(40.18%)
□ Republican:	George Bush	1,894,310	(38.35%)
Independent:	Ross Perot	1,036,426	(20.98%)
	Others:	24,289	(0.49%)
		4,939,967	

1996

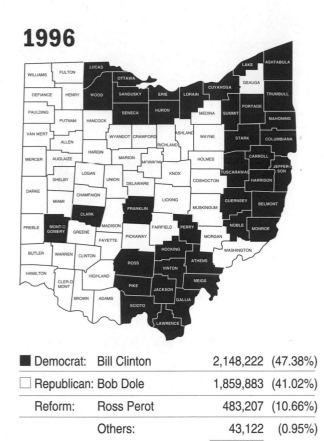

■ Democrat:	Bill Clinton	2,148,222	(47.38%)
□ Republican:	Bob Dole	1,859,883	(41.02%)
Reform:	Ross Perot	483,207	(10.66%)
	Others:	43,122	(0.95%)
		4,534,434	

2000

■ Democrat:	Al Gore	2,186,190	(46.46%)
□ Republican:	George W. Bush	2,351,209	(49.96%)
Green:	Ralph Nader	117,857	(2.50%)
	Others:	50,201	(1.07%)
		4,705,457	

2004

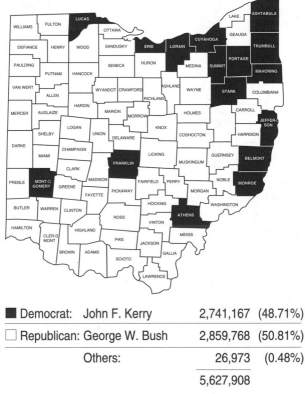

■ Democrat:	John F. Kerry	2,741,167	(48.71%)
□ Republican:	George W. Bush	2,859,768	(50.81%)
	Others:	26,973	(0.48%)
		5,627,908	

Presidential Elections: Ohio vs. Nation

Year	National Winner	Party	%	Carried Ohio	Party	%	Year	National Winner	Party	%	Carried Ohio	Party	%
1804	Thomas Jefferson	(D-R)	N.A.	Thomas Jefferson	(D-R)	N.A.	1908	William H. Taft	(R)	51.6	William H. Taft	(R)	51.0
1808	James Madison	(D-R)	N.A.	James Madison	(D-R)	N.A.	1912	Woodrow Wilson	(D)	41.8	Woodrow Wilson	(D)	41.0
1812	James Madison	(D-R)	N.A.	James Madison	(D-R)	N.A.	1916	Woodrow Wilson	(D)	49.2	Woodrow Wilson	(D)	51.9
1816	James Monroe	(D-R)	N.A.	James Monroe	(D-R)	N.A.	1920	Warren G. Harding	(R)	60.3	Warren G. Harding	(R)	58.5
1820	James Monroe	(D-R)	N.A.	James Monroe	(D-R)	N.A.	1924	Calvin Coolidge	(R)	54.1	Calvin Coolidge	(R)	58.3
1824	John Q. Adams	(D-R)	30.9	Henry Clay	(D-R)	38.5	1928	Herbert Hoover	(R)	58.2	Herbert Hoover	(R)	64.9
1828	Andrew Jackson	(D)	56.0	Andrew Jackson	(D)	51.6	1932	F.D. Roosevelt	(D)	57.4	F.D. Roosevelt	(D)	49.9
1832	Andrew Jackson	(D)	54.2	Andrew Jackson	(D)	51.3	1936	F.D. Roosevelt	(D)	60.8	F.D. Roosevelt	(D)	58.0
1836	Martin Van Buren	(D)	50.8	William H. Harrison	(W)	52.1	1940	F.D. Roosevelt	(D)	54.7	F.D. Roosevelt	(D)	52.2
1840	William H. Harrison	(W)	52.9	William H. Harrison	(W)	54.3	1944	F.D. Roosevelt	(D)	53.4	Thomas E. Dewey	(R)	50.2
1844	James K. Polk	(D)	49.5	Henry Clay	(W)	49.7	1948	Harry S. Truman	(D)	49.5	Harry S. Truman	(D)	49.5
1848	Zachary Taylor	(W)	47.3	Lewis Cass	(D)	47.1	1952	Dwight Eisenhower	(R)	55.1	Dwight Eisenhower	(R)	56.8
1852	Franklin Pierce	(D)	50.8	Franklin Pierce	(D)	47.9	1956	Dwight Eisenhower	(R)	57.4	Dwight Eisenhower	(R)	61.1
1856	James Buchanan	(D)	45.3	John C. Frémont	(R)	48.5	1960	John F. Kennedy	(D)	49.7	Richard M. Nixon	(R)	53.3
1860	Abraham Lincoln	(R)	39.8	Abraham Lincoln	(R)	52.3	1964	Lyndon B. Johnson	(D)	61.1	Lyndon B. Johnson	(D)	62.9
1864	Abraham Lincoln	(R)	56.4	Abraham Lincoln	(R)	56.4	1968	Richard M. Nixon	(R)	43.3	Richard M. Nixon	(R)	45.2
1868	Ulysses S. Grant	(R)	52.7	Ulysses S. Grant	(R)	54.0	1972	Richard M. Nixon	(R)	60.7	Richard M. Nixon	(R)	59.6
1872	Ulysses S. Grant	(R)	55.6	Ulysses S. Grant	(R)	53.2	1976	Jimmy Carter	(D)	50.1	Jimmy Carter	(D)	48.9
1876	Rutherford B. Hayes	(R)	47.9	Rutherford B. Hayes	(R)	50.2	1980	Ronald Reagan	(R)	50.7	Ronald Reagan	(R)	51.5
1880	James A. Garfield	(R)	48.3	James A. Garfield	(R)	51.7	1984	Ronald Reagan	(R)	58.8	Ronald Reagan	(R)	58.9
1884	Grover Cleveland	(D)	48.5	James G. Blaine	(R)	51.0	1988	George Bush	(R)	53.4	George Bush	(R)	55.0
1888	Benjamin Harrison	(R)	47.8	Benjamin Harrison	(R)	49.6	1992	Bill Clinton	(D)	43.0	Bill Clinton	(D)	40.2
1892	Grover Cleveland	(D)	46.1	Benjamin Harrison	(R)	47.7	1996	Bill Clinton	(D)	49.2	Bill Clinton	(D)	47.4
1896	William McKinley	(R)	51.1	William McKinley	(R)	51.9	2000	George W. Bush	(R)	47.9	George W. Bush	(R)	50.0
1900	William McKinley	(R)	51.7	William McKinley	(R)	52.3	2004	George W. Bush	(R)	51.0	George W. Bush	(R)	50.8
1904	Theodore Roosevelt	(R)	56.4	Theodore Roosevelt	(R)	59.8							

D-R: Democratic-Republican   D: Democratic   R: Republican   W: Whig

Sources: Congressional Quarterly ; Columbus Dispatch

CHAPTER 3

The Ohio Presidents

WILLIAM HENRY HARRISON • ULYSSES S. GRANT
RUTHERFORD B. HAYES • JAMES A. GARFIELD
BENJAMIN HARRISON • WILLIAM McKINLEY
WILLIAM HOWARD TAFT • WARREN G. HARDING

William Henry Harrison

9th president (1841)
Born: February 9, 1773, in Charles City County, Va.
Ancestry: English
Religion: Episcopalian
Occupation: soldier
Political party: Whig
Family: wife, Anna Symmes; 10 children
Residence when elected: North Bend, Ohio (Hamilton County)
Served as president: March 4, 1841, to April 4, 1841
Died: April 4, 1841, in Washington, D.C.
Buried: North Bend, Ohio

AFTER HARRISON WAS RIDICULED BY AN OPPOSING NEWSPAPER AS THE "LOG CABIN AND HARD CIDER" CANDIDATE, THE WHIGS HAD THEIR SLOGAN

Although born in Virginia, William Henry Harrison is claimed by Ohio as an adopted son because he spent much of his adult life in Ohio and served it as a U.S. representative, state senator, and U.S. senator before being elected president.

He was the youngest of seven children of Benjamin Harrison, a signer of the Declaration of Independence and governor of Virginia. He attended Hampden-Sydney College in the late 1780s and later studied medicine, but at 18 decided on a military career. In 1791, Harrison was commissioned an ensign in the First U.S. Artillery Regiment at Fort Washington, Ohio, which later became Cincinnati.

As a company leader, Harrison had the task of fighting Indians to help make the Northwest Territory safe for white settlement. He rose to the rank of captain before resigning from the army in May 1798. The next month, Harrison was appointed secretary of the

Northwest Territory by President John Adams. In 1799, he became the territory's first delegate to Congress.

From 1800 to 1812, Harrison served Adams as the first governor of the Indiana Territory, which included what today is Indiana, Illinois, Wisconsin, and parts of Michigan and Minnesota.

On November 7, 1811, at Tippecanoe Creek near the present-day Lafayette, Ind., Harrison led a group of 800 to 900 men against an Indian uprising organized by the Shawnee leader Tecumseh. The victory established Harrison's reputation—one that later would catapult him to the White House.

During the War of 1812, Harrison was appointed brigadier general to lead the Northwestern army against the British and Tecumseh's Indian confederation. Following a promotion to major general, Harrison led American forces to victory at the Battle of the Thames in Ontario. In that battle, on October 5, 1813, Tecumseh was killed. Once more, Harrison won national attention for wartime heroism.

With the northwestern borders secured, Harrison resigned from the military, returned to North Bend, and entered Ohio politics. He was elected to Congress in 1816 but was defeated in his bid for re-election. From 1819 to 1821, he served a term in the Ohio Senate.

After unsuccessful campaigns for Ohio governor and for Congress, Harrison was elected in 1825 by the state legislature to serve in the U.S. Senate. In 1828, the Adams administration tapped Harrison to be the nation's first ambassador to Colombia. At the time, Colombia was headed by Gen. Simon Bolivar. In 1829, Harrison was recalled by Adams's successor, Andrew Jackson.

In 1836, Harrison launched a presidential campaign. Because the Whigs were not unified nationally, the party put up regional candidates—Harrison of Ohio, Daniel Webster of Massachusetts, and Hugh L. White of Tennessee—to oppose Democrat Martin Van Buren. The Whig strategy was to capture enough electoral votes to throw the election into the House of Representatives. Van Buren won the election, but Harrison led the three Whig candidates with 73 electoral votes.

In 1840, the Whigs united behind Harrison in a rematch with Van Buren. The campaign marked the beginning of modern, slogan-driven campaigning as Harrison adopted advisers' warnings to avoid taking positions on slavery and other tough issues.

After Harrison was ridiculed by an opposing newspaper as the "log cabin and hard cider" candidate, the Whigs had their slogan. Turning the taunt to their advantage, the Whigs used those emblems as well as the slogan "Tippecanoe and Tyler Too" to link Harrison to his most famous military victory and his running mate, John Tyler of Virginia.

Portraying Van Buren as a wealthy aristocrat, Harrison campaigned aggressively and won the election by carrying 19 of the 26 states. He garnered 234 electoral votes to Van Buren's 60. Harrison won election at the age of 67 and took office at 68, the oldest president prior to Ronald Reagan. Harrison also was the last president born before the American Revolution.

Inauguration Day—March 4, 1841—was cold and windy. He rode to it bareheaded and delivered an 8,500-word address, during which he promised not to seek a second term. He caught pneumonia and died a month later, the first president to die in office. He also was the first president to lie in state in the White House.

Ulysses S. Grant

18th president (1869–1877)
Born: April 27, 1822, in Point Pleasant, Ohio (Clermont County)
Ancestry: English, Scotch
Religion: Methodist
Occupation: soldier
Political party: Republican
Family: wife, Julia Boggs Dent; four children
Residence when elected: Galena, Ill.
Served as president: March 4, 1869, to March 3, 1877
Died: July 23, 1885, in Mount McGregor, N.Y.
Buried: New York City

ALTHOUGH HE NOMINALLY HAD BEEN A DEMOCRAT, GRANT WAS WOOED BY REPUBLICAN LEADERS TO BE THEIR PRESIDENTIAL CANDIDATE

The first Ohio-born president, Hiram Ulysses Grant was the eldest son of Jesse Root Grant, a tanner, and Hannah Simpson Grant. In the fall of 1823, the family moved to Georgetown in neighboring Brown County. Until 1839, young Ulysses worked with his father on their farm, where he learned to handle horses. That year, Jesse Grant secured an appointment for his son to the U.S. Military Academy at West Point. His name mistakenly had been entered as Ulysses S. Grant; he eventually adopted the name, dropping Hiram.

In 1843, Grant graduated 21st in his class of 39. He was assigned to the Fourth U.S. Infantry at Jefferson Barracks, near St. Louis, as a brevet second lieutenant.

Grant served in the Mexican War (1846 to 1848) under Gen. Zachary Taylor and later Gen. Winfield Scott. He served with distinction, earning brevet commissions as first lieutenant and captain. After the war, Grant was assigned to a series of routine duties. Following transfers to Fort Vancouver in Oregon in 1852 and Fort Humboldt in California in 1853—moves that separated him from his family—Grant grew bored, was reported to be drinking heavily, and finally resigned from the army in 1854 after charges of intemperate drinking.

Grant went to Missouri to farm 80 acres given to his wife by her father, discovered that he wasn't a farmer, then fared no better in a real-estate partnership in St. Louis. In 1860, Grant moved the family to Galena, Ill., to work in his family's leather shop. He was there at the outbreak of the Civil War.

In April 1861, President Lincoln called for volunteers to defend the Union. The following month, Grant, then 39, offered his services. Illinois governor Richard Yates appointed Grant to organize the 21st Illinois Regiment. In August, President Lincoln commissioned Grant as brigadier general of volunteers.

Grant, who was highly successful in waging a number of campaigns, impressed Lincoln and won a series of promotions. In February 1862, he acquired the nickname "Unconditional Surrender" for accepting nothing less in the capture of Forts Henry and Donelson in Tennessee. He was achieving a national reputation.

As a major general, Grant drove off the Confederates at Shiloh Church, near Pittsburg Landing, Tenn., on April 6–7, 1862. He then led the Union advance on Vicksburg, Miss., where the Confederates had their last major stronghold on the Mississippi River. A final victory was achieved on July 4, 1863, effectively cutting the Confederacy in half.

In March 1864, President Lincoln appointed Grant lieutenant general and gave him command of all Union armies. Grant launched an all-out offensive that brought the Civil War to an end with Gen. Robert E. Lee's surrender at Appomattox Court House on April 9, 1865.

As a national hero, the cigar-smoking Grant toured the South at the request of President Andrew Johnson, and Grant initially favored a lenient rather than punitive Reconstruction policy.

After Johnson suspended Secretary of War Edwin M. Stanton to test the constitutionality of the Tenure of Office Act, which required the assent of Congress for such removals, Grant accepted appointment as interim secretary. The Senate refused to concur in Stanton's ouster; Grant resigned from the cabinet rather than remain, as Johnson had wanted, to test the dispute in court. Although he nominally had been a Democrat, Grant was wooed by Republican Party leaders to be their presidential candidate.

Now in an open feud with Johnson, Grant sided with the Radical Republicans in supporting Johnson's impeachment and agreed to become a Republican candidate for president. In May 1868, Grant was unanimously nominated on the first roll call. He easily won election over Democrat Horatio Seymour, a former governor of New York, by capturing 214 electoral votes to Seymour's 80. At 46, Grant was the youngest man elected president up to that time.

During his presidency, most of the Reconstruction of the

South was completed. Grant's first term brought, in 1870, the ratification of the 15th Amendment, which prohibits the denial of the right to vote on the basis of race. Southern states began finding ways to sabotage the amendment and keep blacks from the polls.

Grant easily won re-election in 1872 over New York newspaper editor Horace Greeley, the Democrat and Liberal Republican candidate. Greeley died after the election but before the meeting of presidential electors. Grant won 286 of the 366 electoral votes, with the remainder split among four other candidates.

Several scandals marred Grant's presidency. In 1869, during Grant's first term, financier Jay Gould used inside government information to try to corner the gold market. By Grant's second term, prominent Republican officials had been caught up in the Credit Mobilier scandal (in which Union Pacific Railroad profits were siphoned) and the Whiskey Ring scandal (in which the government was defrauded of millions of dollars in excise taxes).

These scandals and the Panic of 1873, which triggered an economic depression, helped persuade Grant not to seek a third term in 1876. After more than two years of travel, he returned interested in the 1880 presidential election and came close to winning the Republican nomination. James A. Garfield needed 36 ballots at the Republican National Convention to beat Grant, 399 votes to 306.

In retirement, Grant, bankrupt and suffering from throat cancer, began writing his memoirs. The two volumes ultimately provided about $500,000 for his family.

Rutherford B. Hayes

19th president (1877–1881)
Born: October 4, 1822, in
  Delaware, Ohio (Delaware
  County)
Ancestry: Scotch
Religion: Methodist
Occupation: lawyer
Political party: Republican
Family: wife, Lucy Ware
  Webb; eight children
Residence when elected:
  Fremont, Ohio
Served as president:
  March 4, 1877, to
  March 3, 1881
Died: January 17, 1893, in
  Fremont, Ohio
Buried: Fremont, Ohio

WITH A DEAL STRUCK,
BOTH HOUSES
WENT ALONG WITH
THE COMMISSION'S
RECOMMENDATION,
ON AN 8-7 VOTE,
TO AWARD THE
ELECTION TO HAYES—
"RUTHERFRAUD"
TO CRITICS

Rutherford B. Hayes was the first governor of Ohio to become president. Earlier, he had made history as the first Ohio governor to win a third term.

Born three months after the death of his father, Hayes grew up in a family that pushed him to succeed and made sure he had plenty of education to help him do so. He graduated from Kenyon College in 1842 and Harvard Law School in 1845 and then began practicing law in Lower Sandusky (now Fremont), Ohio.

In 1849, Hayes moved to Cincinnati, where he established a successful law practice and earned a reputation for helping fugitive slaves on the Underground Railroad. He was among the activists who formed the Ohio Republican Party, and in 1858, the Cincinnati City Council selected him to fill a vacancy as city solicitor. Hayes had the position until 1861, and he entered the military to serve in the Civil War.

Commissioned a major, Hayes helped organize the 23rd Ohio Volunteers. He eventually rose to the rank of major general by distinguishing himself many times in combat. While in the service, Hayes was nominated for Congress in 1864, although he did not go home to campaign for the office. He was elected and took his seat in Congress in December 1865, where he aligned with the Radical Republicans. He was re-elected in 1866.

In August 1867, Ohio Republicans nominated him for governor. Hayes resigned from Congress and that November won a close gubernatorial election over Democrat A.G. Thurman. Hayes was re-elected in 1869. As governor, he was instrumental in establishing the land-grant agricultural college that would become Ohio State University. He also provided leadership in securing Ohio's support for ratification of the 15th Amendment, giving blacks the right to vote.

After his second term, Hayes, in keeping with custom, declined to seek the nomination for a third term. He ran unsuccessfully for Congress in 1872. He was living on his Fremont estate when Republicans called upon him in 1875 to run for governor again, this time against incumbent Democrat William Allen. Hayes answered the call and won a close election.

In June 1876, the Republican National Convention was held in Cincinnati, and Ohio Republicans supported Hayes as a favorite-son candidate for president. He emerged as a compromise candidate between warring GOP factions and, on the seventh ballot, beat House Speaker James G. Blaine of Maine for the nomination.

The subsequent general election pitting Hayes against New York governor Samuel J. Tilden turned out to be the most controversial—and by some accounts the most corrupt—in the nation's history. Tilden won the popular vote by more than 254,000 votes, only to have Republican Party leaders challenge the result by claiming that blacks had been prevented from voting in Louisiana, Florida, and South Carolina. The Republicans challenged the results in those states as well as in Oregon, and just happened to control the election boards—with the help of federal troops—in the disputed southern states.

The disputed returns put the issue to Congress, which was

divided between a Democratic House and a Republican Senate. Congress appointed a special 15-member commission to arbitrate, and the dealmaking began. Some southern congressional Democrats were willing to accept Hayes as president in return for a promise to withdraw federal troops from the South. With a deal struck, both houses went along with the commission's recommendation, on an 8 to 7 vote, to award the election to Hayes —"Rutherfraud" to critics.

In the White House, Hayes promptly withdrew federal troops from the South, ending Reconstruction and effectively disenfranchising southern blacks for years to come.

His term was notable for advancing the civil service at the expense of the spoils system, putting the nation back on the gold standard, crushing railroad strikes, and banishing liquor from the White House. Hayes's wife, "Lemonade Lucy," was a champion of the Women's Christian Temperance Union and a symbol in the women's movement. She was the first first lady to have a college degree—from Cincinnati's Wesleyan Female College.

Keeping his promise to serve only one term, Hayes left the White House in 1881 and devoted himself to educational, charitable, and public-welfare causes.

James A. Garfield

20th president (1881)
Born: November 19, 1831, in
  Orange Township, Ohio
  (Cuyahoga County)
Ancestry: English
Religion: Disciples of Christ
Occupation: educator,
  lawyer, soldier
Political party: Republican
Family: wife, Lucretia
  Rudolph; seven children
Residence when elected:
  Mentor, Ohio
Served as president: March 4,
  1881, to September 19, 1881
Died: September 19, 1881, in
  Elberon, N.J.
Buried: Cleveland, Ohio

HE DIED AFTER ONLY 200 DAYS AS PRESIDENT. GARFIELD WAS THE SECOND PRESIDENT TO BE KILLED BY AN ASSASSIN

In 1880, James Abram Garfield became the third consecutive Ohioan to be elected president. Until then, only the state of Virginia had accomplished such a feat, sending Thomas Jefferson, James Madison, and James Monroe to the White House as the nation's third, fourth, and fifth presidents. No other state has duplicated Virginia's and Ohio's triple plays.

Garfield, the youngest of five children, was born in a log cabin on a farm in Orange Township near Cleveland. He was not yet two when his father died, and his family was unable to provide him with much early schooling. As a teenager, Garfield worked on a Great Lakes freighter and as a towboy on the Ohio & Erie Canal, driving the horses and mules that pulled boats and barges.

Determined to obtain a college education, Garfield entered the Western Reserve Eclectic Institute in 1851 (now Hiram College), which had been founded the year before by the Disciples of Christ. He studied Greek and Latin and then obtained a loan to enter Williams College in Williamstown, Mass., in 1854. He graduated with honors from Williams in 1856 and returned to the Eclectic Institute to teach Greek and Latin. At 26, Garfield was named to head the institute.

While serving as school president, Garfield was a lay preacher, lecturer, and student of law. He also became involved in politics and was elected in 1859 to the Ohio Senate. He was a fierce opponent of slavery and advocated preservation of the Union. After the outbreak of the Civil War, Garfield was named to lead a company attached to the 42nd Ohio Infantry Volunteers. He rose from lieutenant colonel to become, at 30, the youngest general in the Union army. He was promoted to major general after the Battle of Chickamauga.

In 1862, while on active duty, Garfield was elected to Congress. He resigned his commission in December 1863 to take his seat in the House, where he served for 17 consecutive years. During the Grant administration, he headed several important committees—including appropriations and banking—and rose to Republican leader of the House. He sided with the Radical Republicans and supported impeachment of President Andrew Johnson.

In 1877, Garfield was a member of the special commission that decided the disputed Hayes-Tilden election. In January 1880, the Ohio General Assembly elected Garfield to the U.S. Senate, but events did not give him the opportunity to take his Senate seat.

At the June 1880 Republican convention in Chicago, the party was split into two major factions—the Stalwarts and the Half-Breeds. The Stalwarts wanted to nominate former president Grant; the Half-Breeds were for Sen. James G. Blaine of Maine. Stalemated for 34 ballots, the convention turned to Garfield as a compromise candidate. Garfield, who was heading the Ohio delegation, won on the 36th ballot.

Garfield conducted a front-porch campaign from his Mentor, Ohio, home against the Democratic nominee, Maj. Gen. Winfield Scott Hancock, a hero of Gettysburg. Garfield narrowly won the the popular vote with 4.45 million votes to Hancock's 4.41 million. Garfield had 214 electoral votes to Hancock's 155.

Garfield appointed Blaine as secretary of state. On the morning of July 2, 1881, the two men entered the Baltimore & Potomac railroad station in Washington. Garfield had planned to board a train to travel to the 25th reunion of his Williams College class.

At the train station, Charles J. Guiteau, a mentally imbalanced job seeker, fired two shots at Garfield, wounding him in the arm and in the back. Garfield lay wounded for weeks in the White House before being moved to a seaside residence in Elberon, N.J., to escape the Washington heat. He died on

September 19, after only 200 days as president. Garfield was the second president to be killed by an assassin. Guiteau was hanged on June 30, 1882.

Benjamin Harrison

23rd president (1889–1893)
Born: August 20, 1833, in
   North Bend, Ohio
   (Hamilton County)
Ancestry: English
Religion: Presbyterian
Occupation: soldier, lawyer
Political party: Republican
Family: wife, Caroline Scott;
   two children. Second wife,
   Mary Lord Dimmick;
   one child
Residence when elected:
   Indianapolis, Ind.
Served as president:
   March 4, 1889, to March 3,
   1893
Died: March 13, 1901, in
   Indianapolis
Buried: Indianapolis

BENJAMIN HARRISON WAS INAUGURATED 100 YEARS AFTER GEORGE WASHINGTON AND THUS BECAME KNOWN AS THE CENTENNIAL PRESIDENT

Benjamin Harrison was inaugurated 100 years after George Washington, and thus became known as the centennial president. His great-grandfather, Benjamin Harrison, was a signer of the Declaration of Independence. His grandfather, William Henry Harrison, was the nation's ninth president.

The second of nine children, Harrison was born on his family's farm at North Bend. His father, John Scott Harrison, has been the only American to be the son of one president and the father of another.

Harrison's education began in a one-room schoolhouse on the family farm, under the tutelage of a teacher hired by his father. At 14, the boy was sent to a college preparatory school, Cary's Academy (later Farmer's College), near Cincinnati. After two years there, in the fall of 1850, he registered as a junior at Miami University in Oxford, Ohio.

Upon graduating with honors from Miami, Harrison took up legal studies in a Cincinnati law firm. He was admitted to the bar in 1854 and moved with his wife to Indianapolis. He landed a job as crier of federal court, which paid him $2.50 per day.

Although his father was a Whig congressman from Ohio, Harrison became active in the newly formed Republican Party and campaigned in 1856 for the party's presidential candidate, John C. Frémont. In 1857, Harrison successfully ran for city attorney of Indianapolis. In 1860, he was elected reporter of the Supreme Court of Indiana and was twice re-elected.

In July 1862, Indiana governor Oliver P. Morton asked Harrison to recruit and command the 70th Indiana Regiment. Harrison took the assignment and was commissioned a colonel; his regiment saw heavy fighting in several battles of the Civil War. Cited for bravery on several occasions, Harrison was promoted to brigadier general by President Lincoln in March 1865.

Harrison returned to Indianapolis a war hero and resumed his job at the state supreme court, having been re-elected in 1864 while still serving in the military. He gained attention among the Indiana bar, ran unsuccessfully for Indiana governor in 1876, then became the Republican leader in Indiana. The Indiana legislature in 1881 elected Harrison to the U.S. Senate, where he advocated civil rights for blacks, civil-service reform, regulation of railroads and trusts, and higher tariffs to protect American businesses. In 1887, the legislature failed to re-elect him to the Senate by one vote.

In 1888, James G. Blaine, the Republican presidential nominee of 1884, declined to seek another nomination. The party convention, meeting in Chicago that June, appeared deadlocked in the early balloting between Sen. John Sherman of Ohio and Circuit Judge Walter Q. Gresham of Indiana, the two leading candidates among the 14 who received convention votes. On the eighth ballot, however, the convention nominated Harrison.

President Grover Cleveland was renominated by the Democrats. In a low-key campaign, Harrison lost the popular vote by 90,596 votes among 11.3 million cast. But Harrison carried 20 states to Cleveland's 18 and won the electoral vote count, 233 to 168. Cleveland carried the South, but Harrison nearly swept the East and Midwest.

Harrison took office with Republican majorities in both houses of Congress. The administration and Congress passed the Sherman Antitrust Act to outlaw monopolies and trusts that obstructed trade, the Sherman Silver Purchase Act to increase the coinage of silver, and the McKinley Tariff Act to set very high import duties.

Democrats branded it the "Billion-Dollar Congress" for its free-spending measures to increase Civil War pensions, expand naval construction, and support special-interest programs.

During Harrison's tenure in the White House, six states were admitted to the Union: North Dakota and South Dakota, Montana, Washington, Wyoming, and Idaho. The admissions brought the total number of states to 44 and established that the nation was settled coast to coast.

The 1892 presidential race was a rematch between Harrison and Cleveland, but with the addition of People's Party (Populist) candidate James B. Weaver. The People's Party had been organized in May 1891 in Cincinnati. It was a farmer-labor coalition that protested falling commodity prices and economic hard times, and supported free coinage of silver, labor reforms, and a graduated income tax.

The Populist ticket drew many votes away from the

Republicans, capturing more than one million, or about 8.5 percent of the total cast. In an otherwise dull election, Cleveland defeated Harrison, 46 percent to 43 percent; Cleveland won 277 electoral votes to Harrison's 145.

Harrison returned to Indianapolis to practice law. He died there in 1901, at 67.

William McKinley

25th president (1897–1901)
Born: Jan. 29, 1843, in Niles, Ohio (Trumbull County)
Ancestry: Scotch-Irish
Religion: Methodist
Occupation: lawyer
Political party: Republican
Family: wife, Ida Saxton; two children
Residence when elected: Canton, Ohio
Served as president: March 4, 1897, to September 14, 1901
Died: September 14, 1901, in Buffalo, N.Y.
Buried: Canton, Ohio

THE ACT OF 1890 WAS NAMED FOR MCKINLEY, THE LEADING REPUBLICAN SPOKESMAN OF A HIGH PROTECTIVE TARIFF

From the end of the Civil War to 1900, every winning Republican candidate for president had been an officer of the Union army and an Ohio native. William McKinley was the last in this line, following Ulysses S. Grant, Rutherford B. Hayes, James A. Garfield, and Benjamin Harrison. McKinley was the last Civil War veteran to become president.

The seventh of nine children, McKinley was born in Niles when it was a rural community of only a few hundred residents. McKinley's father operated his own iron foundry there. At nine, McKinley moved with his family to Poland, Ohio, near Youngstown, although his father remained in Niles to run the business. McKinley attended a private school, the Poland Seminary; then, at 17, he entered Allegheny College in Meadville, Pa.

McKinley fell ill, dropped out of Allegheny, returned home, and briefly taught at a country school. A post-office clerk at the outbreak of the Civil War, he volunteered for the army in June 1861 and became a mess sergeant in the 23rd Ohio Volunteer Infantry. He was in a regiment commanded by Maj. Rutherford B. Hayes. McKinley was recognized for bravery in several battles and left the army as a brevet major in 1865.

After the war, McKinley decided to study law and spent about two years in the Youngstown law offices of County Judge Charles E. Glidden. In 1866, he entered law school in Albany, N.Y. He was admitted to the bar the following year, settled in

Canton, and became active in local Republican politics.

In 1869, McKinley was nominated and successfully ran for prosecuting attorney of Stark County. Two years later, he narrowly lost his bid for re-election. He was elected to the U.S. House in 1876 and served until 1891, except for a 10-month break in 1884 to 1885. The break followed a House ruling upholding the claim that Jonathan H. Wallace had defeated McKinley in the 1882 election.

In Congress, McKinley established a national reputation as the leading Republican spokesman on the benefits of a high protective tariff; the tariff act of 1890, raising duties to all-time highs, was named for him. He strongly believed that American industries needed protection from foreign competition to grow, develop, and provide the nation with a diversified economy.

McKinley served as chairman of the House Ways and Means Committee, worked for civil-service reform, and was an advocate of "sound money." He was widely known for being civil and mannerly to a fault. In 1889, he made an unsuccessful bid for House speaker.

McKinley lost his 1890 re-election campaign after the gerrymandering of House districts but the next year was elected governor of Ohio in a close race against Democrat James E. Campbell. He easily won re-election in 1893 over Democrat Lawrence T. Neal.

McKinley had barely begun his first-term gubernatorial duties when Cleveland millionaire Marcus A. Hanna started planning to elevate McKinley to the White House. At the 1892 Republican National Convention in Minneapolis, Hanna was able to secure 182 delegate votes for McKinley, second to Benjamin Harrison.

While governor, McKinley became known for his devotion to his invalid wife. After the death of their two daughters—one during infancy and the other at age four—Ida Saxton McKinley developed a nervous condition and later suffered from epilepsy.

Although Hanna planned to make McKinley president, the millionaire political boss first had to save the governor from financial disaster. McKinley had cosigned on loans totaling $100,000 to help a friend's business venture, which failed. When the banks demanded payment on the notes, Hanna and associates raised the money for them and saved McKinley from political ruin.

At the 1896 Republican convention in St. Louis, McKinley was nominated on the first ballot, as Hanna had lined up a majority of delegates well before the convention's opening ceremonies. Garret A. Hobart, a state senator from New Jersey, was nominated for vice president. Democrats nominated fiery orator William Jennings Bryan.

The currency issue dominated the campaign. Republicans favored a hard-money policy of maintaining the gold standard and opposing free coinage of silver; Democrats demanded a soft-money policy of unlimited coinage of silver and gold. At the Democratic convention in Chicago, Bryan delivered his famous "Cross of Gold" speech in which he declared, "You shall not press down upon the brow of labor this crown of thorns; you shall not crucify mankind upon a cross of gold."

Despite Bryan's oratorical skills, McKinley's "sound money" platform was more attractive to many conservative and eastern Democrats as well as Republicans. McKinley carried the East and Midwest; Bryan carried the South. McKinley won the election with 51.1 percent of the popular vote to Bryan's 45.8 percent. The electoral-vote count: McKinley, 271; Bryan, 176.

Hanna collected more than $3.5 million in campaign funds—an enormous amount then—and arranged McKinley's "front-porch campaign," during which thousands of visitors came to Canton to hear McKinley deliver rehearsed speeches from his front porch.

McKinley showed his gratitude to Hanna by appointing 73-year-old Sen. John Sherman of Ohio secretary of state, thus creating a vacancy in the U.S. Senate, to which the state legislature elected Hanna.

Upon taking office, McKinley confronted the issue of the Cuban revolution against Spanish rule. The uprising had begun in 1895, and popular sentiment in America was with the Cuban rebels—a sentiment fanned furiously by New York publishers William Randolph Hearst and Joseph Pulitzer.

On February 15, 1898, the USS *Maine* was blown up and sunk in Havana Harbor, killing most of the crew. Spain was blamed for it, and McKinley reluctantly yielded to calls for war. Congress declared war on April 25; the conflict lasted 113 days.

With the American flag flying over Cuba, Guam, the Philippines, and Puerto Rico, McKinley led the United States into an era of world leadership and established civil governments in the newly acquired dependencies. Also during McKinley's first term, the nation annexed Hawaii, passed the Gold Standard Act to make gold the basis of the monetary system, and raised protective tariffs to new highs.

At the 1900 Republican convention in Philadelphia, McKinley was renominated by acclamation. Theodore Roosevelt, the governor of New York and hero of the Spanish-American War, received the vice-presidential nomination; Hobart had died in 1899. Democrats again nominated Bryan, but the election wasn't close. Campaigning on the nation's prosperity ("Four more years of the full dinner pail"), McKinley easily won re-election. His plurality of 859,694 votes was the largest among presidential candidates to that time.

On September 5, 1901, McKinley traveled to the Pan-American Exposition in Buffalo, N.Y. The following day, at a public reception at the exposition's Temple of Music, an anarchist named Leon F. Czolgosz approached McKinley and fired two shots from a revolver concealed beneath a handkerchief. McKinley underwent emergency surgery but never recovered. He died on September 14, the third president to be assassinated and the fifth to die in office. Czolgosz was electrocuted.

William Howard Taft

27th president (1909–1913)
Born: September 15, 1857, in Cincinnati (Hamilton County)
Ancestry: English
Religion: Unitarian
Occupation: lawyer, judge
Political party: Republican
Family: wife, Helen Herron; three children
Residence when elected: Cincinnati
Served as president: March 4, 1909, to March 3, 1913
Died: March 8, 1930, in Washington, D.C.
Buried: Arlington, Va.

A JURIST AT HEART, TAFT SOON DISCOVERED HOW MUCH HE DISLIKED THE JOB. HE FREQUENTLY LET FRIENDS AND ASSOCIATES KNOW OF HIS DISTASTE FOR THE RAMPANT INFIGHTING, POMPOSITY, AND PATRONAGE OF WHITE HOUSE POLITICS

William Howard Taft has been the only American to hold both the offices of president and chief justice of the United States. He helped make the Taft name one of the most prominent in American politics. His father, Alphonso Taft, was an attorney who served as secretary of war and attorney general in the administration of President Ulysses S. Grant.

Taft grew up in Cincinnati where he attended Woodward High School. In 1874, he enrolled at Yale in New Haven, Conn. Four years later, after graduating with distinction, Taft entered Cincinnati Law School. In 1880, he received his law degree, was admitted to the bar, and followed his father into Republican politics.

His first public office was that of assistant prosecuting attorney in Hamilton County from 1881 to 1882. In March 1882, Taft was appointed federal tax collector for the first district by President Chester A. Arthur. In 1887, Gov. Joseph B. Foraker appointed Taft to a vacancy on the Cincinnati Superior Court. He was elected to the court the following year.

In 1890, Taft resigned from the court to accept an appointment by President Benjamin Harrison as U.S. solicitor general. Two years later, Harrison named the 34-year-old Taft to the newly established U.S. Court of Appeals for the Sixth Circuit. From 1896 to 1900, Taft also was a professor and dean of the law department at the University of Cincinnati.

In 1900, President William McKinley appointed Taft to head a commission to end U.S. military rule and establish civil rule in the newly acquired Philippines. In 1901, Taft became the first civil governor of the islands and began to gain the national stature that helped elevate him to the presidency. Taft held that position until January 1904, when President Theodore Roosevelt called upon him to become secretary of war after the resignation of Elihu Root.

A trusted friend and ally of Roosevelt, Taft traveled the globe on missions for the president. Taft continued to oversee Philippine affairs, supervised work on the Panama Canal, and assisted in the mediation that ended the Russo-Japanese War.

Keeping a pledge not to seek a third term, Roosevelt urged Taft to seek the Republican nomination. Taft was reluctant because he preferred waiting for an appointment to the U.S. Supreme Court. Pressured by his wife and brothers to accept Roosevelt's urgings, Taft agreed and was nominated on the first ballot at the GOP convention in Chicago. Rep. James S. Sherman of New York was nominated for vice president.

The Roosevelt administration had been popular, and Taft had established himself as an able manager. The Democrats again nominated William Jennings Bryan for the presidency. The result was an easy win for Taft, who carried 30 of the 46 states. Taft received 51.6 percent of the popular vote to Bryan's 43 percent. The electoral vote: Taft, 321; Bryan, 162.

At 6 feet 2 inches tall and weighing more than 300 pounds, Taft has been the largest man ever to serve as president. A jurist at heart, Taft soon discovered how much he disliked the job. He frequently let friends and associates know of his distaste for the rampant infighting, pomposity, and patronage of White House politics.

Taft attempted to carry on many of Roosevelt's policies. His administration began twice as many antitrust suits as had Roosevelt's and succeeded in dissolving the Standard Oil and other trusts. Taft's administration established the Department of Labor and the parcel post and ended the second American occupation of Cuba.

The Taft administration urged Congress to approve constitutional amendments to authorize a federal income tax and to provide for the direct election of U.S. senators. Both passed and went to the states for ratification. The 16th Amendment—to allow an income tax—was ratified February 3, 1913; the 17th Amendment—on direct election of senators—was ratified after Taft left office on April 8, 1913. Taft's tenure also saw the admission of Arizona and New Mexico to the Union, increasing the number of states to 48.

Believing that lower tariffs would help control trusts, Taft called a special session of Congress to pass tariff reductions. The House went along, but the Senate did not. The resulting Payne-Aldrich Tariff Act, approved in August 1909, essentially kept high tariffs. Because Taft declined to confront Congress by vetoing it, he got much of the public blame for the continuing high prices.

The Republican Party was splitting between conservative "Stand-Patters" and progressive or liberal members who thought Taft was too influenced by big money and corporate interests, especially on tariff and conservation issues. The progressives turned to Roosevelt, who challenged Taft for the 1912 Republican nomination. Taft viewed Roosevelt as moving too far to the left. Roosevelt won most of the primaries, but Taft controlled the national committee and was renominated at the June convention in Chicago.

Two months later, Roosevelt was nominated by the newly formed Progressive Party to challenge Taft and Democratic nominee Woodrow Wilson, then governor of New Jersey, for the presidency. The result was disastrous for Taft, who polled just 23 percent of the popular vote, carried only Utah and Vermont, and won only eight electoral votes. It was the worst-ever defeat for an incumbent president. Roosevelt finished second behind Wilson, the first Democrat to win the White House in 16 years.

After his defeat, Taft taught constitutional law at Yale until 1921, when President Warren G. Harding appointed his fellow Ohioan chief justice of the United States after the death of Edward D. White of Louisiana. Taft became the nation's tenth chief justice. He served on the court until February 3, 1930, when he retired because of heart problems. He died on March 8, 1930, in Washington.

Warren G. Harding

29th president (1921–1923)
Born: November 2, 1865, in Blooming Grove, Ohio (Morrow County)
Ancestry: English
Religion: Baptist
Occupation: editor, publisher
Political party: Republican
Family: wife, Florence Kling DeWolfe; no children
Residence when elected: Marion, Ohio (Marion County)
Served as president: March 4, 1921, to August 2, 1923
Died: August 2, 1923, in San Francisco
Buried: Marion, Ohio

Warren G. Harding, the last of Ohio's presidents, was the first president born after the Civil

HARDING SUPPORTERS AND HANGERS-ON BROUGHT SO MANY OF THEIR PALS TO WASHINGTON THAT THE GROUP BECAME KNOWN AS "THE OHIO GANG"

War, the first to be elected while serving in the U.S. Senate, and the first to assume office after the close of World War I. Unfortunately, Harding's brief tenure in the White House is remembered chiefly for the scandals that tarred the administration and may have hastened his death.

Born in Blooming Grove (formerly Corsica), Harding was the oldest of eight children in a family of modest means. His father, George Tryon Harding II, was a farmer, homeopathic doctor, and newspaperman. When Harding was ten, his father moved the family to a farm near Caledonia in Marion County. Harding attended local schools and learned to set type and perform other chores at the *Caledonia Argus*, of which his father had become part owner. At 14, Harding enrolled in Ohio Central College—an undistinguished academy, little more than a high school, in nearby Iberia—and obtained a bachelor of science degree.

At 17, Harding began teaching in a country school for $30 a month but found the job difficult and soon quit. He tried legal work and insurance sales but found himself suited to neither. He took a part-time reporting job at the *Marion Democratic Mirror* but was fired for his enthusiastic support of the 1884 Republican presidential nominee, James G. Blaine.

In November 1884, Harding and two friends purchased the bankrupt *Marion Star*, a small daily, for $300. Within a few years the newspaper was the leading paper in Marion County and one of Ohio's most successful small-town newspapers. Through the years, observers gave much of the credit for the paper's continuing success to Harding's wife, the former Florence Kling DeWolfe, whom he married in 1891. She was a divorcee, a well-to-do daughter of a prominent Marion banker, and more politically ambitious for her husband than he was for himself.

The year after his marriage, Harding lost his campaign for county auditor. In 1899, he was awarded the Republican nomination for a seat in the Ohio Senate and won the election that fall. He served until his election in 1903 as lieutenant governor, an office he held from 1904 to 1906. During his years in the Ohio Statehouse, Harding established a reputation as a good-natured, accommodating man who could mediate opposing Republican factions led by U.S. senators Joseph B. Foraker of Cincinnati and Marcus A. Hanna of Cleveland.

After his service as lieutenant governor, Harding returned to his newspaper office in Marion but was called upon in 1910 to accept the Republican nomination for governor. The party was split between conservative and progressive forces, and Harding was soundly defeated by Democrat Judson Harmon.

Known as a good orator, Harding was asked in 1912 to deliver the Republican convention's nominating speech for President William Howard Taft, who was seeking a second term. In 1916, Harding delivered the keynote speech at the Republican convention that nominated Charles Evans Hughes.

Harding was elected to the U.S. Senate in 1914, the first year senators faced direct election as outlined by the 17th Amendment. Harding defeated Democrat Timothy S. Hogan, who was Ohio attorney general. In the Senate, Harding sided with conservatives and supported Taft, opposed the League of Nations, voted for antistrike legislation, favored high tariffs, and voted for Prohibition even though he liked his drink. He was not identified with any major legislation or accomplishments. In fact, Harding was noted for missing nearly half of the roll-call votes.

Early in 1919, some newspapers began mentioning Harding as a possible compromise candidate for president in 1920. Harry M. Daugherty, an Ohio lobbyist and political strategist who had gotten to know Harding at the Statehouse, had just that in mind. Harding was reluctant to declare his candidacy for president but, urged by his wife and Daugherty, did so.

At the 1920 Republican convention in Chicago, the two leading candidates were Maj. Gen. Leonard Wood of New Hampshire, former army chief of staff; and Gov. Frank O. Lowden of Illinois. A third was Sen. Hiram Johnson of California. With eleven names placed in nomination, no one was able to command a majority of delegate votes. On the first roll call, Harding placed sixth.

Daugherty had spent considerable time collecting promises of second-choice and third-choice delegate votes. After the first day of the convention ended in stalemate, he had his opportunity. The adjournment gave political bosses time to discuss their alternatives. That night, in a legendary "smoke-filled room" in the Blackstone Hotel, the bosses agreed upon Harding as a compromise candidate—"the available man." The next day, Harding was nominated on the tenth ballot. Massachusetts governor Calvin Coolidge was selected as his running mate.

The Democrats later held their convention in San Francisco and nominated Ohio governor James M. Cox, publisher of the *Dayton Daily News,* for president and Franklin D. Roosevelt, assistant secretary of the Navy, for vice president.

From his Marion home, Harding waged a "front-porch campaign" in the style of William McKinley. He capitalized on the public's war weariness and skepticism toward President Woodrow Wilson's international policies. He emphasized the need for a "return to normalcy."

Harding won in a landslide, capturing 37 of 48 states and 60.3 percent of the popular vote in the first election in which women could vote. Harding received 404 electoral votes to Cox's 127. As the nation was entering the radio age, Pittsburgh's KDKA broadcast the election returns.

Harding made many excellent choices in filling his cabinet, including Charles G. Dawes as the first director of the Bureau of the Budget, Herbert Hoover as commerce secretary, Andrew Mellon as treasury secretary, Henry C. Wallace as agriculture secretary, and Charles Evans Hughes as secretary of state.

The new president made some terrible choices as well: he appointed Daugherty attorney general; Charles R. Forbes director of the newly created Veterans Bureau; and campaign contributor and anticonservationist Albert B. Fall, a friend of Western oil interests, interior secretary. Other Harding supporters and hangers-on brought so many of their pals to Washington that the group became known as "the Ohio Gang."

Harding's friends did him in. Forbes was convicted of bribery and conspiracy for a multimillion dollar overpricing scheme in the Veterans Bureau. Charles F. Cramer, the agency's legal adviser, committed suicide. Fall was sent to prison for taking bribes of more than $400,000 from oil magnates E. L. Doheny and Harry F. Sinclair. Fall had leased government-owned oil reserves in Elk Hills, Calif., and Teapot Dome, Wyo., without competitive bidding. Jesse W. Smith, a friend of Harding as well as Daugherty's roommate, committed suicide when it was revealed that he had improperly arranged settlements within the Justice Department. Daugherty avoided prison on charges of accepting bribes after two trials resulted in hung juries. Such widespread criminal conduct was not seen again in the White House until the Watergate scandals under President Richard M. Nixon.

In history books, the scandals obscure Harding's efforts to promote international disarmament, restrain government spending and taxation, implement a national budget system, restrict immigration, create a public welfare department, and end the steel industry's 12-hour workday.

The congressional elections of 1922, in which Democrats made gains in both houses, took place about the time that Harding began to learn of problems in the Veterans Bureau and possibly other offices. In June 1923, Harding began a national speaking tour in an attempt to bolster public confidence. During the trip, he learned that other scandals were about to be exposed.

The national tour had taken Harding to Alaska. As he was returning south, he fell ill, was hospitalized, and died in San Francisco on August 2, 1923. He became the sixth president to die in office. Although Harding had a heart condition, the exact cause of death remains unknown because Mrs. Harding refused to permit an autopsy. After Harding's death, his widow destroyed as much of his correspondence and as many of his records as she could find—leaving Harding's history clouded.

Later, Harding's reputation was scandalized by *The President's Daughter*, a 1927 book by Nan Britton, a woman 30 years younger than Harding who had traveled and carried on an affair with him while he was a senator and president. She had unsuccessfully sued for a share of his estate. The daughter, Elizabeth Ann, was born in 1919.

CHAPTER 4

Governors of Ohio

FROM EDWARD TIFFIN TO BOB TAFT,
60 MEN AND ONE WOMAN HAVE
SERVED AS THE STATE'S CHIEF
EXECUTIVE.

1 Edward Tiffin

(1803–1807)

Born in Carlisle, England, on June 19, 1766, Edward Tiffin came to America with his family in 1783. He was a student of medicine, obtained his degree, and for several years practiced as a country doctor in Virginia. In 1789, he married Mary Worthington, sister of Thomas Worthington, who became Ohio's sixth governor. After the Treaty of Greenville removed the Indian threat in Ohio, Tiffin joined the many settlers moving into the state and settled in Chillicothe in 1798. A strong anti-Federalist, he identified with the Democratic-Republican Party and fought for statehood against the territorial governor, Arthur St. Clair. He was a member from Ross County in the first and second territorial legislatures and was unanimously elected speaker. Tiffin served as president of the state's 1802 constitutional convention, was elected governor almost without opposition in 1803, and was re-elected in 1805. During his second term, Tiffin received thanks from President Thomas Jefferson for his leadership in helping suppress the alleged conspiracy of Aaron Burr. Tiffin was elected by the General Assembly to the U.S. Senate in 1807 but resigned in March 1809, eight months after the death of his wife. In April 1809 he married Mary Porter, with whom he had five children. Later that year, Tiffin was elected to the Ohio House of Representatives and chosen speaker. In 1812, Congress established the General Land Office, and Tiffin was appointed commissioner of the office by President James Madison. When the British burned Washington in 1814, Tiffin was the only department officer who managed to save his records. In the fall of 1814, he was appointed surveyor general of the United States. He served in that office for 15 years and under four presidents. Tiffin died at his home in Chillicothe on August 9, 1829. Tiffin, Ohio, is named in his honor.

TIFFIN WAS ELECTED GOVERNOR ALMOST WITHOUT OPPOSITION IN 1803

1803 Governor's Election
Edward Tiffin
(Democratic-Republican) . . . 4,564
1805 Governor's Election
Edward Tiffin
(Democratic-Republican) . . . 4,783

2 Thomas Kirker

(1807–1808)

When Edward Tiffin resigned the governorship to take his U.S. Senate seat in March 1807, Thomas Kirker became governor by virtue of his position as speaker of the Ohio Senate. Born in County Tyrone, Ireland, in 1760, Kirker came to America with his family when he was 19 and settled in Lancaster, Pa. He married Sarah Smith in 1790 and, around 1792, moved to Manchester in Adams County, where he was one of the pioneer settlers. An anti-Federalist and opponent of Gen. Arthur St. Clair, Kirker was chosen as a delegate from Adams County to the first Ohio constitutional convention in 1802 and was elected to the state senate in the first General Assembly, serving from 1803 to 1815. He served as Senate speaker

HE SERVED AS SENATE SPEAKER FOR SEVEN TERMS

1807 Governor's Election
R.J. Meigs Jr.
(Democratic-Republican)
. . . . 3,299 (58.7)
Nathaniel Massie
(Democratic-Republican)
. . . . 2,317 (41.3)
Total **5,616**

for seven terms. In the gubernatorial election of October 1807, Return Jonathan Meigs Jr. received a majority over Nathaniel Massie, but the General Assembly determined Meigs ineligible because he had not resided continuously in the state for four years prior to the election. Because of the ruling, Kirker continued as governor. The following year, 1808, Kirker ran for governor against Samuel Huntington and Thomas Worthington; all three candidates were Democratic-Republicans. Huntington won the election; Kirker resumed his duties as a state senator. In 1816, Kirker was elected state representative from Adams County and was elected House Speaker for one term. He returned to the state senate and served from 1821 to 1825. He died on his Adams County farm on February 19, 1837.

3 Samuel Huntington
(1808–1810)

Born October 4, 1765, in Coventry, Conn., Samuel Huntington was adopted as a boy by his uncle of the same name, who was governor of Connecticut and a signer of the Declaration of Independence. The younger Huntington attended Dartmouth College and then Yale College, graduating from the latter in 1785. He was married in 1791 to Hannah Huntington, a distant cousin. He studied law and was admitted to the Connecticut bar in 1793. In 1800, at 35, Huntington explored Ohio's Western Reserve and decided to move his family there. He moved to Youngstown in 1801 and soon after settled in Cleveland. He was admitted to the Ohio bar and was appointed lieutenant colonel of the Trumbull County militia by Gen. Arthur St.

THE QUESTION OF JUDICIAL REVIEW WAS THE MAJOR ISSUE

1808 Governor's Election
Samuel Huntington
(Democratic-Republican)
. . . . 7,293 (44.8)
Thomas Worthington
(Democratic-Republican)
. . . . 5,601 (34.4)
Thomas Kirker
(Democratic-Republican)
. . . . 3,397 (20.9)
Total **16,291**

Clair. He was appointed justice of the peace in 1802 and, the same year, elected to represent Trumbull County at the state's first constitutional convention. Huntington became state senator from Trumbull County in the first General Assembly and was chosen Senate speaker. In April 1803, Huntington was appointed by the legislature to the Supreme Court of Ohio. The following year, he succeeded Return Jonathan Meigs Jr. as chief justice. While on the court, a major dispute developed between the judiciary and the state legislature over judicial review of acts of the legislature. The

legislature, trying to subordinate the judiciary, launched impeachment proceedings against George Tod, Huntington's associate on the Supreme Court, and against Calvin Pease, presiding judge in the circuit court of the eastern district. Proceedings also were begun against Huntington but dropped after he was elected governor and resigned his court seat. The question of judicial review was the major issue of the 1808 gubernatorial campaign, won by Huntington over Thomas Worthington and Thomas Kirker. Huntington supported judicial review; Worthington and Kirker split the opposition votes. The attempt to subjugate the judiciary failed when the state senate failed to muster the two-thirds majority needed for conviction of Tod and Pease. Huntington did not seek re-election as governor in 1810. Instead, he ran for the U.S. Senate and was defeated by Thomas Worthington. He served in the Ohio House for the year 1811. In 1813, Huntington was appointed army paymaster under Gen. William Henry Harrison. Huntington died on June 8, 1817.

4 Return Jonathan Meigs Jr.
(1810–1814)

The son of a Revolutionary War soldier, Return Jonathan Meigs Jr. was born in Middletown, Conn., on November 17, 1764. He graduated from Yale College in 1785 in the same class with Samuel Huntington. He studied law and was admitted to the Connecticut bar. At 23, Meigs married Sophia Wright. In 1788, he followed his father to Marietta and practiced law there. Meigs immediately became active in public life and was appointed court clerk in Marietta. In 1794, he was appointed local postmaster and, in 1798, a judge of the territorial court. The following year, Meigs was elected to the territorial legislature. In 1802, the legislature elected him chief justice of the newly organized Supreme Court of Ohio. In October 1803, Meigs resigned from the court to take an appointment from President Thomas Jefferson as an army commander in the Louisiana Territory. Soon thereafter, Meigs was

DURING MEIGS'S GOVERNORSHIP, COLUMBUS WAS CHOSEN THE STATE'S PERMANENT CAPITAL

1810 Governor's Election
R.J. Meigs Jr.
(Democratic-Republican)
. . . . 9,924 (56.2)
Thomas Worthington
(Democratic-Republican)
. . . . 7,731 (43.8)
Total **17,655**

1812 Governor's Election
R.J. Meigs Jr.
(Democratic-Republican)
. . . . 11,859 (60.0)
Thomas Scott
(Democratic-Republican)
. . . . 7,903 (40.0)
Total **19,762**

appointed federal judge in the Michigan Territory. He had hardly begun his duties there before deciding to run for Ohio governor in 1807. Although Meigs defeated Nathaniel Massie in that October's election, the legislature ruled that his out-of-state service disqualified him from meeting the state constitution's four-year residency requirement. Meigs then was appointed to fill a vacancy in the U.S. Senate, created by the resignation of John Smith. Meigs was chosen for a full Senate term, commencing March 4, 1809, but he resigned on May 1, 1810, to run again for governor. Meigs defeated Thomas Worthington in an election dominated once more by the issue of the power of the judiciary to declare legislative acts unconstitutional. He was re-elected in 1812 over Thomas Scott. During Meigs's governorship, Columbus was chosen the state's permanent capital and plans were made for construction of a statehouse and penitentiary. The War of 1812 was the principal event during Meigs's tenure as governor, and he provided leadership in recruiting a state militia. In March 1814, he resigned to take an appointment from President James Madison as postmaster general. He served in that position until 1823. Meigs died in Marietta on March 29, 1825. Meigs County is named in his honor.

5 Othniel Looker
(1814)

Born Oct. 4, 1757, in New York or New Jersey, Othniel Looker was a Revolutionary War private who headed for the Northwest Territory upon receiving a land grant for his wartime services. Looker, who had married Pamela Clark in 1779, settled in Hamilton County around 1804, became a farmer, and, in 1807, was elected to the Ohio House of Representatives. He served in the House until 1809 and in the Ohio Senate from 1810 to 1812 and 1813 to 1817. Looker rose to speaker of the Senate and, by virtue of that office, became governor on March 25, 1814, after the resignation of Return Jonathan Meigs Jr. Looker ran for governor that fall but was defeated decisively by Thomas Worthington. Looker remained in the Senate until 1817, then returned to Hamilton County and became a Common Pleas judge, serving until 1824. He moved to Palestine, Ill., in 1844 to live with a daughter. Looker died on July 23, 1845.

6 Thomas Worthington
(1814–1818)

Thomas Worthington was born into the family of a prominent planter in the Shenandoah Valley on July 16, 1773, in Jefferson County, Va. (present-day Charlestown, W. Va.). Orphaned at the age of seven, he was raised by older brothers and a friend of his father's. At 18, Worthington went to sea for two years on a Scotch merchant ship. He returned to an inheritance of land and slaves. Worthington married Eleanor Van Swearingen on December 13, 1796, released his slaves, and decided to explore the Northwest Territory by making his way to Chillicothe. He was an assistant surveyor of public lands and was elected to the first and second territorial legislatures, where he supported statehood in opposition to Gen. Arthur St. Clair. Worthington was a member of the constitutional convention of 1802 and subsequently was elected to the Ohio House of Representatives from Ross County, but he immediately was chosen one of the first two U.S. senators from Ohio. He served in the U.S. Senate from October 17, 1803, to March 3, 1807, and again from December 1810 to December 1814, having been chosen to fill the vacancy created by the resignation of Return Jonathan Meigs Jr. Between stints in the U.S. Senate, Worthington served one term in the Ohio House (1807). In 1814, he was a candidate for governor against incumbent Othniel Looker. Worthington won handily and was inaugurated December 8, 1814. As governor, Worthington encouraged the establishment of the common school system, proposed state regulation of banks, urged construction of the canal system, and established the State Library of Ohio. In 1816, he easily won re-election against James Dunlap and Ethan Allen Brown. During Worthington's second term, the state capital was moved from Chillicothe to Columbus. In 1818, he became a member of the Canal Commission of Ohio to supervise construction of the canals. He remained a member of the commission until his death in New York City on June 20, 1827. Worthington was the father of James T. Worthington, a member of Ohio's second constitutional convention, and grandfather of Rufus King, vice president of the state's third constitutional convention.

7 Ethan Allen Brown
(1818–1822)

The youngest of seven children of a prosperous farmer and

AS GOVERNOR, WORTHINGTON ENCOURAGED THE ESTABLISHMENT OF THE COMMON SCHOOL SYSTEM

1814 Governor's Election
Thomas Worthington
(Democratic-Republican)
. . . . 15,879 (72.0)
Othniel Looker
(Democratic-Republican)
. . . . .6,171 (28.0)
Total 22,050

1816 Governor's Election
Thomas Worthington
(Democratic-Republican)
. . . . 22,931 (74.3)
James Dunlap
(Democratic-Republican)
. . . . 6,295 (20.4)
Ethan Allen Brown
(Democratic-Republican)
. . . . 1,607 (5.2)
Others 9
Total 30,842

landowner, Ethan Allen Brown was born at Darien, Conn., on July 4, 1766. His early education was interrupted by financial setbacks, but he eventually began studying law and was hired into the New York City law office of Alexander Hamilton. Brown was admitted to the New York bar in 1802 and soon thereafter took a trip down the Ohio and Mississippi rivers to New Orleans in an attempt to sell a load of flour. Finding the market glutted in New Orleans, he sailed to England to sell the flour. Upon returning to the United States, he again traveled down the Ohio River to find a tract of land to purchase. He settled on a plot downriver from Cincinnati, an area that later became Rising Sun, Ind. In 1804, Brown moved to Cincinnati and took up the practice of law. He served one term as prosecuting attorney of Hamilton County. In 1810, Brown was elected by the legislature to the Supreme Court of Ohio. He was re-elected in 1817 and ran for governor in 1818, when he trounced James Dunlap of Chillicothe. Brown assumed

BROWN WAS HAILED
AS "FATHER OF THE
OHIO CANALS"

1818 Governor's Election
Ethan Allen Brown
(Democratic-Republican)
. . . . 30,194 (78.8)
James Dunlap
(Democratic-Republican)
. . . . 8,075 (21.1)
Others 24
Total 38,293

1820 Governor's Election
Ethan Allen Brown
(Democratic-Republican)
. . . . 34,836 (71.3)
Jeremiah Morrow
(Democratic-Republican)
. . . . 9,426 (19.3)
William H. Harrison
(Democratic-Republican)
. . . . 4,348 (9.0)
Others 243 (0.5)
Total 48,853

the governor's office on December 14, 1818; Ohio was in a severe financial depression, brought on by rampant land speculation and the devaluation of overly abundant paper currency issued by Ohio banks. Many Ohioans saw the villain as the Bank of the United States, which was ordering local banks to pay their debts in gold and silver. The state legislature retaliated by imposing an annual tax of $50,000 on each of the federal bank's two branches in Ohio and ordering the state auditor to collect the money. On September 18, 1819, auditor's agents held up the United States Bank in Chillicothe, making off with more than $100,000. The state of Ohio had held up the federal government. The U.S. Supreme Court ruled Ohio's "crowbar law"—which imposed the annual $50,000 tax—unconstitutional. Brown was re-elected in 1820 over Jeremiah Morrow and William Henry Harrison. His governorship was marked by the organization of a seven-member canal commission.

Brown was hailed as "father of the Ohio canals" by supporters; canal opponents dubbed the enterprise "Brown's folly." In 1822, Brown was selected by the legislature to succeed the late William Trimble in the U.S. Senate, where he served until March 1825. In 1830, President Andrew Jackson appointed Brown envoy to Brazil, a post he held until 1834. In July 1835, Brown was appointed commissioner of the General Land Office in Washington—a job he had until October 1836, when he retired to Rising Sun. Brown served in the Indiana House of Representatives from 1841 to 1843. He died on February 24, 1852.

8 and 10
Allen Trimble
(1822, 1826–1830)

The son of a large landowner and slaveholder, Allen Trimble was born on November 24, 1783, in Augusta County, Va. When he was an infant, his family relocated to the area that now is Lexington, Ky. In 1801–1802, he and his father, James Trimble, explored Ohio's Scioto Valley region for land and purchased about 1,200 acres in what became Highland County. The elder Trimble died in 1804, and Allen moved the family to the new estate near Hillsboro. In 1806 he married Margaret McDowell, who died three years later. About 1808, Trimble was appointed common pleas clerk and recorder of Highland County. In 1811, Trimble married Rachel Woodrow. During the War of 1812, he served as a commander of a regiment raised in southern Ohio and led expeditions against Indians on the Eel and Wabash rivers. In 1816, Trimble was elected to the Ohio House of Representatives from Highland County; he served one year before winning election to the Ohio Senate to represent Highland and Fayette

TRIMBLE WAS
THE LAST
OF THE FEDERALISTS

1826 Governor's Election
Allen Trimble
(National Republican)
. . . . 71,475 (84.4)
Alex Campbell
(Democratic-Republican)
. . . . 4,765 (5.6)
Benjamin Tappan
(Democratic-Republican)
. . . . 4,192 (4.9)
John Bigger
(Democratic-Republican)
. . . . 4,114 (4.9)
Others 187 (0.2)
Total 84,733

1828 Governor's Election
Allen Trimble
(National Republican)
. . . . 53,970 (50.9)
John W. Campbell
(Democratic-Republican)
. . . . 51,951 (49.0)
Others 112 (0.1)
Total 106,033

counties. He served in the Senate from 1817 to 1825 and was Senate speaker for the last seven of those years. After Gov. Ethan Allen Brown resigned to become a U.S. senator, Trimble, on January 4, 1822, became acting governor. In previous years, Trimble had called himself a Federalist. He was considered perhaps the last important follower of that party in Ohio although the Democratic-Republican party was firmly in control of state politics. In the 1822 election for governor, Trimble lost to Jeremiah Morrow. Trimble left the governor's office on December 28 that year and returned to his Senate duties. Trimble lost to Morrow again in 1824 in an election in which they agreed on the major issues. In 1826, Trimble was overwhelmingly elected governor over three opponents. Although all four candidates were nominally Democratic-Republicans, Trimble was emerging as a member of the National Republicans, a faction headed by President John Quincy Adams and Henry Clay in opposition to a faction headed by Andrew Jackson. Upon re-election in 1828, Trimble was clearly identified as the National Republican candidate. The National Republicans disbanded after the 1832 election, but they provided the base for the Whigs, a new anti-Jackson party. As governor, Trimble played leadership roles in planning for the construction of Ohio's canals and in establishing a system of common schools. His administration also witnessed the beginnings of the abolition movement in Ohio. Trimble favored African colonization for freed slaves, but the idea was short-lived. After leaving the governor's office on December 18, 1830, Trimble remained active in National Republican and Whig politics. He lost a race for the state legislature in 1832. He helped establish the Ohio State Board of Agriculture and served as its first president from 1846 to 1848. In 1855, Trimble accepted the gubernatorial nomination of the American Party (Know-Nothings) but finished a poor third in the election. Trimble died on February 3, 1870.

9 Jeremiah Morrow
(1822–1826)

Jeremiah Morrow was born October 6, 1771, in Adams County, Pa., near Gettysburg. He was the son of John Morrow, a prosperous farmer and Federalist of Scotch-Irish descent. He received a good education, especially in mathematics, and became a skilled surveyor. In 1794, Morrow ventured into the Ohio country and purchased land in Warren County, where he farmed, surveyed, and taught school. He married Mary Parkhill, a cousin, in February 1799. The following year, Morrow was elected to the territorial legislature, which met in Chillicothe. He was a delegate to Ohio's first constitutional convention in 1802. In 1803, Morrow was a member of the first Ohio Senate. Within six months he was chosen to represent the state in Congress. He served in the U.S. House until 1813, when he was appointed to the U.S. Senate. Morrow served in the upper chamber until 1819. As a federal lawmaker, Morrow was known for his expertise on land and public-land policy; he was chairman of House and Senate committees on the public lands. Morrow was instrumental in passage of the Federal Land Act of 1820, which decreased the minimum price of land to $1.25 per acre and allowed the sale of tracts as small as 80 acres. Morrow served as an Ohio canal commissioner and, in 1822, ran for governor, defeating acting governor Allen Trimble. Morrow won a rematch with Trimble in 1824. During Morrow's governorship, Ohio recovered from economic depression. Completion of the Erie Canal, the extension of the National Road into Ohio, and the onset of canal-building in Ohio all played roles in kindling economic recovery. Morrow's tenure also was marked by enactment of legislation establishing a system of state-supported schools and a method of valuation and taxation of property. Morrow left the governor's office on December 19, 1826. He served in the Ohio Senate from 1827 to 1828 and in the Ohio House from 1829 to 1830 and 1835 to 1836. He also briefly returned to Congress, serving from October 13, 1840, to March 3, 1843. Morrow was among the founders of the Whig Party in Ohio. He also served as president of the Little Miami Railroad Co. from 1837 to 1845. The company built the first railroad out of Cincinnati. Morrow officiated at the laying of the cornerstone of the Statehouse in Columbus on July 4, 1839. He died on March 22, 1852.

11 Duncan McArthur
(1830–1832)

The oldest child in a poor family, Duncan McArthur was born on January 14, 1772, in Dutchess County,

MORROW WAS AMONG THE FOUNDERS OF THE WHIG PARTY IN OHIO

MᶜARTHUR PRESIDED OVER THE LAST OF THE INDIAN WARS

1822 Governor's Election	
Jeremiah Morrow (Democratic-Republican)	26,059 (41.1)
Allen Trimble (Democratic-Republican)	22,899 (36.1)
William W. Irvin (Democratic-Republican)	11,050 (17.4)
Others	3,462 (5.5)
Total	**63,470**

1824 Governor's Election	
Jeremiah Morrow (Democratic-Republican)	39,526 (51.6)
Allen Trimble (Democratic-Republican)	37,108 (48.4)
Total	**76,634**

N.Y. His mother died when he was very young, and McArthur's father moved the family to western Pennsylvania around 1780. As an adventurous youth, McArthur received little formal schooling and worked with pack trains delivering supplies to settlements. In 1790, he enlisted as a private under Gen. Josiah Harmar to serve in the campaign against Indians north of the Ohio River. In the winter of 1792 to 1793, McArthur worked as a salt boiler in Maysville, Ky. Later that year he joined Nathaniel Massie's surveying tour into the Scioto Valley, which made its way to the Chillicothe area. In 1794, McArthur was hired as a scout for the state of Kentucky to keep track of the movements of Indians. He joined Massie again in 1795 to 1796 to help lay out Chillicothe. In February 1796, McArthur married Nancy McDonald and settled on a farm near Chillicothe. He was known as a shrewd and hard bargainer and began to

1830 Governor's Election
Duncan McArthur
(National Republican)
. . . . 49,668 (50.1)
Robert Lucas
(Democratic) 49,186 (49.6)
Others 226 (0.2)
Total 99,080

acquire lands and build considerable wealth in the area. By 1804, McArthur was considered the wealthiest landowner in the Scioto Valley. He was elected to the Ohio Senate in 1805 and served until 1813. He was Senate speaker from 1809 to 1810. Despite his business savvy and political success, McArthur distinguished himself most as a soldier. In 1806 he was made a colonel of the Ohio militia and, in 1808, chosen major general. McArthur had been elected to Congress in 1812, but he resigned to take his place with the Ohio militia during the War of 1812. He commanded a regiment under Gen. William Hull in the march to Detroit. McArthur's troops were included in Hull's surrender to the British, and McArthur was placed on parole and returned to Chillicothe. Upon release from parole on April 5, 1813, McArthur accepted a commission as brigadier general under Gen. William Henry Harrison and was involved in much of the fighting that ended the war in 1815. After Harrison's resignation in May 1814, McArthur was placed in command of the Army of the Northwest. After the war, McArthur resumed his service in the General Assembly. He served in the Ohio House from 1815 to 1818 and from 1826 to 1827, and in the Ohio Senate from 1821 to 1823 and 1829 to 1830. He was elected to Congress in 1822 but served only one term, declining to seek re-election. In 1830, McArthur was a candidate for governor on the National Republican ticket and won narrowly over Robert Lucas, a Jacksonian Democrat. Considered the last of the pioneer governors, McArthur presided over the last of the Indian wars. His administration saw the National Road completed through Zanesville and begun toward Columbus, the operation and continued construction of canals, and the beginnings of the railroad era. In 1832, rather than seek re-election, McArthur ran again for Congress but was defeated—by one vote—by William Allen. McArthur died on April 29, 1839, on his Fruit Hill estate overlooking Chillicothe.

12 Robert Lucas
(1832–1836)

Robert Lucas was born into a prosperous family on April 1, 1781, in Shepherdstown, Va. (now W.Va.). He received lessons in mathematics and surveying from a Scotch tutor. About 1800, the family moved into the Northwest Territory and settled near Portsmouth, an area to become Scioto County. In 1803, Lucas was appointed surveyor of Scioto County and helped establish the boundary between Scioto and Adams counties. In 1810, he married Elizabeth Brown, who died in 1812, leaving an infant daughter. As an officer in the state militia, Lucas served in the War of 1812 and was a member of Gen. William Hull's disastrous campaign into Canada. He had served in the Ohio House of Representatives in 1808–1809 and, after the war, returned to politics, winning election to the Ohio Senate in 1814. In

LUCAS WAS THE FIRST JACKSONIAN DEMOCRAT TO BECOME OHIO GOVERNOR

1832 Governor's Election
Robert Lucas
(Democratic) . . . 71,251 (53.0)
Darius Lyman
(Anti-Mason) . . . 63,185 (47.0)
Others 33
Total 134,469

1834 Governor's Election
Robert Lucas
(Democratic) . . . 70,738 (51.2)
James Findlay
(Whig). 67,414 (48.8)
Others 38
Total 138,190

March 1816, Lucas married Friendly Ashley Sumner and moved to newly organized Pike County. He opened a general store in Piketon, the county seat. Lucas served in the Senate until 1822, then again from 1824 to 1830. An ardent Jacksonian Democrat, he was nominated for governor by like-minded party members in 1830. He lost a very close election to Duncan McArthur, a friend and fellow soldier from the War of 1812. In the 1831 to 1832 legislative session, he served again in the Ohio House. In May 1832, Lucas was elected temporary and permanent chairman of the first Democratic National Convention, which met in Baltimore and nominated Andrew Jackson for a second term. That fall, Lucas again was the Democratic candidate for governor. This time he was elected over Darius Lyman, the candidate supported by National Republicans and Anti-Masons. Lucas was the first Jacksonian Democrat to become Ohio governor. His first term was relatively uneventful, and in 1834 Lucas was re-elected over James Findlay, a Whig. His second term proved very eventful, largely because of the "Toledo War," which pitted Ohio against Michigan in a boundary dispute. The state of Ohio and territory of Michigan both claimed a strip of land along Ohio's northern border, which included the port of Toledo. Lucas summoned the state militia and led them to the border to face Michigan forces headed by Stevens T. Mason, the acting territorial governor. Armed conflict appeared likely until President Jackson intervened. In August 1835, Jackson removed Mason as territorial governor and replaced him with John S. Horner of Virginia. Congress settled the border dispute in Ohio's favor: In June 1836, it passed a law admitting Michigan to the union but with boundaries desired by Ohio. As compensation, Michigan was given its upper peninsula. When Lucas County was established in June 1835, it was named in honor of the governor. In 1836, Lucas ran for the U.S. Senate but was defeated by William Allen. Two years later, President Martin Van Buren appointed Lucas governor and superintendent of Indian affairs in the Iowa Territory. He retired from that job in 1841 and in 1843 lost a campaign for Congress in Ohio's Eighth District. Lucas returned to his farm near Iowa City and participated in the 1844 convention to form an Iowa state constitution. He spent his remaining years in Iowa and died on his farm on February 7, 1853.

13 Joseph Vance
(1836–1838)

Joseph Vance was born into a rather poor family on March 21, 1786, in Washington County, Pa. The family moved to Kentucky in 1788, then to Ohio about 1801—settling on a farm near Urbana in 1805. Vance received little formal schooling but was an industrious worker. He plowed fields and chopped wood and, after buying a team of oxen, sold salt from settlement to settlement. In 1807, Vance married Mary Lemen of Urbana. Upon his father's death in 1809, he took possession of the family farm. About the same time, he organized a rifle company and became its captain. The company became part of the state militia during the War of 1812; Vance helped guide Gen. William Hull's army and supply it with provisions. Vance was elected to the Ohio House of Representatives as a Democratic-Republican in 1812, serving from 1813 to 1816 and again from 1819 to 1820. He laid out the town of Findlay in 1820 and, the same year, was elected to Congress, where he served from 1821 to 1835. In 1836, as a member of the new Whig Party and an admirer of Henry Clay, Vance was elected governor over Democrat Eli Baldwin of Trumbull County—becoming the first

VANCE WAS THE FIRST WHIG ELECTED GOVERNOR

1836 Governor's Election
Joseph Vance
 (Whig) 92,204 (51.6)
Eli Baldwin
(Democratic) . . . 86,158 (48.3)
Others 200   (0.1)
Total 178,562

Whig in the office. As governor, he supported improvements in the public schools and continued canal and road construction. Vance favored abolition of capital punishment and was active in the antislavery movement. He lost the support of many antislavery citizens, however, by honoring Kentucky's request to comply with the Fugitive Slave Law in extraditing John B. Mahan, a Brown County clergyman. Mahan had been accused of assisting runaway slaves on their way to Canada. Although Mahan was found not guilty, Vance's surrender of Mahan to Kentucky authorities contributed to Vance's defeat when he sought re-election in 1838 against Democrat Wilson Shannon. Vance was elected to the Ohio Senate, serving from 1839 to 1840. In 1842, Vance ran for Congress as a Whig and won election over Samuel Mason. He served in Congress from 1843 to 1847 and was chairman of the Committee on Claims. He opposed the annexation of Texas and the Mexican War. Vance was a delegate to the Whig national convention in June 1848 in Philadelphia, which nominated Zachary Taylor for the presidency. He was a delegate to Ohio's second constitutional convention 1850 to 1851. Vance died in Urbana on August 24, 1852.

14 and 16
Wilson Shannon
(1838–1840, 1842–1844)

The youngest of nine children in an Irish family, Wilson Shannon was born February 24, 1802, near Mount Olivet in Belmont County. He attended local schools and helped on the family farm until 1820, when he went to Ohio University in Athens. Two years later, he moved to Lexington, Ky., to live with two brothers, attend Transylvania University, and study law. Shannon returned to Ohio in 1826 and completed his legal studies in the St. Clairsville offices of Charles Hammond and David Jennings. He was admitted to the bar in 1830. Two years later, he won the Democratic nomination to Congress from his eastern Ohio district but lost to the

SHANNON WAS THE FIRST NATIVE OHIOAN TO BECOME GOVERNOR

1838 Governor's Election
Wilson Shannon
(Democratic) . . . 107,884 (51.4)
Joseph Vance
(Whig) 102,146 (48.6)
Others 7
Total 210,037

1842 Governor's Election
Wilson Shannon
(Democratic) . . . 119,774 (49.3)
Thomas Corwin
(Whig) 117,902 (48.5)
Leiscester King
(Liberty) 5,134   (2.1)
Others 40
Total 242,850

Whig candidate. In 1833, Shannon was elected to the first of two terms as prosecuting attorney of Belmont County. In 1838, he was nominated as the Democratic candidate for governor and won 51 percent of the vote to oust Gov. Joseph Vance, a Whig. Shannon was the first native Ohioan to become governor. The major issues of the 1838 campaign were banking, currency, and the state's economic condition. The banks were blamed for the oversupply of bank notes that fueled rampant speculation, risk-taking, and defaults. Campaigning on banking reform, Democrats won both houses of the General Assembly as well as the governor's office. With Shannon as governor, the state enacted a law in 1839 limiting the circulation of bank notes and more closely regulating the banks. Shannon's administration also produced a state fugitive slave law that was more strict than the federal law. In 1840, Shannon was defeated by the popular Whig candidate Thomas Corwin, who captured 53 percent of the vote. Shannon returned to his law practice until 1842, when he recaptured the governor's office by narrowly winning a rematch with Corwin. In April 1844, Shannon resigned as governor to accept an appointment from President John Tyler as minister to Mexico. He was recalled to the United States in March 1845, on the eve of the Mexican War, when diplomatic relations between the two countries were severed. Shannon practiced law again in Ohio until 1849, when he was among a group of Forty-Niners headed for California. He returned to Ohio in 1851. The following year, he was elected to Congress from an eastern Ohio district and served from 1853 to 1855. In 1854, Shannon was one of four Ohio Democrats to vote in favor of the Kansas-Nebraska Act, which repealed the Missouri Compromise, allowed a local option on the slavery question in the newly established Kansas and Nebraska territories, and heightened tensions between proslavery and antislavery forces. In 1855, President Franklin Pierce appointed Shannon governor of the Territory of Kansas. He served until August 21, 1856, when he retired from public life. Shannon settled permanently in Kansas in 1857. Shannon was twice married—first to Elizabeth Ellis, who died a short time after their marriage, and then to Sarah Osbun. Shannon died in Kansas on August 30, 1877.

15 Thomas Corwin
(1840–1842)

Thomas Corwin was born July 29, 1794, in Bourbon County, Ky. By the time he was four, his family moved to a farm near Lebanon, Ohio, in Warren County. He attended a local school, did farm chores, and delivered supplies as a wagon boy during the War of 1812. His father, Matthias Corwin, served in the Ohio House of Representatives and was speaker in the 14th General Assembly. The younger Corwin studied law and was admitted to the bar. He served as Warren County prosecuting attorney and, in 1821, was elected to the Ohio House. The next year he married Sarah Ross, a congressman's daughter. He left the House in 1823

but was elected again in 1829. The following year, Corwin was elected to Congress. As a congressman for a decade, Corwin established a reputation for biting wit and brilliant oratory. In 1840, he was nominated as the Whig candidate for governor. The Whig campaigns that year were conducted in a circuslike atmosphere of parades, rallies, songfests, and assorted amusements. Corwin was promoted in song as "Tom Corwin, the Wagon Boy." Corwin defeated incumbent governor Wilson Shannon but his term as governor was rather unremarkable. Shannon won a rematch in 1842, overcoming Whig charges that the Democrats would use their power to remove the capital from Columbus. In 1844, Corwin was selected for the U.S. Senate, where he led Whig opposition to the Mexican War. In 1850, President Millard Fillmore named Corwin secretary of the Treasury. He served until 1852, when he returned to Ohio to practice law. In 1858, Corwin returned to Washington after being elected as a Republican to the U.S. House. He was re-elected in 1860. In March 1861, President Abraham Lincoln tapped Corwin to serve as minister to Mexico, where he stayed until 1864. Corwin then opened a law practice in Washington. He died December 18, 1865.

CORWIN WAS
PROMOTED IN SONG
AS "TOM CORWIN,
THE WAGON BOY"

1840 Governor's Election
Thomas Corwin
(Whig) 145,442 (52.9)
Wilson Shannon
(Democratic) . . . 129,312 (47.1)
Others. 8
Total 274,762

17 Thomas W. Bartley
(1844)

Thomas W. Bartley was born February 11, 1812, in Jefferson County, Ohio, although he grew up on his family's farm near Mansfield in Richland County. He attended local schools and learned politics under his father, who served in Congress from 1823 to 1831. In 1829, Bartley graduated from Jefferson College in Canonsburg, Pa. After four years of studying law in Mansfield and Washington, he was admitted to the Ohio bar. He was elected prosecuting attorney of Richland County, then to the Ohio House, where he served from 1839 to 1840. Bartley then won election to the Ohio Senate and was serving as Senate speaker (1843–1844) when, by virtue of that position, he became governor on April 15, 1844, following the resignation of Wilson Shannon. At the 1844 Democratic state convention, Bartley lost the gubernatorial nomination to David Tod by one vote. Had Bartley won the nomination, he would have opposed his father, Mordecai Bartley, a Whig, in the fall election. Thomas Bartley served out

Shannon's term, leaving the governor's office on December 3, 1844. From 1845 to 1849, Bartley was U.S. attorney for Ohio's northern district. From 1852 to 1859, he served on the Ohio Supreme Court. He died on June 20, 1885. He was the first person to serve as presiding officer of all three branches of state government.

18 Mordecai Bartley
(1844–1846)

Mordecai Bartley was born December 16, 1783, in Fayette County, Pa. As a boy he attended local schools and worked on his father's farm. He married Elizabeth Welles in 1804. Five years later, he moved to Jefferson County, Ohio, and settled as a farmer. During the War of 1812, Bartley raised and headed a company of volunteers. After the war, he settled on a farm west of Mansfield in Richland County. He established a merchandising house in Mansfield, became prominent in civic life, and, in 1816, was elected to the Ohio Senate. The legislature appointed Bartley register of school lands for the Virginia Military District—an office he held until 1823, when he took a seat in Congress. Affiliated with the National Republicans, Bartley was re-elected three times. After eight years in Congress, he declined to seek another term and returned to Mansfield to pursue his farm and business interests. In 1844, Ohio's Whig Party—the successor of the National Republican Party—nominated Bartley for governor. Bartley won an extremely close election over Democrat David Tod, and the Whigs won control of both houses of the General Assembly. During Bartley's term, a state bank was chartered and the state's system of taxation was revamped to include several previously exempt classes of property on the tax duplicate. In the spring of 1846, the Mexican War erupted and President James Polk issued a call for troops. Bartley and his party opposed the war on the belief that it was intended to create more slaveholding states. Against the advice of fellow party members, Bartley agreed to raise the necessary volunteers—taking the position that, despite personal convictions, the state was constitutionally bound to abide by the federal request. Bartley also

BARTLEY SOUGHT TO REPEAL THE STATE'S BLACK LAWS, WHICH DENIED CERTAIN RIGHTS TO BLACKS

1844 Governor's Election	
Mordecai Bartley (Whig)	146,333 (48.7)
David Tod (Democratic)	145,062 (48.3)
Leiscester King (Liberty)	8,808 (2.9)
Scattering	11
Total	**300,214**

sought to repeal the state's Black Laws, which denied certain rights to blacks, including the right to testify in court against whites. He declined to seek a second term and retired from public life. With the demise of the Whig Party, he joined the Republicans. Bartley died at his Mansfield home on October 10, 1870.

19 William Bebb
(1846–1849)

William Bebb was born into a Welsh family on December 8, 1802, in Butler County, Ohio. He was educated at home and, later, in a local school. When he was about 20, Bebb began teaching, opening a school at North Bend. He was married in 1824 to Sarah Schuck, also a teacher. Bebb and his wife opened a school, which attracted many students from distinguished families. While teaching, Bebb also studied law; in 1831, he was admitted to the Ohio bar. He began practicing law in Hamilton and became active in Whig politics. In the 1840 presidential race, Bebb stumped the state for the "log cabin and hard cider" campaign of William Henry Harrison and John Tyler. In 1846, Bebb was nominated as the Whig candidate for governor. He defeated the Democratic candidate, David Tod, in a close election that was dominated by the issues of banking and currency. Bebb favored the repeal of Ohio's Black Laws but softened his position in response to the hostility it generated. As his predecessor did, Bebb provided for the raising of volunteers for the Mexican War even though he opposed it. He encouraged prison reform, the reduction of state debt, the opening of free schools, and the establishment of turnpikes and railroads. Bebb also recommended holding a second state constitutional convention to update many state-run operations. He declined to seek re-election in 1848, but his term—set to expire in December 1848—was extended to January 22, 1849, because the General Assembly was delayed in organizing a new session. During the administration of President Abraham Lincoln, Bebb served as an examiner of the federal pension department. He resigned the position in 1866 and returned to the 5,000-acre farm near Rockford, Ill., that he had purchased in 1847. He died at his Illinois home on October 23, 1873.

BEBB PROVIDED FOR THE RAISING OF VOLUNTEERS FOR THE MEXICAN WAR

1846 Governor's Election		
William Bebb (Whig)	118,869	(48.3)
David Tod (Democratic)	116,484	(47.3)
Samuel Lewis (Liberty)	10,797	(4.4)
Scattering	46	
Total	**246,196**	

20 Seabury Ford
(1849–1850)

Seabury Ford was born October 15, 1801, in New Haven County, Conn. He was the fifth of seven children in a Scotch family that moved to Burton in Geauga County in 1804. He worked on the family farm, was educated at home for several years, and later attended a local common school, then Burton Academy. In 1821, Ford entered Yale College in New Haven, Conn. He graduated in 1825, returned to Ohio to study law, and was admitted to the bar in 1827. The following year he married a cousin, Harriet Cook. Ford attained the rank of major general in the state militia, worked his farm, and became active in the Whig Party. He was elected to the Ohio House in 1835 and served six terms. During the sixth term, he was chosen House speaker. The following session, Ford was elected to the Ohio Senate. He was defeated for a Whig nomination to Congress in 1838, served again in the House in 1844, then moved back to the Senate. From 1845 to 1846, he served as Senate speaker. In the legislature, Ford led the effort to repeal a law allowing the state to lend money to railroads and invest in the stock of canal and turnpike companies. In 1848, Ford was named the Whig candidate for governor. In the campaign against Democrat John B. Weller, Ford called for the repeal of Ohio's Black Laws and an end to the Mexican War. The election was so close that it was not decided until the General Assembly had examined the returns. On January 22, 1849, the assembly declared Ford the winner by 311 votes; 297,943 were cast. Ford became the last Whig governor of Ohio. The Black Laws were repealed, although a segregation law was enacted. In the fall of 1849, Ohio voters approved the calling of a constitutional convention, which Ford had urged. Convention delegates met in the Statehouse on May 6, 1850, to begin the work that, in 1851, resulted in the adoption of a new Ohio constitution. Ford's term ended December 12, 1850, after which he retired to his Burton home. Soon thereafter, he suffered a stroke; he died at his home May 8, 1855.

21 Reuben Wood
(1850–1853)

The eldest son of a clergyman, Reuben Wood was born in 1792 in Middletown, Vt. He was educated at home until about age 15,

FORD BECAME
THE LAST WHIG
GOVERNOR OF OHIO

1848 Governor's Election
Seabury Ford
(Whig) 148,756 (49.9)
John B. Weller
(Democratic). . . 148,445 (49.8)
Scattering 742 (0.2)
Total 297,943

when he went to Canada to live with an uncle and receive instruction in English and the classics. He began studying law but was forced to flee Canada at the outbreak of the War of 1812, when he was to be drafted to serve for the British against the United States. Wood fled by canoe across Lake Ontario and landed at Sackett's Harbor on the New York shore. He served briefly on the American side during the war, then studied law with Gen. Jonas Clark of Middletown, Vt. In 1816, he married Mary Rice. The family moved to Cleveland in 1818, where Wood established a law practice. He was elected to the Ohio Senate in 1825 and served until 1830, when the legislature elected him presiding judge for the Common Pleas Court of the Third Circuit (which included Cuyahoga County). In December 1832, the legislature elected Wood to the Ohio Supreme Court. He was re-elected in 1839 but denied a third term in 1847 when the Whig majority in the legislature opposed him. In 1850, Wood won the

WOOD VOCALLY
OPPOSED SLAVERY AND
THE FEDERAL FUGITIVE
SLAVE LAW

1850 Governor's Election
Reuben Wood
(Democratic) . . . 133,093 (49.7)
William Johnston
(Whig) 121,105 (45.2)
Edward Smith
(Free-Soil) 13,747 (5.1)
Total 267,945

1851 Governor's Election
Reuben Wood
(Democratic) . . . 145,654 (51.6)
Samuel F. Vinton
(Whig) 119,548 (42.4)
Samuel Lewis
(Free-Soil) 16,918 (6.0)
Scattering 62
Total 282,182

Democratic nomination for governor and captured 49 percent of the vote in the fall election, defeating Whig William Johnston and Free-Soiler Edward Smith. Wood was the last governor elected under the state's first constitution. When he was inaugurated in December 1850, the second constitutional convention was in progress. Adopted by Ohio voters on June 17, 1851, the new constitution provided for the election of governors in odd-numbered years. In the fall of 1851, Wood was re-elected with 52 percent of the vote over Whig Samuel F. Vinton and Free-Soiler Samuel Lewis. As governor, Wood vocally opposed slavery and the federal Fugitive Slave Law, though he counseled obedience to the law. During his tenure, railroads were rapidly being built and the state prospered. In February 1852, while the present Statehouse was under construction, the old Statehouse burned. At the June 1852 Democratic National Convention in Baltimore, Wood was considered a presidential prospect, but his candidacy for the nomination did not materialize. Wood resigned the governorship in July 1853 to become American consul at Valparaiso, Chile. He returned to Ohio in 1855 to practice law in Cleveland and tend his farm. At the beginning of the Civil War, Wood—aligned with Union supporters—was chosen to lead a mass meeting in Cleveland. Wood remained on his farm near Cleveland until his death on October 1, 1864.

22 William Medill
(1853–1856)

William Medill was born into an Irish family in 1802 in New Castle County, Del. He graduated from Delaware College in 1825 and studied law in the office of a local judge. Medill was admitted to the Delaware bar in 1830, and then moved to Lancaster, Ohio, where he resumed his law studies under Judge Philemon Beecher. Medill was admitted to the Ohio bar in 1832 and elected to the Ohio House in 1835. He served for three terms; in 1837, during his third term, he was elected House Speaker. A Democrat, he was elected to Congress in 1838 and re-elected in 1840. Two years later, he was defeated for a third term. In 1845, President James Polk appointed Medill second assistant postmaster general. He served for only a few months before being

MEDILL ENCOURAGED THE SALE OF STATE-OWNED STOCK IN CANALS, TURNPIKES, AND RAILROADS

1853 Governor's Election
William Medill
(Democratic) 147,663 (52.0)
Nelson Barrere
(Whig) 85,857 (30.2)
Samuel Lewis
(Free Soil) 50,346 (17.7)
Total 283,866

appointed commissioner of Indian affairs, a job he held until May 1849, shortly after the end of the Polk administration. Medill returned to Lancaster to practice law. In 1849, he was elected as a delegate to and chosen president of the state's second constitutional convention (1850–1851), which produced a new Ohio constitution, adopted by the electorate on June 17, 1851. Among other things, the constitution created the office of lieutenant governor; Medill was the first person elected to that office in the fall of 1851. When governor Reuben Wood resigned on July 13, 1853, Medill assumed the governor's office. Of the 108 delegates to Ohio's second constitutional convention, Medill was the only one to become governor. He also was the first bachelor to become governor. In the fall of 1853, Medill was elected governor over Whig Nelson Barrere (the last of that party's gubernatorial nominees) and Free-Soil candidate Samuel Lewis. As governor, Medill encouraged the sale of state-owned stock in canals, turnpikes, and railroads. Ohio's political climate was very hot as the slavery issue and anti-immigration sentiment caused deep divisions and spawned new

parties. In 1855, Medill sought re-election but was defeated by Salmon P. Chase, the candidate of the newly formed Republican Party. In March 1857, President James Buchanan, a Democrat, appointed Medill the first comptroller of the U.S. Treasury, a post Medill held until after the start of the Lincoln administration in April 1861. Medill then returned home to Lancaster. In 1863, he presided over the state Democratic convention. Medill died at his home on September 2, 1865.

23 Salmon P. Chase
(1856–1860)

The eighth of 11 children in a farming family, Salmon P. Chase was born January 13, 1808, in Cornish, N.H. His father, Ithamar Chase, was a Federalist who held various state and local offices. Ithamar Chase moved the family to Keene, N.H., when Salmon was seven. Two years later, the elder Chase died and Salmon was sent to Ohio to live with an uncle, Philander Chase, who resided in Worthington and was Episcopal bishop for the diocese of Ohio. In the fall of 1821, Philander Chase was named president of Cincinnati College, where Salmon Chase enrolled. Two years later, Salmon Chase transferred to Dartmouth College in Hanover, N.H.; he graduated in 1826 and went to Washington to teach school and study law. In 1829, he completed his legal studies and was admitted to the bar of the District of Columbia. Chase returned to Cincinnati in 1830, began a legal

CHASE'S ARDENT OPPOSITION TO SLAVERY BECAME HIS NATIONAL TRADEMARK

1855 Governor's Election
Salmon P. Chase
(Republican) 146,770 (48.6)
William Medill
(Democratic) 131,019 (43.4)
Allen Trimble
(American) 24,276 (8.0)
Total 302,065

1857 Governor's Election
Salmon P. Chase
(Republican) 160,568 (48.7)
H.B. Payne
(Democratic) 159,065 (48.2)
P. Van Trump
(American) 10,272 (3.1)
Total 329,905

practice and, as a nominal Whig, became active in the abolitionist movement and local politics. He published the three-volume Statutes of Ohio (1833–1835) and gained attention for defending runaway slaves, arguing in court that people could not be claimed as property. In 1840, Chase joined the newly formed Liberty Party, the first political party to officially adopt an antislavery position. Chase's ardent opposition to slavery later became his national trademark. He was prominent in the Free-Soil movement and, in 1849, was elected to the U.S. Senate by a legislative coalition of Free-Soilers and Democrats. In the Senate, Chase attempted to move the Democratic Party against slavery and campaigned against the Kansas-Nebraska Act, which permitted a local option on slavery. He gravitated toward the newly formed Republican Party, eventually becoming the party's first nominee for Ohio governor in 1855. That fall, Chase ran against Democratic incumbent William Medill and former governor Allen Trimble, running on the American (Know-Nothing) ticket. Chase and other Republican candidates swept the statewide races, overcoming charges that they supported Negro equality and disunion. Chase flirted with the idea of winning the presidential nomination at the first Republican National Convention in 1856 but withdrew before the balloting began. The Chase administration oversaw the passage of several antislavery resolutions, improvement of the common schools, restructuring of the state militia, and establishment of several new bureaus and commissions. On January 6, 1857, the new Statehouse was formally opened with a great celebration presided over by Chase. In the summer of 1857, state government was shaken when it was revealed that the treasury was short by at least $550,000. Interest payments on state bonds were due in July, and Treasurer William H. Gibson disclosed that the state couldn't make the payments. Gibson, a Republican, had been elected the year before, taking over the office from Democrat John G. Breslin, his brother-in-law. An investigation showed that Breslin had embezzled the money; Gibson knew it but had given Breslin time to repay it. Chase demanded and received Gibson's resignation and appointed Republican A.P. Stone to replace him. Democrats used the scandal to tarnish the Republican administration as Breslin fled to Canada without paying back the money. The Chase administration also was hampered by the Panic of 1857, when economic woes wrecked banks, railroads, other businesses, and individuals. Despite the problems, Chase was re-elected by a narrow margin that year over Democrat H.B. Payne, although Democrats captured the General Assembly. The legislature soon passed a measure to create an independent state treasury, divorcing it from banks. After serving two terms as governor, Chase was not a candidate for a third term in 1859. Republicans won the General Assembly that year and decided to send Chase back to the U.S. Senate. Chase was not there long because President Abraham Lincoln appointed him secretary of the Treasury after the 1860 election. Historians give Chase high marks for ensuring that the Union obtained the finances to fight the Civil War and helping institute a national banking system. Chase held the position until July 1864, when Lincoln accepted his fourth offer to resign. Later that year, after the death of Chief Justice Roger B. Taney, Lincoln nominated Chase chief justice. The appointment was confirmed December 6, 1864. As chief justice, Chase presided over the 1868 impeachment trial of President Andrew Johnson and was credited with handling it fairly. Chase continued to aspire to the presidency, but neither major party was interested in nominating him. Chase was married and widowed three times. He died of a stroke in New York City on May 7, 1873.

24 William Dennison, Jr.
(1860–1862)

DENNISON WAS GOVERNOR AT THE OUTBREAK OF THE CIVIL WAR

William Dennison Jr. was born November 23, 1815, in Cincinnati, where his family had moved from New Jersey about ten years earlier. He attended Miami University in Oxford, Ohio, where he distinguished himself in history, literature, and political science; he graduated in 1835. Dennison studied law in the office of Nathaniel G. Pendleton and was admitted to the bar in 1840. Soon thereafter, he married the eldest daughter of William Neil of Columbus, a prominent promoter of stage transportation. In 1848, Dennison was elected as a Whig to the Ohio Senate, where he served one term. He strongly opposed Ohio's Black Laws. Dennison was among the Whig leaders to join the new Republican Party in the mid-1850s. He was a successful businessman and, with the support of much of the business community, was elected governor in 1859 over Democrat Rufus P. Ranney. Dennison was governor at the outbreak of the Civil War and found it difficult to maintain public support while making strong decisions about the war effort. He sent George McClellan with state troops to western Virginia to help the area's residents drive out Confederates. Dennison also took control of the state's railways, telegraph companies, and express companies to manage the flow of war supplies and war news. In a deal with War Democrats, the Ohio Republican leaders did not renominate Dennison in 1861. They chose David Tod instead, as Republicans joined War Democrats in forming the Union Party. Dennison returned to his business affairs but frequently was consulted by Tod. In 1864, Dennison served as chairman of the Republican National Convention and was appointed postmaster general by President Abraham Lincoln; he held that position until 1866. In 1880, Dennison sought the Republican nomination to the U.S. Senate but was defeated by James Garfield. Dennison was remembered much more for his business success: He was president of the Exchange Bank of Columbus, an organizer of the Hocking Valley and Columbus and Xenia railroads, and a leader in the development of the Columbus Rolling Mills. For a time, Dennison also served on the Columbus City Council. He died June 15, 1882.

1859 Governor's Election	
William Dennison (Republican)	184,557 (51.9)
Rufus P. Ranney (Democratic)	171,226 (48.1)
Total	**355,783**

25 David Tod
(1862–1864)

David Tod was born February 21, 1805, near Youngstown, grew up on his father's farm, and attended local schools before entering Burton Academy in Geauga County. His father, George Tod, was a judge of the Supreme Court of Ohio from 1806 to 1810. The son followed his father in the study of law, was admitted to the bar in 1827, served as postmaster of Warren from 1830 to 1838, and served one term in the Ohio Senate from 1838 to 1840. He married Maria Smith in 1832; they had seven children. Although his father was a Whig, Tod was an admirer of Andrew Jackson and became a Democrat. As the Democratic nominee, Tod unsuccessfully ran

TOD WAS ACTIVE IN FORMATION OF THE UNION PARTY AND WAS SELECTED ITS NOMINEE FOR GOVERNOR IN 1861

1861 Governor's Election
David Tod
(Unionist) 206,997 (57.7)
Hugh J. Jewett
(Democratic) . . . 151,794 (42.3)
Scattering 109
Total 358,900

for governor in 1844 and in 1846. Both races, although close, went to Whig candidates: the first to Mordecai Bartley, the second, William Bebb. From 1847 to 1851, Tod served as minister to Brazil in the administration of President James Polk. He had considerable business interests in the Youngstown area and built a fortune in coal and iron. He was among the founders of Youngstown's iron industry and of the Cleveland and Mahoning Valley Railroad, of which he served as president. In 1858, Tod lost a congressional race to Republican John Hutchins. Tod was a presidential delegate for Stephen A. Douglas in 1860 and, in June, served as chairman of the Democratic convention when it reconvened in Baltimore after the tumultuous session that began in April in Charleston, S.C. At the outbreak of the Civil War, Tod supported President Lincoln and the war effort. He was active in formation of the Union Party and was selected its nominee for governor in 1861. Tod easily defeated Democrat Hugh J. Jewett in the fall election. Upon taking office, he was consumed by the war effort—drafting troops, recruiting medical personnel, putting down outbreaks of armed resistance, securing Ohio's borders, and meeting many other needs. During Tod's tenure, Confederate general John Hunt Morgan conducted his raids into southern Ohio. Because of public dissatisfaction with the war, political unhappiness with some of Tod's appointees, and other problems, Union Party leaders in 1863 nominated John Brough for governor instead of Tod. Tod declined President Lincoln's offer to become secretary of the Treasury in 1864, after the resignation of Salmon P. Chase. Tod died on November 13, 1868.

26 John Brough
(1864–1865)

The second of five children, John Brough was born September 17, 1811, in Marietta, Ohio. He attended local schools and, after the death of his father, apprenticed in a Marietta print shop. Brough attended Ohio University in Athens, worked on the *Athens Mirror*, then began studying law. He was an adherent of Jacksonian democracy and brought that viewpoint to editorial positions at several newspapers. He edited the *Washington County Republican* in Marietta, and then, with his brother Charles, purchased the *Ohio Eagle* of Lancaster in 1833. In 1835, he began serving as clerk of the Ohio Senate. Brough was twice married and had seven children. His first wife was Achsah P.

BROUGH HELPED SUPPORT TROOPS FOR THE WAR AND IMPROVED INSPECTION OF FIELD HOSPITALS

1863 Governor's Election
John Brough
(Unionist) 288,374 (60.6)
Clement L. Vallandigham
(Democratic) 187,492 (39.4)
Total 475,866

Pruden of Athens; his second, Caroline A. Nelson of Columbus. In 1838, Brough was elected to the Ohio House from Fairfield County. He served one term before being elected state auditor in 1839, a post he held until 1845. While auditor, Brough purchased a Cincinnati newspaper and renamed it the *Enquirer*, which he ran with his brother. In 1848, Brough was chosen president of the Madison and Indianapolis Railroad and gave up editorship of the *Enquirer*. At the beginning of the Civil War, Brough became active in the Union cause, opposing the Copperheads or Peace Democrats. In 1863, he became the Union Party candidate for governor against Clement L. Vallandigham, a leader of the Peace Democrats. Brough won handily, capturing nearly 61 percent of the vote. As governor, he obtained passage of tax levies to support soldiers' families and state and local government. He helped raise troops for the war and improved inspection of field hospitals. Brough announced that he would not seek re-election in 1865 because of ill health. He died in Cleveland on August 29, 1865, four months before his term was to expire.

27 Charles Anderson

(1865–1866)

AT THE CLOSE OF THE CIVIL WAR, ANDERSON CALLED FOR A GENERAL AMNESTY

Charles Anderson was born June 1, 1814, at his father's estate, Soldiers' Retreat, Ky., near present-day Louisville. Col. Richard Clough Anderson was a prominent soldier and land surveyor who left Virginia to help survey the Virginia Military District of Ohio. His son Charles received excellent schooling as a youth and, in 1829, entered Miami University in Oxford, Ohio. He graduated in 1833 and began studying law in the Louisville firm of Pirtle & Anderson. He was admitted to the bar in 1835, then moved to Dayton. Soon thereafter, he married Eliza Jane Brown, whom he had met at his college commencement. They had a son and two daughters. In Dayton, Anderson served as town clerk, superintendent of common schools, and Montgomery County prosecutor. He later served one term (1844–1845) in the Ohio Senate, where he advocated repeal of the state's discriminatory Black Laws. He identified with the Whig politics of Henry Clay. Suffering from asthma, Anderson took an extended vacation to Europe in search of better care. He returned to Ohio about 1848, moved his family to Cincinnati, and began practicing law with Rufus King. Anderson migrated back to Dayton before heading south to Texas in 1859. There he obtained notoriety, making enemies by publicly supporting the Union in the face of the prevailing Texan sentiment for secession. At the outbreak of the Civil War, Anderson extricated himself from unfriendly circumstances and moved his family back to Ohio. He was appointed a colonel of the 93rd Regiment of Ohio Volunteers and was wounded in the Battle of Stone River. In 1863, Anderson was elected lieutenant governor on the Union ticket with John Brough, who was elected governor. Upon Brough's death on August 29, 1865, Anderson was elevated to governor. At the close of the Civil War, Anderson called for a general amnesty. He served as governor for less than five months, fulfilling Brough's term, until January 8, 1866. Thereafter, Anderson resumed his law practice in Dayton. He later moved to Kentucky, where he died on September 2, 1895.

28 Jacob D. Cox

(1866–1868)

Jacob D. Cox was born October 27, 1828, in Montreal while his father, a New York building contractor, was supervising the roof construction of the Basilica of Notre Dame in the Canadian city. In 1842, the younger Cox began a law apprenticeship. Two years later, he switched interests and worked in the office of a banker and broker. In 1846, Cox entered Oberlin College, where he began studying theology. In 1849, he married Helen Finney, the eldest daughter of the college's president. Graduating in 1851, Cox became superintendent of schools in Warren, Ohio, while continuing to study law. He was admitted to the bar in 1852 and started a practice. Politically, Cox identified with the Whigs, though he became a delegate to the 1855 convention in Columbus that organized the Ohio Republican Party. In 1859, he was elected to the Ohio Senate from a district representing Mahoning and Trumbull counties. In the Senate, Cox was considered part of a radical antislavery group. At the beginning of the Civil War, he was active in organizing volunteers and was commissioned a brigadier general of the Ohio militia. After commanding forces in several important campaigns, he advanced to major general. In June 1865, he was nominated for governor as the Union Party candidate. The following month he was put

COX OPPOSED SUFFRAGE FOR BLACKS AND CALLED FOR FORCED RACIAL SEGREGATION

1865 Governor's Election
Jacob D. Cox
(Unionist) 223,633 (53.5)
George W. Morgan
(Democratic) . . . 193,797 (46.4)
Scattering 360
Total 417,790

in charge of mustering out and discharging the Ohio troops. In the fall election, Cox defeated the Democratic nominee, Gen. George W. Morgan of Licking County. Cox's tenure as governor was unremarkable, but he surprised some with his strong opposition to suffrage for blacks and his call for forced racial segregation. Cox was not renominated in 1867. After his term as governor, he moved to Cincinnati to resume practicing law. In March 1869, he accepted the post of secretary of the interior in the administration of Ulysses S. Grant. Cox served in the job only 18 months, resigning to protest his inability to enact reforms in the face of political considerations and the spoils system. In 1873, Cox moved to Toledo to become president of the Wabash Railway. In 1876, he was elected to Congress from the Toledo district and served one term. Cox became dean of the Cincinnati Law School in 1881, a position he held until 1897. He also served as president of the University of Cincinnati from 1885 to 1889. Cox gained recognition as a military historian and, from 1874 until his death, was military book critic for *The Nation*. He died August 4, 1900, in Magnolia, Mass.

29 and 32
Rutherford B. Hayes
(1868–1872, 1876–1877)

Rutherford B. Hayes was born in Delaware, Ohio, on October 4, 1822, three months after the death of his father, a farmer who had arrived in 1817 from Windham County, Vt. An uncle, Sardis Birchard, helped the family raise Hayes and provide him an education. He graduated from Kenyon College in 1842, studied law in Columbus, and attended Harvard Law School. Hayes was admitted to the Ohio bar on March 10, 1845. He began practicing law in Lower Sandusky (Fremont),and then moved to Cincinnati in 1849 and opened a law office. Hayes enjoyed the intellectual and literary offerings of Cincinnati, got involved in local politics as a Whig, and, on December 30, 1852, married Lucy Ware Webb of Chillicothe. He was a delegate to the state Republican convention in 1855, which launched the party in Ohio. The Cincinnati City Council appointed him city solicitor in 1858. Hayes was not as forceful in his opposition to slavery as many others in the Republican Party, but he opposed slavery's extension. He had hoped to see war avoided but entered the military at the outbreak of the Civil War and was chosen major in the 23rd Ohio Volunteers. He eventually rose to the rank of major general. In July 1864, he was nominated for Congress, although he continued his military service rather than return home to campaign. He was elected but did not take his seat until December 1865. He was re-elected in 1866. In June 1867, Republicans nominated Hayes for governor. He resigned from Congress and ran against Democrat Allen G. Thurman of Chillicothe. The major campaign issue was whether to

DURING HAYES'S REIGN, THE STATE ESTABLISHED THE COLLEGE THAT WOULD BECOME OHIO STATE UNIVERSITY

1867 Governor's Election
Rutherford B. Hayes
(Republican) 243,605 (50.3)
Allen G. Thurman
(Democratic) 240,622 (49.7)
Total 484,227

1869 Governor's Election
Rutherford B. Hayes
(Republican) 236,082 (50.7)
George H. Pendleton
(Democratic) 228,581 (49.1)
Samuel Scott
(Prohibition) 629 (0.1)
Total 465,292

1875 Governor's Election
Rutherford B. Hayes
(Republican) 297,817 (50.2)
William Allen
(Democratic) 292,273 (49.3)
Jay Odell
(Prohibition) 2,593 (0.4)
Scattering 17
Total 592,700

grant black males the right to vote. In a campaign that attracted national attention, Hayes eked out a victory with 50.3 percent of the vote. The proposed amendment to grant universal manhood suffrage was defeated, however, and Democrats won control of the state legislature. Much of Hayes's first-term agenda was thwarted by the Democrats, but he won re-election in 1869 with 50.7 percent of the vote over Democrat George H. Pendleton of Cincinnati. In the election, Republicans regained control of the legislature. During Hayes's reign as governor, the state established the college that would become Ohio State University, a geologic survey, and the Soldiers' and Sailors' Orphans Home in Xenia. Hayes improved the preservation of state historical records, expanded the powers of the State Board of Charities, began a program of reducing the state debt, and warned of the dangers of excessive taxation and government power. Hayes's leadership also was instrumental in Ohio's ratification of the 15th Amendment, giving all men the right to vote, regardless of color. After unsuccessfully running for Congress in 1872, Hayes resided on his estate near Fremont and devoted himself to his law and real-estate business. In June 1875, Republicans again turned to Hayes for the gubernatorial nomination. Hayes dreamed of winning the presidency and saw the governor's race as a stepping-stone toward that goal. That fall, in yet another extremely close race, Hayes defeated incumbent Democrat William Allen and became Ohio's first three-term governor. Hayes's foresight paid off, for he served just one year of his third term before winning election as the 19th president of the United States (see Chapter 3). Hayes served one term as president. He died January 17, 1893, in Fremont.

30 Edward
F. Noyes
(1872–1874)

Edward F. Noyes was born October 3, 1832, in Haverhill, Mass. His parents, Theodore and Hannah Noyes, died before he was three. He was cared for by his maternal grandparents and, later, a guardian. At 14, Noyes became an apprentice at a Dover, N.H., newspaper, the *Morning Star,* published by Free Will Baptists. He attended an academy in Kingston, N.H., and entered Dartmouth College in 1853. In

NOYES WAS HAMPERED BY ALLEGATIONS OF STATEHOUSE IMPROPRIETIES

the 1856 presidential election, Noyes campaigned for John C. Frémont, the nominee of the newly formed Republican Party. He began studying law, graduated from Dartmouth in 1857,and then traveled to Ohio to visit a classmate in Cincinnati. Noyes resumed his law studies in Cincinnati and, in 1858, graduated from the law school of Cincinnati College. He had hardly begun practicing law when the Civil War broke out. He entered the Union army, was made a major in the 39th Ohio Infantry and later was promoted to colonel. On February 15, 1863, during a leave from the army, Noyes married Margaret Wilson Proctor of Kingston, N.H. In July 1864,

1871 Governor's Election
Edward F. Noyes
(Republican). . . . 238,273 (51.7)
George W. McCook
(Democratic) 218,105 (47.4)
Gideon T. Stewart
(Prohibition) 4,084 (0.9)
Total 460,462

during fighting near Ruff's Mills, Ga., Noyes was wounded in the left ankle by gunfire and lost the leg to amputation. He was assigned to command Camp Dennison, Ohio, and was brevetted brigadier general. Noyes resigned from the military in April 1865 to become city solicitor of Cincinnati, a job he held for three years until elected probate judge of Hamilton County. In 1871, Noyes accepted the Republican Party's offer of its gubernatorial nomination and defeated the Democratic nominee, Col. George W. McCook. Noyes won 52 percent of the vote in an election that also included Gideon T. Stewart, a Prohibition candidate. Noyes's administration was rather uneventful. Seeking re-election in 1873, Noyes was hampered by an economic depression, dissatisfaction with the Grant administration in Washington, and allegations of Statehouse improprieties. The Democratic nominee, 69-year-old William Allen, defeated Noyes by 817 votes; 448,878 were cast. Allen became the first Democrat in the governor's office since 1856. Noyes remained active in Republican politics and, in 1877, was appointed minister to France by President Rutherford B. Hayes. Noyes held the post for four years, returning to Cincinnati in 1881. He practiced law and was elected in 1889 to the Superior Court of Cincinnati. Noyes died a year later, on September 4, 1890.

31 William Allen
(1874–1876)

William Allen was born December 18, 1803, in Edenton, N.C., to Nathaniel Allen, a Revolutionary War officer, and the elder Allen's third wife, Sarah Colburn Allen. Both parents died when William was an infant; the boy was raised by a half-sister in Lynchburg, Va.,

where, as a youth, Allen worked as an apprentice saddler. At 16, he moved to Chillicothe, Ohio, to rejoin his half-sister, who had moved there with her husband, the Rev. Pleasant Thurman. Allen began his first formal schooling at the Chillicothe Academy and two years later began studying law in the office of Col. Edward King, the son of Rufus King. At 21, he was admitted to the bar and became a partner of King's. Allen was a Jacksonian Democrat who became known for his oratorical and debating skills. In 1832, he was nominated by the Democrats for Congress and defeated Gen.

Duncan McArthur, the National Republican candidate, by one vote. Ten years later, Allen married McArthur's only daughter, Effie Coons. Allen served one term in the House and was defeated for re-election in 1834. In 1837, the Democratic-controlled state legislature sent Allen to the U.S. Senate to succeed Thomas Ewing, a Whig. In 1843, Allen was re-elected to a second term, during which he was chairman of

ANSWERING THE CALL TO "RISE UP, WILLIAM ALLEN," HE RAN AND WON

1873 Governor's Election
William Allen
(Democratic) 214,654 (47.8)
Edward F. Noyes
(Republican) 213,837 (47.6)
Gideon T. Stewart
(Prohibition) 10,278 (2.3)
Isaac C. Collins . . . 10,109 (2.3)
Total 448,878

the Committee on Foreign Relations and spokesman for President James Polk on Mexican War matters. After 12 years in the Senate, Allen was replaced by Republican Salmon P. Chase, retiring to his 1,400-acre farm near Chillicothe. A student of history and philosophy, Allen remained active in public affairs. During the Civil War, he identified with the Peace Democrats and strongly criticized the Lincoln administration. In 1873, as Allen approached his 70th birthday, Ohio Democrats saw an opportunity to capitalize on public frustration with the Grant administration in Washington and the severe economic conditions—the Panic of 1873. Answering the call to "Rise Up, William Allen"—popularized by the *Cincinnati Commercial*—Allen ran for governor and won an extremely close election over the Republican incumbent, Edward F. Noyes. Allen had supported the issuance of greenbacks, a policy of inflation, to counter low prices for commodities and unemployment. Allen's term was unremarkable, though he was widely considered an honest man. In 1875, he was narrowly defeated by Republican Rutherford B. Hayes, who was considered the sound-money candidate. Allen again retired to his estate, where he died July 11, 1879.

33 Thomas L. Young
(1877–1878)

Thomas L. Young was born December 14, 1832, in Killyleagh, Ireland. At 12, he immigrated to the United States with his parents and lived in New York City, where he attended public schools. At 16, Young enlisted in the army as a musician. Ten years later, in 1858, he left the army as a sergeant and soon settled in Cincinnati. He became an

instructor at a reform school for youth. In August 1861, Young was commissioned a captain in an outfit of Missouri Volunteers that served as bodyguard for Gen. John C. Frémont. The guard disbanded at the end of 1861, and Young spent the next six months editing a Democratic newspaper in Sidney, Ohio. In August 1862, he was commissioned a major in the 118th Ohio Infantry. Young rose to the rank of colonel and served until September 1864, when he was honorably discharged because of a sickness. He returned to Cincinnati to study law and was admitted to the bar in April 1865. That October he was elected as a Republican to the Ohio House of Representatives, where he served one term. In 1867, he was elected recorder of Hamilton County. The following year, President Andrew Johnson appointed Young supervisor of internal revenue for the southern district of Ohio. Young resigned the position one year later and began a real-estate practice. In 1871, he was elected to the Ohio Senate, where he served one term. In 1875, Young was the Republican nominee for lieutenant governor on a ticket headed by Rutherford B. Hayes; both were elected. When Hayes assumed the presidency in March 1877, Young ascended to the governor's office. That July Young called out the state militia in response to rioting during railroad and mining strikes, which had begun in Pennsylvania and spread to other states. Peace was restored in August. In 1878, Young was elected to Congress from the second district. He served for four years before failing to win nomination to a third term. He practiced law in Cincinnati and served on that city's board of public affairs. He died in Cincinnati on July 20, 1888. Young had been married three times and had eight children.

WHEN HAYES ASSUMED THE PRESIDENCY, YOUNG BECAME GOVERNOR

34 Richard M. Bishop
(1878–1880)

Richard M. Bishop was born November 4, 1812, in Fleming County, Ky. He received a common-school education and, as a teenager, worked in a country store, learning the merchant's trade. He and a brother later operated a pork business that eventually failed. In 1848, he moved to Cincinnati and opened a wholesale grocery business that flourished. Bishop later became the senior member of R.M. Bishop and Co., in partnership with his three sons. Bishop was not an energetic office-seeker, but he responded to the political urgings of members of Cincinnati's business community. In 1857, he was elected to the Cincinnati City Council. Two years later, Bishop was elected mayor of Cincinnati, but he declined re-nomination in 1861. He was very active in Christian church leadership and, from 1859 to

BISHOP ALLOWED A SON TOO MUCH INFLUENCE IN THE GRANTING OF PARDONS

1869, served as president of the Ohio Missionary State Society. He served as board president of the Home for the Friendless and Foundlings. Bishop served many other business, charitable, and educational institutions. He was a trustee of the Cincinnati Southern Railway and a director of the First National Bank of Cincinnati. He was a Democratic delegate to the state constitutional convention of 1873, although the constitution it proposed was rejected by the people. In 1877, the Ohio Democratic Party turned to Bishop—then 65—to be its gubernatorial nominee, although the party did not have great expectations of victory. To the surprise of many, Bishop won the five-man race with 49 percent of the vote. The Republican nominee, Judge William H. West of Bellefontaine, got just less than 45 percent of the vote. Bishop's tenure as governor was unremarkable, and he got into political trouble with Democratic insiders by too often failing to confer with them about political appointments. In addition, the governor was criticized for allowing one of his sons to exert too much influence in the granting of pardons to convicts. At the Democratic state convention in 1879, Bishop was not renominated. He died on March 2, 1893, in Jacksonville, Fla.

1877 Governor's Election	
Richard M. Bishop (Democratic)	271,625 (48.9)
William H. West (Republican)	249,105 (44.9)
Stephen Johnson	16,912 (3.0)
Lewis H. Bond	12,489 (2.3)
Henry A. Thompson	4,836 (0.9)
Total	554,967

35 Charles Foster
(1880–1884)

Charles Foster was born April 12, 1828, in Seneca County. He was the son of Charles W. Foster, a pioneer merchant after whom the city of Fostoria was named in 1854, when the adjacent villages of Rome and Risdon were combined. The younger Foster attended local schools but discontinued his formal education at 18, when he became a partner with his father in the family dry-goods business. He married Ann M. Olmsted in 1853 and had two daughters. Having amassed a small fortune, Foster entered politics by winning election to Congress in 1870. He was re-elected three times before losing his bid for a fourth term in 1878, following a redistricting. The next year, Foster was nominated as the Republican candidate for governor. He was a skilled political

HE WAS A SKILLED POLITICAL PRACTITIONER, INTRODUCING AN EARLY VERSION OF THE PRE-ELECTION POLL

practitioner, introducing an early version of the pre-election poll, identifying areas where he was weak, and spending large amounts of money in those areas to shore up support. Democratic newspapers criticized Foster for having sat out the Civil War. An oft-repeated attack: Foster was "a man who knew no higher occupation during the war than measuring calico." He was dubbed "Calico Charlie." In response, Foster's backers took to wearing calico garments in a show of support. Foster, considered the sound-money candidate, won the election with just more than 50 percent of the vote in a five-man race; Democrat Thomas Ewing of Lancaster, who had been a Civil War general, finished 17,129 votes behind and collected 48 percent. Two years later, Foster won a second term by 24,309 votes over Democrat John W. Bookwalter, a Clark County farmer-businessman. As governor, Foster appointed bipartisan boards to control public institutions and promoted forest protection, mine inspections, and revision of the tax system. He also took a hard stance toward the liquor industry, favoring stricter regulation and higher taxes on saloons. The unpopularity of such antiliquor aggressiveness led to the defeat of the entire Republican ticket in 1883, although Foster was not on it. Foster remained active in politics and, in March 1891, entered the cabinet of President Benjamin Harrison as secretary of the Treasury. In the position, he remained an advocate of sound-money policies. The Panic of 1893 and its resulting financial depression cost Foster a sizable share of his fortune. For many years he served as board president of the Toledo Asylum for the Insane. He died January 9, 1904, in Springfield, Ohio, en route to the inauguration of governor Myron T. Herrick.

36 George Hoadly
(1884–1886)

George Hoadly was born July 31, 1826, in New Haven, Conn. His grandfather was a member of the Connecticut legislature and his father, George Hoadly, served as mayor of New Haven. The family moved to Cleveland

1879 Governor's Election
Charles Foster
(Republican) 336,261 (50.3)
Thomas Ewing
(Democratic) 319,132 (47.7)
A. Sanders Piatt
(Greenback) 9,072 (1.4)
Gideon T. Stewart
(Prohibition) 4,145 (0.6)
John Hood 547
Total 669,157

1881 Governor's Election
Charles Foster
(Republican) 312,735 (50.1)
John W. Bookwalter
(Democratic) 288,426 (46.2)
Abraham R. Ludlow
(Prohibition) 16,597 (2.7)
John Seitz
(Greenback) 6,330 (1.0)
Scattering 138
Total 624,226

---

about 1830. Hoadly attended public schools and, at 14, entered Western Reserve College in Hudson, Ohio. At 18, he graduated in the class of 1844. He went to Harvard Law School the following year, entered the Cincinnati law office of Salmon P. Chase in 1846, and was admitted to the bar in 1847. Hoadly soon made partner in the firm, which became Chase, Ball and Hoadly. In 1851, the state legislature elected Hoadly to the Superior Court of Cincinnati. The same year, Hoadly married Mary Burnet Perry;

1883 Governor's Election
George Hoadly
(Democratic) 359,693 (49.9)
Joseph B. Foraker
(Republican) 347,164 (48.1)
F. Schumacher
(Prohibition) 8,362 (1.2)
Charles Jenkins
(Greenback) 2,937 (0.4)
Scattering 3,154 (0.4)
Total 721,310

they had two sons and a daughter. In 1855, he became city solicitor of Cincinnati, then was re-elected to the Superior Court in 1859. Hoadly served on the bench until 1866, resigning to form the law firm of Hoadly, Jackson and Johnson. Before the Republican Party was formed, Hoadly was a Democrat. Slavery and his association with Chase moved him to the Republicans, although he became uneasy with some party policies, particularly Reconstruction. Hoadly moved to the Liberal Republicans, a faction of the Republican Party, but was disappointed with the party's nomination of Horace Greeley in 1872 as he supported the re-election of President Ulysses S. Grant. Hoadly returned to the Democratic Party in 1876 and supported Samuel J. Tilden in that year's presidential election. He also represented Tilden before the special electoral commission appointed by Congress to settle the disputed election, which went to Ohioan Rutherford B. Hayes, the Republican candidate. Hoadly became the Democratic candidate for governor in 1883 against Republican Joseph B. Foraker. In the campaign, Democrats were aided by public resentment over Republican-passed legislation taxing saloons and forbidding Sunday liquor sales. Hoadly defeated Foraker by 12,529 votes; Democrats also won a majority in the legislature. Hoadly had a difficult time in the governor's office, partly because of his action —or lack of action—in responding to rioting in Cincinnati and labor disturbances in a mining strike in the Hocking Valley. In March 1884, a Cincinnati mob marched to the jail after a murderer was convicted of the lesser offense of manslaughter. Seeking to hang the prisoner, the mob became further enraged upon learning that the prisoner was en route to the penitentiary in Columbus. The rioters burned the courthouse, and critics charged Hoadly with being indecisive in delaying the call for the state militia to quell the disturbances. The next month, Hoadly sent troops to a labor uprising by striking coal miners in the Hocking Valley. The move angered labor organizers but did not placate those who thought Hoadly weak and indecisive. The 1885 election offered a Hoadly-Foraker rematch; this time Foraker prevailed by 17,451 votes. Hoadly resumed his law practice and, in 1887, moved to New

York City. There he established Hoadly, Lauterbach and Johnson and was a leading corporate lawyer. Hoadly handled many high-profile cases, including one involving the Jefferson Davis estate. He died August 26, 1902, in Watkins, N.Y.

37 Joseph B. Foraker
(1886–1890)

Joseph B. Foraker was born July 5, 1846, on a farm near the village of Rainsboro in Highland County. He spent his boyhood on the family farm, attending local schools. At 15, he worked for his uncle in the Highland County auditor's office. The following year, in July 1862, he enlisted as a private in the 89th Ohio Infantry. Foraker participated in Gen. William T. Sherman's march to the sea in 1864 and, by the time he left the army in June 1865, had risen to the rank of captain. He pursued studies at Salem Academy, Ohio Wesleyan University, and Cornell University. He was a member of Cornell's first graduating class in 1869. That October, Foraker was admitted to the bar and began practicing law in Cincinnati. In October 1870, he married Julia Bundy of Jackson County; they had five children. From 1879 to 1882, Foraker was a judge of the Superior Court of Cincinnati. In 1883, he won the first of four Republican gubernatorial nominations but was defeated by Democrat George Hoadly. In an 1885 rematch, Foraker was victorious in a close election; he won a second term in 1887 by defeating Democrat Thomas E. Powell. The election was Ohio's tenth consecutive gubernatorial race to include a Prohibition candidate; Morris Sharp received 29,700 votes, the best showing for a Prohibition candidate in a governor's contest. A great and fiery orator, Foraker was nicknamed "Fire Alarm" for his campaigning

A GREAT AND FIERY ORATOR, FORAKER WAS NICKNAMED "FIRE ALARM"

1885 Governor's Election
Joseph B. Foraker
(Republican) . . . 359,281 (49.0)
George Hoadly
(Democratic). . . . 341,830 (46.6)
Adna B. Leonard
(Prohibition) 28,081 (3.8)
John W. Northrop
(Greenback). 2,001 (0.3)
Scattering. 2,774 (0.4)
Total 733,967

1887 Governor's Election
Joseph B. Foraker
(Republican) 356,534 (47.7)
Thomas E. Powell
(Democratic). . . . 333,205 (44.6)
Morris Sharp
(Prohibition). 29,700 (4.0)
John Seitz
(Union Labor) 24,711 (3.3)
Scattering. 2,820 (0.4)
Total 746,970

style. As governor, he secured passage of legislation to regulate the liquor traffic, establish a state board of health, require bipartisan boards of elections and registration of voters in large cities, and establish a board of pardons. Foraker's second term was marked by celebrations of the centennial of the settlement of the Northwest Territory. He was nominated again in 1889 but defeated in the fall by Democrat James E. Campbell. Foraker returned to his law practice, which involved extensive corporate representation. In 1896, the legislature chose him to represent Ohio in the U.S. Senate, where he served from 1897 to 1909. As a member of the Committee on Foreign Relations, Foraker supported President William McKinley's Philippines policy and was instrumental in the organization of a civil government for Puerto Rico. In September 1908, publisher William Randolph Hearst revealed that Foraker had received $29,500 from the Standard Oil Company during his first term in the Senate. Foraker said the money was payment for legal services, but the disclosure did enough damage to prompt his exit from the public stage. The legislature selected fellow Republican Theodore E. Burton to replace Foraker. He attempted a comeback in 1914 by seeking the Republican Senate nomination but lost to Warren G. Harding. Foraker died May 10, 1917.

38 James E. Campell
(1890–1892)

James E. Campbell was born July 7, 1843, in Middletown, Ohio, the son of a surgeon who died eight years later. Raised by his mother, Laura Reynolds, Campbell attended local schools and had a private tutor. He began studying law but enlisted in the navy in the summer of 1863. He served on a gunboat for one year before his discharge, necessitated by breakbone fever. After his recovery, Campbell resumed his law studies, was admitted to the bar in 1865, and began a practice in Hamilton. In 1870, he married Libby Owens; they had four

CAMBELL WAS GREATLY HELPED BY A FALSE ALLEGATION AGAINST HIM—"THE BALLOT-BOX HOAX"

children. He was elected prosecuting attorney of Butler County in 1875 and re-elected in 1877. In 1882, Campbell was elected to Congress from a Dayton-area district; he was twice re-elected. In 1889, he won the Democratic nomination for governor over Lawrence T. Neal of Chillicothe and Virgil P. Kline of Cleveland. Republican governor Joseph B. Foraker was running for a third term. Because political tradition discouraged third terms, the Democrats emphasized that point during the campaign. They employed the slogan: "What Washington wouldn't have and Grant couldn't get, Foraker oughtn't to ask for." An extremely energetic campaigner, Campbell covered the state like few others. He condemned third terms, blasted Foraker for appointing some dishonest members of municipal boards, and championed home rule for cities. At the time, the governor appointed members of municipal boards of public affairs. The Democratic platform called for home rule; to emphasize the point, Campbell's campaign workers distributed miniature carpenter's rules at rallies. Campbell's bid was greatly helped by a false allegation against him —"the ballot-box hoax." Richard Wood, the inventor of a ballot box, offered to supply the Foraker campaign with a document showing that Campbell was an original investor in the ballot box at the time he was sponsoring a ballot-box law in Congress. Campbell was accused of using his congressional influence for personal gain. In exchange for the document, Wood wanted to be appointed smoke inspector of Cincinnati. Wood and two assistants forged Campbell's name on a fake contract and supplied it to Foraker. After the Foraker campaign leaked it to the press, every major newspaper in the state carried a story about Campbell's alleged conflict of interest. Upon investigation, Wood's helpers admitted the forgery. Foraker's campaign was castigated, and Campbell won the election by 10,872 votes. Campbell was the first governor in the state's 87-year history whose parents were both Ohio natives. Campbell's administration was not particularly eventful, although he pressed the General Assembly in special session to pass a portion of his home-rule plan. The legislature also passed a law requiring all children to attend school for a certain period and labor laws to protect workers. The assembly also adopted the Australian ballot system—to ensure secrecy and improve uniformity in the elections process. Campbell was nominated for a second term in 1891 but ran into a formidable Republican machine constructed by political boss Marcus A. Hanna, who backed the up-and-coming William McKinley as the GOP gubernatorial nominee. After serving several terms in Congress and achieving national notoriety for his tariff act of 1890, McKinley was defeated in his re-election bid that year because of Democratic-led gerrymandering of districts. In the 1891 governor's race, McKinley defeated Campbell by 21,511 votes in an election dominated by national issues. Campbell resumed his law practice but, in 1895, was again drafted to become the Democratic nominee for governor. He ran but was soundly defeated by Republican Asa S. Bushnell. Campbell later served on a commission to revise Ohio laws and as president of the Ohio Historical Society. He died December 17, 1924.

1889 Governor's Election
James E. Campbell
(Democratic) . . . 379,423 (48.9)
Joseph B. Foraker
(Republican) . . . 368,551 (47.5)
John B. Helwig
(Prohibition) 26,504 (3.4)
John H. Rhodes
(Union Labor). 1,048 (0.1)
Scattering. 195
Total 775,721

39 William McKinley
(1892–1896)

The seventh of nine children, William McKinley was born January 29, 1843, in Niles, Ohio. His father and grandfather had operated small iron foundries in Pennsylvania and Ohio. At nine, McKinley started his schooling in Poland, Ohio, near Youngstown, later attending Allegheny College in Meadville, Pa. He fell ill and returned home, taught in a country school, and, in June 1861, volunteered for the army. He became a mess sergeant with the 23rd Ohio Volunteers, an outfit containing many men who gained national fame. In 1865, McKinley was mustered out as a brevet major and studied law in the Youngstown office of County Judge Charles E. Glidden. In 1866, he attended Albany (N.Y.) Law School. The next year he was admitted to the bar and began practicing law in Canton, his home for the rest of his life. In 1869, he married Ida Saxton, daughter of a prominent banker. The same year McKinley was elected prosecuting attorney of Stark County; two years later, he was defeated for re-election. In 1876, he was elected to Congress, where he served until 1891— except for a break between 1884 to 1885, when he lost an election due to gerrymandering of districts. Chairman of the House Ways and Means Committee and champion of a high protective tariff, McKinley had established a national reputation by the late 1880s. In 1890, the tariff act bearing

MARCUS A. HANNA, A CLEVELAND-BASED POLITICAL BOSS AND MILLIONAIRE, WAS BUSY PLANNING MCKINLEY'S RISE TO THE PRESIDENCY

1891 Governor's Election
William McKinley
(Republican) . . . 386,739 (48.6)
James E. Campbell
(Democratic) . . . 365,228 (45.9)
John J. Seitz
(People's) 23,472 (2.9)
John J. Ashenhurst
(Prohibition) 20,190 (2.5)
Scattering 2
Total 795,631

1893 Governor's Election
William McKinley
(Republican) . . . 433,342 (51.9)
Lawrence T. Neal
(Democratic). . . 352,347 (42.2)
Gideon P. Macklin
(Prohibition) 22,406 (2.7)
Edward J. Bracken
(People's) 15,563 (1.9)
Scattering 11,946 (1.4)
Total 835,604

his name was enacted, raising duties to all-time highs. A month after the law was passed, he lost his re-election bid, largely because of a Democratic gerrymander. Gerrymandering by successive legislatures—in the wake of takeovers by one party or the other—was commonplace. In 1891, McKinley was the Republicans' unanimous choice for the gubernatorial nomination. He won the governorship in the fall—by 21,511 votes—over incumbent Democrat James E. Campbell. McKinley's first term was unexciting; he was re-elected in 1893 by a comfortable margin over Democrat Lawrence T. Neal. His second term was complicated by the Panic of 1893 and the resulting financial depression. Large-scale unemployment, strikes, and hunger caused much distress, and on several occasions McKinley called out the state militia to restore order. During the winter of 1894 to 1895, McKinley organized relief efforts to prevent starvation in the Hocking Valley, home to thousands of unemployed miners. Marcus A. Hanna, a Cleveland-based political boss and millionaire, was busy planning McKinley's rise to the presidency—a goal he achieved in the 1896 election (see Chapter 3). McKinley served one full term as president. He was re-elected to a second term but was shot by an anarchist on September 5, 1901, and died September 14. He is buried in Canton, Ohio.

40 Asa S. Bushnell
(1896–1900)

DURING BUSHNELL'S TENURE, THE STATE BEGAN USING THE ELECTRIC CHAIR

Asa S. Bushnell was born September 16, 1834, in Rome, N.Y., where his father, Daniel Bushnell, was a school teacher. His great-uncle, William Bushnell, was among the original Marietta settlers. In 1845, the family moved to Cincinnati, where Bushnell attended public schools. At 17, he moved to Springfield and became a dry-goods clerk, and then a bookkeeper in a factory. In 1857, he married Ellen Ludlow and soon became a partner with her father in a drugstore business. In the summer of 1864, he served as a captain in the 162nd Ohio Volunteer Infantry, which was assigned to guard and picket duty in the Shenandoah Valley. After the war, Bushnell returned to business interests in Springfield and, in 1867, became a partner in a company that manufactured mowers and reapers—Warder, Bushnell and Glessner Co. Years later, Bushnell sold the business to International Harvester. A strong Republican, Bushnell became a leading public figure in Springfield and had leadership roles in banking and public utility companies. He belonged to the wing of the Republican Party led by Joseph B. Foraker; in 1885, as chairman of the Republican State Executive Committee, he managed Foraker's successful campaign for governor. During Foraker's two terms as governor—1886 to 1890—Bushnell served as state quartermaster general. He declined a nomination for lieutenant governor in 1887. With the party split by factions, the Republican State Convention met in Zanesville in May 1895 to nominate a gubernatorial candidate. The Foraker faction took control of the convention, winning the nomination for Bushnell over the opposition led by Marcus A. Hanna. In the fall, Bushnell won a sweeping victory over Democrat James E. Campbell and Republicans carried all state offices. Bushnell was renominated and won re-election in 1897 over Democrat Horace L. Chapman, although by that year the Hanna faction controlled the state Republican organization. Hanna at the time was more interested in state legislative campaigns—to ensure his return to the U.S. Senate. Yielding to political realities, Bushnell reluctantly appointed Hanna to the Senate in March 1897 to succeed John Sherman, who had been named U.S. secretary of state by President William McKinley. During Bushnell's tenure as governor, the state advanced the merit system for civil service, set the stage for enactment of the corporate franchise tax in 1902, passed an antitrust act, and began using the electric chair instead of a hangman's noose for executions. The state also began more strictly regulating the employment of minors, working conditions for women, and the practice of medicine. In 1898, under Bushnell's leadership, Ohio became the first state to mobilize volunteers and field troops for the Spanish-American War. About the same time, construction work began on the Statehouse Annex, then called the Judiciary Annex, on the structure's east side. At the close of his second term, in January 1890, Bushnell returned to his business interests in Springfield. On January 11, 1904, he suffered a stroke. Four days later, on January 15, 1904, Bushnell died in a Columbus hospital.

41 George K. Nash
(1900–1904)

George K. Nash was born August 14, 1842, on a Medina

1895 Governor's Election		
Asa S. Bushnell (Republican)	427,141	(51.0)
James E. Campbell (Democratic)	334,519	(39.9)
Jacob S. Coxey (People's)	52,675	(6.2)
Seth H. Ellis (Prohibition)	21,264	(2.5)
William Watkins (Socialist Labor)	1,867	(0.2)
Scattering	3	
Total	**837,469**	

1897 Governor's Election		
Asa S. Bushnell (Republican)	429,915	(50.3)
Horace L. Chapman (Democratic)	401,750	(47.0)
John C. Holiday (Prohibition)	7,555	(0.9)
Jacob S. Coxey (People's)	6,276	(0.7)
William Watkins (Socialist Labor)	4,246	(0.5)
John Richardson (Liberty)	3,105	(0.4)
Julius Dexter (National Democrat)	1,662	(0.2)
Samuel J. Lewis (Negro Protection)	477	
Total	**854,986**	

County farm, studied at Western Reserve Academy, and, in 1862, entered Oberlin College. Two years later, he enlisted in the Union army, becoming a private in the 150th Ohio Infantry. After the war, he moved to Columbus, taught school, and studied law. Nash was admitted to the bar in 1867; two years later, he earned a Republican appointment as chief clerk to the secretary of state. In 1870, he won the first of two terms as Franklin County prosecutor. He ran unsuccessfully for Ohio attorney general in 1877 but won the office in 1879; he served from 1880 to 1883, and then was appointed to the Supreme Court Commission. The panel was created by constitutional amendment to help clear the court's docket. Nash belonged to the Republican faction controlled by Marcus A. Hanna and was Hanna's choice for governor in 1895, although the Foraker-led faction still controlled the party. By 1897, Hanna took control of the party and, in 1899, the gubernatorial nomination went to Nash. In the fall, Nash defeated Democrat John R. McLean, owner of the *Cincinnati Enquirer,* and several other candidates—most notably Samuel M. "Golden Rule" Jones, the reformist mayor of Toledo. Nash was re-elected in 1901 over Democrat James Kilbourne of Columbus and several other candidates. During Nash's tenure as governor, Ohio voters approved a 1903 constitutional amendment giving the governor veto authority for the first time. The veto could be overridden by a vote of two-thirds of each house of the legislature. Nash was loyal to the Hanna machine, which then included George B. Cox ("Boss Cox") of Cincinnati. Siding with the machine bosses, Nash

DURING NASH'S TENURE, OHIO VOTERS GAVE THE GOVERNOR VETO AUTHORITY

1899 Governor's Election
George K. Nash
(Republican). . . . 417,199 (45.9)
John R. McLean
(Democratic). . . . 368,176 (40.5)
Samuel M. Jones
(Independent). . . 106,721 (11.8)
Seth H. Ellis
(Union Reform). . . . 7,799 (0.9)
George M. Hammell
(Prohibition) 5,825 (0.6)
Robert Bandlow
(Socialist Labor) . . . 2,439 (0.3)
Total 908,159

1901 Governor's Election
George K. Nash
(Republican). . . . 436,092 (52.7)
James Kilbourne
(Democratic). . . . 368,525 (44.5)
E. Jay Pinney
(Prohibition) 9,878 (1.2)
Harry C. Thompson
(Socialist). 7,359 (0.9)
John H.T. Juergens
(Socialist Labor) . . . 2,994 (0.4)
John Richardson
(Union Reform) . . . 2,718 (0.3)
Total 827,566

opposed efforts by municipal reformers to give more executive authority to mayors instead of governor-appointed boards. Although friendly to business, Nash confronted revenue problems by getting the legislature to enact new taxes. The corporate franchise tax was enacted in 1902 at a rate of one mill on the value of capital stock invested in Ohio. Out-of-state insurance companies that sold policies in Ohio also were taxed for the first time, at a rate of $2\frac{1}{2}$ percent on gross premiums. The new taxes allowed the state to end its reliance on property taxes for the general fund. Nash died nine months after leaving office—on October 28, 1904. He was preceded in death by his wife and daughter.

42 Myron T. Herrick
(1904–1906)

Myron T. Herrick was born October 9, 1854, in Lorain County, Ohio, in a log cabin on the farm operated by his father, Timothy R. Herrick. The younger Herrick attended local schools and, about the age of 16, began teaching in a district school. He later studied at Oberlin Academy, traveled to St. Louis to pursue business ventures, worked as a newspaper reporter, and returned to Ohio to study at Ohio Wesleyan University in Delaware. Two years later, in 1875, Herrick moved to Cleveland to study law and work in a law office. He was admitted to the bar in 1878 and later opened a law office. He joined the Cleveland Grays, a military organization, and on June 30, 1880, married Carolyn M. Parmely of Dayton. Herrick's honesty and industriousness impressed many people; before long, he

HERRICK WAS A FRIEND OF CONSERVATIVE BUSINESSMEN

1903 Governor's Election
Myron T. Herrick
(Republican) 475,560 (54.9)
Tom L. Johnson
(Democratic) 361,748 (41.8)
Nelson D. Creamer
(Prohibition) 13,505 (1.6)
Isaac Cowan
(Socialist) 13,467 (1.6)
John D. Goerke
(Socialist Labor) 2,071 (0.2)
Total 866,351

was involved in many business enterprises. In 1886, he was appointed secretary and treasurer of the Society for Savings, a Cleveland bank, and later became its president and chairman. In 1885, Herrick was elected to the first of two terms on the Cleveland City Council. He controlled the 1888 district convention to name delegates to the Republican National Convention; he could have been first delegate but insisted that Marcus A. Hanna have the honor. The two developed a friendship that helped Herrick's political career. Herrick was an adviser to President William McKinley and was instrumental in McKinley's 1896 nomination and election. In 1901, Herrick was elected president of the American Bankers Association. In June 1903, the Republican State Convention met in Columbus with Hanna as its temporary chairman. Herrick was nominated for governor; he faced Democrat Tom L. Johnson, the reformist mayor of Cleveland. Herrick won 55 percent of the vote in a five-man race during a big year for Republicans and was inaugurated January 11, 1904. The next month, Hanna died. Herrick's administration was considered the friend of conservative businessmen. Although Herrick was credited with sound financial policies, he made enemies for using the veto and supporting certain provisions in local option legislation for liquor questions. The Anti-Saloon League and various church leaders opposed Herrick's re-election, as did sportsmen who were angered by his veto of legislation to allow betting at racetracks. In 1905, the Democrats nominated John M. Pattison to oppose Herrick. Pattison, considered a temperance supporter, denounced boss rule in urban politics and backed municipal ownership of public utilities. Pattison won the election, breaking the string for Democrats after four consecutive Republican governors. Herrick returned to his business interests, including the reorganization of railroads. On February 15, 1912, he was appointed ambassador to France by President William Howard Taft — an appointment that marked the beginning of a distinguished diplomatic career for Herrick. He served as ambassador until December 1914. In 1916, he lost a bid for the U.S. Senate. His wife died on September 15, 1918. Appointed by President Warren G. Harding, Herrick returned to the American embassy in France in July 1921. Herrick was at Le Bourget Field in May 1927 to greet Charles A. Lindbergh at the conclusion of the first solo flight across the Atlantic. Herrick died March 31, 1929—Easter Sunday—in the embassy. His body was returned home for burial in Cleveland.

43 John M. Pattison
(1906)

John M. Pattison was born June 13, 1847, near Owensville in Clermont County. The son of a country merchant, he worked in his father's store and on neighboring farms. In 1864, before his 17th birthday, Pattison joined the 153rd Ohio Volunteer Infantry. At the close of the Civil War, Pattison entered Ohio Wesleyan University and took the classical course of studies. He graduated in 1869 and took a job in the Bloomington, Ill., office of the Union Central Life Insurance Co. A short time later, he returned to Ohio and entered Cincinnati Law School. He graduated in 1872 and was admitted to the bar. He became a member of the law firm of Yaple,

PATTISON ATTACKED BOSSISM IN OHIO'S MAJOR CITIES

Moos and Pattison and served as attorney for the Cincinnati and Marietta Railroad. In 1873, he was elected to the Ohio House of Representatives, where he served one term. From 1874 to 1876, Pattison was attorney for the Committee of Safety of Cincinnati, a civic welfare group. On December 10, 1879, he married Aletheia Williams

of Delaware, Ohio; they had three children. She preceded him in death and Pattison later married her sister, Anna Williams. In 1881, Williams was elected vice president of Union Central Life Insurance. In February 1890, he was nominated to fill a vacancy in the Ohio Senate. Before the term expired, he was elected to Congress. He served from 1891 to 1893 and was defeated for re-election after a redistricting. In 1891, Pattison also became president of Union Central Life. In 1905, he was chosen the Democratic nominee for governor to oppose incumbent Republican Myron T. Herrick. Pattison was considered a strong supporter of the temperance movement, which was unhappy with Herrick; Pattison also was a strong advocate of Sunday closing laws. His campaign attacked bossism in Ohio's major cities and called for municipal ownership of utilities. In November, he defeated Herrick and was the only winner on the Democrat statewide ticket. Pattison was inaugurated January 8, 1906, but lived only five months longer; the exhausting campaign seemed to have weakened the frail Pattison. In April, he entered Christ Hospital in Cincinnati. He died June 18, 1906, at his Clermont County home.

44 Andrew L. Harris
(1906–1909)

Andrew L. Harris was born November 17, 1835, on a farm in Butler County in southwestern Ohio. In 1838, the family moved to Preble County, one county north, where Harris maintained a home for the rest of his life. Harris attended public schools and, in 1857, entered Miami University in Oxford, Ohio. He graduated in 1860, returned home, and began studying law in the firm of Thompson and Harris in Eaton. In April 1861, Harris enlisted as a private in the Union army and saw considerable action during the Civil War. His right arm was

HARRIS WAS THE LAST CIVIL WAR VETERAN TO SERVE AS GOVERNOR

47

permanently disabled by a gunshot wound during the Battle of McDowell in Virginia. When his regimental commander was killed at Chancellorsville, Harris was made commander. He was mustered out of the army on January 15, 1865, and later given the honorary title of brigadier general. Harris continued his legal studies, was admitted to the bar in April 1865, and set up

1908 Governor's Election

Judson Harmon (Democratic)	552,569	(49.3)
Andrew L. Harris (Republican)	533,197	(47.6)
Robert Bandlow (Socialist)	28,573	(2.5)
John B. Martin (Prohibition)	7,665	(0.7)
John Kircher (Socialist Labor)	797	
Andrew F. Otte (Independence)	397	
Total	**1,123,198**	

practice in Eaton. In October 1865, he married Caroline Conger of Preble County; they had one son. That same fall, he was elected to the Ohio Senate, serving from 1866 to 1867. Harris later served two terms as Preble County probate judge. In 1885, he was elected to the Ohio House of Representatives and, in 1887, re-elected. In 1891 and again in 1893, Harris was elected lieutenant governor on the Republican ticket headed by William McKinley. His association with McKinley continued when McKinley became president; McKinley appointed Harris to the federal industrial commission on trusts and industrial combinations. In 1905, Harris returned to the Republican statewide ticket as a candidate for lieutenant governor. Harris won the office again, but the incumbent Republican governor, Myron T. Herrick, was defeated by Democrat John M. Pattison. The same year, an amendment to the Ohio Constitution was approved, providing for the election of state and county officers in even-numbered years; the next election for governor was in 1908. When Pattison died on June 18, 1906, Harris became governor; he was the last Civil War veteran to serve in the office. The period was marked by progressive and reformist political movements, which elevated concerns about corporate control of elected officials and the use of public money for private gain. In addition, the state treasurer's office was investigated because the interest on deposits apparently had been funneled into private accounts. During Harris's tenure as governor, this environment prompted a law prohibiting the use of corporate cash in political campaigns. The General Assembly also passed legislation regulating building and loan associations and improving food and drug standards for purity. Harris was nominated for governor at the 1908 Republican State Convention and was opposed by Democrat Judson Harmon that fall. Harris battled the suspicion of graft at the Statehouse and faced opposition from the liquor interests, who were enraged by a local-option law that saw more than half of Ohio's counties go ''dry.'' Harmon defeated Harris, and the Republican Party also lost the treasurer's office for the first time since 1886. Harris returned to his home in Eaton, where he died September 13, 1915.

45 Judson Harmon
(1909–1913)

The oldest of eight children, Judson Harmon was born February 3, 1846, in the village of Newton in Hamilton County. His father was a teacher and Baptist preacher. Educated at home and in public schools, he entered Denison University at 16, graduated four years later, and then entered Cincinnati Law School. He received a law degree in 1869, was admitted to the bar, and, in 1870, married Olivia Scobey of Hamilton. After practicing law for seven years, Harmon was elected to the Hamilton County Common Pleas Court. He subsequently was elected judge of the Superior Court of Cincinnati, resigning in 1887 to replace ex-governor George Hoadly, who had moved to New York City, in a prominent Cincinnati law firm. Originally supportive of the Republican Party, Harmon could not support the party's Reconstruction

HARMON BROUGHT MUCH-NEEDED REFORMS TO STATE GOVERNMENT

1910 Governor's Election

Judson Harmon (Democratic)	477,077	(51.6)
Warren G. Harding (Republican)	376,700	(40.7)
Tom Clifford (Socialist)	60,637	(6.6)
Henry A. Thompson (Prohibition)	7,129	(0.8)
J.R. Malley (Socialist Labor)	2,920	(0.3)
Total	**924,463**	

program; he moved to the Liberal Republican Party, and, later, to the Democratic Party. In June 1895, Harmon was appointed U.S. attorney general by President Grover Cleveland. He distinguished himself in defending the Sherman Antitrust Act of 1890 from legal assaults. Harmon served until 1897, when he returned to his Cincinnati law practice. In 1905, during the administration of Theodore Roosevelt, he was chosen to investigate charges of illegal rebating by the Atchison, Topeka & Santa Fe Railroad. He uncovered more than $1 million in kickbacks and planned to indict company officers until Roosevelt interceded. The president insisted that the company—not individual officers—be held responsible for any illegal acts. Harmon withdrew from the case and wrote in a public letter: "The evils with which we are now confronted are corporate in name but individual in fact. Guilt is always personal. So long as officials can hide behind their corporations, no remedy can be effective. When the government searches out the guilty men and makes corporate wrongdoing mean personal punishment and dishonor, the laws will be obeyed." Considered a leading conservative in the party, Harmon was chosen the Democratic nominee for governor in May 1908 over the objections of Cleveland mayor Tom L. Johnson. At 62, Harmon defeated Republican incumbent Andrew L. Harris, whose administration had been damaged by a scandal involving the deposit of state funds. In the same election, Ohioan William Howard Taft, a Republican, was elected president. Amid a spirit of progressivism, Harmon's administration brought much-needed reforms to state government, including changes in depository laws. When the Republican-controlled legislature refused to enact some of his proposals, Harmon appealed to the voters and led Democrats to a resounding victory in 1910. In that election, Harmon won re-election over Republican challenger Warren G. Harding, led the entire Democratic ticket to victory, and saw Democrats win a majority of both houses of the legislature. The progressive mood spawned many new laws. The state enacted a workers' compensation act to pay Ohioans for workplace injuries and deaths, created a Tax Commission to equalize real-estate taxes, limited to ten mills the amount of taxes that could be levied without a vote of the people, provided for nonpartisan elections of judges, adopted the Oregon plan for direct election of U.S. senators, ratified the federal income-tax amendment, created a public utility commission, approved the initiative and referendum for cities, and limited the work week for women to 54 hours. In 1912, Harmon was promoted as a favorite-son candidate for president. He lost the support of some progressive Democrats, however, by opposing, at the 1912 Ohio Constitutional Convention, the proposal for the statewide initiative and referendum. The presidential nomination went to Woodrow Wilson. Harmon left the governor's office in January 1913. He resumed practicing and teaching law in Cincinnati, where he died on February 22, 1927. He was survived by three daughters.

46 and 48
James M. Cox
(1913–1915, 1917–1921)

James M. Cox was born March 31, 1870, on a farm near Dayton. As a young man, he worked in a print shop, taught school, was a reporter, and served as secretary to U.S. Rep. Paul Sorg, an Ohio Democrat. Cox's politics were those of the populists, reformers, and muckrakers. By 1898, he was the editor and publisher of the *Dayton Daily News*; he acquired the *Springfield News* in 1905. He was elected in 1908 to the first of two terms in Congress. The Progressive movement was reaching high tide in the Midwest, and Ohio Democrats chose Cox, then in his second congressional term, as the party's 1912 nominee

COX WAS THE FIRST OHIO GOVERNOR TO SERVE THREE FULL TERMS

for governor. In 1910, Ohio voters had authorized a constitutional convention, which convened January 9, 1912, and adjourned June 7, 1912. The convention submitted 41 proposed amendments for the September 1912 ballot—proposals that formed much of the Progressive platform of Cox's candidacy. In the election, Cox buried Republican challenger Robert B. Brown of Zanesville and Progressive Party candidate Arthur L. Garford of Elyria; Ohio voters approved 33 amendments, including the statewide initiative and referendum, compulsory workers' compensation, a merit system for civil service, municipal home rule, and the line-item veto for the governor on appropriations acts. Cox spent much of his first term implementing the amendments, although other reforms included the introduction of child labor laws and lobbyist registration, the addition of a seventh justice to the Ohio Supreme Court, the requirement of only a three-fourths jury vote for awards in civil cases, and the implementation of a new state budget system. The legislature also ratified the 17th Amendment, providing for direct election of U.S. senators. The period was most notable, though, for the 1913 floods, which killed more than 400 people, destroyed more than 20,000 homes, and swept away $300 million in property. Most of the devastation occurred in the Miami and Scioto valleys. The rains, which began on Easter Sunday, forced Cox to call out 8,000 members of the state militia to lead relief efforts. The General Assembly responded with legislation to construct dams. In 1914, Cox sought re-election on a platform of "promises fulfilled." But Ohio voters, perhaps weary of the cost of so much progress, rejected Cox in favor of Frank B. Willis, a Republican congressman from Delaware County. Cox

1912 Governor's Election
James M. Cox
(Democratic) 439,323 (42.4)
Robert B. Brown
(Republican) 272,500 (26.3)
Arthur L. Garford
(Progressive). . . . 217,903 (21.0)
C.E. Ruthenberg
(Socialist) 87,709 (8.5)
Daniel A. Poling
(Prohibition). 16,607 (1.6)
John Kircher
(Socialist Labor) . . . 2,689 (0.3)
Total **1,036,731**

1914 Governor's Election
Frank B. Willis
(Republican) 523,074 (46.3)
James M. Cox
(Democratic) 493,804 (43.7)
James R. Garfield
(Progressive). 60,904 (5.4)
Scott Wilkins
(Socialist) 51,441 (4.6)
Total **1,129,223**

1916 Governor's Election
James M. Cox
(Democratic) 568,218 (48.4)
Frank B. Willis
(Republican) 561,602 (47.8)
Tom Clifford
(Socialist) 36,908 (3.1)
John H. Dickason
(Prohibition) 7,347 (0.6)
Total. **1,174,075**

1918 Governor's Election
James M. Cox
(Democratic) 486,403 (50.6)
Frank B. Willis
(Republican) 474,459 (49.4)
Total **960,862**

defeated Willis in a 1916 rematch, by fewer than 7,000 votes, and afterward seemed better attuned to Ohioans' penchant for economy in government. His second term was not nearly as ambitious as his first, although he made improvements in several areas. In 1918, Cox once more defeated Willis, becoming the first Ohio governor to serve three full terms. Three months into Cox's second term, the United States entered World War I (April 6, 1917), and Ohio's industries were crucial to the wartime effort. Cox was instrumental in preventing work stoppages but also fanned anti-German sentiment in the state. After the war, he prompted the General Assembly to enact legislation banning the teaching of German in the schools—laws later declared unconstitutional. In 1920, nearing the end of his third term, Cox won the Democratic presidential nomination but was decisively defeated in the fall by Republican Warren G. Harding, a fellow Ohioan. After his defeat, Cox returned to his newspaper business and expanded his chain of publications. He died on July 15, 1957, in Dayton. He had been married twice and was the father of six.

47 Frank B. Willis
(1915–1917)

Frank B. Willis was born December 28, 1871, into a Delaware County farm family. He grew up doing farm chores and attending a local school. He worked his way through Ohio Northern University, graduated in 1893, and then became a teacher there. Willis soon became involved in Republican politics, winning election in 1899 to the Ohio House of Representatives. As a state representative, he led efforts to enact Ohio's first corporate franchise tax, which became law in 1902. In 1904, Willis unsuccessfully sought the GOP

AS STATE REPRESENTATIVE, WILLIS LED EFFORTS TO ENACT OHIO'S FIRST CORPORATE FRANCHISE TAX

nomination for a congressional seat, returned to the Ohio Northern faculty, continued studying law, and passed the bar in 1906. Four years later, he won election to Congress; he was re-elected in 1912. In 1914, Willis won the Republican nomination for governor; he defeated incumbent Democrat James M. Cox. The election also included Progressive candidate James R. Garfield, son of the Ohio-born president. Having campaigned on a platform of economy in government, Willis advanced little of an agenda in the Statehouse. He concentrated instead on consolidating and managing many of the new programs enacted under Cox. In a 1916 rematch with Cox, Willis lost an extremely close election. Willis made a political comeback in 1920, winning the U.S. Senate seat vacated by Warren G. Harding upon Harding's election as president. A member of the

GOP's conservative wing, Willis supported Harding's "back to normalcy" policies, was an isolationist, and opposed the League of Nations. After eight years in the Senate, Willis fixed his sights on the 1928 presidential race and began campaigning for the Republican nomination. He suffered a heart attack during a political rally at Ohio Wesleyan University and died on March 30, 1928. He was survived by a wife and daughter.

49 Harry L. Davis
(1921–1923)

The son of a steelworker, Harry L. Davis was born January 25, 1878, in Cleveland. He attended public schools until age 13 and then joined his father in the steel mill while attending night school and, later, business college. As a youth, Davis also spent some time as a page in the Ohio House of Representatives after his father, Evan H. Davis, won election to the assembly; the elder Davis served from 1888 to 1900. Harry Davis married Lucy V. Fegan of Cleveland on July 16, 1902; they had one son. Active in Republican politics, Davis was elected Cleveland treasurer in 1909 and Cleveland mayor in 1915; he was re-elected mayor in 1917 and 1919. In 1920, Davis won the Republican nomination for governor and defeated Democrat A. Victor Donahey. It was a huge year for Republicans: Warren G. Harding won the presidency in a landslide, and

DAVIS'S ADMINISTRATION SPONSORED AN ACT TO ENFORCE PROHIBITION

1920 Governor's Election
Harry L. Davis
(Republican). . . 1,039,835 (51.9)
A. Victor Donahey
(Democratic). . . . 918,962 (45.9)
Frank B. Hamilton
(Socialist) 42,889 (2.1)
Earl H. Foote
(Single Tax) 1,497
Total **2,003,183**

Republicans took 113 of 125 seats in the Ohio House and 36 of 37 seats in the Ohio Senate. As governor, Davis reorganized the state bureaucracy into seven cabinet departments with directors responsible to the governor. Passed as an emergency measure in April 1921, the act was challenged but upheld by the Ohio Supreme Court. In September 1922, in a special two-day session of the legislature, Davis won the authority to appoint a fuel administrator to cope with strikes by coal miners. The administrator could seize the mines, if necessary, to ensure a continued supply of coal. The office was abolished in December after the crisis had passed. Davis's administration claimed to have paved more roads than all previous administrations, sponsored an act to enforce Prohibition, and got the legislature to approve a two-year levy to finance the expansion of Ohio State University, Ohio University, and Miami University. The administration also opened Ohio's first state game preserve, the 15,000-acre Roosevelt Game Preserve in Scioto County. In 1922, Davis declined to run for re-election, saying he could not take time from reorganizing state government. He won the Republican gubernatorial nomination in 1924 but was handily defeated by incumbent Donahey. Davis returned to Cleveland, tended his insurance business, and led an effort to abolish Cleveland's city manager form of government—a goal he accomplished in 1931. Davis won election again as Cleveland mayor, serving from 1933 to 1935. He died May 21, 1950, in his Shaker Heights home.

50 A. Victor Donahey
(1923–1929)

Alvin Victor Donahey was born July 7, 1873, on a farm near Cadwallader in Tuscarawas County. He was one of three sons of John C. and Catherine Donahey. Donahey's father was a schoolteacher and farmer who was elected county clerk in the 1880s. A. Victor Donahey began his schooling in West Chester and continued it in New Philadelphia, the county seat, after the family moved there upon his father's election. He began

DONAHEY ACHIEVED A STATEWIDE REPUTATION FOR SHARP SCRUTINY OF GOVERNMENT EXPENSES

high school in New Philadelphia but dropped out after two years to work in a print shop. On January 5, 1897, Donahey married Mary Edith Harvey of Canal Dover (now Dover); the couple had 12 children. While still in his twenties, Donahey opened a print shop and was elected a Goshen Township trustee. In 1905, he was elected to the first of two terms as county auditor and gave up the printing business. In 1911, he was elected a district delegate to the 1912 Ohio Constitutional Convention. In 1912, he was elected to the first of two terms as state auditor, an office in which Donahey achieved a statewide reputation for sharp scrutiny of government expenses. He knew how to play to the press, as when he called in newsmen to announce that he would refuse to reimburse a Cleveland judge for a 35-cent baked potato submitted as an expense. "That's too much for a baked potato," Donahey said. "That is as much as a farmer gets for a whole bushel of them." Donahey agreed to reimburse the judge ten cents, the judge filed a mandamus action against Donahey, and the story received so much publicity that the judge withdrew the suit. After two terms as auditor, Donahey won the 1920 Democratic nomination for governor without opposition. In a big year for Republicans, Donahey lost to Republican Harry L. Davis—Donahey's only defeat during his political career. In 1922, he tried again and defeated Republican Carmi A. Thompson, a Cleveland Republican.

Donahey had acquired the nickname "Honest Vic," a reputation he nurtured with a homespun style of speech, disdain for pomp, and a preference for fishing and other common recreations. Donahey also rigidly opposed tax increases, vetoing virtually every tax measure that crossed his desk. In constant battle with the Republican-controlled legislature, Donahey acquired a new nickname —"Veto Vic"—by nixing 151 bills and appropriations while governor. Most of his vetoes were overridden. In a 1931 book, *The Beak and Claws of America,* Donahey explained his views on taxation: "We must reduce the tax burden and see that public money shall be touched with the great

1922 Governor's Election	
Vic Donahey (Democratic)	821,948 (50.6)
Carmi A. Thompson (Republican)	803,300 (49.4)
Scattering	551
Total	**1,625,799**

1924 Governor's Election	
Vic Donahey (Democratic)	1,064,981 (54.0)
Harry L. Davis (Republican)	888,139 (45.0)
Virgil D. Allen (Com. Land)	11,776 (0.6)
Franklin J. Catlin (Socialist Labor)	8,468 (0.4)
Total	**1,973,364**

1926 Governor's Election	
Vic Donahey (Democratic)	702,733 (50.3)
Myers Y. Cooper (Republican)	685,957 (49.1)
Joseph W. Sharts (Socialist)	5,985 (0.4)
Walter Freeman (Socialist Labor)	1,597 (0.1)
Total	**1,396,272**

scrupulousness of honor." Donahey easily won re-election in 1924 over Harry Davis and won a third term in 1926 over Republican Myers Y. Cooper. Donahey was the first governor elected to three successive terms. In 1928, he announced that he would not seek a fourth term. Upon leaving the governor's office, Donahey became president of Motorists Mutual Insurance Co. in Columbus and lived in a house on Governor's Island at Indian Lake. In 1934, Donahey returned to politics to run for the U.S. Senate. In the Democratic primary, he defeated Gov. George White and U.S. Rep. Charles West. In the general election, Donahey defeated incumbent Republican Simeon D. Fess of Greene County. He played a low-key role in the Senate, introducing only three bills during his term. Opting not to seek re-election in 1940, he returned to his insurance business. Donahey died April 8, 1946, in Grant Hospital in Columbus. He was buried in New Philadelphia.

51 Myers Y. Cooper
(1929–1931)

Myers Y. Cooper was born November 25, 1873, in a farmhouse in Newton

Township, a few miles from Newark in Licking County. The son of a country schoolteacher, he was the youngest of 11 children. Cooper attended a one-room school in the neighborhood before heading to National Normal University in Lebanon, Ohio. National Normal later became part of Wilmington College. Cooper attended the university for two years, became a salesman, and, in 1894, joined two brothers in the real-estate business in Cincinnati. In 1898, he married Martha Kinney, the daughter of a Cincinnati lawyer; the couple had a son and a daughter. Cooper developed extensive business interests in Cincinnati. His real-estate company built thousands of homes, and he became president of Hyde Park Lumber Co. and of Norwood National Bank. He served on the Hyde Park City Council before the village was annexed to Cincinnati and was a co-founder of the Hyde Park Business Club. He served as president of the Ohio Council of Churches for three years and, for nearly a dozen years, was president of the Ohio Fair Managers' Association. In the latter capacity, Cooper traveled the state and gained familiarity with its diversity. Since the early 1900s, Cooper was involved in Republican politics. He was the party's nominee for governor in 1926 but lost a close election to Democratic incumbent Vic Donahey, who won a third term. Two years later, Cooper won the governor's office over Democrat Martin L. Davey. The year was big for Republicans nationally and in Ohio: The GOP won all state administrative offices, every seat in the Ohio Senate, and all but 11 seats in the Ohio House of Representatives. Cooper had been in office nine months when, on October 29, 1929, the stock market crashed. The Great Depression completely overshadowed the accomplishments of the Cooper administration. During Cooper's term, the state approved construction of the $6.5 million State Departments Building at 65 S. Front Sreet expanded the regulatory powers of the Public Utilities Commission, revised the criminal code, and revamped the state budgeting process. In April 1930, a fire killed 318 inmates at the Ohio Penitentiary. That fall, as worsening economic conditions turned the political climate in favor of the Democrats, Cooper was defeated by Democratic challenger George White. Cooper returned to his business interests in Cincinnati. He sought the Republican gubernatorial nomination in 1932 but lost to David S. Ingalls of Cleveland. In 1933, Cooper was appointed chairman of the Little Miami Conservancy District. From 1949 to 1951, he was a member of Ohio's "Little Hoover

> ## COOPER HAD BEEN IN OFFICE NINE MONTHS WHEN, ON OCTOBER 29, 1929, THE STOCK MARKET CRASHED

1928 Governor's Election
Myers Y. Cooper
(Republican) 1,355,517 (54.8)
Martin L. Davey
(Democratic) 1,106,739 (44.7)
Joseph W. Sharts
(Socialist) 7,149 (0.3)
William Patterson
(Workers Communist) . . 2,184 (0.1)
John D. Goerke
(Socialist Labor) 1,272
Frank W. Stanton
(Prohibition) 1,085
Total 2,473,946

Commission," which recommended improvements in state operations. He died December 7, 1958, and was buried in Cincinnati.

52 George White
(1931–1935)

George White was born August 21, 1872, in Elmira, N.Y., the older of two children of Charles W. and Mary White. His father was a small businessman who went broke during the Panic of 1873—the year the family moved to Titusville, Pa., where Charles White worked as a jeweler and watchmaker. George White attended public schools and, in 1891, entered Princeton University, where he studied political science under Woodrow Wilson. During the summers, White worked in lumber camps and on farms. He obtained a bachelor of arts degree from Princeton in 1895 and later earned a master of arts at Marietta College. White spent time working in lumber camps and oil fields and teaching before he and some friends, in early 1898, joined in the gold rush to the Klondike region of Alaska. After two years of prospecting, White returned to Titusville; soon thereafter, on September 25, 1900, he married Charlotte McKelvy. They moved to Woodsfield, Ohio, where White was an independent oil producer. In 1903, they moved to Marietta and

> ## UNDER WHITE, THE STATE'S FIRST GENERAL SALES TAX WAS APPROVED

1930 Governor's Election
George White
(Democratic) . . . 1,033,168 (52.8)
Myers Y. Cooper
(Republican) 923,538 (47.2)
Total 1,956,706

1932 Governor's Election
George White
(Democratic) . . . 1,356,518 (52.8)
David S. Ingalls
(Republican) . . . 1,151,933 (44.8)
Joseph W. Sharts
(Socialist) 32,288 (1.3)
Aaron S. Watkins
(Prohibition) 19,575 (0.8)
John Marshall
(Communist) 6,349 (0.2)
William Woodhouse
(Socialist Labor) 1,784
Total 2,568,447

White got involved in Democratic politics. He later served as vice president and director of the People's Bank and Trust Co. of Marietta. White was elected in 1905 to the Ohio House of Representatives, where he sponsored a resolution asking Congress to submit a constitutional amendment providing for the direct election of U.S. senators. In 1906 and 1908, White lost races for Congress. But he was successful in 1910 and was re-elected in 1912. He was defeated for a third term in 1914 but won again in 1916. Known as a "dry," White twice voted for Prohibition. He continued to support the direct election of U.S. senators, a reform that in 1913 became the 17th Amendment to the U.S. Constitution. From 1920 to 1921, White chaired the Democratic National Committee; he also directed James M. Cox's unsuccessful 1920 presidential campaign. White's next political campaign was in 1928, when he unsuccessfully sought the Democratic nomination for governor. His wife died in 1929. The following year, White again entered the governor's race, defeated Stephen M. Young of Cleveland in the primary, and defeated incumbent Republican Myers Y. Cooper in the general election. Although White campaigned on reducing state spending and improving highways and bridges, his election primarily was due to voter frustration over worsening economic conditions. In his first term, White ordered 15 percent spending cuts in state departments, got the legislature to enact a cigarette tax (two cents a pack) and an intangible personal property tax, and pushed through other measures to meet the growing demands brought on by the economic crisis. In 1932, White started Frank J. Lausche's political career by appointing him a municipal judge in Cleveland. White won re-election in 1932 over Republican David S. Ingalls. Again, the economy dominated his second term, during which the state's first general sales tax was approved. The tax was enacted in December 1934 at three cents on the dollar; it became effective in 1935. The legislature imposed a tax on beer and malt beverages, too. Also created during White's tenure were the State Highway Patrol, a liquor-control system, a five-day waiting period for marriage licenses, legislation to build flood-control dams, and many other programs. In January 1934, White announced that he would seek the Democratic nomination for the U.S. Senate; he lost to former governor Vic Donahey. White tried but failed again in 1938. Blaming his losses on a lack of support from President Franklin D. Roosevelt and fellow New Dealers, he supported Republican Wendell L. Willkie in the 1940 presidential election. After Roosevelt's re-election, White withdrew from politics. He had married for the second time in April 1936; Agnes Hofman Baldwin of Parkersburg, W.Va., survived him. White died December 15, 1953, in West Palm Beach, Fla.; he was buried in Marietta.

53 Martin L. Davey
(1935–1939)

Martin L. Davey was born July 25, 1884, in Portage County and was raised in Kent. He was the son of John Davey, founder of the Davey Tree Expert, a tree-surgery company that the younger Davey later headed. Martin Davey graduated from Kent High School and attended Oberlin Academy before becoming general manager of his father's business in 1907. He was elected mayor of Kent in 1913, becoming known as the "boy mayor." In 1918, Davey entered Congress to fill an unexpired term; he was defeated in the 1920 election. He returned to win the seat in 1922 and was re-elected in 1924 and 1926. Two years later, Davey won the Democratic nomination for governor but was defeated in the fall by Republican Myers Y. Cooper. Davey returned to run for governor in 1934 and defeated Republican Clarence J. Brown, who had served two terms as Ohio secretary of state. Dapper in dress and flamboyant in political style, Davey had one of the most colorful tenures in the history of the governor's office. He constantly feuded with the legislature. When the assembly refused to appropriate $1,000 for new carpeting in his Statehouse office, Davey led a statewide campaign to collect money for his "rug fund." When the legislature refused to buy him a limousine, Davey purchased one with Ohio National Guard money since he was commander-in-chief. When he launched a cleanup of the prison system, Davey ordered the eviction of Preston E. Thomas, warden of the Ohio Penitentiary, and had the National Guard carry Thomas's belongings to the street. The Davey administration often was investigated for scandal. During his first term, Federal Relief Administrator Harry L. Hopkins accused Davey campaign aides of trying to shake down contractors doing business with the relief administration. Davey charged Hopkins with criminal libel and threatened to have him arrested if he set foot in Ohio; the charge was later dropped. In 1936, Davey was challenged for the Democratic nomination by Congressman-at-large Stephen M. Young. Davey

DAPPER IN DRESS AND FLAMBOYANT IN POLITICAL STYLE, DAVEY HAD ONE OF THE MOST COLORFUL TENURES IN THE HISTORY OF THE GOVERNOR'S OFFICE

1934 Governor's Race
Martin L. Davey
(Democratic)... 1,118,257 (51.1)
Clarence J. Brown
(Republican)... 1,052,851 (48.1)
I.O. Ford
(Communist)..... 15,854 (0.7)
Scattering 64
Total 2,187,026

1936 Governor's Race
Martin L. Davey
(Democratic)... 1,539,461 (52.0)
John W. Bricker
(Republican)... 1,412,773 (47.7)
Andrew R. Onda
(Communist)...... 7,372 (0.2)
Total........ 2,959,606

won but had been hammered by Young on the issue of Ohioans having to pay the state's new sales tax on groceries. Davey got the message: He urged the legislature to repeal the sales tax on food purchased for off-premise consumption. After the legislature refused, Davey headed a petition drive to put the issue on the November ballot—an amendment that was approved 2-to-1. In the same election, Davey won re-election over Republican John W. Bricker, the Ohio attorney general. In the summer of 1937, Davey called out the National Guard to maintain order during the Republic Steel strike in the Mahoning Valley. His second term was marked by many investigations led by the Ohio Senate, including one that produced evidence of price-fixing on road-paving contracts. The investigations hindered Davey's political future. In the 1938 Democratic primary for governor, he was defeated by Charles

Sawyer of Cincinnati, a former lieutenant governor. Sawyer lost in the fall to Bricker. Davey ran for governor once more, in 1940, but was handily defeated by Bricker. Davey returned to his home and business in Kent, where he died March 31, 1946. He was survived by his wife, Berenice, and a son and daughter.

54 John W. Bricker
(1939–1945)

The son of Lemuel and Laura King Bricker, John W. Bricker was born September 6, 1893, on a small farm north of Mount Sterling in Madison County. He and his twin sister, Ella, attended a nearby one-room school, and then Mount Sterling High School. After high school, Bricker taught in an elementary school for a year to earn money for college. In September 1912, he enrolled at Ohio State University, where he was a catcher on the baseball team and a member of the debate team. He graduated in 1916 and entered the university's college of law. He passed the bar exam in June 1917, despite having another year of law school ahead of him. His studies were interrupted by World War I, during which he served as an army chaplain. On September 4, 1920, he married Harriet Day of Urbana, Ohio; they later adopted a son. Also in 1920, Bricker received his law degree, began a practice, and was appointed solicitor of Grandview Heights, a Columbus suburb. In 1923, he was named an assistant Ohio attorney general and counsel for the Public Utilities Commission of Ohio. In 1928, Bricker unsuccessfully sought the Republican nomination for attorney general. The following year, he was appointed to the Public Utilities Commission; he served until 1932, when he was elected attorney general. He was re-elected to that post in 1934. Two years

BRICKER WAS THE FIRST REPUBLICAN GOVERNOR TO SERVE THREE CONSECUTIVE TERMS

1938 Governor's Race
John W. Bricker
(Republican). . . . 1,265,548 (52.4)
Charles Sawyer
(Democratic) . . . 1,147,323 (47.6)
Total 2,412,871

1940 Governor's Race
John W. Bricker
(Republican). . . . 1,824,863 (55.5)
Martin L. Davey
(Democratic) . . . 1,460,396 (44.5)
Total 3,285,259

1942 Governor's Race
John W. Bricker
(Republican). . . . 1,086,937 (60.5)
John McSweeney
(Democratic). 709,599 (39.5)
Total 1,796,536

later, Bricker was the Republican nominee for governor against incumbent Democrat Martin L. Davey. Davey prevailed in a big year for Democrats: President Franklin D. Roosevelt was re-elected in a landslide, and Democrats won all statewide executive offices. In 1938, Bricker again won the Republican gubernatorial nomination. Davey lost the Democratic nomination that year to Charles Sawyer, a former lieutenant governor, after disclosures of contract price fixing and shakedowns in the Davey administration. Bricker, campaigning on the slogan "Ohio Needs a Change," defeated Sawyer in the fall; the entire Republican ticket was elected. Upon taking office, Bricker discovered a $40 million state deficit. He ordered many measures of economy and department reorganizations, prompting the firing of more than 2,000 state employees. A strong conservative who preached against big government, Bricker easily won re-election in 1940 and 1942. He was the first Republican governor to serve three consecutive terms. In his first term, much attention was focused on relief for the poor, especially in Ohio's cities, while Bricker was trying to wipe out the state's deficit and build a surplus. Bricker considered care of the poor primarily a local obligation. The rest of Bricker's tenure as governor was overshadowed by World War II and efforts to ensure that the state was doing its part. During Bricker's administrations, the state increased workers' compensation benefits, re-established the governor's authority to appoint the adjutant general, established a Division of Conservation and Natural Resources and the Ohio Water Supply Board, revised the state's traffic code and juvenile and probate laws, and required venereal-disease testing before the issuance of marriage licenses. In 1944, Bricker was the Republican nominee for vice president on the ticket headed by New York governor Thomas E. Dewey. The Republican ticket carried Ohio but lost to Franklin D. Roosevelt, who won a fourth term. After that loss, Bricker organized a law firm in Columbus. In 1946, he was elected to the first of two terms in the U.S. Senate. As a senator, Bricker gained national attention for his unsuccessful effort in 1953 to pass an amendment to the U.S. Constitution limiting the treaty-making powers of the president. In his bid for a third term in 1958, Bricker was defeated by Democrat Stephen M. Young. That year, boosted by the right-to-work issue, Democrats won every statewide office except secretary of state, posting their biggest political gains in 20 years.

Bricker returned to his law firm and remained active in Republican politics. From 1948 to 1969, he served on the Ohio State University board of trustees. He died in Columbus on March 22, 1986.

55 and 57
Frank J. Lausche
(1945–1947, 1949–1957)

Frank J. Lausche was born November 14, 1895, in

Cleveland, the second of ten children of parents who arrived in the United States from Slovenia in 1885. Lausche's father, a steelworker, and his older brother died when Frank was 12. Left as the oldest man in the family, Lausche sold newspapers and became a neighborhood lamplighter, earning $2 a week while his mother operated a wine shop. As a youth, he was an excellent baseball player and later played semiprofessional baseball with Duluth of the Northern League and Lawrence (Mass.) of the Eastern League. In 1918, he joined the army as a private and was stationed at Camp Gordon, Ga., during World War I. He rose to the rank of second lieutenant before his discharge in 1919. Although offered a position with the Atlanta baseball club of the Southern Association, Lausche opted to study law at Cleveland's John Marshall Law School. He completed his studies in 1920, passed the Ohio bar, and became an assistant in the Cleveland law firm headed by Cyrus Locher, who was appointed to fill an unexpired term in the U.S. Senate in 1928. Lausche lost bids for an Ohio House seat in 1922 and an Ohio Senate seat in 1924. On May 17, 1928, he married Jane Sheal of Cleveland. In 1932, Gov. George White appointed Lausche a judge of the Cleveland Municipal Court; the next year, Lausche won election to the seat. In 1936, Lausche was elected judge of the Cuyahoga County Common Pleas Court, a post in which he attacked gambling and racketeering. In 1941, Lausche was elected mayor of Cleveland—the city's first of eastern European descent. As mayor, he continued the attacks on gambling along with the city's safety director, Eliot Ness. He was re-elected mayor in 1943. The next year, Lausche won the Democratic nomination for governor; he captured 52 percent of the vote in defeating Republican James Garfield Stewart, mayor of Cincinnati. Lausche became Ohio's first governor born to immigrants from southern or eastern Europe. As Cleveland's mayor, Lausche had established a reputation for independence from his party and from interest groups. He soon established the same reputation statewide. When he took over the governor's office, he did not replace all Republicans with Democrats; he retained many holdovers, including a Republican finance director. A conservative who was frequently at odds with organized labor, Lausche also built a reputation for being tightfisted with the public purse. In 1946, a huge year for Republicans, Lausche was narrowly defeated for re-election by Republican Thomas J. Herbert, a former Ohio attorney general. Two years later, in 1948, Lausche came back to defeat Herbert. Lausche won re-election three more times, becoming Ohio's only five-term governor. During his administrations, the state constructed mental institutions in Lima, Apple Creek, and Tiffin, a medical center at Ohio State University, and the Ohio Turnpike across northern Ohio. A 1952 riot at the Ohio Penitentiary caused more than $1 million in damage and prompted Lausche to develop plans for prison improvements. A 23-member State Board of Education was created, and the office-type ballot was adopted to discourage straight-ticket voting. Also, a constitutional amendment was approved in 1954 to extend the governor's term to four years

TIGHTFISTED WITH THE PUBLIC PURSE, LAUSCHE BECAME OHIO'S ONLY FIVE-TERM GOVERNOR

1944 Governor's Election . . . . . Counties
■ Frank J. Lausche
(Democratic) 1,603,809 (51.8) 18
❑ James G. Stewart
(Republican) 1,491,450 (48.2) 70
Total 3,095,259

1946 Governor's Election . . . . . . Counties
❑ Thomas J. Herbert
(Republican) . . . . . 1,166,550 (50.6) . . . 70
■ Frank J. Lausche
 (Democratic). . . . . 1,125,997 (48.9) . . . 18
Arla A. Albaugh
(Socialist Labor) 11,203   (0.5). 0
Total. 2,303,750

1948 Governor's Election . . . . . Counties
■ Frank J. Lausche
(Democratic) . . . 1,619,775 (53.7) 35
❑ Thomas J. Herbert
(Republican) . . . 1,398,514 (46.3) 53
Total 3,018,289

1950 Governor's Election . . . . . Counties
■ Frank J. Lausche
(Democratic) . . . 1,522,249 (52.6) 21
❑ Don H. Ebright
(Republican) . . . 1,370,570 (47.4) 67
Total. 2,892,819

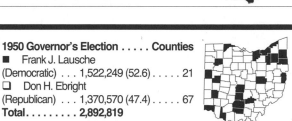

1952 Governor's Election . . . . . Counties
■ Frank J. Lausche
(Democratic) . . . 2,015,110 (55.9) 53
❑ Charles P. Taft
(Republican) . . . 1,590,058 (44.1) 35
Total. 3,605,168

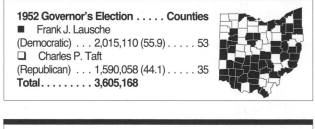

1954 Governor's Election . . . . . Counties
■ Frank J. Lausche
(Democratic) . . . 1,405,262 (54.1) 25
❑ James A. Rhodes
(Republican) . . . 1,192,528 (45.9) 63
Total. 2,597,790

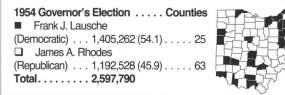

and limit him to two successive terms; it took effect in January 1959. Near the end of his fifth term, in November 1956, Lausche defeated U.S. Rep. George H. Bender, a Cleveland Republican, for a U.S. Senate seat. Lausche was re-elected in 1962 over Republican John Marshall Briley. His political career, spanning 36 years, ended in 1968. Frustrated for years by Lausche's opposition to its goals, organized labor made him a target, strongly supporting John J.

Gilligan of Cincinnati in that year's Democratic primary. Gilligan defeated Lausche, then 73, but lost in the general election to Republican William B. Saxbe. In his retirement years, Lausche often endorsed Republicans in state and national elections. His wife died November 24, 1981. They had no children. Lausche died April 21, 1990, in Cleveland.

56 Thomas J. Herbert
(1947–1949)

Thomas J. Herbert was born October 28, 1894, in Cleveland, the son of John T. and Jane A. Herbert, who had come from the Welsh community of Oak Hill in Jackson County. He attended Cleveland public schools, received a bachelor's degree in 1915 from Western Reserve University, and enrolled in the university's law school. On May 15, 1917, Herbert interrupted his law studies to enlist in officers' training camp at Fort Benjamin Harrison, Ind. He transferred to aviation

HERBERT DEALT
LAUSCHE
HIS ONLY DEFEAT
IN SIX CAMPAIGNS
FOR GOVERNOR

training, attended ground school at Ohio State University, and, in the fall of 1917, was sent to England as one of 150 cadets to be trained by the Royal Flying Corps. Herbert was commissioned first lieutenant in March 1918. Three months later, he was attached to the 56th Pursuit Squadron of the Royal Air Force, stationed in Doullens, France. On August 8, 1918, he was shot down in aerial combat over Cambrai, France. Wounded in the leg, Herbert spent five months in a London hospital and two more years in U.S. hospitals. He was awarded the British Distinguished Flying Cross, the American Distinguished Service Cross, and, later, the Purple Heart. On April 30, 1919, Herbert married Jeannette Judson of Cleveland; they had three children. He was honorably discharged from the military in May 1920. The same year, he received his law degree from Western Reserve University and was named an assistant law director of Cleveland. In 1922, he was appointed assistant Cuyahoga County prosecutor, serving through 1923. Herbert then entered a private law practice. In 1927, he was commissioned a major to organize and command the Ohio National Guard's 112th Observation Squadron, 37th Division. In January 1929, he became an assistant Ohio attorney general and was counsel for the Public Utilities Commission. He remained with the National Guard until 1933, when he resigned as a lieutenant colonel and became special counsel to the attorney general. He held the post

until 1937. Herbert was defeated in his first race for attorney general in 1936 but won the office in 1938 and served for three terms, from 1939 to 1945. In 1944, he had sought the Republican nomination for governor but lost to James G. Stewart, who lost to Democrat Frank J. Lausche. Jeannette Herbert died December 30, 1945. In 1946, Herbert won the Republican gubernatorial nomination and defeated Lausche in a year that proved big for Republicans. It was the only defeat for Lausche in six campaigns for governor. Herbert's two years as governor were marked by the construction of roads and mental-health facilities, the elimination of sales tax on sales of less than 41 cents, and the appropriation of $45 million for veteran bonuses. One year into his term, on January 3, 1948, Herbert married Mildred Stevenson of Indianapolis. That November, Lausche returned to defeat Herbert, who returned to Cleveland to practice law. In May 1953, Herbert was appointed by President Dwight Eisenhower to the five-member Subversive Activities Control Board, which was charged by a 1950 act with determining whether organizations were subversive. Herbert was serving on that panel when elected in November 1956 to the Ohio Supreme Court. While sitting on the bench, Herbert suffered a stroke on March 21, 1961. Because of health problems stemming from the stroke, he did not seek re-election to the court in 1962. Herbert died October 26, 1974, in a Columbus-area nursing home and was buried in Cleveland.

58 John W. Brown
(1957)

The son of a Scottish immigrant coal miner, John W. Brown was born December 28, 1913, in Athens, Ohio. He attended public schools in Athens and Fairfield counties, graduating in 1932 from Lancaster High School. He worked at the Palace Theater in Lancaster, and then managed the Civic Theater in Wellston from 1939 to 1941. In 1941, Brown joined the State Highway Patrol and was assigned to the patrol's Medina district. The

BROWN WAS THE
FIRST EX-GOVERNOR
TO SERVE IN THE
OHIO LEGISLATURE
SINCE 1840

following year, he entered the U.S. Coast Guard and served through World War II. He then worked in a pharmacy and purchased a Medina appliance company. In July 1943, Brown married Violet A. Cameron of Lakewood. In 1949, he was elected mayor of Medina, serving from 1950 to 1953. He was elected lieutenant governor in November 1952 and re-elected in 1954. In 1956, Brown lost the Republican gubernatorial primary to C. William O'Neill, then Ohio's attorney general. In November 1956, Gov. Frank J. Lausche was elected to the U.S. Senate. Lausche took his Senate seat on January 3, 1957, but O'Neill wasn't sworn in until January 14. During that 11-day period, Brown—by virtue of his position as lieutenant governor —served as governor. He was the first lieutenant governor to succeed to the governor's office since June 18, 1906, when Gen. Andrew L. Harris replaced governor John M. Pattison, who died five months after taking office. As governor, Brown commuted the sentences of five persons convicted of first-degree murder. In 1958, Brown was elected to the Ohio House and, two years later, to the Ohio Senate. He was the first ex-governor to serve in the Ohio legislature since 1840. In 1962, Brown again was elected lieutenant governor. He was re-elected to four-year terms in 1966 and 1970. In 1974, he was defeated for re-election by Democrat Richard F. Celeste. Brown spent a total of 16 years in the lieutenant governor's office. Just before leaving office, he was a central player in the "six-day war," a political battle during which the General Assembly convened on January 6, 1975, a week before the incoming Republican governor—James A. Rhodes—was to be sworn in. The Democratic-controlled assembly, with Democrat John J. Gilligan still in the governor's office, saw an opportunity to rush six partisan bills to passage. The Ohio Constitution provided that the lieutenant governor sign all bills before presentation to the governor. The legislative leaders, however, bypassed Brown, fearing that he would sit on the bills until Rhodes took office. The Ohio Supreme Court later ruled that the bills were not legally enacted because they lacked Brown's signature. Brown later served as administrator of Ohio Lake Lands (1975–1981) and state director of the Farmers Home Administration (1981–1983). Brown died October 29, 1993, in Medina. He was survived by his second wife, LaRue, and three run in stepdaughters.

59 C. William O'Neill
(1957–1959)

C. William O'Neill was born February 14, 1916, in Marietta. He was the son of Charles O'Neill, an Irish-American lawyer and justice of the peace. The boy's mother died when he was four. Reared by his father, O'Neill was encouraged to study law. He graduated in 1934 from Marietta High School and was on the team that won the state debating championship that year. O'Neill went on to Marietta College, where he

O'NEILL IS THE ONLY PERSON ELECTED TO HOLD THE TOP POSITION IN THE LEGISLATIVE, EXECUTIVE, AND JUDICIAL BRANCHES

1956 Governor's Election . . . . . Counties		
☐ C. William O'Neill (Republican)	1,984,988 (56.0)	83
■ Michael V. DiSalle (Democratic)	1,557,103 (44.0)	5
Total.	**3,542,091**	

was president of his junior and senior classes. Just before graduating in 1938, O'Neill began campaigning for Washington County's seat in the Ohio House of Representatives, which he won; at 22, O'Neill was the youngest member of the House. He served six consecutive terms; during his first two terms, he worked his way through Ohio State University's law school. He enlisted in the army in 1943 and won the 1944 House election while overseas with the 976th Engineers Co., a unit in Gen. George Patton's 3rd Army. In 1945, he married Betty Hewson, a proofreader at the *Marietta Times* and daughter of a Marietta grocer. O'Neill was discharged from the army in 1946 as a staff sergeant. He became House Speaker in 1947 at 30, Ohio's youngest Speaker. He served as speaker from 1947 to 1948 and as minority leader the next two years. In 1950, a 34-year-old O'Neill successfully ran for Ohio attorney general—the youngest man to hold the job. He was re-elected in 1952 and 1954. In 1956, O'Neill won the Republican nomination for governor, defeating Lt. Gov. John W. Brown. In the general election, O'Neill defeated Democrat Michael V. DiSalle, a former mayor of Toledo. The 1956 campaign marked the emergence of television advertising in Ohio gubernatorial contests. O'Neill, who was just 40, spent $59,952 on TV ads; DiSalle spent $18,281. O'Neill was the last governor to serve a two-year term. In November 1954, Ohio voters had approved a constitutional amendment establishing four-year gubernatorial terms effective January 1959. The O'Neill family mansion in Bexley, a private residence donated to the state in 1955. Having pledged to operate the state with no increase in taxes, O'Neill was unable to expand state services, though he pushed highway building projects. At the urging of business and manufacturing leaders, O'Neill agreed to support a right-to-work initiative in the 1958 election. The proposal would have prohibited the adoption of labor contracts that established union membership as a condition of employment. Organized labor mobilized to defeat the initiative—and, with it, O'Neill. The opposition, combined with an economic recession that pushed unemployment to a post-Depression high, led to O'Neill's defeat in a rematch with DiSalle—O'Neill's only loss in a 40-year political career. The 1958 election gave Democrats their biggest gains in 20 years. Ohio Republicans lost U.S. senator John W. Bricker's seat, the Ohio House, the Ohio Senate, and every statewide office except secretary of state. O'Neill returned to Marietta to practice law and taught at Bethany College in West Virginia during the 1959 to 1960 school year. In 1960, he won an Ohio Supreme Court seat vacated by the death of James G. Stewart. O'Neill joined the court December 1, 1960, and was re-elected to a full, six-year term in November 1964. O'Neill has been the only person elected to the top position in the legislative, executive, and judicial branches of Ohio government. He served on the Supreme Court, including eight years as chief justice, until his death on August 20, 1978.

60 Michael V. DiSalle
(1959–1963)

The oldest of seven children of Italian immigrants, Michael V. DiSalle was born in New York City on January 6, 1908. In 1911, the family moved to Toledo, where DiSalle attended public and parochial schools. His father, Anthony C. DiSalle, was a factory worker who later headed his own plating company. Michael DiSalle studied law at Georgetown University. While a junior in law school, he married Myrtle England of Washington D.C.; they had four daughters and a son. He completed his legal education at Georgetown in 1931 and began practicing law the next year in Toledo. In 1936, he was elected to the Ohio House of Repre-

CONSIDERING HIMSELF A REFORMER, DISALLE LAID OUT AMBITIOUS PLANS FOR IMPROVING STATE SERVICES. REPUBLICANS DUBBED HIM "TAX-HIKE MIKE"

sentatives. Two years later, he was defeated in a race for the Ohio Senate. From 1939 to 1941, he was assistant law director of Toledo; in 1941, he was elected to the first of five terms on Toledo City Council. In 1946, he was defeated in a race for Congress. While on the council, he served two terms as vice mayor. From 1948 to 1950, he served as Toledo mayor. The city then had a city-manager form of government. In 1950, DiSalle lost to Joseph T. Ferguson in a race for the Democratic nomination for the U.S. Senate. In November 1950, President Harry Truman appointed DiSalle director of the federal Office of Price Stabilization to oversee a temporary general freeze on prices. With the outbreak of the Korean War earlier that year, consumer prices had been rising an average of 8.5 percent annually. DiSalle kept the job of "price czar" until February 1952. In November 1952, DiSalle lost a second U.S. Senate bid to Republican U.S. Sen. John W. Bricker. When Gov. Frank J. Lausche decided to run for the U.S. Senate in 1956, DiSalle sought the Democratic nomination for governor and defeated four other candidates in the May primary. In November, DiSalle lost to Republican C. William O'Neill, the state's three-term attorney general. Two years later, in a rematch with O'Neill, DiSalle capitalized on O'Neill's disastrous decision to align with the right-to-work initiative. Organized labor mobilized like seldom before in Ohio to defeat O'Neill and right-to-work. DiSalle was the state's

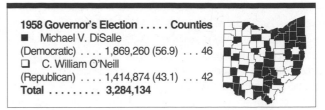

1958 Governor's Election . . . . . Counties		
■ Michael V. DiSalle (Democratic) . . . . 1,869,260 (56.9) . . . 46		
❑ C. William O'Neill (Republican) . . . . 1,414,874 (43.1) . . . 42		
Total 3,284,134		

first chief executive from Toledo. He entered office with fellow Democrats in control of both the Ohio Senate and Ohio House. Considering himself a reformer, DiSalle laid out ambitious plans for improving state services to the aged, the poor, the mentally retarded, and criminals. He also proposed higher payments for education assistance, unemployment compensation, and workers' compensation. He pushed through a package of tax increases on corporations, gasoline, cigarettes, alcoholic beverages, and horse racing. The state's two-year budget was increased by $500 million. Legislative Republicans dubbed him " Tax-Hike Mike." DiSalle also drew widespread criticism from many newspapers for his strident opposition to capital punishment. In 1962, DiSalle lost his bid for re-election to State Auditor James A. Rhodes. After leaving the governor's office, DiSalle set up a law practice in Washington D.C. In March 1963, he became chief administrator of the model city project of Reston, Va. He resigned from that job in November 1963. DiSalle maintained his law practice until he died on September 16, 1981, while vacationing in Pescara, Italy.

61 and 63
James A. Rhodes
(1963–1971, 1975–1983)

The third of five children of James and Susie Howe Rhodes, James A. Rhodes was born September 13, 1909, in Coalton, Ohio. The elder Rhodes was a coal miner and mine operator as well as a Republican precinct committeeman. In 1910, the family moved to Jasonville, Ind., which offered better mining opportunities. The elder Rhodes died in Jasonville in 1918. Not long afterward, the family returned to Jackson County, Ohio, settling in Jackson, about five miles south

RHODES SERVED AS OHIO'S GOVERNOR LONGER THAN ANYONE IN THE STATE'S HISTORY

of Coalton. Susie Rhodes supported the family by working in a cigar factory and operating a boardinghouse. About 1923, the family moved to Springfield, where Rhodes played football and basketball for Springfield High School. As a youth, Rhodes was a salesman and promoter: he sold advertising for ink blotters, booked bands for dances, and worked at a grocery store. Rhodes left high school for a year and took a railroad job; he returned to school and graduated in 1930. He attended Ohio State University in 1932 but spent most of his time working and promoting. He established a restaurant, Jim's Place, near the university. He organized a campus Republican club and, in 1934, successfully ran for his first office: ward committeeman. It was the start of a 50-year political career. In 1937, he was elected to the Columbus Board of Education and, in 1939, to the first of two terms as Columbus city auditor. On December 18, 1941, Rhodes married Helen Rawlins of Jackson County; the couple had three daughters. In 1943, Rhodes, at 34, was elected to the first of three terms as mayor of Columbus. During his second term, he won approval of the city's first income tax, a 0.5 percent levy that took effect in January 1948. From the mayor's office, he launched campaigns for state jobs—unsuccessfully for the 1950 Republican nomination for governor, then successfully in 1952 for state auditor against incumbent Democrat Joseph T. Ferguson. He was re-elected auditor in 1956 and 1960. During his first term as auditor, Rhodes lost a bid for governor in 1954 to incumbent Democrat Frank J. Lausche. In 1962, Rhodes defeated Democratic governor Michael V. DiSalle, whom Rhodes had attacked as "Tax-Hike Mike." In 1966, Rhodes easily won re-election over Frazier Reams Jr. During those first two terms as governor, Rhodes embarked on massive building programs, financed with $1.2 billion in voter-approved bond issues. The borrowings supported highways, airports, colleges and universities, technical schools, mental hospitals, parks, and lodges. Ohio and the nation enjoyed economic prosperity, low unemployment, and low inflation. In the final year of his second term, Rhodes sought the Republican nomination for the U.S. Senate against Robert Taft Jr. On May 4, 1970—the day before the primary—Ohio National Guardsmen opened fire on antiwar protesters at Kent State University, killing four students and wounding several others. Rhodes had sent the guard to Kent State to quell rioting over the Vietnam War. The next day, Rhodes lost the Senate primary to Taft. During the turbulent 1960s, the governor had called out the guard at least 40 times to counter strikes and rioting. In 1971, Rhodes, who by law could not seek a third successive term for governor, turned his attention to making money through James A. Rhodes & Associates, a development and consulting firm. In 1974, Rhodes re-emerged on the political stage to challenge incumbent Democrat John J. Gilligan. Rhodes won an extremely close election—by less than one vote per precinct. Four years later, he won another squeaker over lieutenant governor Richard F. Celeste. The political and economic climates were much different in Rhodes's second two terms. Unlike his first two, when Republicans controlled the legislature, Democrats controlled the House for all eight years of Rhodes's second two terms. Democrats controlled the Senate for six of those eight years. In addition, the state's economy struggled and Ohio voters no longer were willing to approve massive bond issues. Although "no new taxes" had been Rhodes's political trademark, he had to seek tax increases three times in his last term to keep state-funded programs running in the face of a national recession and record unemployment. The month before Rhodes left office—on December 5, 1982—a bronze statue of him was dedicated on the northeast corner of the Statehouse grounds. Rhodes, who had served as Ohio's governor

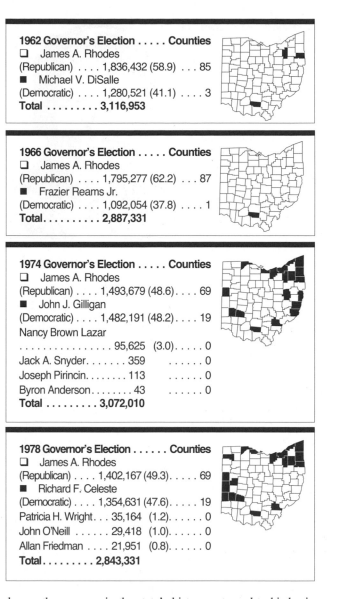

longer than anyone in the state's history, returned to his business ventures, but Ohio voters had not heard the last of him. In the summer of 1985, Rhodes made it clear that he would seek the 1986 Republican nomination for governor. He won a three-man primary, defeating Ohio Senate president Paul E. Gillmor of Port Clinton and state senator Paul E. Pfeifer of Bucyrus. In the November election, however, Rhodes sustained his largest-ever defeat. Celeste, who had been elected governor in 1982, won re-election over Rhodes by a landslide, 651,000-vote margin. Rhodes's wife, who became ill during the campaign, died December 9, 1987. The former governor continued his work with James A. Rhodes & Associates. Rhodes died March 4, 2001, at age 91, at Ohio State University Medical Center.

62 John J. Gilligan
(1971–1975)

The son of Harry J. and Blanche Joyce Gilligan, John J. Gilligan was born March 22, 1921, in Cincinnati. He graduated from St. Xavier High School in 1939, earned a bachelor's degree from the

University of Notre Dame in 1943, and was commissioned as an ensign in the navy. He served 27 months as a gunnery officer and won a Silver Star for gallantry while aboard a destroyer, the USS *Rodman* off Okinawa in the Pacific during World War II. The honor recognized Gilligan's efforts in saving several shipmates after the destroyer was set ablaze by enemy fire. Discharged in 1945, he returned to Cincinnati. He married Mary Kathryn Dixon on June 28, 1945; they later had four children. Gilligan joined his family's business, Gilligan Funeral Homes, and enrolled in the University of Cincinnati, earning a master's

AS GOVERNOR, GILLIGAN SUPPORTED— AND THE LEGISLATURE APPROVED—OHIO'S FIRST PERSONAL INCOME TAX

degree in 1947. From 1948 to 1953, Gilligan taught literature at Xavier University. He was elected to the Cincinnati City Council in November 1953 and re-elected five times to two-year terms. Gilligan lost a 1962 campaign for Ohio congressman-at-large but, in 1964, was sent to Congress from Ohio's first district. In 1966, Gilligan was defeated for re-election by Republican Robert Taft Jr. In 1967, he again was elected to the Cincinnati City Council. The next year, he challenged U.S. Sen. Frank J. Lausche in the Democratic primary. Strongly backed by organized labor, Gilligan defeated Lausche but lost the 1968 general election to Republican William B. Saxbe. Gilligan became a partner in the insurance firm of Sauter-Gilligan Associates, then made plans to seek the 1970 Democratic nomination for governor. In a year when the Ohio Constitution prohibited Republican governor James A. Rhodes from seeking a third four-year term, Gilligan won a three-man primary for the Democratic nomination; state auditor Roger Cloud defeated two major challengers for the Republican nomination. The year was big for Ohio Democrats, as Republicans were victimized by the Crofters loan scandal. Crofters, Inc., a Columbus loan-arranging company with ties to the state Republican Party, had persuaded the state treasurer's office to make questionable loans to two private companies. Gilligan easily defeated Cloud, and Democrats also won the offices of attorney general, auditor, and treasurer. As governor, Gilligan supported—and the legislature approved—Ohio's first personal income tax in December 1971. The tax, which took effect in 1972, ranged from .5 percent to 3.5 percent. The tax was challenged in a November 1972 referendum but upheld by Ohio voters. Gilligan reorganized state government by creating the Department of Administrative Services and the Ohio Environmental Protection Agency, merging several agencies into the Ohio Department of Transportation and splitting mental health and mental retardation into

1970 Governor's Election . . . . . Counties		
■ John J. Gilligan (Democratic)	1,725,560 (54.2)	 34
❑ Roger Cloud (Republican)	1,382,659 (43.4)	 54
Edwin G. Lawton (American Ind.)	61,300 (1.9)	 0
Joseph Pirincin (Socialist Labor). . . .	14,087 (0.4)	 0
John A. Crites	321	 0
Maria Sweetenham . . .	106	 0
Donald R. Lesiak	100	 0
Total	**3,184,133**	

separate departments. In 1974, most political observers considered Gilligan the favorite to win re-election against the comeback effort of Rhodes; Rhodes, however, pulled off the upset by 11,488 votes. Gilligan, who had been considered a possible 1976 presidential contender, left elective politics for 25 years. Upon leaving the governor's office, he became a fellow with the Woodrow Wilson International Center for Scholars in Washington, D.C. In 1976, he returned to his insurance business in Cincinnati. He later briefly served as administrator of the Agency for International Development in the administration of President Jimmy Carter. In 1979, Gilligan became a law instructor at Notre Dame, where he later became director of the Institute for International Peace Studies. He retired from the university in June 1991 and returned to Cincinnati to study, write, and lecture. He taught at the University of Cincinnati College of Law. His wife died October 10, 1996 in Cincinnati. In 1999, at age 78, Gilligan re-entered elective politics. Citing the challenges of urban education, he ran for a seat on the Cincinnati Board of Education and finished first; he was re-elected in 2003. Gilligan was remarried on September 30, 2000, to Susan Fremont, a family physician and native of Brazil.

64 Richard F. Celeste
(1983–1991)

Richard F. Celeste was born November 11, 1937, in Lakewood, Ohio, a Cleveland suburb where his Italian immigrant father, Frank P. Celeste, was elected mayor in 1955 and re-elected in 1959. The younger Celeste graduated from Lakewood High School in 1955 and, that fall, enrolled in Yale University, where he majored in American and African history. In 1959, he was elected president of the National Methodist Student Movement. After graduation in 1959, Celeste taught for a year at Yale as a Carnegie fellow. In 1961, he went to Oxford University in England as a Rhodes scholar and studied American diplomatic history. While at Oxford, Celeste met Dagmar Braun of Durnstein, Austria. They were married August 24, 1962, in Austria; they later had six children. They divorced in 1995. In 1963, Celeste went to work in Washington as a staff liaison officer for the Peace Corps. Later that year, he was appointed executive assistant to Chester Bowles, the ambassador to India. After four years in New Delhi, Celeste returned to Cleveland in 1967 and joined his father's housing business, the National Housing Corp. In 1970, Celeste was elected to the first of two terms in the Ohio House of Representatives. In 1974, he won a five-man primary for the Democratic nomination for lieutenant governor. In the fall, Celeste defeated incumbent Republican John W. Brown to win the lieutenant governor's office; the election was the last in which Ohio's lieutenant governor was chosen independently of the governor. An amendment to the Ohio Constitution, approved by voters on June 8, 1976, required that the governor and lieutenant governor be elected as a team beginning in 1978. That year, after one term as lieutenant governor, Celeste challenged Republican governor James A. Rhodes but lost an extremely close race. In 1979, President Jimmy Carter appointed Celeste director of the Peace Corps; Celeste served for 22 months and visited 23 countries before returning to Ohio to plan his 1982 gubernatorial campaign. To win the Democratic nomination, Celeste defeated Ohio Attorney General William J. Brown and Cincinnati City Councilman Jerry Springer. In the fall, Celeste led a Democratic sweep of statewide executive offices by crushing Republican congressman Clarence J. Brown Jr. of Urbana. In a huge Democratic year, Democrats kept control of the Ohio House and won back the Ohio Senate from Republicans. Taking office amid a national recession, with unemployment at a post-Depression high, Celeste faced a projected budget deficit of $528 million. With Democratic majorities in the House and Senate, Celeste quickly pushed through legislation to make permanent a 50 percent income tax surcharge imposed under Rhodes, and to add 40 percent to it. The combined income tax increase, 90 percent over prerecessionary rates, became a major political issue and enabled Republicans to recapture the Ohio Senate in 1984. The tax increases, combined with a recovering economy, enabled Celeste to dramatically increase state funding for education and other programs. Those advances, however, often were overshadowed by a series of scandals that plagued the Celeste administration. The most severe involved James E. Rogers, the director of the Ohio Department of Youth Services, who was imprisoned on convictions of soliciting bribes, accepting kickbacks, and theft in office. Rogers is believed to be the first Ohio cabinet member ever indicted. Celeste got better

TAX INCREASES, COMBINED WITH A RECOVERING ECONOMY, ENABLED CELESTE TO DRAMATICALLY INCREASE STATE FUNDING FOR EDUCATION AND OTHER PROGRAMS

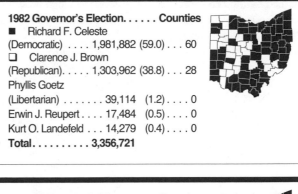

1982 Governor's Election. . . . . . Counties
■ Richard F. Celeste
(Democratic) . . . . 1,981,882 (59.0) . . . 60
❑ Clarence J. Brown
(Republican). . . . . 1,303,962 (38.8) . . . 28
Phyllis Goetz
(Libertarian) 39,114 (1.2) 0
Erwin J. Reupert 17,484 (0.5) 0
Kurt O. Landefeld . . . 14,279 (0.4) 0
Total. 3,356,721

1986 Governor's Election . . . . . . Counties
■ Richard F. Celeste
(Democratic) . . . . . . 1,858,372 (60.6). . .55
❑ James A. Rhodes
(Republican) . . . . . . 1,207,264 (39.4). . .33
Thomas V. Brown 803   0
Guy Templeton Black 92   0
Roberta L. Scherr 80   0
Total 3,066,611

marks for his handling of Ohio's 1985 savings and loan crisis, touched off by the March 1985 collapse of Cincinnati-based Home State Savings Bank. The collapse triggered a panic among depositors in the state's 69 other privately insured savings and loans. Celeste closed the savings and loans until they secured federal deposit insurance. Heading into his 1986 re-election campaign, Celeste was politically weakened by his administration's ethics problems. It soon became apparent, however, that Ohio voters did not view Republican challenger James A. Rhodes, then 77, as an attractive alternative. For the second consecutive election, Celeste led a Democratic sweep of statewide executive offices. Celeste became the first Democrat to win re-election as governor since Frank J. Lausche. For several months in 1987, Celeste openly considered entering the race for the 1988 Democratic presidential nomination but ultimately decided against it. Celeste's tenure as governor gave Ohio its first collective-bargaining law for public employees, the Thomas Edison program to link universities and businesses to create jobs of the future, the beginnings of a community-based mental-health system, and a cabinet-level agency on drug- and alcohol-recovery services. Four days before leaving office in January 1991, Celeste commuted the death sentences of eight convicted murderers—four men and four women. The commutations sparked a political uproar. After leaving office, Celeste established a business consulting firm, Celeste and Sabety Ltd. In 1993, he was named chairman of the National Health Care Campaign, an arm of the Democratic National Committee charged with promoting President Bill Clinton's healthcare program. Celeste remarried on October 28, 1995, to Jacqueline Lundquist, a former Washington D.C. public-relations consultant. In July 1997, they became parents of a son. On November 6, 1997, Celeste was confirmed by the U.S. Senate as ambassador to India; he served until 2001. On July 1, 2002, Celeste became president of Colorado College, a liberal-arts college in Colorado Springs.

65 George V. Voinovich
(1991– 1998)

George V. Voinovich was born July 15, 1936, in Cleveland. He was the oldest of six children of Josephine and George Voinovich, a prominent Cleveland-area architect. He attended parochial and public schools, graduating in 1954 from Collinwood High School. Voinovich earned a bachelor's degree in government in 1958 from Ohio University. In 1961, he graduated from Ohio State University's College of Law and was president of his graduating class.

DURING HIS TEN YEARS AS MAYOR, VOINOVICH SAW CLEVELAND PROCLAIMED AS A "COMEBACK CITY"

Voinovich married Janet Kay Allan of Lakewood, Ohio, on September 8, 1962; they had four children. In 1966, he won the first of three terms in the Ohio House of Representatives. In 1971, he lost in Cleveland's mayoral primary. When fellow Republican Ralph J. Perk was elected mayor, Voinovich was appointed to replace Perk as Cuyahoga County auditor. In 1972, Voinovich was elected to Perk's unexpired term and, in 1974, to a full term. In 1976, Voinovich was elected Cuyahoga County commissioner; two years later, he planned to run for state auditor but was asked and agreed to run for lieutenant governor on a ticket headed by Gov. James A. Rhodes. The election was the first in which Ohio voters would choose a governor-lieutenant governor team, and Rhodes wanted a strong running mate from northeastern Ohio to counter the challenge from lieutenant governor Richard Celeste, a Clevelander. Rhodes and Voinovich were elected in an extremely close contest, but Voinovich wasn't lieutenant governor for long. Within months of taking office, he was encouraged by many business and civic leaders in Cleveland to run for mayor against Democrat Dennis J. Kucinich, a populist who waged fierce battles with the city's business community. In December 1978, Cleveland had become the first American city to default since the Great Depression. In Cleveland's 1979 mayoral election, Voinovich defeated Kucinich for a two-year term. Two weeks before the election, the Voinoviches' youngest child, nine-year-old Molly, was struck by a van and killed. After a change in Cleveland's city charter, Voinovich was re-elected to four-year terms in 1981 and 1985. During his ten years as mayor, Voinovich persuaded Cleveland voters to raise the city income tax from 1.5 percent to 2 percent, got the city out of debt, presided over a $2 billion building boom downtown, and saw Cleveland proclaimed in many national

1990 Governor's Election		Counties
George V. Voinovich (Republican)	1,938,103 (55.7)	76
Anthony J. Celebrezze Jr. (Democratic)	1,539,416 (44.3)	12
David Marshall	82	0
James E. Attia	49	0
Total	**3,477,650**	

1994 Governor's Election		Counties
George V. Voinovich (Republican)	2,401,572 (71.8)	86
Robert L. Burch (Democratic)	835,849 (25.0)	2
Billy Inmon	108,745 (3.2)	0
Others	72	0
Total	**3,346,238**	

publications as a "comeback city." In 1988, Voinovich unsuccessfully challenged Democratic U.S. senator Howard M. Metzenbaum. Having received only 43 percent of the vote in the race, Voinovich faced gloomy statewide political prospects. He wasted little time, however, launching a comeback bid: On April 27, 1989, Voinovich became the first to announce a candidacy for the 1990 governor's race. His early start helped him outmaneuver Robert A. Taft II of Cincinnati for Republican support; Voinovich went on to defeat Democratic nominee Anthony J. Celebrezze Jr. the state's two-term attorney general, in the November election. In 1994, Voinovich ran for re-election against Democrat Robert L. Burch Jr. a three-term state senator from Dover; and Billy R. Inmon, who had been fired by Voinovich as manager of the Ohio State Fair. Burch practically won the Democratic nomination by default, as no big-name Democrat chose to oppose Voinovich. In the election, Voinovich received nearly 72 percent of the vote—a 20th century record—and carried 86 of the state's 88 counties. During his first two years as governor, Ohio had a sagging economy and a projected deficit of $1 billion. Voinovich reduced spending, eliminated the General Assistance welfare program, and pushed $1 billion in tax increases through the legislature. The changes included raising the state's top tax bracket—for income above $200,000—to 7 percent. On April 11, 1993—Easter Sunday —a prison riot erupted at the Southern Ohio Correctional Facility, the state's maximum-security prison near Lucasville. At the end of 11 days, the longest state prison riot in U.S. history, guard Robert Vallandingham and 10 prisoners were dead. On July 5, 1996, Voinovich presided over the dedication of the renovated Statehouse, a $120.9 million restoration begun during the previous administration. On March 24, 1997, the Ohio Supreme Court, in a 4-3 decision, ruled unconstitutional Ohio's system of financing public education. The court ruled that heavy reliance on local real-estate taxes for education produced too much financial disparity among school districts. In response, Voinovich urged Ohioans in May 1998 to approve a one-cent increase in the state sales tax; the proposal was crushed, 80-20. On October 9, 1997, Paul C. Mifsud,

Voinovich's former chief of staff, was sentenced to six months in jail for an ethics violation stemming from a home-remodeling deal with a contractor. During his two terms, Voinovich held state spending to its lowest growth rate in 30 years, curbed welfare, reformed the workers' compensation system, provided historic levels of support to Head Start and other preschool programs, converted all state liquor stores to private enterprise, and built seven new prisons at a cost of $271 million. In November 1998, Voinovich defeated Democrat Mary O. Boyle, a former Cuyahoga County commissioner and state legislator, to win the U.S. Senate seat previously held by John Glenn, a four-term Democrat who retired. Voinovich won re-election in 2004.

66 Nancy P. Hollister
(1998–1999)

Nancy Putnam Hollister became Ohio's first woman governor on December 31, 1998. She previously was the state's first woman lieutenant governor and the first woman mayor of Marietta. The oldest of five children, Nancy Putnam was born May 22, 1949, into a family whose ancestors led the establishment of the first permanent white settlement in Ohio. Cousins Rufus and Israel Putnam, Revolutionary War veterans, led the settlers

HOLLISTER BECAME OHIO'S FIRST WOMAN GOVERNOR

who arrived in Marietta on April 7, 1788. She graduated from Marietta High School and attended Kent State University. On March 21, 1970, she married Jeff Hollister, an attorney and businessman whom she had dated since high school; they had five children. In 1977, she was appointed to a vacancy on the Marietta City Council; she was elected to a full term in 1979. In 1983, Hollister was elected Marietta's mayor; she was re-elected in 1987. In 1991, Gov. George V. Voinovich appointed Hollister as director of the Governor's Office of Appalachia to oversee programs affecting the state's 29 Appalachian counties. In 1994, when Lt. Gov. Michael DeWine decided to run for the U.S. Senate, Gov. Voinovich asked Hollister to be his lieutenant-governor running mate as Voinovich sought and won re-election. In November 1998, Hollister unsuccessfully ran for Ohio's 6th Congressional District seat against Democrat Ted Strickland. In the same election, Voinovich was elected to the U.S. Senate seat being vacated by four-term Democrat John Glenn. Voinovich resigned as governor December 31, 1998, to assume his Senate seat; Hollister was sworn in to replace Voinovich shortly after noon that day. She served as governor for 11 days until Bob Taft, who had been elected in November, was sworn in on January 11. On February 2, 1999, Hollister was appointed the the 96th District seat in the Ohio House of Representatives to replace Tom Johnson, who had become Taft's

budget director. Hollister was elected to the seat in 2000, re-elected in 2002, and defeated in 2004.

67 Bob Taft
(1999–2007)

Robert Alphonso Taft II was born January 8, 1942 in Boston, where his father was enrolled at Harvard Law School. The oldest of four children of Robert Jr. and Blanca Taft, he was the son of a future U.S. senator, grandson of a U.S. senator and three-time candidate for the Republican nomination for president, and great-grandson of William Howard Taft, the nation's 27th president and later chief justice

TAFT LED THE STATE'S MASSIVE SCHOOL-BUILDING PROGRAM

of the United States. Taft's great-great grandfather was Alphonso Taft, a secretary of war and attorney general under President Ulysses S. Grant. Taft grew up in a farmhouse on the family estate in Indian Hill, a Cincinnati suburb. His high-school years were spent at the Taft School in Connecticut. In 1963, he earned a bachelor's degree in English from Yale University. He then enrolled in the Peace Corps, and for two years taught school in Tanzania, East Africa. In 1967, he earned a master's degree in government from Princeton University. While doing research at Princeton, Taft travelled to Central America, where in 1966 he met Janet Hope Rothert of Camden, Ark., at the Guatemala City airport. They married on June 17, 1967. A daughter, Anna, was born in 1979. Following the marriage, Taft took a teaching job with the U.S. Agency for International Development in Saigon, Vietnam. In 1969, he returned to the United States to become a budget analyst for the state of Illinois, and later became assistant budget director. Taft returned to Cincinnati where, in 1976, he earned a law degree from the University of Cincinnati. The same year, he was appointed to a vacancy in the Ohio House of Representatives; he was elected to the seat that November. In 1980, Taft was elected Hamilton County commissioner; he was re-elected in 1984. Two years later, he ran for lieutenant governor on the Republican ticket headed by former Gov. James A. Rhodes, who was crushed in the landslide re-election of Democratic Gov. Richard F. Celeste. In 1990, Taft made an early bid for the Republican nomination for governor but stepped aside for former Cleveland mayor George V. Voinovich. Taft ran instead for secretary of state and ousted Democratic incumbent Sherrod Brown. In 1994, Taft was re-elected. In 1998, Republicans considered it Taft's turn to run for governor. That November, he defeated Democrat Lee Fisher, a former Ohio attorney general and state senator. Taft took office in January 1999 amid a strong economy, and his first biennial budget called for back-to-back, billion-dollar spending increases. Taft especially focused on improving education and urban renewal. On February 19, 1999, Ohio carried out its first execution in 36 years as convicted murderer Wilford Berry was given a lethal injection. The state began carrying out death sentences with regularity. On February 26, 1999, the Ohio Supreme Court ruled the state's revamped school-funding system still was unconstitutional. The state embarked on a 10-year, $12 billion program to build and repair schools. Much of the money came from national tobacco-settlement funds. By the end of 2002, about $2.5 million was being spent per day on school construction. Taft also led efforts to impose higher academic standards and competency tests in Ohio's primary and secondary schools. In November 2002, Taft easily won re-election over Democrat Timothy Hagan, a former Cuyahoga County commissioner. In 2003, Taft presided over the state's bicentennial celebrations. In June 2003, Taft signed a $48.8 billion, two-year budget requiring $3 billion in new or added taxes. To fund the program, the General Assembly raised the state sales tax from 5 percent to 6 percent and extended the tax to many previously untaxed services. In November 2003, Taft suffered a political setback when Ohioans rejected a proposed $500 million bond issue to help finance his $1.6-billion Third Frontier project designed to stimulate high-tech business development. Throughout Taft's second term, Ohio lost manufacturing jobs and struggled to adjust to a stagnating economy.

Trying to revive the state's economic fortunes, Taft and the General Assembly enacted, on July 1, 2005, a budget with the most far-reaching tax reform in decades. The budget eliminated the corporate-franchise tax, replacing it with a commercial-activities tax based on gross receipts; cut personal income taxes across the board by 21 percent over five years; reduced the state sales tax to 5.5 percent; and phased out the tangible personal property tax on business equipment, machinery, inventory, furniture, and fixtures.

1998 Governor's Election . . . . . Counties
☐   Robert A. Taft
(Republican). . . . 1,678,721 (50.0%). . . 68
■   Lee Fisher
(Democratic) . . . 1,498,956 (44.7%). . . 20
John R. Mitchel . . . 111,468   (3.3%) . . . 0
Zanna Feitler 65,068   (1.9%) 0
Total 3,354,213

2002 Governor's Election . . . . . Counties
☐   Robert A. Taft
(Republican). . . . . 1,865,007 (57.8%). . . 82
■   Timothy Hagan
(Democratic). . . . . 1,236,924 (38.3%). . . . 6
John Eastman. 126,686   (3.9%). . . . 0
Others. 375   0
Total 3,228,992

The second Taft administration was plagued by a series of scandals, most notably investment boondoggles by the Bureau of Workers' Compensation. The bureau gave $50 million to Thomas Noe, a Republican fundraiser and rare-coin dealer who converted millions to his personal use. The bureau lost additional millions through ill-considered investments with other politically connected individuals. Compounding his problems, on August 18, 2005, Taft was found guilty of four misdemeanor ethics charges in Franklin County Municipal Court. In his annual financial-disclosure statements, Taft had failed to report the receipt of 52 gifts valued at $5,800; most of the gifts were golf outings. Taft was fined $4,000 and became the first Ohio governor to be convicted of a crime in office.

CHAPTER 5

The Ohio General Assembly

THE FIRST LEGISLATURE, CONSISTING OF 30 REPRESENTATIVES AND 14 SENATORS, CONVENED IN CHILLICOTHE ON MARCH 1, 1803.

Ohio's bicameral legislature descends from a territorial legislature authorized by the Northwest Ordinance of 1787. The ordinance, establishing a government for the Northwest Territory, granted legislative powers to the governor of the territory and three judges of the territorial court until the territory contained "five thousand free male inhabitants of full age." The governor (Arthur St. Clair) and judges (Samuel H. Parsons, James M. Varnum, and John Cleves Symmes) were empowered to select laws of the original states that might be suitable for the new territory. In December 1798, St. Clair determined that 5,000 white males inhabited the territory and issued a proclamation calling for the election of representatives to a General Assembly. The ordinance called for an elected House of Representatives and a five-member Legislative Council (analogous to an upper house), appointed by the president of the United States from a list of ten candidates submitted by the territorial House of Representatives. The two houses were to choose a congressional delegate.

In February 1799, the lower house of 22 representatives met in Cincinnati to nominate the 10. From that list, the five selected to the Legislative Council by President John Adams were: Jacob Burnet of Hamilton, James Findlay of Cincinnati, Henry Vanderburgh of Vincennes (Ind.), Robert Oliver of Marietta, and David Vance of Vanceville. In September 1799, the first territorial legislature met in Cincinnati; it selected William Henry Harrison as the territory's delegate to Congress and began making laws. Burnet was speaker of the Legislative Council; Edward Tiffin of Ross County was Speaker of the House.

Because of friction between St. Clair and the legislature, senti-

The Statehouse, begun in 1838, was completed in 1861. Its total cost was $1.6 million.

ment started to grow for a constitutional convention and statehood. After the second territorial legislature adjourned in January 1802, the conditions were ripe for movement to statehood. On April 30, 1802, President Thomas Jefferson approved an act enabling the people of Ohio to form a constitution and state government. The Ohio Constitutional Convention met November 1, 1802, in Chillicothe and, within a month, prepared a constitution.

The new constitution established executive, judicial, and legislative branches of state government. It called for a General Assembly consisting of a Senate and a House of Representatives, with senators chosen for two-year terms and representatives for one-year terms. About half of the senators were to be elected each year. Assemblies would meet annually. The number of representatives and senators would vary depending on the population of the state; the number of senators would be no less than one-third and no more than one-half the number of representatives. The county was the basis of each legislative district, with the more populous counties being allotted more legislators in a system that approximated equal representation by population. The first constitution vested virtually all state power in the General Assembly; the governor, largely a figurehead, had no veto authority. The legislature chose all state executive officers except the governor, and appointed state and county judges. The first legislature—consisting of 30 representatives and 14 senators—convened in Chillicothe on March 1, 1803. Forty-nine general assemblies convened under the provisions of the 1802 constitution; the Senate and House each called the presiding officer of the chamber a Speaker.

The state's second constitution was adopted by the people in June

1851, and took effect September 1, 1851. Judges and state executive officeholders were to be chosen by the people rather than appointed by the assembly. Retroactive laws were prohibited; legislative powers were limited in other ways, too. Senators and representatives would be chosen every two years, and general assemblies would be biennial rather than annual. A Speaker would continue to lead the House, but a new officer—the lieutenant governor—would preside over the Senate. The Senate majority leader became the president pro tem.

The new constitution also contained a complicated formula for apportionment, the so-called "major fraction rule." Under it, the state's population was divided by 100, with the resulting quotient being the ratio of representation in the House of Representatives. Any county with a population equal to at least half the ratio was entitled to one representative; a county with a population of less than half the ratio was grouped with an adjacent county for districting; a county containing a population of at least one and three-fourths the ratio was entitled to two representatives; a county with a population equal to three times the ratio was entitled to three representatives. To determine Senate districts, a similar procedure was followed; the starting point, however, was figured by dividing the state's population by 35. The ratios for the House and Senate and the resulting apportionment were determined by a board consisting of the governor, auditor, and secretary of state. Because of the complex formula, the number of seats in the House and Senate varied from session to session.

The apportionment system was modified in 1903 by the Hanna Amendment to the state constitution, which provided each county at least one representative, with all members being elected at large. Another significant amendment in 1903 established the veto power of the governor, which shifted the balance of power between the governor and the General Assembly.

The next wave of change in the state's legislative system occurred in 1912, when the last state constitutional convention was held. The convention produced 41 proposed amendments to the 1851 constitution; 33 were approved by voters in November 1912. For lawmaking purposes, the most significant amendments were those authorizing the initiative and referendum—giving Ohioans the power to directly initiate laws and overturn those enacted by lawmakers. Another change expanded the governor's veto authority, allowing him to line-item veto specific items in appropriations bills. The legislative majority needed to override a gubernatorial veto, however, was reduced from two-thirds to three-fifths.

In November 1956, Ohio voters approved a constitutional amendment increasing the terms of state senators to four years from two years.

For decades, the Hanna Amendment of 1903 assured that Ohio's legislature would be dominated by rural interests even as the state was rapidly becoming urbanized. In the 1960s, however, the U.S. Supreme Court issued a series of rulings requiring states to apportion their legislatures on the basis of population only, thus rendering the Hanna Amendment unconstitutional. In its 1962 *Baker v. Carr* ruling, the court held that federal courts had the right to consider state apportionment cases. By June 1964, states were ordered to apportion their legislatures only on the basis of population. In Ohio, districts of approximately equal population went into effect in 1966. The following year, a constitutional amendment established a 99-member House and a 33-member Senate. Each Senate district was to consist of three House districts. Since those rulings and subsequent changes in apportionment, a majority of lawmakers in the Ohio General Assembly have come from urban and suburban districts instead of rural areas.

In the second half of the 20th century, state legislatures—including Ohio's—began to add specialized staff and professionalize operations. The Legislative Service Commission was established September 16, 1953 to provide impartial and in-depth research services to the General Assembly. The commission staffs legislative committee meetings, drafts bills and resolutions, and produces studies on topics of legislative interest. In 1973, the commission was expanded to include a Legislative Budget Office to provide fiscal expertise. The Legislative Reference Bureau, which had been in existence since 1910 and maintained files on laws and resolutions, was abolished in 1981; its duties were given to the Legislative Service Commission.

The growth of staff enabled lawmakers to more easily obtain information and take a more active role in forming public policy. From 1967 to 1985, the number of staff employees serving the General Assembly grew from 34 to 121. In the same span, the assembly expanded its number of committees from 24 to 38.

In June 1976, Ohio voters approved a constitutional amendment —effective with the 1978 election—requiring the lieutenant governor to be elected in tandem with the governor and to relieve the lieutenant governor of the duty of presiding over the Senate. Since January 1979, the presiding officer of the Senate has been the Senate president.

In 1988, the 99 members of the Ohio House moved out of the Statehouse and into new offices across the street—in the 31-story Vern Riffe Center for Government and the Arts at State and High streets.

In November 1992, Ohio voters approved a state constitutional amendment to limit the terms of state legislators to eight consecutive years in office—four two-year terms for House members and two four-year terms for Senate members. Gone are the days of the "career legislator" who served for decades. When the 124th General Assembly was convened in January 2001, nearly half of the previous legislature—with 211 years of combined experience—was gone. Ohio, which had ranked among the states with the lowest turnover of state lawmakers, joined those with the highest. The wisdom of term limits continues to be debated across the state, with much speculation about whether voters will be asked to modify or repeal the eight-year limit.

IN THE 1960s
THE U.S. SUPREME
COURT ISSUED A SERIES
OF RULINGS REQUIRING
STATES TO APPORTION
THEIR LEGISLATURES
ON THE BASIS OF
POPULATION ONLY

House Speakers

GENERAL ASSEMBLY	CONVENED	SPEAKER*	COUNTY
1	Mar. 1, 1803	Michael Baldwin	Ross
2	Dec. 5, 1803	Elias Langham	Ross
3	Dec. 3, 1804	Michael Baldwin	Ross
4	Dec. 2, 1805	John Sloane	Jefferson
5	Dec. 1, 1806	Abraham Shepherd	Adams
6	Dec. 7, 1807	Philemon Beecher	Fairfield
7	Dec. 5, 1808	Alexander Campbell	Adams
8	Dec. 4, 1809	Edward Tiffin	Ross
9	Dec. 3, 1810	Edward Tiffin	Ross
10	Dec. 2, 1811	Matthias Corwin	Warren
11	Dec. 7, 1812	John Pollock	Clermont
12	Dec. 6, 1813	John Pollock	Clermont
13	Dec. 5, 1814	John Pollock	Clermont
14	Dec. 4, 1815	Matthias Corwin	Warren
15	Dec. 2, 1816	Thomas Kirker	Adams
16	Dec. 1, 1817	Duncan McArthur	Ross
17	Dec. 7, 1818	Joseph Richardson	Columbiana
18	Dec. 6, 1819	Joseph Richardson	Columbiana
19	Dec. 4, 1820	Joseph Richardson	Columbiana
20	Dec. 3, 1821	John Bigger	Warren
21	Dec. 2, 1822	Joseph Richardson	Columbiana
22	Dec. 1, 1823	Joseph Richardson	Columbiana
23	Dec. 6, 1824	Micajah T. Williams	Hamilton
24	Dec. 5, 1825	William W. Irvin	Fairfield
25	Dec. 4, 1826	David Higgins	Butler
26	Dec. 3, 1827	Edward King	Ross
27	Dec. 1, 1828	Edward King	Ross
28	Dec. 7, 1829	Thomas L. Hamer	Brown
29	Dec. 6, 1830	James M. Bell	Guernsey
30	Dec. 5, 1831	William B. Hubbard	Belmont
31	Dec. 3, 1832	David T. Disney	Hamilton
32	Dec. 2, 1833	John H. Keith	Muskingum
33	Dec. 1, 1834	John M. Creed	Fairfield
34	Dec. 7, 1835	William Sawyer	Montgomery
35	Dec. 5, 1836	William Medill	Fairfield
36	Dec. 4, 1837	Charles Anthony	Clark
37	Dec. 3, 1838	James J. Faran	Hamilton
38	Dec. 2, 1839	Thomas J. Buchanan	Clermont
39	Dec. 7, 1840	Seabury Ford	Geauga
40	Dec. 6, 1841	Rufus P. Spalding	Summit
41	Dec. 5, 1842	John Chaney	Fairfield
42	Dec. 4, 1843	John M. Gallagher	Madison
43	Dec. 2, 1844	John M. Gallagher	Clark
44	Dec. 1, 1845	Elias F. Drake	Greene
45	Dec. 7, 1846	William P. Cutler	Washington
46	Dec. 6, 1847	Joseph S. Hawkins	Preble
47	Dec. 4, 1848	John G. Breslin	Seneca
48	Dec. 3, 1849	Benjamin F. Leiter	Stark
49	Dec. 2, 1850	John F. Morse	Ashtabula
50	Jan. 5, 1852	James C. Johnson	Medina
51	Jan. 2, 1854	Francis C. LeBlond	Mercer
52	Jan. 7, 1856	Nelson H. VanVorhes	Athens
53	Jan. 4, 1858	William B. Woods	Licking
54	Jan. 2, 1860	Richard C. Parsons	Cuyahoga
55	Jan. 6, 1862	James R. Hubbell	Delaware
56	Jan. 4, 1864	James R. Hubbell	Delaware
57	Jan. 1, 1866	Edwin A. Parrott	Montgomery
58	Jan. 6, 1868	John F. Follett	Licking
59	Jan. 3, 1870	A.J. Cunningham	Hamilton
60	Jan. 1, 1872	Nelson H. VanVorhes	Athens
61	Jan. 5, 1874	George L. Converse	Franklin
62	Jan. 3, 1876	Charles H. Grosvenor	Athens
63	Jan. 7, 1878	James E. Neal	Butler
64	Jan. 4, 1880	Thomas A. Cowgill	Champaign
65	Jan. 2, 1882	Orlando J. Hodge	Cuyahoga
66	Jan. 7, 1884	Archeleus D. Marsh	Mercer
67	Jan. 4, 1886	John C. Entrekin	Ross
68	Jan. 2, 1888	Elbert L. Lampson	Ashtabula
69	Jan. 6, 1890	Nial R. Hysell	Perry
70	Jan. 4, 1892	Lewis C. Laylin (R)	Huron
71	Jan. 3, 1894	Alexander Boxwell (R)	Warren
72	Jan. 6, 1896	David L. Sleeper (R)	Athens
73	Jan. 3, 1898	Harry C. Mason (R)	Cuyahoga
74	Jan. 1, 1900	Arlington G. Reynolds (R)	Lake
75	Jan. 6, 1902	William S. McKinnon (R)	Ashtabula
76	Jan. 4, 1904	George T. Thomas (R)	Huron
77	Jan. 1, 1906	Carmi A. Thompson (R)	Lawrence
		Freeman T. Eagleson (R)	Guernsey
78	Jan. 4, 1909	Granville W. Mooney (R)	Ashtabula
79	Jan. 2, 1911	Samuel J. Vining (D)	Mercer
80	Jan. 6, 1913	Charles L. Swain (D)	Hamilton
81	Jan. 4, 1915	Charles D. Conover (R)	Champaign
82	Jan. 1, 1917	E.J. Hopple (D)	Cuyahoga
83	Jan. 6, 1919	Carl R. Kimball (R)	Lake
84	Jan. 3, 1921	Rupert R. Beetham (R)	Harrison
85	Jan. 1, 1923	H.H. Griswold (R)	Geauga
86	Jan. 5, 1925	Harry D. Silver (R)	Preble
87	Jan. 3, 1927	O.C. Gray (R)	Harrison
88	Jan. 7, 1929	O.C. Gray (R)	Harrison
89	Jan. 5, 1931	Arthur Hamilton (R)	Warren
90	Jan. 2, 1933	Frank Cave (D)	Richland
91	Jan. 7, 1935	J. Freer Bittinger (D)	Ashland
92	Jan. 4, 1937	Frank R. Uible (D)	Cuyahoga
93	Jan. 2, 1939	Wm. M. McCulloch (R)	Miami
94	Jan. 6, 1941	Wm. M. McCulloch (R)	Miami
95	Jan. 4, 1943	Wm. M. McCulloch (R)	Miami
96	Jan. 1, 1945	Jackson E. Betts (R)	Hancock
97	Jan. 6, 1947	C. William O'Neill (R)	Washington
98	Jan. 3, 1949	John F. Cantwell (D)	Mahoning
99	Jan. 1, 1951	Gordon Renner (R)	Hamilton
100	Jan. 5, 1953	William B. Saxbe (R)	Champaign
101	Jan. 3, 1955	Roger Cloud (R)	Logan
102	Jan. 7, 1957	Roger Cloud (R)	Logan
103	Jan. 5, 1959	James A. Lantz (D)	Fairfield
104	Jan. 2, 1961	Roger Cloud (R)	Logan
105	Jan. 7, 1963	Roger Cloud (R)	Logan
106	Jan. 4, 1965	Roger Cloud (R)	Logan
107	Jan. 2, 1967	Charles F. Kurfess (R)	Wood
108	Jan. 6, 1969	Charles F. Kurfess (R)	Wood
109	Jan. 4, 1971	Charles F. Kurfess (R)	Wood
110	Jan. 1, 1973	A.G. Lancione (D)	Belmont
111	Jan. 6, 1975	Vernal G. Riffe Jr. (D)	Scioto
112	Jan. 3, 1977	Vernal G. Riffe Jr. (D)	Scioto
113	Jan. 2, 1979	Vernal G. Riffe Jr. (D)	Scioto
114	Jan. 5, 1981	Vernal G. Riffe Jr. (D)	Scioto
115	Jan. 3, 1983	Vernal G. Riffe Jr. (D)	Scioto
116	Jan. 7, 1985	Vernal G. Riffe Jr. (D)	Scioto
117	Jan. 5, 1987	Vernal G. Riffe Jr. (D)	Scioto
118	Jan. 3, 1989	Vernal G. Riffe Jr. (D)	Scioto
119	Jan. 7, 1991	Vernal G. Riffe Jr. (D)	Scioto
120	Jan. 4, 1993	Vernal G. Riffe Jr. (D)	Scioto
121	Jan. 3, 1995	Jo Ann Davidson (R)	Franklin
122	Jan. 6, 1997	Jo Ann Davidson (R)	Franklin
123	Jan. 4, 1999	Jo Ann Davidson (R)	Franklin
124	Jan. 2, 2001	Larry Householder (R)	Perry
125	Jan. 6, 2003	Larry Householder (R)	Perry
126	Jan. 3, 2005	Jon Husted (R)	Montgomery

* In some general assemblies, the House elected one Speaker for its regular session and, later, another Speaker for an adjourned or extraordinary session. For purposes of this list, attempts were made to list only the Speaker for the regular session.

The first legislature—
30 representatives and
14 senators—con-
vened in Chillicothe on
March 1, 1803.

Ohio Senate Leaders*

GENERAL ASSEMBLY	CONVENED	SENATE SPEAKER	COUNTY
1	Mar. 1, 1803	Nathaniel Massie	Ross
2	Dec. 5, 1803	Daniel Symmes	Hamilton
3	Dec. 3, 1804	Daniel Symmes	Hamilton
4	Dec. 2, 1805	James Pritchard	Jefferson
5	Dec. 1, 1806	Thomas Kirker	Adams
6	Dec. 7, 1807	Thomas Kirker	Adams
7	Dec. 5, 1808	Thomas Kirker	Adams
8	Dec. 4, 1809	Duncan McArthur	Ross
9	Dec. 3, 1810	Thomas Kirker	Adams
10	Dec. 2, 1811	Thomas Kirker	Adams
11	Dec. 7, 1812	Thomas Kirker	Adams
12	Dec. 6, 1813	Othniel Looker	Hamilton
13	Dec. 5, 1814	Thomas Kirker	Adams
14	Dec. 4, 1815	Peter Hitchcock	Geauga
15	Dec. 2, 1816	Abraham Shepherd	Adams
16	Dec. 1, 1817	Abraham Shepherd	Adams
17	Dec. 7, 1818	Robert Lucas	Pike
18	Dec. 6, 1819	Allen Trimble	Highland
19	Dec. 4, 1820	Allen Trimble	Highland
20	Dec. 3, 1821	Allen Trimble	Highland
21	Dec. 2, 1822	Allen Trimble	Highland
22	Dec. 1, 1823	Allen Trimble	Highland
23	Dec. 6, 1824	Allen Trimble	Highland
24	Dec. 5, 1825	Allen Trimble	Highland
25	Dec. 4, 1826	Abraham Shepherd	Adams
26	Dec. 3, 1827	Samuel Wheeler	Geauga
27	Dec. 1, 1828	Samuel Wheeler	Geauga
28	Dec. 7, 1829	Robert Lucas	Pike
29	Dec. 6, 1830	Samuel R. Miller	Hamilton
30	Dec. 5, 1831	William Doherty	Franklin
31	Dec. 3, 1832	Samuel R. Miller	Hamilton
32	Dec. 2, 1833	David T. Disney	Hamilton
33	Dec. 1, 1834	Peter Hitchcock	Geauga
34	Dec. 7, 1835	Elijah Vance	Butler
35	Dec. 5, 1836	Elijah Vance	Butler
36	Dec. 4, 1837	George J. Smith	Warren
37	Dec. 3, 1838	William Hawkins	Morgan

GENERAL ASSEMBLY	CONVENED	SENATE SPEAKER	COUNTY
38	Dec. 2, 1839	William McLaughlin	Richland
39	Dec. 7, 1840	William McLaughlin	Richland
40	Dec. 6, 1841	James J. Faran	Hamilton
41	Dec. 5, 1842	James J. Faran	Hamilton
42	Dec. 4, 1843	Thomas W. Bartley	Richland
43	Dec. 2, 1844	David Chambers	Muskingum
44	Dec. 1, 1845	Seabury Ford	Geauga
45	Dec. 7, 1846	Edson B. Olds	Pickaway
46	Dec. 6, 1847	Charles B. Goddard	Muskingum
47	Dec. 4, 1848	Brewster Randall	Ashtabula
48	Dec. 3, 1849	Harrison G. Blake	Medina
49	Dec. 2, 1850	Charles C. Convers	Muskingum
		PRESIDENT PRO TEM	
50	Jan. 5, 1852	Joel W. Wilson	Sandusky
		George Rex	Wayne
51	Jan. 2, 1854	Robert J. Atkinson	Carroll
52	Jan. 7, 1856	Robert W. Taylor	Trumbull
53	Jan. 4, 1858	Edward M. Phelps	Defiance
54	Jan. 2, 1860	Richard A. Harrison	Madison
55	Jan. 6, 1862	James Monroe	Lorain
56	Jan. 4, 1864	Samuel Humphreyville	Medina
57	Jan. 1, 1866	H.S. Martin	Stark
58	Jan. 6, 1868	Thomas J. Godfrey	Mercer
59	Jan. 3, 1870	Samuel F. Hunt	Hamilton
60	Jan. 1, 1872	Allen T. Brinsmade	Cuyahoga
61	Jan. 5, 1874	Emory D. Potter	Lucas
62	Jan. 3, 1876	H.W. Curtiss	Cuyahoga
63	Jan. 7, 1878	James W. Owens	Licking
64	Jan. 4, 1880	Reese G. Richards	Jefferson
65	Jan. 2, 1882	R.A. Horr	Lorain
66	Jan. 7, 1884	Elmer White	Defiance
67	Jan. 4, 1886	John O'Neill	Muskingum
		Silas A. Conrad	Stark
68	Jan. 2, 1888	Theodore F. Davis	Washington
69	Jan. 6, 1890	Perry M. Adams	Seneca
70	Jan. 4, 1892	Elbert L. Lampson	Ashtabula
71	Jan. 3, 1894	Thomas H. McConica (R)	Hancock

GENERAL ASSEMBLY	CONVENED	PRESIDENT PRO TEM	COUNTY
72	Jan. 6, 1896	John C. Hutsinpiller (R)	Gallia
73	Jan. 3, 1898	Thaddeus E. Cromley (D)	Pickaway
74	Jan. 1, 1900	Oscar Sheppard (R)	Preble
75	Jan. 6, 1902	Frank B. Archer (R)	Belmont
76	Jan. 4, 1904	G.H. Chamberlain (R)	Lorain
77	Jan. 1, 1906	James M. Williams (D)	Cuyahoga
78	Jan. 4, 1909	Nation O. Mather (R)	Summit
79	Jan. 2, 1911	William Green (D)	Coshocton
80	Jan. 6, 1913	William Green (D)	Coshocton
81	Jan. 4, 1915	C.J. Howard (R)	Belmont
82	Jan. 1, 1917	J.H. Miller (D)	Licking
83	Jan. 6, 1919	Frank E. Whittemore (R)	Summit
84	Jan. 3, 1921	Frank E. Whittemore (R)	Summit
85	Jan. 1, 1923	George E. Kryder (R)	Henry
86	Jan. 5, 1925	Joseph R. Gardner (R)	Hamilton
87	Jan. 3, 1927	Chester C. Bolton (R)	Cuyahoga
88	Jan. 7, 1929	Allan G. Aigler (R)	Sandusky
89	Jan. 5, 1931	Earl R. Lewis (R)	Belmont
90	Jan. 2, 1933	D.H. DeArmond (D)	Hamilton
91	Jan. 7, 1935	Paul P. Yoder (D)	Montgomery
92	Jan. 4, 1937	Keith Lawrence (D)	Cuyahoga
93	Jan. 2, 1939	Frank E. Whittemore (R)	Summit
94	Jan. 6, 1941	Frank E. Whittemore (R)	Summit
95	Jan. 4, 1943	Frank E. Whittemore (R)	Summit
96	Jan. 1, 1945	Frank E. Whittemore (R)	Summit
97	Jan. 6, 1947	Frank E. Whittemore (R)	Summit
98	Jan. 3, 1949	Margaret A. Mahoney (D)	Cuyahoga
99	Jan. 1, 1951	Roscoe R. Walcutt (R)	Franklin
100	Jan. 5, 1953	C. Stanley Mechem (R)	Athens
101	Jan. 3, 1955	C. Stanley Mechem (R)	Athens

GENERAL ASSEMBLY	CONVENED	PRESIDENT PRO TEM	COUNTY
102	Jan. 7, 1957	C. Stanley Mechem (R)	Athens
103	Jan. 5, 1959	Frank W. King (D)	Lucas
104	Jan. 2, 1961	C. Stanley Mechem (R)	Athens
105	Jan. 7, 1963	C. Stanley Mechem (R)	Athens
106	Jan. 4, 1965	Theodore M. Gray (R)	Miami
107	Jan. 2, 1967	Theodore M. Gray (R)	Miami
108	Jan. 6, 1969	Theodore M. Gray (R)	Miami
109	Jan. 4, 1971	Theodore M. Gray (R)	Franklin
110	Jan. 1, 1973	Theodore M. Gray (R)	Franklin
111	Jan. 6, 1975	Oliver Ocasek (D)	Summit
112	Jan. 3, 1977	Oliver Ocasek (D)	Summit
		SENATE PRESIDENT	
113	Jan. 2, 1979	Oliver Ocasek (D)	Summit
114	Jan. 5, 1981	Paul E. Gillmor (R)	Ottawa
115	Jan. 3, 1983	Harry Meshel (D)	Mahoning
116	Jan. 7, 1985	Paul E. Gillmor (R)	Ottawa
117	Jan. 5, 1987	Paul E. Gillmor (R)	Ottawa
118	Jan. 3, 1989	Stanley J. Aronoff (R)	Hamilton
119	Jan. 7, 1991	Stanley J. Aronoff (R)	Hamilton
120	Jan. 4, 1993	Stanley J. Aronoff (R)	Hamilton
121	Jan. 3, 1995	Stanley J. Aronoff (R)	Hamilton
122	Jan. 6, 1997	Richard H. Finan (R)	Hamilton
123	Jan. 4, 1999	Richard H. Finan (R)	Hamilton
124	Jan. 2, 2001	Richard H. Finan (R)	Hamilton
125	Jan. 6, 2003	Doug White (R)	Adams
126	Jan. 3, 2005	Bill Harris (R)	Ashland

* From 1803 to 1851, the presiding officer of the Senate was the Senate Speaker. When the state's second constitution took effect on September 1, 1851, the lieutenant governor began presiding over the Senate although the effective leader in the Senate was the president pro tem (the majority leader). In January 1979, when a constitutional amendment took effect, the lieutenant governor was relieved of the duty of presiding over the Senate and the presiding officer became the Senate president (the majority leader).

From 1810 to 1812, Zanesville served as the state capital. A commission was appointed to determine the permanent capital "not more than 40 miles from the center of the state." Chillicothe and Zanesville were just outside this range.

In 1816, the legislature voted that the capital should be located on "the high banks of the Scioto." With the new site having no name, the General Assembly voted that the future capital would be "known and distinguished by the name of Columbus." With a town plan drawn, surveyors began staking out High and Broad streets. The city's first Statehouse was at the southwest corner of the square—at State and High streets.

Ohio General Assembly Political Control

1872–2006

ASSEMBLY	YEARS	HOUSE DEM.	REP.	OTHER	SENATE DEM.	REP.	OTHER
60	1872-73	48	57		18	18	
61	1874-75	56	46		22	14	
62	1876-77	47	64	3	17	20	
63	1878-79	66	41		26	10	
64	1880-81	45	69		15	22	
65	1882-83	35	70		11	22	
66	1884-85	60	45		22	11	
67	1886-87	43	67		20	17	
68	1888-89	45	64		11	25	
69	1890-91	60	54		19	17	
70	1892-93	35	72		10	21	
71	1894-95	21	86		5	26	
72	1896-97	25	87		6	30	
73	1898-99	47	62		18	17	1
74	1900-1901	45	62	3	11	19	1
75	1902-3	42	68		12	21	
76	1904-5	22	88		4	29	
77	1906-8	57	62		18	18	1
78	1909-10	45	71	1	14	20	
79	1911-12	70	49		19	15	
80	1913-14	87	33	3	26	7	
81	1915-16	50	72	1	13	20	
82	1917-18	72	56		25	11	
83	1919-20	47	77		12	21	
84	1921-22	12	113		1	36	
85	1923-24	27	103		4	31	
86	1925-26	20	110		2	33	
87	1927-28	33	103		2	35	
88	1929-30	11	122		0	31	
89	1931-32	58	70		14	18	
90	1933-34	84	51		16	16	
91	1935-36	67	68		19	13	
92	1937-38	103	33		31	5	
93	1939-40	31	100		8	27	
94	1941-42	60	78		17	19	
95	1943-44	25	111		5	28	
96	1945-46	47	89		13	20	
97	1947-48	16	123		4	32	
98	1949-50	69	66		19	14	
99	1951-52	36	99		7	26	
100	1953-54	34	102		10	23	
101	1955-56	47	89		12	21	
102	1957-58	42	97		12	22	
103	1959-60	78	61		20	13	
104	1961-62	55	84		18	20	
105	1963-64	49	88		13	20	
106	1965-66	62	75		16	16	
107	1967-68	37	62		10	23	
108	1969-70	35	64		12	21	
109	1971-72	45	54		13	20	
110	1973-74	58	41		16	17	
111	1975-76	59	40		21	12	
112	1977-78	62	37		21	12	
113	1979-80	62	37		18	15	
114	1981-82	56	43		15	18	
115	1983-84	62	37		17	16	
116	1985-86	59	40		15	18	
117	1987-88	60	39		15	18	
118	1989-90	59	40		14	19	
119	1991-92	61	38		12	21	
120	1993-94	53	46		13	20	
121	1995-96	43	56		13	20	
121	1995-96	43	56		13	20	
122	1997-98	39	60		12	21	
123	1999-2000	40	59		12	21	
124	2001-2002	40	59		12	21	
125	2003-2004	37	62		11	22	
126	2005-2006	40	59		11	22	

Sources: Annual Reports, Ohio secretary of state; Ohio House journals; Ohio Senate journals

CHAPTER 6

The Ohio Judiciary

OHIO'S SECOND CONSTITUTION, ADOPTED IN 1851, REQUIRED THE ELECTION OF ALL JUDGES. SINCE THEN, OHIOANS TWICE HAVE REJECTED APPOINTMENT PROPOSALS.

The Ohio Judiciary

Ohio's judicial system consists of three levels—the trial courts, the appeals courts, and the Supreme Court of Ohio. The Ohio Constitution designates certain courts as "constitutional courts" (the Supreme Court, the courts of appeals, and the common pleas courts and their divisions) and others as "statutory courts" (municipal courts, county courts, mayor's courts), which can be created by legislative acts.

The Supreme Court of Ohio

The Ohio Constitution of 1802 created a Supreme Court of three judges appointed for seven-year terms by a joint ballot of the legislature. To bring the justice system close to the people, the court was required to hold sessions at least once a year in each county (Ohio had 17 at the time). In 1808, the General Assembly increased the number of judges to four, as allowed by the constitution, and divided the state into two judicial circuits. The court was reduced to three judges in 1810 but increased again to four in 1824. In the early years of statehood, Ohio law assigned both original and appellate jurisdiction to the Supreme Court in many cases, especially those involving disputed amounts exceeding $1,000 – then a sizable sum. The court also had exclusive jurisdiction in capital punishment cases.

Ohio's second constitution, adopted in 1851, required the election of all judges, including five Supreme Court judges for terms of five years. The new constitution ended the Supreme Court's role as a county court and established it as the state's court of last resort. For many years, the requirement that the court meet annually in each county had been impossible to satisfy; by 1849, the state had 85 counties. In 1892, the General Assembly, as authorized by a constitutional amendment, increased the number of judges to six and lengthened judicial terms to six years. Another amendment, adopted in 1912, established a seven-member court, including a chief justice, who would be elected separately to the office.

The Modern Courts Amendment of 1968 designated that Ohio Supreme Court judges be called "justices" and charged the court with adopting uniform rules and regulations for all courts in the state. The amendment also provided that—beginning with the 1970 elections —

no judge could be appointed or elected to a term after reaching age 70; retired judges could be assigned to temporary court duty. The amendment also reduced—to a simple majority—the number of justices required to declare a law unconstitutional; the previous requirement was six of the seven justices. In addition, the legislature was granted the authority to increase the number of justices.

As Ohio's court of last resort, the Supreme Court mostly handles appeals from the state's 12 district courts of appeals. The court must accept appeals involving interpretations of the Ohio Constitution or U.S. Constitution, cases in which the death penalty was imposed, cases initiated in a court of appeals, and cases in which appellate-court decisions conflict. The Supreme Court also is required to accept appeals from the Board of Tax Appeals and the Public Utilities Commission.

The Supreme Court has original jurisdiction for writs of habeus corpus (for the release of people who have been improperly imprisoned), writs of mandamus (ordering a lower court or public official to perform an act), writs of procedendo (ordering a lower court to proceed to judgment), writs of prohibition (ordering a judge or public official to cease an unlawful act), and writs of quo warranto (alleging misuse of an office or franchise). In cases involving contested elections, the Supreme Court may take a case directly from a common pleas court.

The Supreme Court establishes admission rules for lawyers to practice in Ohio and has exclusive jurisdiction to discipline lawyers and judges for misconduct.

The chief justice and justices are elected in even-numbered years to six-year terms on a nonpartisan ballot, although they are nominated in partisan primaries. Court vacancies that occur between elections are filled by gubernatorial appointment.

Court of Appeals

Ohio's appellate courts originated as district courts created by the 1851 Ohio Constitution. The district courts were to consist of one Supreme Court judge and several common pleas judges in each district. The district courts were given original jurisdiction in the same matters as the Supreme Court and appellate jurisdiction for cases originating in the common pleas courts. The legislature created five judicial districts;

at the time, the state had nine common pleas districts.

As Ohio grew and caseloads expanded, Supreme Court judges had less and less time to preside over the district courts. In 1865, the Supreme Court judges were relieved of this duty, and the district-court system began to decline. An 1883 amendment to the Ohio Constitution replaced the district courts with circuit courts, which were given much the same jurisdiction as the district courts. The legislature divided the state into seven circuits and authorized the election of three judges in each.

The 1912 amendments to the Ohio Constitution renamed the circuit courts as courts of appeals. Circuit judges became appellate judges, and all pending cases proceeded toward judgment. Terms of office were fixed at six years. The amendments specified that no judgment of a common pleas court or other court of record could be reversed except by the concurrence of all three appellate judges. Ohio's appeals courts consisted of three judges in each of nine districts. In 1959, Ohio voters approved an amendment authorizing the General Assembly to increase the number of appellate judges in any district whenever a heavy caseload requires it.

As of 2005, Ohio had 12 appellate districts, with the number of judges in each district ranging from 4 to 12. Each appellate case is heard and decided by a three-judge panel. The cases are appeals from Ohio's common pleas, municipal, and county courts. In most cases, appellate court decisions are final. While the concurrence of all three judges is needed to reverse a lower-court decision, only a majority is necessary on all other questions. In 1994, Ohio voters approved a constitutional amendment removing from courts of appeals all jurisdiction over the review of death penalty cases.

Common Pleas Courts

Before Ohio became a state, a territorial act of 1788 authorized the establishment of a common pleas court in each county of the Northwest Territory. The courts, consisting of three to five judges appointed by the territorial governor, had jurisdiction in all civil matters. The first Ohio Constitution maintained the common pleas courts but altered their makeup to two or three associate judges and one president judge. The state was divided into three circuits, each with a president judge. The common pleas judges were appointed to seven-year terms by the General Assembly. An act of 1803 gave common pleas courts original jurisdiction in cases involving disputes that exceeded the jurisdiction of justices of the peace. In addition, the courts heard appeals from justices of the peace, county commissioners, and other lower courts. In 1810, cases in which a common pleas court had original jurisdiction became appealable to the Ohio Supreme Court.

The constitution of 1851 reduced the terms of common pleas judges to five years. The state was divided into nine common pleas districts, each containing at least three counties; each district was subdivided into three parts with a judge elected from each part. The General Assembly could change the number of districts and judges in any district. Common pleas judges were called upon to perform appellate work in conjunction with a Supreme Court judge within five appellate districts. This system did not work well, however; common pleas judges were relieved of appellate duties in 1883. Starting in 1853, common pleas courts were given original jurisdiction over most criminal cases.

The constitutional amendments of 1912 provided for the election of at least one common pleas judge in each county. In 1917, the legislature approved a law requiring that common pleas judges have at least six years of experience practicing law. Beginning in 1910, the establishment and growth of municipal courts relieved the common pleas courts in many counties of some civil cases.

Today, common pleas courts have original jurisdiction in all criminal felony cases and all civil cases in which the amount in dispute exceeds $15,000. Common pleas courts also have appellate jurisdiction over decisions of some state administrative agencies. Most Ohio common pleas courts have divisions to handle cases involving domestic relations, juveniles, and probate. Judges are elected to six-year terms on a nonpartisan ballot, although they are nominated for office in partisan primaries.

Common Pleas: Probate Division

Probate courts in Ohio were first established in August 1788 by an act of the Northwest Territory. The act authorized a probate court for each county, with a probate judge ruling on wills, guardianships, and other probate cases and two common pleas judges ruling with the probate judge on contested matters and final judgments.

When Ohio became a state, its first constitution did not provide for probate courts in the judicial system. The constitution gave common pleas courts the powers exercised by the probate courts in the territorial period. Ohio's second constitution, adopted in 1851, re-established a probate court in each county with a judge elected to a three-year term. The probate courts were given jurisdiction in probate and testamentary matters; the appointment of administrators and guardians; the settlement of accounts of executors; the issuance of marriage licenses; the sale of land by executors, administrators, and guardians; and other matters.

In subsequent years, the probate courts were charged with determining mental competency and making commitments to mental institutions, issuing adoption orders, deciding delinquency cases, and keeping vital statistics. With the enactment of Ohio's direct-inheritance tax law in 1919, the probate court began assessing the tax after the county auditor determined the value of a decedent's estate. From time to time, Ohio's probate courts had concurrent jurisdiction with common pleas courts in some criminal cases; the criminal jurisdiction of probate courts was abolished in 1931.

The Modern Courts Amendment of 1968 established probate courts as divisions of common pleas courts, although probate judges continued to be elected separately. Probate judges are elected to six-year terms.

Common Pleas: Division of Domestic Relations

Prior to 1913 in Ohio, cases involving family matters were heard in various courts. In 1913, the General Assembly approved legislation providing for the election of a common pleas judge in Hamilton County to be designated as a domestic-relations judge. The judge handled cases of divorce, alimony, child neglect, illegitimacy, nonsupport, and other domestic-relations and juvenile matters. In subsequent years, similar acts were passed establishing domestic-relations judges in most of Ohio's major counties. By 1929, at least seven of the state's largest counties had separate domestic-relations divisions; by 1960, at least 13

Ohio Judicial System Structure

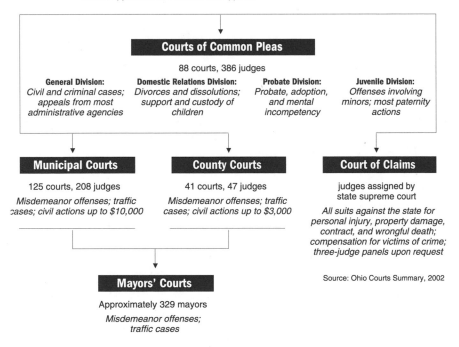

Supreme Court

Chief justice and six justices

Original jurisdiction in select cases; court of last resort on state constitutional questions and questions of public or great general interest; appeals from Board of Tax Appeals and Public Utilities Commission, and death penalty cases.

Court of Appeals

12 courts, 68 judges
three-judge panels

Original jurisdiction in select cases; appellate review of judgment of common pleas, municipal, and county courts; appeals from Board of Tax Appeals

Courts of Common Pleas

88 courts, 386 judges

General Division:
Civil and criminal cases; appeals from most administrative agencies

Domestic Relations Division:
Divorces and dissolutions; support and custody of children

Probate Division:
Probate, adoption, and mental incompetency

Juvenile Division:
Offenses involving minors; most paternity actions

Municipal Courts

125 courts, 208 judges

Misdemeanor offenses; traffic cases; civil actions up to $10,000

County Courts

41 courts, 47 judges

Misdemeanor offenses; traffic cases; civil actions up to $3,000

Court of Claims

judges assigned by state supreme court

All suits against the state for personal injury, property damage, contract, and wrongful death; compensation for victims of crime; three-judge panels upon request

Source: Ohio Courts Summary, 2002

Mayors' Courts

Approximately 329 mayors

Misdemeanor offenses; traffic cases

---

counties had them. By 2002, the number was 17. In some counties, the domestic-relations division handles both adult domestic-relations cases and juvenile cases; in others, a separate juvenile division—as a branch of the common pleas or the probate court—handles juvenile matters.

Common Pleas: Juvenile Division

The first juvenile courts in Ohio were created in 1904. In most counties, the juvenile court was a branch of the common pleas or the probate court. In Cuyahoga County, a separate juvenile court was established. The juvenile courts handle cases involving minors and those involving unruly, abused, and neglected children. Today, juvenile courts in most Ohio counties are branches of the probate or domestic-relations divisions of the common pleas court. Nine counties have separate juvenile divisions of the common pleas court.

Municipal and County Courts

Municipal courts were established in Ohio in the early 1900s to begin replacing township-based justice-of-the-peace courts, which had become unworkable in the rapidly growing state—especially in the largest urban areas. The General Assembly set up the first municipal court in Cleveland in 1910. Three years later, the legislature created similar courts in Cincinnati, Columbus, Dayton, and Youngstown. In criminal cases, the courts supplanted local police courts. In 1951, the legislature passed a Municipal Court Act to set uniform procedures for Ohio's 51 municipal courts. By 1955, Ohio had 69 municipal courts; by 1960, there were 92; by 2004, the number had grown to 125. Municipal courts conduct preliminary hearings in felony cases and have jurisdiction over misdemeanors and traffic offenses. The courts also can handle civil cases involving disputes not exceeding $15,000—an amount the General Assembly periodically has raised. Municipal judges, who serve six-year terms, may have jurisdiction in one municipality, in additional parts of a county, or over an entire county. The geographic jurisdictions are established by state statute.

The General Assembly created county courts in 1957 to continue phasing out justice-of-the-peace courts and serve areas of a county not covered by municipal courts. The jurisdiction of county courts is similar to that of municipal courts. In civil cases, county courts as of 2004 could handle disputes not exceeding $15,000. Like municipal judges, county court judges are elected to six-year terms and empowered to perform marriages.

The Court of Claims

The General Assembly created the Court of Claims in 1975 to hear suits against the state for money damages. The court has exclusive jurisdiction in all such civil actions against the state. A 1912 amendment to the Ohio Constitution established that the state could be sued "in such courts and in such manner as may be provided by law." Such suits often involve personal injury, property damage, contract disputes, and wrongful-death actions. Judges for the Court of Claims—who must be incumbent or retired justices or judges—sit by temporary assignment per the appointment of the chief justice of the Ohio Supreme Court. The court has jurisdiction over compensation claims from victims of crime. A Victims of Crime Division was created within the court in 1976 to reimburse crime victims for personal injuries and loss of wages; the compensation fund is financed by court fees. Compensation claims are heard by a commissioner of the Court of Claims; commissioners are lawyers appointed by the Ohio Supreme Court. Decisions can be appealed to a panel of three commissioners, then to the Court of Claims.

Mayors's Courts

Mayors' courts, established in 1852 in Ohio, today have jurisdiction in cases involving violations of municipal ordinances within municipal corporations that do not have a municipal court. For the most part, mayors' courts serve Ohio's villages; presided over by elected or appointed mayors, the courts usually handle traffic and parking violations. Jurisdiction over drug- or alcohol-related traffic offenses is limited to first-time violations. Decisions of a mayor's court may be appealed to a municipal court or county court. In 2004, Ohio had 329 mayors' courts, down from about 500 in the previous decade.

Merit Selection Proposals

In Ohio, judges at the county, appellate, and state levels are nominated for office in partisan primaries but are elected in November on a nonpartisan ballot. In other words, judges run with party labels in primaries and without party labels in general elections.

Periodically, reform-minded groups have attempted to abolish the direct election of judges and replace it with an appointment or "merit selection" system. Under such a system, a nominating council would review applicants for a judicial vacancy and provide the governor with a list of recommended candidates; the governor would be required to choose from the list.

Ohio voters twice have rejected proposed constitutional amendments to adopt appointment systems for Supreme Court and appellate judgeships.

Voters rejecting appointment systems

November 8, 1938
"To provide for the original appointment of judges of the Supreme Court and Courts of Appeals."

YES 621,011 (33.4%) NO 1,237,443 (66.6%)

November 3, 1987
"To change the way Ohio selects its Supreme Court and appeals court judges by abolishing the direct election method and replacing it with an appointment system."

YES 878,683 (35.4%) NO 1,600,588 (64.6%)

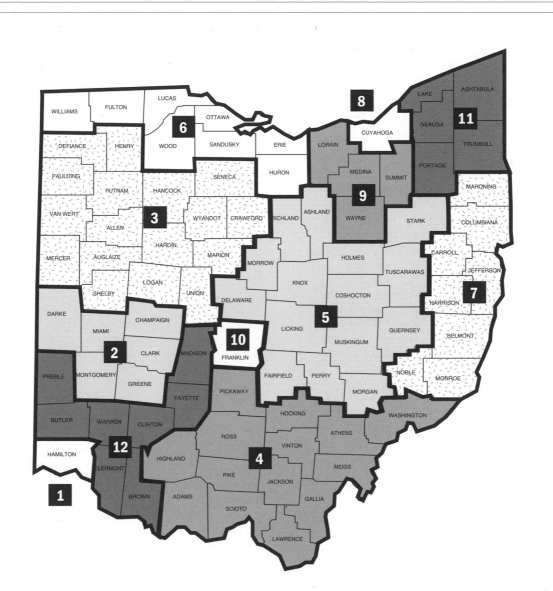

Court of Appeals Districts

DISTRICT	JUDGES	COUNTIES	POPULATION	POPULATION PER JUDGE
1	6	1	845,303	144,371
2	5	6	1,042,757	208,551
3	4	17	782,234	195,559
4	4	14	616,789	154,197
5	6	15	1,364,704	272,941
6	5	8	899,206	179,841
7	4	8	587,680	146,920
8	12	1	1,393,978	116,165
9	5	4	1,090,222	218,044
10	8	1	1,068,978	133,622
11	5	5	798,311	199,578
12	4	8	862,978	215,745
TOTAL:	68	88	11,353,140	AVERAGE: 172,017

Source: Ohio Courts Summary, 2002

Judges of the
Supreme Court of Ohio

Served under the 1802 Constitution

JUDGE	COUNTY	TERM OF SERVICE
Samuel Huntington	Trumbull	Apr. 1803–Dec. 1808
R.J. Meigs Jr.	Washington	Apr. 1803–Dec. 1804
William Spriggs	Jefferson	Apr. 1803–Apr. 1806
Daniel Symmes	Hamilton	Jan. 1805–Jan. 1808
George Tod	Trumbull	Apr. 1806–1810
William Spriggs	Jefferson	Feb. 1808–1810
R.J. Meigs Jr.	Washington	Feb. 1808–Jan. 1809
Thomas Scott	Ross	Feb. 1809–Feb. 1816
Thomas Morris	Clermont	Feb. 1809–1809
William W. Irvin	Fairfield	Feb. 1810–Feb. 1816
Ethan Allen Brown	Hamilton	Feb. 1810–Dec. 1818
Jessup N. Couch	Ross	Feb. 1816–1821
John McLean	Warren	Feb. 1816–1822
Calvin Pease	Trumbull	Feb. 1816–Feb. 1830
Peter Hitchcock	Geauga	Feb. 1819–Feb. 1833
Jacob Burnet	Hamilton	1821–Dec. 1828
Charles R. Sherman	Fairfield	Jan. 1823–1829
Joshua Collett	Warren	Feb. 1829–Feb. 1836
Elijah Hayward	Hamilton	Feb. 1830–1830
John Milton Goodenow	Jefferson	Feb. 1830–1830
Henry Brush	Ross	1830–1831
Gustave Swan	Franklin	1830–1831
Ebenezer Lane	Huron	Dec. 1830–Dec. 1844
John C. Wright	Jefferson	1831–Feb. 1835
Reuben Wood	Cuyahoga	Feb. 1833–Feb. 1847
Peter Hitchcock	Geauga	Feb. 1835–Feb. 1842
Frederick Grimke	Ross	Feb. 1836–1842
Matthew Birchard	Trumbull	Feb. 1842–Feb. 1849
Nathaniel C. Reed	Hamilton	Mar. 1842–1849
Peter Hitchcock*	Geauga	Dec. 1844–Feb. 1852
Edward Avery	Wayne	Feb. 1847–1851
Rufus P. Spalding*	Summit	Mar. 1849–Feb. 1852
William B. Caldwell*	Hamilton	Mar. 1849–Feb. 1852
Rufus P. Ranney*	Trumbull	Mar. 1851–Feb. 1852

* Served until the second Monday in February 1852, when the terms of the judges elected under the Constitution of 1851 commenced.

Served under the 1851 Constitution

JUDGE	COUNTY	TERM OF SERVICE
William B. Caldwell	Hamilton	Feb. 1852–Dec. 1854
Thomas W. Bartley	Richland	Feb. 1852–Feb. 1859
John A. Corwin	Champaign	Feb. 1852–Dec. 1854
Allen G. Thurman	Ross	Feb. 1852–Mar. 1856
Rufus P. Ranney	Trumbull	Feb. 1852–Feb. 1857
Robert B. Warden	Franklin	Dec. 1854–Feb. 1855
William Kennon	Belmont	Dec. 1854–Mar. 1856
Joseph R. Swan	Franklin	Feb. 1855–Nov. 1859
Jacob Brinkerhoff	Richland	Mar. 1856–Feb. 1871
Charles C. Convers	Muskingum	Mar. 1856–May 1856
Ozias Bowen	Marion	May 1856–Feb. 1858
Milton Sutliff	Trumbull	Feb. 1858–Feb. 1861
Josiah Scott	Butler	Feb. 1857–Feb. 1872
William Y. Gholson	Hamilton	Nov. 1859–Dec. 1863
William V. Peck	Scioto	Feb. 1859–Feb. 1864
Horace Wilder	Ashtabula	Dec. 1863–Feb. 1865
Rufus P. Ranney	Trumbull	Feb. 1863–Feb. 1865
John Welch	Athens	Feb. 1865–Feb. 1878
Hocking Hunter	Fairfield	Feb. 1864–Feb. 1864
William White	Clark	Feb. 1864–Mar. 1883
Luther Day	Portage	Feb. 1865–Feb. 1875
George W. McIlvaine	Tuscarawas	Feb. 1871–Feb. 1886
William H. West	Logan	Feb. 1872–1873
Walter F. Stone	Erie	1873–Sept. 1874
George Rex	Wayne	Sept. 1874–Feb. 1877
William J. Gilmore	Preble	Feb. 1875–Feb. 1880
W.W. Boynton	Lorain	Feb. 1877–Nov. 1881
Nicholas Longworth	Hamilton	Nov. 1881–Mar. 1883
John W. Okey	Hamilton	Feb. 1878–July 1885
William H. Upson	Summit	Mar. 1883–Dec. 1883
Selwyn N. Owen	Williams	Dec. 1881–Feb. 1889
William W. Johnson	Lawrence	Feb. 1880–Nov. 1886
John H. Doyle	Lucas	Mar. 1883–Dec. 1883
Martin D. Follett	Washington	Dec. 1883–Feb. 1887
Gibson Atherton	Licking	Aug. 1885–Dec. 1885
William T. Spear	Trumbull	Dec. 1885–Jan. 1913
Franklin J. Dickman	Cuyahoga	Nov. 1886–Feb. 1895
Thaddeus A. Minshall	Ross	Feb. 1886–Feb. 1902
Marshall J. Williams	Fayette	Feb. 1887–July 1902
Joseph P. Bradbury	Gallia	Feb. 1889–Jan. 1900
Jacob F. Burnett	Hancock	Feb. 1893–Feb. 1904
William Z. Davis	Marion	Jan. 1900–Feb. 1913
John A. Shauck	Montgomery	Feb. 1895–Dec. 1914
James L. Price	Allen	Feb. 1902–Mar. 1912
William B. Crew	Morgan	July 1902–Jan. 1911
Augustus N. Summers	Clark	Feb. 1904–Jan. 1911
Joseph W. O'Hara	Hamilton	Apr. 1912–Nov. 1912
J. Foster Wilkin	Tuscarawas	Nov. 1912–Dec. 1914
Maurice H. Donahue	Perry	Jan. 1911–Nov. 1919

JUDGE	COUNTY	TERM OF SERVICE
James G. Johnson	Clark	Jan. 1911–Aug. 1922
Oscar W. Newman	Scioto	Jan. 1913–Dec. 1918
R.M. Wanamaker	Summit	Jan. 1913–June 1924

(In November 1914, as provided by a 1913 law, Ohio voters began selecting a chief justice of the Supreme Court. Chief justices are designated in boldface.)

JUDGE	COUNTY	TERM OF SERVICE
Hugh L. Nichols	Clermont	Jan. 1915–Dec. 1920
Thomas A. Jones	Jackson	Jan. 1915–Aug. 1937
Edward S. Matthias	Van Wert	Jan. 1915–Nov. 1953
Stanley W. Merrill	Hamilton	Nov. 1919–June 1920
Coleman Avery	Hamilton	June 1920–Nov. 1920
Benson W. Hough	Delaware	Nov. 1920–Dec. 1922
George H. Clark	Stark	Aug. 1922–Dec. 1922
James E. Robinson	Union	Jan. 1919–Jan. 1932
Harry L. Conn	Van Wert	June 1924–Dec. 1924
Carrington T. Marshall	Muskingum	Jan. 1921–Dec. 1932
Florence E. Allen	Cuyahoga	Jan. 1923–Apr. 1934
Robert H. Day	Stark	Jan. 1923–Sept. 1933
Reynolds R. Kinkade	Lucas	Jan. 1925–May 1933
Robert N. Wilkin	Tuscarawas	Apr. 1934–Dec. 1934
William L. Hart	Stark	Nov. 1934–Dec. 1934
Charles B. Zimmerman	Clark	Oct. 1933–Nov. 1934
W.F. Garver	Holmes	Nov. 1934–Dec. 1934
Will P. Stephenson	Adams	Jan. 1932–Dec. 1936
Howard L. Bevis	Hamilton	May 1933–Nov. 1934
Roy H. Williams	Erie	Nov. 1934–Dec. 1946
Carl V. Weygandt	Cuyahoga	Jan. 1933–Dec. 1962
Robert N. Gorman	Hamilton	Sept. 1937–Nov. 1938
William C. Dixon	Cuyahoga	Nov. 1938–Dec. 1938
Arthur H. Day	Cuyahoga	Jan. 1935–Dec. 1940
Charles B. Zimmerman	Clark	Jan. 1935–Dec. 1946
George S. Myers	Cuyahoga	Jan. 1937–May 1940
Edward C. Turner	Franklin	Oct. 1940–Oct. 1950
William L. Hart	Stark	Jan. 1939–Jan. 1957
Gilbert Bettman	Hamilton	Jan. 1941–July 1942
Charles S. Bell	Hamilton	Nov. 1942–Mar. 1947
Robert M. Sohngen	Butler	Dec. 1946–Dec. 1948
James Garfield Stewart	Hamilton	Mar. 1947–Apr. 1959
Howard E. Fought	Guernsey	Oct. 1950–Nov. 1950
Henry A. Middletown	Lucas	Nov. 1950–1954
Kingsley A. Taft	Cuyahoga	Jan. 1949–Dec. 1962
John H. Lamneck	Tuscarawas	Nov. 1953–Nov. 1954

JUDGE	COUNTY	TERM OF SERVICE
John M. Matthias	Franklin	Nov. 1954–Sept. 1970
Charles B. Zimmerman	Clark	Jan. 1953–June 1969
James F. Bell	Madison	Jan. 1955–Oct. 1962
Thomas J. Herbert	Cuyahoga	Jan. 1957–Jan. 1963
John W. Peck	Hamilton	Jan. 1959–Apr. 1959
C. William O'Neill	Washington	Nov. 1960–Apr. 1970
Lynn B. Griffith	Trumbull	Oct. 1962–Nov. 1964
Louis J. Schneider Jr.	Hamilton	Nov. 1964–Dec. 1972
Rankin Gibson	Franklin	Jan. 1963–Nov. 1964
Paul W. Brown	Mahoning	Nov. 1964–Dec. 1968
Kingsley A. Taft	Cuyahoga	Jan. 1963–Mar. 1970
Paul M. Herbert	Franklin	Jan. 1963–Jan. 1969
J.J.P. Corrigan	Cuyahoga	Sept. 1969–Dec. 1976
Leonard J. Stern	Franklin	Aug. 1970–Jan. 1977
Robert M. Duncan	Franklin	Jan. 1969–Nov. 1971
Lloyd O. Brown	Cuyahoga	Dec. 1971–Jan. 1973
C. William O'Neill	Washington	Apr. 1970–Aug. 1978
Robert E. Leach	Franklin	Sept. 1970–Aug. 1978
Frank D. Celebrezze	Cuyahoga	Dec. 1972–Dec. 1978
Thomas M. Herbert	Franklin	Jan. 1969–July 1980
William B. Brown	Ross	Jan. 1973–Dec. 1984
Paul W. Brown	Franklin	Jan. 1973–Sept. 1981
Robert E. Leach	Franklin	Aug. 1978–Dec. 1978
Frank D. Celebrezze	Cuyahoga	Dec. 1978–Dec. 1986
Robert E. Holmes	Franklin	Dec. 1978–Dec. 1992
David D. Dowd	Stark	July 1980–Jan. 1981
A. William Sweeney	Hamilton	Jan. 1977–Dec. 1994
Ralph S. Locher	Cuyahoga	Jan. 1977–Dec. 1986
Blanche Krupansky	Cuyahoga	Sept. 1981–Dec. 1982
Clifford F. Brown	Huron	Jan. 1981–Jan. 1987
James P. Celebrezze	Cuyahoga	Jan. 1983–Dec. 1984
Andrew Douglas	Lucas	Jan. 1985–Dec. 2002
Craig Wright	Franklin	Jan. 1985–Mar. 1996
Thomas J. Moyer	Franklin	Jan. 1987–
Herbert R. Brown	Franklin	Jan. 1987–Dec. 1992
Alice Robie Resnick	Lucas	Jan. 1989–
Paul E. Pfeifer	Crawford	Jan. 1993–
Francis E. Sweeney	Cuyahoga	Jan. 1993–Dec. 2004
Deborah Cook	Summit	Jan. 1995–May 2003
Evelyn L. Stratton	Franklin	Mar. 1996–
Maureen O'Connor	Summit	Jan. 2003–
Terrence O'Donnell	Cuyahoga	May 2003–
Judith Lanzinger	Lucas	Jan. 2005–

CHAPTER 7

The Ohio Constitution

MEANS OF AMENDING THE CONSTITUTION

(1) By a joint resolution of the legislature, when three-fifths of the members of each house of the General Assembly vote to place the issue before the people.

(2) By initiative petition, signed by a number of eligible voters equal to at least 10 percent of the number who voted in the last gubernatorial election.

(3) By constitutional convention.

The Ohio Constitution is among the nation's oldest state constitutions. Although substantially amended through the years, the basic document now serving as Ohio's fundamental law was adopted by the people in 1851 to replace the state's first constitution of 1802. The Northwest Ordinance, adopted by Congress in 1787, specified that each state formed from the Northwest Territory should have a republican government and constitution. Most state constitutions, including Ohio's, are much longer than the U.S. Constitution. In time, state constitutions became more detailed than the U.S. Constitution because, besides establishing a framework for state government, their drafters attempted to more specifically limit and define governmental powers. When Ohio was formed, men identifying with the Democratic-Republican Party controlled public affairs in the state. As a group, they were more distrustful of a strong central government than were the Federalists, who dominated the federal government when the U.S. Constitution was designed in 1787. Like many early state constitutions, the first Ohio Constitution was drafted to guard against excessive and arbitrary power, especially in the executive branch.

The 1802 Constitutional Convention

Where: Chillicothe
Convened: November 1, 1802
Delegates: 35
(Democratic-Republican, 26;
Federalist, 7; Unknown, 2)
In session: 25 days
Constitution length: about 3,800 words
Convention cost: $4,556

The Northwest Ordinance dictated that "60,000 free inhabitants" would be necessary to form a state from the territory. Although the 1800 federal census showed only 45,365 people living in the Ohio portion of the territory, political leaders strongly favored statehood. They successfully urged Congress to pass legislation to enable statehood—an act signed on April 30, 1802, by President Thomas Jefferson. Thirty-five delegates to a constitutional convention were elected on October 12 from districts within the counties. Eligible voters were adult male taxpayers who had resided in the territory at least one year. The delegates met in Chillicothe on November 1. Edward Tiffin, a doctor and businessman from Ross County, was president of the convention. The delegates remained in session until November 29, when the constitution was completed after 25 working days.

The state's first constitution was not submitted to the people for a vote. A majority of the delegates was confident the document reflected the desires of the population. The convention's majority Democratic-Republican members, who defeated a Federalist proposal to submit the constitution to the people, were wary of delays and campaign tactics the Federalists might employ. At the time, adopting a constitution without popular ratification was common among the states.

The document vested virtually all power in the legislative branch. The General Assembly would choose all state executive officers except the governor and appoint state and county judges. The governor would have no veto authority and could serve no more than six years in any eight-year period. The constitution provided one method of amendment —via a convention called by the people upon the recommendation of a two-thirds vote of the General Assembly. The constitution enfranchised "all white male inhabitants above the age of 21 years, having resided in the state one year next preceding the election, and who have paid or are charged with a state or county tax." It also established Chillicothe as the seat of state government until 1808.

The constitution contained a Bill of Rights, similar to that of the U.S. Constitution, to guarantee the right to free speech, free press, religious liberty, trial by jury, private property, peaceful assembly, and other basic freedoms. It also declared: "There shall be neither slavery nor involuntary servitude in this state."

Proposal to hold a constitutional convention
Voted upon October 12, 1819
For. 6,987
Against. 29,315

In Ohio's first two decades of statehood, its population multiplied to more than a half-million. Because of the rapid growth, the General Assembly considered the state's original constitution no longer adequate, especially in providing for an efficient court system. In December 1818, the assembly approved a joint resolution recommending that a constitutional convention be convened to deal with this and other issues. Voters, however, rejected the convention call by a 4-to-1 vote.

By midcentury, with the state's population approaching two million, a majority of Ohioans clearly saw the need for a constitution overhaul. At the time, the state had 85 counties and the Supreme Court no longer could be expected to serve as a county court. Another major issue was public alarm over massive state debts, particularly indebtedness for canal construction and unwise state investments in railroad stock and other private ventures. The General Assembly submitted a convention proposal that, in October 1849, was approved by a substantial majority. An election to select delegates was held April 1, 1850.

The 1850–51 Constitutional Convention

Where: Columbus and Cincinnati
Convened: May 6, 1850
Delegates: 108 (Democrats, 64; Whigs, 41; Free-Soilers, 3)
In session: 163 days
Constitution length: about 6,700 words
Convention cost: $95,364
Approved by voters: June 17, 1851

> For 125,564
> Against 109,276

The state's second constitutional convention convened in May 1850 in Columbus and met until July, when it adjourned because of an outbreak of cholera. The convention reconvened in December in Cincinnati, and met until final adjournment on March 10, 1851. The convention produced a constitution nearly twice the length of the original—the better to limit legislative power, restrain special interests, and expand popular sovereignty. Approved in a special election in June 1851 (the electorate at the time was still limited to adult white males with one year of residence), the second constitution took effect September 1, 1851.

Notable changes:

• Require that state executive officeholders, county officeholders, and state and local judges be elected by the people.
• Revamp the judicial system by adding one judge to the Supreme Court, relieving it of the duty to hold sessions in each county, creating appellate (district) courts, and re-establishing county probate courts.
• Establish a debt limit of $750,000 and prohibit state investment in private enterprises.
• Require that taxation of real and personal property be uni-

---

Proposal to hold a constitutional convention
Voted upon October 9, 1849

For 145,698
Against 51,167

---

form, so the same tax rate would apply to all classes of property.
• Mandate the establishment of a thorough and efficient system of public schools to be supported by the state.
• Establish that in 1871 and every 20 years thereafter, Ohioans vote on whether to call a convention to "revise, alter, or amend" the constitution.
• Empower the General Assembly to submit proposed amendments to the people by a three-fifths vote of each house.
• Mandate that all laws apply uniformly throughout the state, be general in nature, have only one subject, not be retroactive, and not grant special privileges or immunities.

The new constitution also created the offices of attorney general and lieutenant governor, adopted a new system of legislative apportionment, and called for biennial rather than annual legislative sessions. Although legislative power was diminished by many of these reforms, the new constitution—by continuing to withhold veto power from the governor—still gave the General Assembly the upper hand. The second constitution remains the essential framework for Ohio's government, although it has been amended repeatedly through the years and many of the 1851 provisions no longer exist. Between 1851 and 1867, the legislature placed seven proposed amendments on the statewide ballot. Six of the seven proposals received more affirmative than negative votes, but none was adopted. At the time, amending the constitution required a majority vote among all who cast ballots in the election, not just among those who voted on the amendment question. The difference between total electors and those voting on amendments often was quite high, making the passage of amendments very difficult.

Twenty years after the state's second constitution was adopted, Ohio voters for the first time faced the mandatory convention question in 1871. Since the last convention, Ohio had added nearly 750,000 inhabitants. The court system still was bogged down, sentiment was growing for a license system to control the liquor traffic, and frustration had built up over the extreme difficulty of amending the constitution. With both major parties supporting a convention, the question was approved by a sizable majority of voters. The delegates were chosen in an election on April 6, 1873.

Proposal to hold a constitutional convention
Voted upon October 10, 1871

For 267,618
Against 104,231

The 1873–74 Constitutional Convention

Where: Columbus and Cincinnati
Convened: May 13, 1873
Delegates: 105 (Republicans, 50; Democrats, 46; Liberals or Independents, 9)
In session: 188 days
Constitution length: about 15,000 words
Convention cost: $236,088

Rejected by voters: August 18, 1874

For 102,885

Against 250,169

The state's third constitutional convention convened in Columbus in May 1873 and met until August, when it recessed; the convention reconvened in December in Cincinnati, where it met until final adjournment on May 15, 1874. Toledo lawyer Morrison R. Waite was the convention's president until January 1874, when he resigned to become chief justice of the United States; Rufus King of Cincinnati replaced Waite. The convention produced a proposed constitution more than twice as long as the existing constitution. Among its many provisions, the proposal called for the following:

- Revising the judicial system to extend Supreme Court terms to ten years from five years, appoint a commission to eliminate the backlog of Supreme Court cases, create more judicial districts and judgeships, and make many other changes.
- Providing the governor with the veto.
- Making women eligible for election to school boards.
- Limiting the maximum indebtedness of municipalities.
- Requiring that each county have at least one representative in the General Assembly.
- Moving state elections to November from October.
- Designating the chief justice as presider in the event of a governor's impeachment.

The delegates also submitted to the electorate three separate issues to be voted upon in the election: one to guarantee minority party representation on the Supreme Court and in the circuit courts; a second to provide for aid to railroads; a third to establish a liquor-control system.

The three issues as well as the proposed constitution were defeated.

> **Proposal to hold a constitutional convention**
>
> Voted upon November 3, 1891
>
> For 99,789
> Against 161,722

Between 1874 and the 1912 constitutional convention, Ohio voters adopted 9 of 25 offered amendments. Several of the adopted amendments were part of the proposed constitution defeated in 1874. Some amendments targeted improvements in the judicial system, including measures to create a commission to eliminate the backlog of Supreme Court cases and replace the district courts with circuit courts.

Ohioans rejected the convention call in 1891. In ensuing years, they rejected numerous amendments but in 1903 approved two far-reaching changes: one was the so-called Hanna Amendment, approved by an overwhelming majority, to guarantee each county at least one representative in the Ohio House of Representatives; the second, adopted by a less-resounding majority, gave the veto power to the governor. In 1905, voters approved an amendment to elect state and county

> **Proposal to hold a constitutional convention**
>
> Voted upon November 8, 1910
>
> For 693,263
> Against 67,718

officials in November of even-numbered years. Ohioans were scheduled to vote on the convention call again in 1911, but the General Assembly sped up the process by placing the question before them a year early.

Since the 1873 to 1874 convention, Ohio had added two million residents. The state was rapidly becoming industrialized and urbanized. By 1910, the Progressive movement was at its height in Ohio, with much of the country demanding more citizen participation in government, consumer protection, an end to child labor, civil-service reform, regulation of big business and monopolies, recognition of labor unions, and safe working conditions. It was in this atmosphere that Ohioans voted overwhelmingly in favor of a constitutional convention. The selection of delegates took place in the election of November 7, 1911.

The 1912 Constitutional Convention

Where: Columbus
Convened: January 9, 1912
Delegates: 119 (Democrats, 65; Republicans, 48; Independents, 3; Socialists, 3)
In session: 82 days
Convention cost: $330,463
Amendments voted upon: September 3, 1912

Because of the defeat of the last proposed constitution in 1874 and the contention over many of the issues being debated, delegates to the 1912 convention decided to submit separate amendments to the people rather than rewrite the entire constitution. With Cincinnati minister Herbert Bigelow presiding, delegates considered hundreds of amendment proposals. They finally agreed to submit 41 to the people; 33 were adopted.

Notable changes:
- Provide for the initiative and referendum, allowing voters to check the legislature.
- Establish municipal home rule.
- Provide for the recall of elected officials.
- Limit the veto power by reducing from two-thirds to three-fifths the legislative majority needed to override the governor.
- Give the governor the line-item veto on appropriations measures.
- Establish primary elections for nominations for elective state, district, county, and municipal offices.
- Reform the civil jury system.
- Allow the state to be sued.
- Establish a system of compulsory workers' compensation.
- Establish the eight-hour day for public work.
- Abolish prison contract labor.
- Regulate expert testimony in criminal trials.
- Revise the judicial system, including renaming the circuit courts as courts of appeals and providing for the election of at least one common pleas judge in each county.
- Enable a majority of those voting on a proposed constitutional amendment to amend the constitution.

Among the eight losing amendments were proposals to provide

for women's suffrage, abolish capital punishment, omit the word "white" from the section on voting eligibility (even though blacks had been voting since 1870), allow women to serve in offices that care for women and children, and regulate outdoor advertising.

Given access to the initiative petition to amend the Constitution, Ohioans in modern times have not seen a need to call for a constitutional convention. The convention call was soundly defeated in 1932, 1952, 1972, and 1992. Since 1912, more than 160 amendments have been proposed; almost 100 have been adopted. Because of the $750,000 debt limit adopted in 1851—an all-but-ignored relic still on the books—many of the post-1912 amendments have been to authorize additional state debts for specific capital improvements and special programs.

In addition, state leaders periodically have proposed amendments to update the constitution and delete old sections. In August 1969, Gov. James A. Rhodes signed legislation to create a Constitutional Revision Commission, which met from 1970 to 1977. It resulted in the recommendation of 18 amendments, 15 of which were adopted over nine years. Since 1912, changes in the constitution have been gradual and piecemeal, but their cumulative effect through the decades has been dramatic. Below are some of the more notable changes have been to:

- Allow the General Assembly to classify property for tax purposes (1918).
- Eliminate the words "white male" from voter qualifications (1923).
- Establish a 15-mill limit on unvoted real estate taxes (1929).
- Lower to ten mills from 15 mills the limit on unvoted real-estate taxes (1933).
- Prohibit sales tax on food sold for off-premises consumption (1936).
- Establish six-year terms for county probate judges (1947).
- Require that gasoline taxes be used for highway and related purposes (1947).
- Eliminate straight-ticket voting by requiring separate votes for each office (1949).
- Authorize a $500 million bond issue for highways—the first of many such debt issues (1953).
- Establish four-year terms for governor, lieutenant governor, attorney general, and secretary of state, and limit the governor to two successive terms (1954).
- Extend to four years from two years the terms of state senators (1956).
- Permit county voters to adopt county charters (1957).
- Adopt a legislative apportionment plan for a 99-member House and a 33-member Senate with districts of approximately equal population (1967).
- Enact a Modern Courts Amendment to reorganize the state judicial system (1968).
- Authorize the state to conduct lotteries (1973).
- Require ballot rotation of candidates' names (1975).
- Require that the lieutenant governor be elected jointly with the governor and revise the lieutenant governor's duties (1976).
- Authorize the General Assembly to classify real property for tax purposes (1980).
- Adopt a procedure for filling a vacancy in the office of lieutenant governor (1989).
- Establish term limits for state executive officeholders, state legislators, and U.S. senators and representatives (1992).
- Expedite the appeals process in death-penalty cases (1994).
- Limit the governor's authority to reduce criminal sentences when granting commutations (1995).
- Establish that only a union between one man and one woman may be a recognized marriage by the state and its political subdivisions (2004).

Vote Totals

For selected amendments, 1912 to 2004

Nov. 4, 1913
* To make women eligible to serve on boards or commissions, and in departments and institutions caring for women and children. (Passed)
Yes 435,222 (63.1)
No 255,036 (36.9)
690,258

November 3, 1914
* To give women the right to vote. (Failed)
Yes 335,390 (39.3)
No 518,295 (60.7)
853,685

* To prohibit the manufacture, import, and sale of intoxicating beverages. (Failed)
Yes 504,177 (46.1)
No 588,329 (53.9)
1,092,506

November 2, 1915
* To prohibit the manufacture and sale of intoxicating beverages. (Failed)
Yes 484,969 (47.3)
No 540,377 (52.7)
1,025,346

November 6, 1917
* To prohibit the manufacture and sale of intoxiating beverages. (Failed)
Yes 522,590 (47.0)
No 588,382 (53.0)
1,110,972

November 5, 1918
* To reserve to the people the referendum authority to approve or reject an action of the General Assembly in ratifying any proposed amendment to the U.S. Constitution.

(Passed)
Yes 508,282 (61.7)
No 315,030 (38.3)
823,312

* To prohibit the manufacture and sale of intoxicating beverages. (Passed)
Yes 463,354 (51.4)
No 437,895 (48.6)
901,249

* To provide for the classification of property for taxation purposes. (Passed)
Yes 336,616 (52.5)
No 304,399 (47.5)
641,015

November 8, 1921
* To authorize the levying of a poll tax.
(Failed)
Yes 244,509 (26.7)
No 672,581 (73.3)
               917,090

November 6, 1923
* To eliminate the words "white male" from the Ohio Constitution to conform to federal amendments. (Passed)
Yes 536,762 (56.0)
No 421,744 (44.0)
               958,506

November 7, 1933
* To repeal statewide prohibition. (Passed)
Yes 1,250,923 (68.4)
No 578,035 (31.6)
             1,828,958

* To provide a 10-mill limitation on unvoted real estate tax. (Passed)
Yes 979,061 (59.7)
No 661,151 (40.3)
             1,640,212

November 3, 1936
* To prohibit the levy or collection of an excise tax on the sale or purchase of food for human consumption off the premises where sold. (Passed)
Yes 1,585,327 (68.8)
No 719,966 (31.2)
             2,305,293

November 8, 1938
* To provide for the appointment of judges of the Supreme Court and Courts of Appeals. (Failed)
Yes 621,011 (33.4)
No 1,237,443 (66.6)
             1,858,454

November 4, 1947
* To prohibit the expenditure of revenue from motor vehicle license taxes and gasoline taxes for other than highway and related purposes. (Passed)
Yes 1,037,650 (60.8)
No 669,718 (39.2)
             1,707,368

November 8, 1949
* To eliminate straight-ticket voting by requiring separate votes for each office on the ballot. (Passed)
Yes 1,007,693 (57.3)
No 750,206 (42.7)
             1,757,899

November 3, 1953
* To authorize the issuance of bonds up to $500 million for highway construction. (Passed)
Yes 1,035,869 (60.5)
No 676,496 (39.5)
             1,712,365

* To create a State Board of Education with power to appoint a superintendent of public instruction. (Passed)
Yes 913,134 (56.8)
No 693,624 (43.2)
             1,606,758

* To remove the word "white" as a designation from those eligible to serve in the state militia. (Passed)
Yes 905,059 (58.2)
No 650,567 (41.8)
             1,555,626

November 2, 1954
* To establish four-year terms of office for governor, lieutenant governor, attorney general, and secretary of state, and to limit the governor to two successive terms. (Passed)
Yes 1,165,650 (55.5)
No 933,716 (44.5)
             2,099,366

November 6, 1956
* To increase to four years, from two years, terms of members of the Ohio Senate. (Passed)
Yes 1,636,449 (57.4)
No 1,214,643 (42.6)
             2,851,092

November 5, 1957
* To permit the electors of counties to adopt county charters. (Passed)
Yes 832,912 (51.0)
No 799,094 (49.0)
             1,632,006

November 4, 1958
* To forbid labor contracts which established union membership as a condition for continuing employment (right-to-work). (Failed)
Yes 1,160,324 (36.7)
No 2,001,512 (63.3)
             3,161,836

November 6, 1962
* To limit the power of the state to forbid the sale of certain goods and services on Sunday. (Failed)
Yes 1,274,792 (42.9)
No 1,697,433 (57.1)
             2,972,225

November 7, 1967
* To provide a method for the apportionment of the House of Representatives and Senate into single member districts (creating a 99-member House and a 33-member Senate). (Passed)
Yes 1,315,736 (59.2)
No 908,010 (40.8)
             2,223,746

May 7, 1968
* To revise the administration and organization of the Ohio judicial system (Modern Courts Amendment). (Passed)
Yes 925,481 (62.4)
No 556,530 (37.6)
             1,482,011

November 4, 1969
* To lower the voting age to 19 from 21. (Failed)
Yes 1,226,592 (49.0)
No 1,274,334 (51.0)
             2,500,926

November 7, 1972
* To repeal the state income tax, prohibit any state or county graduated income tax, and provide for a public referendum on any future flat-rate state or county income tax. (Failed)
Yes 1,164,653 (31.2)
No 2,571,516 (68.8)
             3,736,169

May 8, 1973
* To authorize the state to conduct lotteries, the net proceeds of which shall be paid into the general fund. (Passed)
Yes 973,956 (64.0)
No 547,655 (36.0)
             1,521,611

November 6, 1973
* To permit agricultural land to be valued for taxation in accordance with its agricultural use. (Passed)
Yes 1,810,630 (76.1)
No 567,189 (23.9)
             2,377,819

November 4, 1975
* To require that candidate names be given reasonably equal treatment on the ballot by rotation of names or other methods. (Passed)
Yes 1,619,219 (63.9)
No 915,599 (36.1)
             2,534,818

June 8, 1976
* To require the lieutenant governor to be elected jointly with the governor, and to provide for the duties of the lieutenant governor.
(Passed)
Yes. 1,085,175 (61.2)
No 689,244 (38.8)
1,774,419

November 8, 1977
* To prohibit the use of leghold traps or any trapping device causing prolonged suffering. (Failed)
Yes. 1,169,068 (36.6)
No 2,027,642 (63.4)
3,196,710

November 4, 1980
* To authorize the General Assembly to classify business and agricultural-residential into two separate categories for tax purposes. (Passed)
Yes. 1,973,344 (53.0)
No 1,751,277 (47.0)
3,724,621

November 3, 1981
* To authorize the sale of workers' compensation insurance coverage by private insurance companies. (Failed)
Yes. 572,227 (20.9)
No 2,164,395 (79.1)
2,736,622

November 2, 1982
* To authorize the Ohio Rail Transportation Authority to build a high-speed rail system and levy a 1 percent sales tax to build it. (Failed)
Yes. 708,605 (22.6)
No 2,420,593 (77.4)
3,129,198

* To provide for electing members of the Public Utilities Commission and provide public financing of their campaigns. (Failed)
Yes. 1,053,274 (32.6)
No 2,175,893 (67.4)
3,229,167

November 8, 1983
* To raise the minimum age to 21 years for the consumption of beer. (Failed)
Yes. 1,386,959 (41.4)
No 1,965,469 (58.6)
3,352,428
* To require a three-fifths majority of the General Assembly to raise taxes. (Failed)
Yes. 1,354,320 (40.8)
No 1,965,469 (59.2)
3,319,789

* To repeal all taxes passed since 1982. (Failed)
Yes. 1,452,061 (43.5)
No 1,883,270 (56.5)
3,335,331

November 5, 1985
* To allow the state to issue bonds to finance coal research. (Passed)
Yes. 1,439,344 (64.1)
No 807,647 (35.9)
2,246,991

November 3, 1987
* To require the entire net proceeds of state lotteries to be used solely for the support of education programs. (Passed)
Yes. 1,984,905 (77.9)
No 564,421 (22.1)
2,549,326

* To change the way Ohio selects Supreme Court and appeals court judges by abolishing the direct election method and replacing it with an appointment system. (Failed)
Yes. 878,683 (35.4)
No 1,600,588 (64.6)
2,479,271

November 6, 1990
* To allow the state and political subdivisions to provide or assist in providing housing and housing assistance. (Passed)
Yes. 1,705,528 (52.9)
No 1,517,466 (47.1)
3,222,994

November 3, 1992
* To require businesses to provide labels and warnings in the use or release of toxic chemical substances. (Failed)
Yes. 1,007,882 (21.9)
No 3,587,734 (78.1)
4,595,616

November 2, 1993
* To authorize the state to issue bonds for improvements of state and local parks and recreation areas. (Passed)
Yes. 1,547,841 (60.6)
No 1,008,172 (39.4)
2,556,013

November 8, 1994
* To repeal the state's wholesale tax on soft drinks and to prohibit future wholesale taxes on soft drinks, carbonated nonalcoholic beverages, food for human consumption, and their ingredients and packaging. (Passed)
Yes. 2,228,874 (66.4)
No 1,126,728 (33.6)
3,355,602

* To remove jurisdiction from the courts of appeals to review death penalty cases on direct appeal and provide for direct appeals to the Ohio Supreme Court. (Passed)
Yes. 2,199,791 (70.1)
No 936,323 (29.9)
3,136,114

November 7, 1995
* To limit the governor's authority to reduce criminal sentences by requiring the governor to follow regulations prescribed by law when granting commutation to a person convicted of a crime. (Passed)
Yes. 1,816,213 (71.0)
No 742,590 (29.0)
2,558,803

November 5, 1996
* To authorize the establishment of riverboat casino gambling in Ohio. (Failed)
Yes. 1,639,955 (38.1)
No 2,659,076 (61.9)
4,299,031

November 2, 1999
* To authorize the issuance of bonds and other obligations for the construction and renovation of Ohio's public schools and state-supported colleges and universities. (Passed)
Yes 1,303,830 (60.8)
No 840,240 (39.2)
2,144,070

November 5, 2002
* To require a court to order treatment instead of incarceration for first-time or second-time offenders charged with or convicted of illegal possession or use of a drug who request treatment. (Failed)
Yes 1,012,682 (33.1)
No 2,048,770 (66.9)
3,061,452

November 4, 2003
* To authorize state and local governments to issue bonds and provide other financial assistance to support science-and technology-based research and development purposes.(Failed)
Yes 1,195,706 (49.2)
No 1,235,323 (50.8)
· 2,431,029

November 4, 2004
* To establish that only a union between one man and one woman may be a marriage valid in or recognized by the state or its political subdivisions. (Passed)
Yes 3,329,335 (61.7)
No 2,065,462 (38.3)
5,394,797

CHAPTER 8

Democrats and Republicans

THE PRESIDENTIAL CANDIDATES ATTEMPTED TO HAVE
COMMITTEES IN AS MANY COUNTIES AS POSSIBLE,
UNDER THE UMBRELLA OF A STATE COMMITTEE. SUCH WERE
THE BEGINNINGS OF PARTY ORGANIZATION IN OHIO.

For nearly a century and a half, a two-party system of Democrats and Republicans has dominated politics in Ohio and the nation. The story of party development in Ohio is rich and detailed, largely because the state's rapid growth after admission to the Union made its expanding electoral vote a prize in presidential elections. At the beginning of the 19th century, the ascendant Democratic-Republican Party of Thomas Jefferson was considered the party of the common man. The party arose in the 1790s as a congressional caucus and, by the early 1800s, had developed a national following. Its members believed in limiting the power of the federal government and allowing as much direct popular control as possible.

As Ohio approached statehood, some settlers aligned with the Federalist Party, but they were vastly outnumbered by those who wanted a government based on Jeffersonian principles. In Ohio's first quarter-century of statehood, most of the candidates for elective office belonged to the Democratic-Republican Party. The Federalist Party was dying—and eventually disappeared in the 1820s. Party organizations per se did not exist; instead, parties represented sets of beliefs and principles associated with leading national figures, often candidates for president.

Until 1824, the congressional caucus was the customary method of nominating presidential candidates. Under the system, members of Congress called a caucus to vote on nominations. For several years before 1824, however, citizens in Ohio and other states had been agitating for more direct involvement in the nomination process. With the Democratic-Republican Party monopolizing national affairs, several of its leaders with presidential aspirations capitalized on the public mood and turned to state legislatures, mass meetings, and local and state committees for nominations. The Democratic-Republican Party's presidential aspirants were John Quincy Adams, John C. Calhoun, Henry Clay, William H. Crawford, and Andrew Jackson. Crawford was the choice of the congressional caucus, but the caucus process had lost its legitimacy—so much so that it did not reappear in 1828.

In Ohio, supporters of anticaucus candidates—especially Jackson and Clay—held county meetings in 1823 and 1824 to begin building a delegate selection and convention process. With the Democratic-

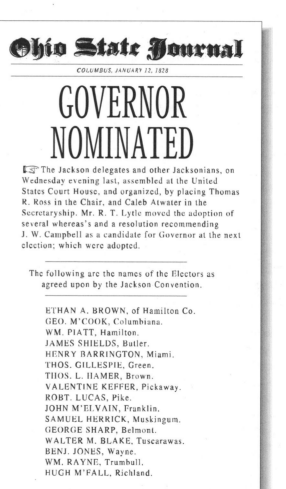

Ohio State Journal

COLUMBUS, JANUARY 12, 1828

GOVERNOR NOMINATED

☞ The Jackson delegates and other Jacksonians, on Wednesday evening last, assembled at the United States Court House, and organized, by placing Thomas R. Ross in the Chair, and Caleb Atwater in the Secretaryship. Mr. R. T. Lytle moved the adoption of several whereas's and a resolution recommending J. W. Campbell as a candidate for Governor at the next election; which were adopted.

The following are the names of the Electors as agreed upon by the Jackson Convention.

ETHAN A. BROWN, of Hamilton Co.
GEO. M'COOK, Columbiana.
WM. PIATT, Hamilton.
JAMES SHIELDS, Butler.
HENRY BARRINGTON, Miami.
THOS. GILLESPIE, Green.
THOS. L. HAMER, Brown.
VALENTINE KEFFER, Pickaway.
ROBT. LUCAS, Pike.
JOHN M'ELVAIN, Franklin.
SAMUEL HERRICK, Muskingum.
GEORGE SHARP, Belmont.
WALTER M. BLAKE, Tuscarawas.
BENJ. JONES, Wayne.
WM. RAYNE, Trumbull.
HUGH M'FALL, Richland.

Republicans split into factions, each presidential candidate had his own "party," or network of supporters. The county meetings appointed delegates to attend district and state conventions on behalf of the favored candidate and to form a ticket of presidential electors. In 1824, Ohio had 64 counties, and the presidential candidates attempted to have committees in as many as possible—under the umbrella of a state committee. Such were the beginnings of party organization in Ohio.

PARTIES TAKE ROOT

The nation's founders created the Electoral College as the device for selecting the chief executive, intending for established leaders in each state to use their independent judgment in selecting a president and vice president. The founders, however, had not envisioned the rise of political parties and the power the parties would wield in choosing electors. By 1824, candidate committees in Ohio and other states were nominating slates of electors. That year, Ohio was entitled to 16 electoral votes. The 1820 census and the resulting reapportionment doubled Ohio's electoral clout, stirring interest—among the public and the candidates—in the state's role in the 1824 presidential contest.

In the presidential balloting on October 29, 1824, Clay narrowly defeated Jackson in the popular vote in Ohio, capturing the state's 16 electoral votes; nationally, though, Jackson won more popular and electoral votes. Jackson had not received a majority of the nation's electoral votes, however, so the election was decided by the House of Representatives. With Clay supporting John Quincy Adams, the House named Adams president.

Between the 1824 and 1828 presidential elections, Ohio saw an expansion of its network of ward, township, county, and district political meetings and conventions. At the meetings, candidates for state and local offices were recommended, delegates to state conventions chosen, and committees to prepare for the next presidential election established. In 1827, conventions were held in dozens of counties in preparation for a Jackson statewide convention on January 8 and 9, 1828, in Columbus. The convention, with 160 delegates from across the state, selected a slate of 16 Jackson presidential electors and recommended John W. Campbell for governor. Meetings also were held across Ohio that year for Adams, whose faction of the Democratic-Republican Party had taken the name National Republican Party. Jackson's Ohio supporters led the way in grass-roots organization, and Jackson narrowly carried Ohio in the fall, when he was elected president.

With Jackson in the White House, the Democratic-Republican Party dropped the word *Republican* from its name and became simply the Democratic Party. In the 1830s, Ohio Democrats routinely held state conventions—with delegates having been chosen in county conventions—to nominate candidates for governor and other state offices and to choose presidential electors. At the 1830 state convention, held July 12 in Columbus, Robert Lucas was nominated for governor. He was the Ohio Democratic Party's first gubernatorial candidate. Although he lost in 1830 to the National Republican candidate, Duncan McArthur, Lucas ran again—successfully—in 1832. County conventions became a more common method of nominating candidates for county offices; district conventions became more common for nominating congressional candidates.

DEMOCRATS LEAD THE WAY

On January 9 and 10, 1832, the Democrats held a state convention in Columbus to renominate Lucas for governor and choose 32 delegates to the party's first national convention, scheduled for May 21 through the 23 in Baltimore, Md. Ohio was among 23 states represented at the convention, which ratified the various state nominations of Jackson for re-election. The convention decided to establish committees of corre-

spondence in each state, which formed the basis of the first national party committee. In Ohio, no permanent party organization functioned between elections. Each state convention appointed a state central committee to serve until the next convention, although party activity generally subsided after one election before gearing up for another.

During Jackson's second administration, the Whig Party arose from the old National Republican Party to challenge Jackson and the Democrats. The Whigs were a coalition of businessmen, conservatives, Southerners, and various interest groups, and each had its reasons for opposing Jackson. For about 20 years—from the mid-1830s to the mid-1850s—the Whigs were a competitive force in Ohio and national politics.

Jackson believed in a strong party system and the use of patronage (federal appointments) to reward loyal supporters. He used patronage more extensively than his predecessors, and those who followed him in the presidency used it even more. For decades to come, patronage would be fundamental to the operations of party politics at the national, state, and local levels.

By the 1840s, the state party was known as the Democracy of Ohio, with local organizations in virtually every county. There were ward and township Democratic clubs, Hickory Clubs that sponsored public meetings and published newspapers, and ethnic Democratic clubs for Germans and Irishmen. The convention system became well established, with the delegate-selection process starting at the ward or township level and working up to the state convention. More than 900 delegates from 72 counties attended the January 8, 1840, Democratic state convention in Columbus to renominate Wilson Shannon for governor and select 21 presidential electors. Democrats and Whigs traded the Ohio governor's office back and forth during the 1840s—as they did the presidency on the national level. During the decade, the two parties were of comparable strength in Ohio, though the Whigs did not rival the Democrats in party organization.

DEMOCRATS SPLINTER; REPUBLICANS ARISE

An infusion of German and Irish immigrants into the state promised to strengthen the Democracy of Ohio, but the slavery issue increasingly dominated political debate and threatened to split the party. The 1840 Democratic National Convention, held May 5 and 6 in Baltimore, produced the nation's first party platform. It emphasized strict interpretation of the Constitution and limited federal authority and noninterference in states' rights, including the right to permit slavery. William Henry Harrison, an Ohio Whig, was elected president in 1840 with a campaign that introduced sloganeering, parades, placards, and other forms of political hoopla.

In the 1844 presidential election, Whig candidate Henry Clay carried Ohio but Democrat James K. Polk narrowly won the presidency. A continuing influx of immigrants led to the founding of anti-immigrant, anti-Catholic parties, and other nativist organizations, some of which attracted many Whigs. Northern Democrats and Whigs opposed the 1845 annexation of Texas out of fear that it would become another slaveholding state. Ohioans strongly opposed the extension of slavery, and Texas's annexation and the resulting war with Mexico alienated many Ohio Democrats and Whigs from their party brethren in the South. The slavery issue split both parties: The Whigs did not survive, and the Democrats would not recover fully in Ohio until after the turn of the century, when memories of the Civil War had faded and waves of immigrants eventually found a political home in the party.

Antislavery activity, evident in Ohio since the state's founding, became much more prevalent during the 1840s and 1850s. The Liberty Party (founded in 1839) and the successor Free-Soil Party (founded in 1848) attracted modest followings in Ohio and spawned candidates for elective state offices. Salmon P. Chase—a Cincinnati lawyer, an antislavery organizer, and a future governor—helped prominently in the founding of the Free-Soilers. Although neither the Liberty Party nor the Free-Soil Party rivaled the Democrats or Whigs in attracting votes, both antislavery parties signaled a forthcoming eruption in the political landscape.

The spark that ignited the explosion was congressional passage in 1854 of the Kansas-Nebraska Act. The measure repealed the Missouri Compromise, which had restricted the extension of slavery into the territories, and authorized the territories to make their own decisions on slavery. Anti-Nebraska coalitions sprang up throughout the North. Some activists were motivated by antislavery sentiment; perhaps more were motivated by a fear that the act would allow southern planters to compete with free farmers in the new territories.

The anti-Nebraska meetings, sometimes referred to as Fusion meetings, drew support across the Midwest and across the political spectrum—from Democrats, Whigs, Free-Soilers, abolitionists, and nativists. From the meetings, the Republican Party was born. The Ohio Republican Party's founding can be traced to a meeting on February 14, 1854, in First Presbyterian Church in Columbus. Meeting organizers agreed to plan a statewide anti-Nebraska convention, to be held March 22. It attracted an estimated 1,200 delegates, who approved a resolution stating, "We say deliberately, on behalf of an immense majority of the people of the State of Ohio, and, as we believe, of the whole North, that they will, under no

The Columbus Gazette

FRIDAY... JANUARY 25, 1861

OFFICIAL PAPER OF THE CITY

Democratic State Convention

This body assembled in Armory Hall, on Wednesday morning, a large number of delegates in attendance. Hon. H. J. Jewett was chosen President. A large number of Vice Presidents and Secretaries were appointed. Speeches were made by Messrs. Jewett, Thurman, Ranney, Carter, Warden, Medary and Buffalo Taylor. The following resolutions were passed:

☞ 1st. *Resolved*, That since the admission of Ohio as one of the United States, the Democratic party of the United States has uniformly shown devotion to the Union, allegiance to the Constitution, obedience to the Federal laws, and respect for the constitutional rights, and regard for the interests of each of her sister States; and that same views and sentiments now animate the Democracy of Ohio.

☞ 2d. *Resolved*, That while we gratefully acknowledge the services of those of our public men in Congress who are striving to preserve the Union, and thus to promote the best interest of our nation and the cause of constitutional liberty among mankind; and while we would accept with joy the compromise measures known as the Crittenden resolutions — or the propositions of Senator Bigler or Douglas, or those known as the "Border States" resolutions as a basis of settlement of our national difficulties; or any other settlement of our affairs honorable to us all, all of which can be effected by conciliation and compromise, and mutual concessions of all concerned to secure the safety and perpetuity of the Union; yet we believe that the questions that disturb the country are of such character, and have existed for so long a period that the time has arrived when people of the whole country should avail themselves of that provision of the Constitution which requires Congress, upon the application of two-thirds of the legislatures of the several States, to call a Convention of all the States for proposing amendments thereto.

☞ 3d. *Resolved*, That this Convention does recommend and request the General Assembly of this State, now in session, to make application to Congress to call a Convention, pursuant to the fifth article of the Constitution of the United States, for the proposing amendments thereto.

☞ 4th. *Resolved*, That the President of this Convention be instructed to communicate the forgoing 3d resolution to the presiding officers of the General Assembly, with the request that they present the same to their respective Houses.

☞ 5th. *Resolved*, That the two hundred thousand Democrats of Ohio send to the people of the United States, both North and South, greeting; and when the people of the North shall have fulfilled their duties to the Constitution and the South; — then, and not till then, will it be proper for them to take into consideration the question of the right and propriety of coercion.

The Convention ordered that copies of the resolutions be sent to the Governors of all the States.

circumstances whatever, suffer slavery to obtain a foothold in the proposed Territories of Kansas and Nebraska. The heart of this continent is the choicest heritage of the free laborers of the United States. The slaveholders are not equal in number to the voters of the State of Ohio. We say to these misguided men: 'Be not deceived: you are sowing the wind, and you will reap the whirlwind.'"

On July 13, 1854—the 67th anniversary of the passage of the Northwest Ordinance—the first state Republican nominating convention was held in Columbus. Convention participants did not adopt the name *Republican*; it was adopted exactly one year later—July 13, 1855—at a convention in Columbus's Town Street Methodist Church. In the October 1855 election, Republican Salmon Chase was elected governor. In 1856, Republican presidential candidate John C. Frémont carried Ohio.

A Republican county headquarters in the mid-1800s, location undetermined.

By 1860, Republicans controlled all of Ohio's statewide offices and both houses of the General Assembly. In the presidential race that year, Ohio Democrats and other Northern Democrats supported Sen. Stephen A. Douglas of Illinois while Southern Democrats favored John C. Breckinridge of Kentucky. With the Democrats split, Republican Abraham Lincoln carried Ohio and other northern states to become the party's first president. Republicans also won the U.S. Senate in 1860, after having taken control of the U.S. House of Representatives in 1858.

THE UNION PARTY

In 1861, with the Civil War dominating the nation's attention, the Ohio Republican Party issued a call for a nominating convention to unite with Democrats and others who favored the war to preserve the Union. In convention on September 5 in Columbus, the Union Party was formed; it nominated for governor David Tod, a Youngstown industrialist and Democrat who twice had lost gubernatorial bids. The Ohio Democratic Party was split between "Peace Democrats" and "War Democrats," with the latter joining the Union Party ranks and the former firmly controlling the Democratic Party.

The Union Party dominated the state. In the 1861 governor's election, Tod's 57.7 percent of the vote was the biggest majority received by a gubernatorial candidate in 35 years. Two years later, Union Party gubernatorial nominee Charles Brough—also a former Democrat—did even better, capturing more than 60 percent of the vote against Democrat Clement L. Vallandigham, a former congressman from Dayton and fervent antiwar orator. Vallandigham's oratory so infuriated Maj. Gen. Ambrose Burnside, commander of the Department of Ohio, that Burnside issued an order on April 13, 1863, proclaiming that all persons "within our lines who commit acts for the benefit of the enemies of our country will be tried as spies or traitors, and if convicted will suffer death."

In response, Vallandigham stepped up his antiwar rhetoric. He was arrested at his Dayton home, taken before a military tribunal in Cincinnati, and—to avoid making him a martyr—sent into exile in the Confederacy. Enraged by the action, the Ohio Democratic Party on June 11, 1863, nominated Vallandigham for governor despite his absence. Shortly after his nomination, Vallandigham left North Carolina for Niagara Falls, Ontario. He later moved to Windsor. Vallandigham was the first and only candidate for Ohio governor to wage a campaign from Canadian soil. After the Civil War, Republicans boasted the political majority in Ohio, although the Democrats won back many of those who had left the party for the Union cause. During the late 1860s and through the 1870s and 1880s, Democrats and Republicans traded control of the Ohio General Assembly. In gubernatorial contests, however, Republicans dominated, winning 16 of 20 gubernatorial elections between 1865 and 1903. Many of the races were close, though: In 9 of the 16 Republican wins, the victory margin was less than 4 percentage points.

In the half-century after the Civil War, Ohio dominated presidential politics. Starting with Ulysses S. Grant, the state sent seven men—all Republicans—to the White House between 1868 and 1920. Warren G. Harding ended the string. In the postwar years, Ohio Republicans sold an image of having saved the Union and casted Democrats as unpatriotic rebels. To counter, Democrats were as active as Republicans in seeking to nominate Union Army veterans for elective offices.

Ohio Democratic leaders warned voters of the dangers of large numbers of freed blacks entering the state and opposed granting them suffrage; state Republican platforms favored universal manhood suffrage. Also during the Reconstruction era, Ohio politics centered on national policy toward the South, cheap money v. sound money, and the traffic of liquor. Republicans favored harsher policies toward the South, sound money (gold) instead of paper, and stricter controls on the liquor trade.

ERA OF BOSS RULE

Between the end of the Civil War and the turn of the century, the United States was transformed from a predominantly agricultural country to an industrial one. No state better exemplified this revolution than Ohio, whose location and resources energized development in iron, steel, coal, machinery, and other industries. Industrialists, bankers, and assorted business tycoons amassed great wealth. Some created giant monopolies and trusts by merging previously competing companies, lessening competition, and fixing prices. In the 1880s and 1890s, captains of industry exercised great influence over state and local government. Business interests wanted to continue high tariffs on imported goods, ensure sound money, and avoid government regulation.

Factories replaced farms as the primary source of jobs, leading to the urbanization of Ohio. At the start of the Civil War in 1861, nearly five times as many Ohioans lived on farms as in cities; by 1900, the state's population was almost equally divided between rural and urban areas; by 1920, almost twice as many Ohioans lived in cities as in the countryside. The urban-industrial revolution transformed Ohio politics. Having amassed fortunes, some business leaders were willing to spend large amounts to elect and support friendly officeholders. With more voters living in cities, political entrepreneurs emerged to build organizations ward by ward, compete for the unofficial title of city boss, and win financial rewards from alliances with business leaders. Although the Ohio Republican Party was dominated more by business leaders than was the Ohio Democratic Party, both parties became more conservative and pro-business during the period.

Marcus Alonzo Hanna, a Republican, was the political boss of Cleveland. Having made a fortune in coal, iron, and steel, Hanna bought the city's street railway system, became dominant in Cleveland politics in the 1870s, and established himself as a major power in the state Republican organization during the 1880s. Always willing to spend money on cooperative politicians, Hanna encouraged other business leaders to join him in paying for the kind of government they wanted. Hanna was the primary force behind the 1891 election of William McKinley as governor, McKinley's re-election in 1893, and McKinley's election as president in 1896. Hanna was chosen chairman of the Republican National Committee at the same time McKinley won the party's nomination for president. From the late 1880s until just before his death on February 15, 1904, Hanna had unrivaled influence in Ohio Republican politics.

In Cincinnati, boss rule was personified by Democrat John R. McLean, publisher of the *Cincinnati Enquirer,* and two Republicans—Sen. Joseph B. Foraker, a corporation lawyer, and businessman George B. Cox. The conservative McLean characterized the state's Democratic leadership of the time. Foraker proved to be emblematic of the corrupt relationships between business and politics. In 1908, the Hearst newspapers revealed that Foraker had been on the payroll of the Standard Oil Co. during his first U.S. Senate term. The disclosure forced Foraker to withdraw his re-election bid. Other notable city bosses were Guy G. Major, a Republican mayor of Toledo, and Joseph E. Lowes, a Republican of Dayton.

Republicans reigned in Ohio during the 1890s, which marked the height of boss rule. From 1892 through 1900, Republicans controlled every statewide office. From 1892 through 1910, Republicans held a majority in the Ohio House; for 14 of those 18 years, Republicans controlled the Ohio Senate. State campaigns usually were conducted on national issues, but Republican strength in Ohio was built on local organization. The party structure was developed block by block in cities and quartersection by quartersection in townships. Ohio had no prohibition on the use of corporate money in politics. In much of the state, cash was used to buy officeholder loyalty and build party organization, especially Republican organization.

DEMOCRATS TRY REORGANIZING

Throughout the era of boss rule, the Ohio Democratic Party had been disorganized. It had no permanent state headquarters and essentially was a loose confederation of county party organizations, each seeming to care more about local power than statewide races. Thomas E. Powell, who edited *The Democratic Party of Ohio* (1913), lamented that state Democratic chairmen, upon opening campaign offices in late August or early September, "inherited from their predecessors a few old desks and broken chairs, but no records whatsoever. They were fortunate if they ascertained the names of members of the various county central committees before election day."

Eventually recognizing the problem, the Ohio Democratic Party opened its first permanent state headquarters in January 1902 in Columbus—in the new Hayden Building on E. Broad Street, just across from the Statehouse. Taking note, the Republican *Ohio State Journal* published a story headlined "Democrats Are Going to Take a Leaf from Book of Republicans and Try Organization." To get started, the party solicited donations of $100 each from 25 leading Democrats, and then began selling general memberships for $10.

Harvey C. Garber of Greenville, the Democratic state chairman, told the *Ohio State Journal*, "We mean business. We are going to hand an organization over to the next state executive committee such as the party has not had in years. It will be an organization for the whole party and not for any leader in it. . . . The plain truth is that the Democratic Party of Ohio hasn't votes enough to afford it the luxury of factionalism and this committee will have none of it."

Some observers viewed the efforts to build a statewide organization as instrumental in helping Democrats win four consecutive gubernatorial elections between 1905 and 1912—though other factors probably were more influential. In later decades, academic analysts and Democratic activists repeatedly identified the party's inability to sustain a strong statewide organization as an important factor in election losses to Republicans.

PROGRESSIVE SPIRIT BLAZES

As boss rule and machine politics spread during the 1890s, more people began to reject what they viewed as official corruption, social irresponsibility, and excessive concentration of wealth. In 1900, about 1 percent of the population controlled an estimated half of the nation's wealth. A reform movement—progressivism—began to develop across the country; it bloomed rapidly in Ohio. Reform-minded Samuel M. Jones, an independent Republican elected mayor of Toledo in 1897, had attracted wide notice for his anticorruption efforts. On a similarly progressive platform, Democrat Tom L. Johnson was elected mayor of Cleveland in 1901. The two mayors won national recognition for championing civil-service reform, business regulation and competition, public control of utilities, home rule for cities, and increased citizen control of state government through measures such as the initiative and referendum.

Both political parties sprouted progressive wings. Within the Ohio Democratic Party, the progressive Johnson bested Boss McLean for control; inside the Republican state organization, the reform spirit moved leaders to denounce the type of boss rule represented by Hanna, Cox, and Foraker. At the state Democratic convention of July 9, 1901, delegates adopted a platform calling for municipal home rule and the nomination of U.S. senators in open convention. By 1905, the state Democratic platform endorsed the initiative and referendum and the direct election of U.S. senators.

The Democrats' quicker start in the race to embrace reform helped

John M. Pattison win the 1905 governor's election over incumbent Republican Myron T. Herrick. Acknowledging the public mood, William Howard Taft—then secretary of war under President Theodore Roosevelt—attempted to help Herrick's candidacy by distinguishing him from Boss Cox. While campaigning for Herrick, Taft publicly denounced Cox and boss rule in Cincinnati, but the effort was enough to turn the tide that swept out Herrick. Pattison died after only five months in the governor's office, but Democrat Judson Harmon won the next two governor's elections in 1908 and 1910. In February 1908, the General Assembly responded to public concern over the cozy relationship between big business and elected officials by outlawing the use of corporate money to finance candidates and political parties. In the 1910 election, Democrats enjoyed a sweeping victory, capturing the entire statewide ticket and 16 of 21 congressional seats. Harmon presided over the enactment of many progressive laws, including a workers' compensation act and a measure providing for the nonpartisan election of judges, but he wasn't progressive enough for many in the party. Harmon disappointed Johnson and others by opposing the statewide initiative and referendum.

On November 3, 1911, about 300 reform-minded Republicans met in Cleveland to create the Ohio Progressive Republican League. The following year, like-minded Democrats founded the Ohio Progressive Democratic League. Nationally, the progressive v. conservative split in the Republican Party resulted in the formation of the Progressive (Bull Moose) Party, led by former president Theodore Roosevelt. The Republican split that year enabled a progressive Democrat, Woodrow Wilson, to win the presidential election.

Columbus Evening Dispatch

COLUMBUS, OHIO, WEDNESDAY, NOVEMBER 9, 1938

TAFT, BRICKER WIN

Every Republican on the state ticket moves into office behind ballot leaders

Legislature goes strongly Republican

Chief Justice Carl V. Weygandt was the only Democrat to triumph in judicial races

Through 1912, nominations for Ohio's statewide offices were decided at party conventions. The process changed with a 1912 amendment to the Ohio Constitution, which provided that "all nominations for elective state, district, county, and municipal offices shall be made at direct primary elections or by petition as provided by law ... [and] all delegates from this state to the national conventions of political parties shall be chosen by direct vote of the electors." On August 11, 1914, Ohio held its first statewide direct primary election. Other 1912 amendments that dramatically changed Ohio's political system provided for the initiative and referendum, a method for the recall of elected officials, and municipal home rule. Cleveland adopted the state's first home-rule charter in 1913.

In Ohio, the three gubernatorial administrations of Democrat James M. Cox (1913–1915 and 1917–1921) marked the high point and tail end of the Progressive Era. Cox, a Dayton newspaper publisher, was elected in 1912 on a platform that included many of the proposed constitutional amendments adopted that year. His first administration, aided by Democratic majorities in both houses of the General Assembly, carried out many of the reforms. His last two terms were far less ambitious, as the public's attention turned to the nation's involvement in World War I.

REPUBLICAN RESURGENCE

Progressivism had been good to the Ohio Democratic Party. When the country entered World War I on April 6, 1917, Democrats held all of Ohio's statewide executive offices, controlled both houses of the

General Assembly, and had 13 of 22 U.S. House seats and one of two U.S. Senate seats. The Democrats's good fortune, however, did not last long: the Republicans regained their dominance during the war and postwar years.

German-Americans, the state's largest immigrant group, had been wed mostly to the Democratic Party, but they began to reject the party when anti-German sentiment was fanned during Wilson's presidency and Cox's gubernatorial administration. Street and village names with German origins were changed, and German books were burned. Though Cox, a Democratic governor, supported the ban on German language instruction, the Republican-controlled assembly, in May 1919, passed the legislation (the Ake Law) that prohibited the teaching of German in grade schools.

Cox had narrowly won re-election in November 1918, but Republicans had retaken the offices of lieutenant governor, attorney general, secretary of state, and treasurer. Republicans also regained control of both houses of the General Assembly, ushering in 14 years of GOP superiority. In the same election, Ohioans approved a ban on the manufacture and sale of liquor. The amendment for state prohibition was approved on the fourth try; it had failed in 1914, 1915, and 1917. The liquor question was ever-present in Ohio politics in the early decades of the 20th century, just as it had been in the late 19th century; activists were more interested in "wets" v. "drys" than Democrats v. Republicans. The 18th Amendment, requiring national prohibition, was ratified in January 1919 and took effect in January 1920. It remained effective until December 5, 1933, when ratification of the 21st Amendment repealed prohibition.

The November 2, 1920, election was the first in which women had full voting rights. The year was huge for Republicans: Ohioan Warren G. Harding won the presidency in a landslide, and Republicans captured 113 of 125 seats in the Ohio House and 36 of 37 seats in the Ohio Senate. Americans, eager to forget the war, embraced Harding's call for a "return to normalcy." Republicans controlled the national and state political agendas and promoted a pro-business climate. In 1922, Democrat A. Victor Donahey bucked the Republican trend to win Ohio's governorship, but his brand of politics was decidedly conservative and thrifty. A hard-line opponent of tax increases, Donahey was rewarded by Ohio voters, who made him the state's first governor to win three straight elections.

In 1926, Ohioans rejected a proposed state constitutional amendment to eliminate the compulsory primary; approval would have resurrected the convention system for nominating candidates. Republicans enjoyed another banner year in 1928, winning all of the state's administrative offices, all 31 seats in the Ohio Senate, and 122 of the 133 seats in the Ohio House. Herbert Hoover won the presidency in a landslide over Democrat Alfred E. Smith.

DEPRESSION AND REALIGNMENT

The prosperity of the 1920s had been fueled by excessive buying on credit and speculation in the stock market. Many people spent beyond their means, while wages did not keep pace with prices. Once signs of trouble became readily apparent in the economy, public confidence slipped and demand for goods and services declined rapidly. Stock prices, which had spiraled upward throughout most of the 1920s, began to decline on October 21, 1929. Eight days later—Black Tuesday—the stock market crashed and the Great Depression began. Millions of people suffered economic ruin. Businesses failed; banks closed; wages plummeted; unemployment soared. Amid the worst economic crisis to hit the United States and the Western world, President Hoover opposed government relief. He contended that the crisis was mostly psychological and that churches and other private charities should lead relief efforts. In Ohio, Republican governor Myers Y. Cooper had been in office only nine months when the stock market crashed, and the worsening economic conditions doomed his governorship. Democrat George White won nearly 53 percent of the vote in the November 1930 governor's election. Fellow Democrats picked up 47 seats in the Ohio House and 14 seats in the Ohio Senate, setting the stage for a takeover of the General Assembly in the 1932 election.

Between 1930 and 1934, Democrats regained control of Ohio's two U.S. Senate seats, as well as the offices of governor, lieutenant governor, and secretary of state. In the 1929 to 1930 session of the General Assembly, Republicans held 153 of 164 seats; four assemblies later, in the 1937 to 1938 session, Democrats controlled 134 of 172 seats. During the same two years, Democrats held both of Ohio's U.S. Senate seats and all six of the state's executive offices—the strongest showing by Ohio Democrats since the 1917 to 1919 period, when Democrats held all of the offices except one U.S. Senate seat. In 1932, 1936, and 1940, Ohio joined the nation in voting for Franklin D. Roosevelt for president. Those elections mark the only time in the state's history that it has voted three consecutive times for a Democratic presidential candidate. In 1944, FDR won a fourth term, but Ohio voted for Republican Thomas E. Dewey, whose vice-presidential running mate was Ohio's Republican governor, John W. Bricker.

The Depression and the New Deal era that followed made the Democratic Party the nation's majority party. In Ohio, Democrats became more competitive, but the Republican Party still had a broader base and maintained its majority status. The state's growing black population and the bulk of other urban immigrants, helped by New Deal relief programs, firmly aligned with the Democrats, especially in northeastern Ohio—a region that has been the state's Democratic bastion since 1932. The growth of Ohio's major cities, heavy industries, and labor class provided the Democratic Party with an expanded natural constituency. By 1930, twice as many Ohioans lived in urban areas as

in rural areas.

Although the economic conditions of the 1930s made Ohio more competitive politically, the 1938 election proved again the solidity of the state's Republican base. The recession of 1936–1937, caused by the reduction of government relief spending, helped Republicans gain seats in both houses of Congress, although Democrats retained control. In Ohio, however, Republicans enjoyed a banner year: Republican Robert A. Taft of Cincinnati unseated Democratic U.S. senator Robert J. Bulkley of Cleveland; Republican John W. Bricker of Columbus defeated Charles Sawyer of Cincinnati for governor; Republicans retook the offices of lieutenant governor, attorney general, secretary of state, and treasurer; and Republicans achieved a stunning reversal in the Ohio General Assembly. In the 1937 to 1938 legislative session, Democrats had enjoyed a 103–33 advantage in the House and a 31–5 advantage in the Senate. In the next session (1939–1940), Republicans controlled the House (100–31) and the Senate (27–8).

OHIO'S PARTY CHAIRMEN
1930s–2005

DEMOCRATIC

1935–1938	Henry Brunner	Mansfield
1938–1940	Arthur Limbach	New Philadelphia
1940–1948	Albert A. Horstman	Dayton
1948–1956	Eugene H. Hanhart	Dover
1956–1966	William L. Coleman	Milford Center
1966–1968	Morton Neipp	Toledo
1968–1971	Eugene P. O'Grady	Cleveland
1971–1974	Bill Lavelle	Athens
1974–1982	Paul Tipps	Dayton
1983–1990	James M. Ruvolo	Toledo
1991–1993	Eugene Branstool	Utica
1993–1995	Harry Meshel	Youngstown
1995–2002	David J. Leland	Columbus
2002–2005	Dennis L. White	Columbus
2005–	Chris Redfern	Catawba Island

REPUBLICAN

1930–1944	Ed. D. Schorr	Cincinnati
1945–1948	Fred H. Johnson	Zanesville
1949–1965	Ray C. Bliss	Akron
1965–1973	John S. Andrews	Toledo
1973–1977	Kent B. McGough	Lima
1977–1982	Earl T. Barnes	Cincinnati
1982–1988	Michael F. Colley	Columbus
1988–	Robert T. Bennett	Cleveland

THE WORLD WAR II ERA

When Bricker was sworn in on January 9, 1939, Adolf Hitler was only months away from conquering Czechoslovakia and invading Poland. Europe was at war, and Americans were dividing between interventionists and isolationists. With his eye on a possible presidential campaign in 1940, Bricker emphasized economy in government, pledged not to increase taxes, and denounced the New Deal's centralization of government power in Washington. He laid off about 2,000 state employees, balanced the budget, and resisted appeals from city leaders to increase relief payments to the poor. In July 1939, Bricker shelved his presidential ambition for 1940 and signaled his support for fellow Ohioan Robert Taft, who sought the Republican nomination but lost to Wendell L. Willkie of Indiana.

With Taft and Bricker at the top of the party hierarchy, Republicans were in nearly complete charge of Ohio's political system during the war years. Bricker became the first Republican to win three terms as governor; Taft won three terms in the U.S. Senate; and Republicans controlled the General Assembly for five consecutive sessions from 1939 through 1948. During his third term—on November 15, 1943—Bricker declared his 1944 candidacy for president. He later withdrew to run as vice president on the Republican ticket headed by New York governor Thomas E. Dewey. The Dewey-Bricker ticket narrowly carried Ohio but lost nationally to FDR, who won a fourth presidential term.

With Bricker exiting the Statehouse, Cleveland mayor Frank J. Lausche, a conservative and independent Democrat, won the 1944 governor's race over Republican James G. Stewart, mayor of Cincinnati. Lausche had an appeal that crossed party lines. Ohio Democrats were divided and disorganized at the time, although the steady growth of organized labor, the immigration of many eastern and southern Europeans, and the northward migration of southern blacks continued to enlarge the party's potential base of voters.

The 1935 passage of the National Labor Relations (Wagner) Act, which established collective-bargaining rights, greatly aided union organizing; in the 1940s and 1950s, Ohio became known as a state of strong unions and strike activity. Militant unionism concerned many, especially conservatives, prompting Taft to co-author the Taft-Hartley Act of 1947, which amended the Wagner Act to outlaw the closed shop (wherein union membership was required for employment) and forbid unions from contributing to political campaigns. The Taft-Hartley Act was passed over the veto of President Harry S. Truman, who had been elevated to the presidency on April 12, 1945, upon Roosevelt's death.

Republicans won majorities in both houses of Congress in the 1946 elections, as voters protested against spiraling inflation, tax increases, and wartime controls that caused shortages of housing, meat, and many other desired goods. The big Republican year enabled Thomas J. Herbert, a former Ohio attorney general, to narrowly defeat Lausche; Bricker was elected to the U.S. Senate; and Republicans captured 155 seats in the General Assembly, to the Democrats' 20.

Two years later, Democrats made a remarkable comeback—nationally and in Ohio. Truman, thought by many to be headed for defeat, rallied late in the campaign to defeat Dewey, who had bested Taft for the Republican nomination. Truman carried Ohio by a razor-thin margin, while Lausche easily defeated Herbert in a gubernatorial rematch. Nationally, Democrats recaptured both houses of Congress. In Ohio, Democrats captured 12 congressional seats, up from only four seats in the 1946 election. Democrats also won every statewide executive office except treasurer, which had been held for ten years by Republican Don H. Ebright. For the first time in a decade, Democrats won control of both houses of the General Assembly.

REPUBLICANS TURN TO BLISS

Angered by the Democrats's near-sweep of statewide offices in November 1948, the Ohio Republican Party ousted Fred H. Johnson of Zanesville from the chairman's job in February 1949 and replaced him with Ray C. Bliss, chairman of the Summit County Republican Party. As the county chairman since 1941, Bliss had learned how to build a party at the precinct, city, and county levels. He was a skilled political tactician who preached the importance of an effective, permanent party organization. He launched registration drives, boosted fund-raising, emphasized diversity and inclusiveness rather than ideological purity, maintained neutrality in primary contests, extensively used public-opinion surveys, began using television in campaigns, and did not concede the rank-and-file union voter to the Democrats. Bliss also established divisions within state Republican headquarters to handle public relations, field work, legislative matters, and other political specialties.

Guiding the Ohio Republican Party for 16 years, Bliss set a standard by which each of his successors has been judged. He led the Republican comeback in 1950, when Taft won re-election in the face of an all-out attack from organized labor. Republicans also regained the offices of attorney general and secretary of state, and retook both houses of the General Assembly. For Bliss, constant organizing—not issues—was the key to winning elections. In the 1950s, Republicans took charge of all statewide executive offices except the governor's office—the province of Lausche, who was popular with Democratic and Republican voters. From 1951 through 1958, Republicans held lopsided majorities in the Ohio Senate and Ohio House of Representatives. In the 1952 and 1956 presidential elections, Republican Dwight D. Eisenhower carried Ohio even more impressively than his landslide-proportion national majorities.

In the 1950s, both major parties recognized that voters were growing more independent of party labels. In Ohio, the movement was speeded by voter approval—in November 1949—of a state constitutional amendment to eliminate straight-ticket voting, by requiring separate votes for each contest on the ballot.

While Bliss was building an Ohio Republican bulwark, the Ohio Democratic Party was torn between pro-Lausche and anti-Lausche forces. Lausche, on his way to becoming Ohio's only five-term governor, attributed his popularity—probably correctly—to his reputation of independence from party and interest groups, coupled with fiscal conservatism. Lausche did little to encourage party-building at the state or local levels. He had ignored Albert A. Horstman, the Democratic state chairman since 1940, controlled patronage from the governor's office, and angered Democratic loyalists by retaining Republicans in many state jobs. In 1948, Lausche picked Eugene H. Hanhart, a Dover insurance executive, to replace Horstman as party chairman.

Ray Bliss

Organized labor and other anti-Lausche factions within the Democratic Party charged that Hanhart devoted himself only to Lausche and not to other Democratic candidates. They were kept in check, however, by Lausche loyalists who controlled the state Democratic committee until 1956, when Lausche was elected to the U.S. Senate. Lausche was the first Democrat to win a U.S. Senate seat from Ohio since 1934, when Vic Donahey was elected. With Lausche out of the governor's office, Hanhart's days were up as state Democratic chairman. In May 1956, the Democratic committee—led by gubernatorial nominee Michael V. DiSalle—selected William L. Coleman, a lawyer from Union County, to lead the party. Starting then, the Ohio Democratic Party and organized labor formed a working partnership, although it has waxed and waned through the years. Lausche's departure allowed Republicans to retake the governor's office, as C. William O'Neill, Ohio's three-term attorney general, defeated DiSalle. The win gave Republicans control of all of the state's executive offices.

THE RIGHT-TO-WORK ERUPTION

In 1958, with Republicans in charge of the entire state government, Ohio Democrats needed a break. They got a huge one: The state's big business leaders, led by the Ohio Chamber of Commerce and the Ohio Manufacturers' Association, persuaded O'Neill to endorse a proposed right-to-work amendment. He did so despite warnings by Bliss to stay away from the issue. At the time, many southern states had such laws, which prohibit the adoption of labor contracts that establish union membership as a condition of employment. Backed by the business groups, an initiative petition committee qualified the issue for the statewide ballot. The business leaders and O'Neill vastly underestimated the potential opposition.

Organized labor saw the amendment as a union-busting tool that must be defeated. Unions that had been at odds for years put aside their differences, formed United Organized Labor of Ohio, registered voters across the state, and whipped up a storm of protest. Union membership was near its peak in Ohio, which helped inspire groups such as the Ohio Council of Churches and many veterans' clubs to join in opposing the amendment. The right-to-work issue dominated the 1958 campaigns, but Democrats also were helped by an economic downturn that had pushed the unemployment rate to a post-Depression high.

Riding both waves, DiSalle won 57 percent of the vote to defeat O'Neill; fellow Democrats made their biggest gains in 20 years, winning every statewide office on the ballot except secretary of state. Democrat Stephen M. Young ousted Bricker from the U.S. Senate; Democrats won the Ohio House and Ohio Senate; the right-to-work amendment was pummeled, receiving just 37 percent of the vote. Nationally, Democrats also scored big, taking 22 of 33 governor's races.

Coleman, the state Democratic chairman, attempted to build and strengthen the Democratic-labor alliance at the state and local levels but found—in the absence of a galvanizing issue such as right-to-work—many obstacles. Because Ohio's industry always has been decentralized among many cities, the labor unions also have been decentralized, hampering efforts to build a strong, statewide labor movement such as those that existed in some other midwestern states. In addition, many Ohio Democrats—especially in the southern areas of the state—did not share the activist government goals of a liberal-labor coalition. Fiscal conservatism, for example, has been a long-standing characteristic of many Ohio Democrats as well as Republicans. In the 1950s, polls repeatedly showed that more Ohioans identified with the Democratic Party than the Republican Party, but the Democrats were a more heterogenous lot—and not easily held together.

REPUBLICAN REDUX

Furious over the right-to-work disaster, Bliss delivered an ultimatum to the state Republican committee and Ohio business leaders: leave the job to the pros. He began rebuilding the party, which regained dominance in Ohio in the 1960s. In the 1960 presidential election, he was the chief strategist for Richard M. Nixon's Ohio campaign, which captured a surprising 53 percent of the vote, though Democrat John F. Kennedy narrowly won the presidency. During the same election year, Republicans regained control of the Ohio House and Ohio Senate. In 1962, Republicans retook the offices of governor, lieutenant governor, and treasurer, once again giving the party complete control of the state executive branch. Ohio Republicans also won 18 of the state's 24 seats—a gain of two—in the U.S. House of Representatives.

In the 1962 governor's race, state auditor James A. Rhodes toppled Michael DiSalle. For 16 of the next 20 years, Rhodes held the governor's office. Bliss and Rhodes had a polite but not friendly relationship. From Bliss's perspective, Rhodes was more concerned with preventing potential rivals from rising within the Republican Party than helping with partybuilding. Bliss remained chairman of the Ohio Republican Party until April 1, 1965, when he went to Washington to head the

Republican National Committee. Nationally, Republican leaders hoped Bliss could provide the leadership the party needed to recover from its disastrous showing in the 1964 presidential election, in which GOP nominee Barry Goldwater received just 38.5 percent of the vote. The Ohio Republican Party chose John S. Andrews, who had been Lucas County Republican chairman, to replace Bliss.

In 1966, Coleman ran for lieutenant governor and was replaced as state Democratic chairman by Toledo's Morton Neipp, who had been Lucas County Democratic chairman and was a law partner of Frazier Reams Jr., the party's nominee for governor. Neipp inherited a party that was in debt and poorly organized. He devoted himself to fund-raising and rebuilding the alliance with organized labor, with whom he shared a goal of ousting Lausche from the U.S. Senate. Neipp also hired Eugene (Pete) O'Grady, a long-time Cleveland political leader, as the party's executive director to run the Columbus office.  Although Republicans swept all statewide executive offices again in 1966, the seeds were being sown for a Democratic comeback in the 1970s.

When Lausche ran for the U.S. Senate in 1956, he openly supported the re-election of Republican Dwight D. Eisenhower. During his two terms as a U.S. senator, Lausche frequently supported Republican candidates, shunning his party's state and national tickets. Organization Democrats and labor leaders viewed him as a major impediment to the building of an effective statewide party. In 1968, the state Democratic committee, backed by organized labor, selected a Cincinnati city councilman, John J. Gilligan, to challenge Lausche in the Democratic primary. For organized labor, the mission was almost as important as the right-to-work battle a decade earlier. The primary goal was accomplished: In defeating Lausche, Gilligan won 55 percent of the vote. Gilligan lost the general election in November to Republican William B. Saxbe, but he and the Democratic-labor coalition had laid the foundation for a party reawakening.

DEMOCRATIC DOMINANCE

In May 1968, the Ohio Democratic Party had selected O'Grady to replace Neipp as chairman. O'Grady, instrumental in orchestrating the anti-Lausche coalition, achieved a reputation for his nuts-and-bolts organizational skills. The party nurtured its relationship with organized labor, built liaisons with county Democratic organizations, increased fund-raising efforts, and attracted young, liberal activists. In May 1970, O'Grady was re-elected chairman, and Gilligan easily won a three-man primary for the Democratic gubernatorial nomination. With Gilligan at the top of its 1970 ticket, the Ohio Democratic Party was entering a two-decade period of unprecedented success. For most of those years—in a historic reversal of roles—the Democratic state organization was superior to that of the Republicans.

In 1970, the Ohio Republican Party did its share to help Democrats. Prevented by law from seeking a third consecutive term as governor, Rhodes sought his party's nomination for the U.S. Senate, as did Robert Taft Jr. The Rhodes-Taft primary was bitter, dividing a party unaccustomed to such acrimony. Worse, Republicans fell victim to the Crofters, Inc., loan scandal. The Columbus loan-arranging company, which had ties to the state Republican organization, helped arrange $12 million in questionable loans from the state treasury to two private companies that went bankrupt shortly after borrowing the money. John S. Andrews, the state Republican chairman, sought to contain the scandal by urging the withdrawal of John D. Herbert, an eight-year state treasurer who was seeking the 1970 GOP nomination for attorney general, and Robin T. Turner, the GOP nominee for treasurer. Herbert and Turner were among those who had received campaign contributions from Crofters. In all that year, the company contributed $33,000 to Republican state candidates.

Herbert and Turner refused to get off the ticket and, in November, were soundly defeated by Democrats William J. Brown and Gertrude W. Donahey, respectively. The scandal also boosted other Democratic candidates: Gilligan swamped state auditor Roger Cloud in the governor's race, while 78-year-old Joseph T. Ferguson came out of political retirement to narrowly win the auditor's office over Republican Roger W. Tracy Jr. The only Republicans to survive the 1970 election were Taft, who defeated Democrat Howard M. Metzenbaum in the U.S. Senate race, lieutenant governor John W. Brown, and secretary of state Ted W. Brown.

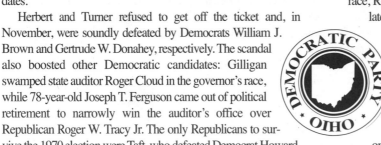

The 1970 victories paved the way for a Democratic takeover of the Ohio General Assembly. After winning the offices of governor and auditor, Democrats held two of the three offices (the third is secretary of state) that control the state's apportionment board, which draws state legislative districts. Besides having the power to draw the legislative map, Democrats were helped by a series of U.S. Supreme Court rulings from the 1960s that required states to apportion their legislatures on population only. Starting with the 1966 elections, state representatives no longer were elected at large from entire counties; no longer was each county guaranteed at least one representative, which had weighted the General Assembly in favor of rural and Republican interests.

The apportionment changes enabled the Democrats to draw districts with more representation from urban and minority areas, increasing the party's chances of winning the General Assembly. In 1972, Democrats won control of the Ohio House for the first time since 1958. In 1974, Democrats took over the Ohio Senate, also for the first time since 1958. For 11 consecutive sessions—from 1973 through 1994—Democrats controlled the Ohio House. The party was less successful in holding the Senate: after controlling the upper chamber from 1975 through 1980 and again in 1983 through 1984, Democrats lost it to Republicans, who ruled from 1985 through 1996.

The Democratic trend of the 1970s was not without interruptions. The party's major setback was Gilligan's failure to win re-election in 1974 against former governor James A. Rhodes. A liberal, Gilligan had won passage of Ohio's personal income tax in December 1971, reorganized state government, and expanded services. He entered the 1974 campaign as a heavy favorite but made several mistakes against the canny Rhodes, who pulled out an 11,488-vote victory. Gilligan had an academic bearing that bordered on arrogance, while Rhodes showcased a down-home folksiness. The morning after the election, Gilligan cited his personality as a reason for his defeat, calling the loss a "personal repudiation."

In other 1974 statewide races, Democrats retained the offices of attorney general, auditor, and treasurer; former astronaut John Glenn won a U.S. Senate seat, and Richard F. Celeste, a state representative from Cleveland, took the lieutenant governor's office from 16-year vet-

eran John W. Brown.

In 1976, Metzenbaum won a rematch against Taft in the U.S. Senate race. For the next 18 years, Metzenbaum and Glenn had a lock on Ohio's two seats in the U.S. Senate. In 1978, Democrat Anthony J. Celebrezze Jr. won the office of secretary of state from Ted W. Brown, who had held it for 28 years.

For the time being, only Rhodes stood in the way of total Democratic domination of state government. In the 1978 governor's race, Rhodes withstood a vigorous challenge from Celeste. Four years later, Celeste came back to win the governor's office in a landslide year for Democrats. The Democratic resurgence begun in 1970 was complete; the party controlled every statewide executive office. In 1986, Democrats again swept the statewide races. Celeste—easily rebuffing a comeback bid by Rhodes—became the first Democrat to win re-election as governor since Frank Lausche in 1954, and the first to do it after a first term since Martin L. Davey in 1936. Through the 1980s, the only Statehouse breakthrough for Republicans was in the Ohio Senate, where a resourceful GOP caucus used Celeste's tax hikes as an effective campaign issue, retook the Senate in 1984, and remained in control through the mid-2000s. Celeste, working through Chairman James M. Ruvolo, for eight years worked to build perhaps the most effective Democratic state organization in Ohio's history.

REPUBLICANS, ONCE MORE

In 1990, the pendulum of Ohio politics began to swing back in favor of the Republicans. Although Celeste had won an easy re-election victory in 1986, most political analysts saw it more as a rejection of the comeback attempt by Rhodes, then 77, than an affirmation of Celeste's leadership. Starting in his first term and continuing into his second, Celeste took a pounding in Ohio's major newspapers for alleged ethical lapses. Many accusations linked state contracts and other governmental favors to political contributions. Under Celeste, the state Democratic Party had been more successful than ever raising funds to support party operations and candidates; the flip side was that more questions than ever were asked about fund-raising methods.

In 1990, with Celeste prevented by law from seeking a third consecutive term, Ohio's editorial drumbeat demanded a change in executive leadership. Republican George V. Voinovich, for ten years the mayor of Cleveland, was the beneficiary of the mood for change. For the first time in modern history, and perhaps all of Ohio history, every major newspaper statewide endorsed the same candidate for governor—Voinovich, who was facing Democratic nominee Anthony J. Celebrezze Jr., the two-term attorney general. Seizing the ethics issue, Voinovich promised to "restore trust, honesty and efficiency in government." He won the election comfortably.

The same year, Republican Robert A. Taft II—a Hamilton County commissioner, son of former U.S. senator Robert Taft Jr., and great-grandson of President William Howard Taft—ran for secretary of state against the two-term Democratic incumbent, Sherrod Brown. The Ohio Republican Party, under Chairman Robert T. Bennett, had persuaded Taft to drop out of a campaign against Voinovich for the party's gubernatorial nomination. The secretary of state's race was a priority because of its representation on the apportionment board. Taft defeated Brown, giving Republicans two of the three apportionment board offices—and control of the legislative map-making process for the first time in two decades.

Democrats retained the offices of attorney general, auditor, and treasurer, but Republicans had won the two big prizes on the 1990 ballot.

In 1992, races for the Ohio General Assembly were conducted in new, Republican-drawn districts. The Republicans gained eight seats in the Ohio House, trimming the Democratic majority to 53–46, while keeping the Senate with a comfortable 20–13 majority.

The Republican gains served as a harbinger for 1994, when the Ohio GOP enjoyed its greatest election successes in more than a quarter century. At the top of the ballot, no big name Democrat challenged Voinovich; a little-known state senator from Dover, Robert L. Burch Jr., won the Democratic gubernatorial nomination almost by default. As a result, the popular and well-financed Voinovich piled up nearly 72 percent of the vote—a 20th century record—and led Republicans to a sweep of the statewide executive offices. In January 1995, elected Republicans—Betty Montgomery, Jim Petro, and J. Kenneth Blackwell, respectively—held the offices of attorney general, auditor, and treasurer for the first time since 1970. Blackwell, who had been appointed treasurer in March 1994 by Voinovich, was Ohio's first black to hold statewide executive office.

Voinovich's lieutenant governor, Mike DeWine, was elected to the U.S. Senate seat of retiring Democrat Howard M. Metzenbaum; in defeating Metzenbaum's son-in-law Joel Hyatt, DeWine became the first Republican to represent Ohio in the U.S. Senate since 1976. In state legislative races, Republicans retained their 20–13 control of the Ohio Senate and gained nine seats in the Ohio House of Representatives to take control (56–43) for the first time since 1972.

In 1995, with control of both legislative houses and the governor's office, Republicans responded to concerns about campaign fund-raising abuses and big-dollar contributions. Voinovich signed legislation limiting individual contributions to $2,500 to state candidates, $5,000 to a county political party or legislative caucus, and $15,000 to a state political party. The governor promised the law would bring "sweeping reform that will help bring the staggering costs of campaigns under control."

The legislation failed to do that, partly because of loopholes exempting from limits all in-kind contributions and party loans to candidates. Such "loans" could be forgiven and often were.

In addition, corporate money could be donated to a political party's "building fund" or "operating fund" as well as to so-called "issue advocacy groups." There were no requirements for disclosure of the sources of these contributions—a recipe for political money-laundering and other abuses. State Treasurer Joseph T. Deters was caught in such a scandal when it was revealed that Frank Gruttadauria, a Cleveland investment broker, provided $50,000 to Deters's campaign fund in 2001 by routing it through the Hamilton County Republican Party's operating fund. Gruttadauria was jailed for defrauding investment clients out of $125 million.

As a result of the campaign-finance scandals, Deters returned to his previous office of Hamilton County prosecutor and resigned from the treasurer's office. And, in December 2004, Governor Taft signed legislation requiring the disclosure of all political donations. The bill also quadrupled individual contribution limits to $10,000.

In 1996, with the national economy humming, President Bill Clinton coasted to re-election over Republican U.S. senator Bob Dole. In capturing Ohio in both 1992 and 1996, Clinton became the first Democrat since Franklin Delano Roosevelt (in 1936 and 1940) to win the state in successive presidential elections. Despite Clinton's success at the top of the ticket, Ohio Republicans gained four seats in the Ohio House and one seat in the Ohio Senate. For the first time in 25 years, Republicans maintained control of both houses of the General Assembly in back-to-back elections. The bright spot for Democrats was a gain of two seats in the U.S. House of Representatives, reducing the GOP advantage from 13–6 to 11–8.

Flush with success, the Ohio Republican Party—on May 16, 1997—dedicated its new headquarters on S. Fifth Street in downtown Columbus. Utilizing corporate contributions, the GOP spent $1.5 million renovating the building and equipping it with modern computers and equipment for producing high-speed mailings, radio ads, polls, graphics, and telemarketing. The state-of-the-art headquarters expanded the already sizable advantage the Republican Party had built in political infrastructure.

In 1998, in the last gubernatorial election of the 20th century, Republican Bob Taft, the two-term secretary of state, easily outdistanced Democrat Lee Fisher, a former state attorney general. As in 1994, Republicans swept the statewide executive offices. The GOP also picked up the U.S. Senate seat of four-term Democrat John Glenn, who retired, as outgoing governor George V. Voinovich defeated Democrat Mary O. Boyle, a former Cuyahoga County commissioner. The repeat sweep by Republicans prompted party loyalists to begin comparing party chairman Robert T. Bennett to the legendary Ray C. Bliss.

Republicans continued their dominance in Ohio in the 2000, 2002, and 2004 elections. Texas governor George W. Bush, son of the 41st president, carried Ohio in 2000 enroute to his disputed presidential election victory over Vice President Al Gore. Gore ran well in Ohio's most populated counties, but Bush piled up impressive vote totals in most of Ohio's small and medium-sized counties. The election also marked the advent of legislative term limits, as Ohio Senate and House members elected in 1992 or earlier were prevented from seeking re-election.

In June 2002, in an attempt to change its fortunes, the Ohio Democratic Party elected a new chairman—Dennis L. White, who had successfully led the Franklin County Democratic Party since 1994. Nevertheless, in November Republicans swept the state's executive offices for the third consecutive election. Led by Taft's re-election as governor, Republicans became the first political party in Ohio history to control all of state government for 10 consecutive years.

Democrats pinned their hopes on rebounding in the 2004 presidential election. Both parties conducted unprecedented registration and get-out-the-vote campaigns, leading to voter turnout of about 70 percent—or nearly 5.5 million voters, compared to 4.7 million four years earlier. Despite the huge turnout, historically a good sign for Democrats, George W. Bush won Ohio by 2 percentage points over Democratic U.S. senator John Kerry of Massachusetts. Capturing Ohio's 20 electoral votes was pivotal for Bush, who won the national electoral vote over Kerry, 286–252.

The election caused Democrats to begin rethinking Ohio's electoral math, because Kerry outperformed all the traditional benchmarks for Democratic success in the state. Kerry dominated the vote in Ohio's largest counties, but the biggest increases in voter turnout occurred in suburban and rural counties which strongly favored Bush.

THE TIDES OF OHIO POLITICS

Democratic-Republican Control of Ohio Statewide Offices, 1900–2005

DEMOCRAT
REPUBLICAN

U.S. SENATE
U.S. SENATE
GOVERNOR
LT. GOVERNOR
ATTORNEY GENERAL
AUDITOR
SECRETARY OF STATE
TREASURER

1900 1906 1912 1918 1924 1930 1936 1942 1948 1954 1960 1966 1972 1978 1984 1990 1996 2002

* John W. Brown, by virtue of his position of lieutenant governor, served as governor for 11 days—January 3-14, 1957. It was the period between Lausche taking his U.S. Senate seat and the inauguration of O'Neill as governor.

96

CHAPTER 9

Ohio's Political Demographics

ECONOMICALLY, CULTURALLY,
AND POLITICALLY,
OHIO IS TREMENDOUSLY DIVERSE.

There are many Ohios. The state is both foundry and breadbasket, metropolis and backwoods, boom center and rusting burg. Ohio ranks seventh in the nation in gross state product and third in the nation in industrial output. It ranks sixth or higher in the production of corn, soybeans, chickens, eggs, and Swiss cheese. The state has six metropolitan areas among the 100 most populous in the nation yet has vast stretches of sparsely populated Appalachia. Several counties in central and southwestern Ohio are attracting people and jobs at a record pace, while others in northeastern and southeastern Ohio continue their steady decline.

Economically, culturally, and politically, Ohio is tremendously diverse. The state has cities and counties that vote Democratic religiously, and it has cities and counties as rock-ribbed in their Republicanism as any in the nation. Ohio also has independent-minded, swing counties that—in combination with the Democratic and Republican strongholds—make for a state renown for its ticketsplitting.

Ohio's diversity, in part, is a reflection of its dispersed population. Among the six regions outlined in this analysis, none delivers a majority or nearmajority of the statewide vote. The most populous region, northeastern Ohio, accounted for 39 percent of the state's vote in the 2004 presidential election. This Democratic-oriented section of Ohio is counterbalanced by the next three most populous regions—central, southwestern, and western Ohio—which usually vote Republican and together supplied 47 percent of the state's vote in 2004. To illustrate the counterbalance, northeastern Ohio in 2004 preferred Democrat John F. Kerry by 280,625 votes; central, southwestern, and western Ohio in combination preferred Republican George W. Bush by 373,336 votes.

Any attempt to divide Ohio into political regions requires some subjective judgments as to which region should get certain counties. For example, Ohio has 29 counties officially designated as part of Appalachia by the Appalachian Regional Commission. However, some of those counties—such as Clermont County near Cincinnati—today are known more for exclusive suburbs than for their Appalachian heritage.

This study divides Ohio by groupings of media markets. In cases where a media market is too small to be considered a political region unto itself, it is grouped with an adjacent media market. The political regions and the media markets included are

- **Northeast**—Cleveland and Youngstown
- **Central**—Columbus and Zanesville
- **Southwest**—Cincinnati
- **West**—Dayton, Lima, and Fort Wayne, Ind.
- **Northwest**—Toledo
- **Southeast**—Charleston–Huntington, W. Va., and Wheeling, W. Va.–Steubenville

Together, the six regions form a politically balanced and competitive state. Between 1944 and 2002, Republicans won 10 of 19 gubernatorial elections; between 1944 and 2004, Republicans carried Ohio in 11 of 16 presidential elections.

For most of the 20th century, the winning formula for a Democratic candidate remained the same: capture at least 60 percent of the vote in Cuyahoga County and make similar gains in the rest of northeastern Ohio; win big in Lucas County; win the river counties of southeastern Ohio. For a Republican, who almost always wins a majority of Ohio's counties, the formula was: capture 40-45 percent of the vote in Cuyahoga County; do marginally better in the rest of northeastern Ohio; win about 55 percent of the vote in the downstate regions.

That old electoral math began changing in the 1980s and 1990s, as many of Ohio's largest counties lost population to their surrounding counties and to rural counties. This shift has benefited Republicans in recent statewide elections, challenging Democrats to reshape their appeal to suburban and rural Ohio.

For four consecutive decades, central and southwestern Ohio—ever so gradually—have gained voting clout at the expense of northeastern Ohio. In 1960, northeastern Ohio delivered 1.6 votes for every ballot cast in central and southwestern Ohio; in 2004, the advantage was down to 1.1 to 1—near parity. Between 1990 and 2000, six of Ohio's 10 fastest-growing counties were in central and southwestern Ohio. State demographers, projecting population trends to 2020, expect those two regions to gradually increase their shares of Ohio's population at the expense of the other four regions.

In each region of Ohio, there has been a gradual shifting of populations. Within major urban counties, between 1940 and 2000, suburbs gained at the expense of central cities; within regions, between 1970 and 2000, nonmetropolitan counties and suburban counties gained at the expense of central counties.

Ohio's economic base also has been substantially transformed in recent decades. By 2000, only one-fifth of Ohio workers were employed in manufacturing industries, compared to about one-half four decades earlier. Although manufacturing remains the main engine of Ohio's economy, contributing twice as much to the gross state product as any other sector, it is a smaller and more efficient engine than in the past. Many displaced blue-collar workers have been forced to exchange a high-wage manufacturing job for a low-wage service-industry job. Major consequences have been declines in Ohio's real income levels and increases in the state's poverty rate.

Presidential Vote 2004

Northwest
Bush 52%
Kerry 48%
Provides 9% of state's vote

West
Bush 58%
Kerry 42%
Provides 13% of state's vote

Central
Bush 54%
Kerry 46%
Provides 19% of state's vote

Northeast
Bush 44%
Kerry 56%
Provides 39% of state's vote

Southwest
Bush 61%
Kerry 39%
Provides 15% of state's vote

Southeast
Bush 52%
Kerry 48%
Provides 5% of state's vote

Party Self-Identification among Ohio Voters

	REPUBLICAN	DEMOCRAT	INDEPENDENT	SAMPLE SIZE
June 1994	34%	33%	28%	800
September 1996	31%	33%	32%	800
June 1998	30%	28%	37%	800
October 2000	34%	33%	32%	600
October 2002	32%	31%	33%	800
October 2004	36%	32%	30%	800
January 2005	34%	36%	30%	800

Source: Public Opinion Strategies

Share of Statewide Vote by Region

(Selected presidential years)

	2004	1992	1980	1972	1960	1944	1924	1888	1860
Northeast	39%	41%	42%	43%	44%	42%	36%	26%	26%
Central	19%	17%	17%	16%	14%	15%	17%	19%	21%
Southwest	15%	14%	14%	13%	14%	13%	14%	16%	17%
West	13%	13%	13%	12%	12%	12%	13%	15%	13%
Northwest	9%	9%	9%	9%	9%	10%	11%	11%	9%
Southeast	5%	6%	6%	6%	6%	8%	9%	12%	13%

(Percentages may total 99 or 101 due to rounding)

Source: Ohio secretary of state

Largest Metropolitan Areas in Ohio

	2000	1990	% CHANGE
Cleveland–Akron	2,945,831	2,859,644	3.0
Cincinnati–Hamilton*	1,979,202	1,817,571	8.9
Columbus	1,540,157	1,345,450	14.5
Dayton–Springfield	950,558	951,270	-0.1
Toledo	618,203	614,128	0.7
Youngstown–Warren	594,746	600,895	-1.0
Canton–Massillon	406,934	394,106	3.3

* Includes population in Indiana and Kentucky

Source: Ohio Department of Development

Major City Share of County Populations

COUNTY	MAJOR CITY	2000	1990	1980	1970	1960	1950	1940
Cuyahoga	Cleveland	34.3	35.8	38.3	43.6	53.2	65.8	72.1
Franklin	Columbus	65.7	65.8	65.0	64.8	69.0	74.7	78.7
Hamilton	Cincinnati	39.2	42.0	44.1	48.9	58.1	69.6	73.2
Montgomery	Dayton	29.7	31.7	33.8	39.9	49.7	61.2	71.3
Lucas	Toledo	68.9	72.0	75.2	79.2	69.6	76.7	81.9
Summit	Akron	40.0	43.3	45.2	49.7	56.5	66.9	72.1
Stark	Canton	21.4	22.8	24.6	29.6	33.4	41.3	46.2
Mahoning	Youngstown	31.8	36.2	39.8	46.3	55.4	65.3	69.8

Source: U.S. Bureau of the Census

Democratic Vote Strength

Strongest to weakest by percentage, 1996–2004

COUNTY	KERRY 04	GORE 00	CLINTON 96	HAGAN 02	FISHER 98	TOTAL	AVERAGE
1. Cuyahoga	66.565 %	62.617 %	60.751 %	59.528 %	58.317 %	307.779 %	61.556 %
2. Mahoning	62.597	60.649	61.531	49.552	56.323	290.652	58.130
3. Trumbull	61.651	59.896	58.688	49.326	57.451	287.012	57.402
4. Athens	63.232	51.707	56.016	51.403	51.946	274.304	54.861
5. Lucas	60.207	57.830	57.724	38.342	59.073	273.176	54.635
6. Belmont	52.746	53.017	57.786	45.982	56.476	266.007	53.201
7. Monroe	54.897	50.668	56.179	47.611	55.195	264.550	52.910
8. Lorain	56.110	53.315	52.369	49.085	51.182	262.061	52.412
9. Summit	56.669	53.264	52.069	48.936	49.460	260.398	52.080
10. Jefferson	52.304	50.491	56.038	39.846	51.748	250.427	50.085
11. Portage	53.068	49.994	50.553	47.455	46.977	248.047	49.609
12. Erie	53.439	50.641	50.016	42.752	48.510	245.358	49.072
13. Pike	47.622	46.619	51.377	43.817	53.480	242.916	48.583
14. Ashtabula	52.987	50.241	49.948	41.876	45.382	240.434	48.087
15. Franklin	54.353	48.788	48.137	39.270	45.034	235.581	47.116
16. Harrison	46.615	46.795	50.270	40.767	50.658	235.106	47.021
17. Montgomery	50.603	49.612	49.996	36.944	47.422	234.577	46.915
18. Scioto	47.800	46.742	48.011	40.591	51.231	234.375	46.875
19. Stark	50.588	47.113	46.378	39.167	44.116	227.362	45.472
20. Ottawa	47.801	47.501	49.349	33.886	46.718	225.254	45.051
21. Perry	47.778	45.954	46.750	37.754	46.929	225.165	45.033
22. Columbiana	47.365	46.496	47.482	36.934	45.303	223.581	44.716
23. Ross	44.135	44.826	49.033	36.668	48.238	222.901	44.580
24. Clark	48.738	48.618	48.251	33.042	44.087	222.735	44.547
25. Tuscarawas	43.940	42.780	43.861	42.403	49.595	222.580	44.516
26. Vinton	44.720	41.185	48.846	38.176	47.212	220.139	44.028
27. Lake	48.471	45.335	44.186	40.782	40.659	219.433	43.887
28. Lawrence	43.735	46.242	48.462	35.484	42.654	216.576	43.315
29. Hocking	46.784	41.595	44.863	37.933	44.558	215.733	43.147
30. Wood	46.413	43.467	46.983	30.409	45.130	212.402	42.480
31. Guernsey	43.543	43.052	44.553	37.267	41.182	209.597	41.919
32. Sandusky	43.728	43.296	45.437	32.309	42.215	206.985	41.397
33. Carroll	44.643	40.453	40.645	35.462	40.527	201.730	40.346
34. Jackson	39.766	41.081	45.788	32.579	41.638	200.851	40.170
35. Marion	40.775	41.789	42.482	32.986	42.743	200.775	40.155
36. Hamilton	47.091	42.757	43.126	30.345	37.207	200.526	40.105
37. Noble	40.581	38.343	42.909	38.011	40.282	200.126	40.025
38. Medina	42.734	39.823	40.157	38.255	37.986	198.955	39.791
39. Richland	39.842	38.978	40.489	36.728	41.755	197.791	39.558
40. Muskingum	42.250	41.120	41.893	27.990	39.127	192.381	38.476
41. Huron	41.349	38.310	41.860	30.756	39.200	191.475	38.295
42. Meigs	41.203	37.509	45.166	28.592	38.348	190.819	38.164
43. Seneca	40.595	39.062	42.720	28.767	39.545	190.690	38.138
44. Washington	41.495	39.159	42.133	33.080	34.349	190.215	38.043

Democratic Vote Strength (continued from page 100)

Strongest to weakest by percentage, 1996–2004

COUNTY	KERRY 04	GORE 00	CLINTON 96	HAGAN 02	FISHER 98	TOTAL	AVERAGE
45. Coshocton	42.640 %	39.207 %	41.905 %	28.519 %	36.981 %	189.252 %	37.850 %
46. Gallia	38.348	38.134	43.206	29.853	39.345	188.885	37.777
47. Hardin	36.522	37.761	41.512	33.731	39.171	188.697	37.739
48. Morgan	42.891	37.727	39.943	29.737	35.480	185.779	37.156
49. Paulding	36.542	37.827	40.123	31.442	39.097	185.031	37.006
50. Defiance	37.670	38.019	39.911	30.293	38.930	184.822	36.964
51. Pickaway	37.542	37.193	40.238	31.768	38.055	184.795	36.959
52. Greene	38.509	38.432	40.598	27.482	37.101	182.122	36.424
53. Adams	35.675	34.988	41.586	32.133	37.353	181.734	36.347
54. Geauga	39.352	35.979	36.182	35.595	34.283	181.390	36.278
55. Brown	35.894	36.350	41.117	27.541	40.032	180.934	36.187
56. Champaign	37.111	37.978	40.220	27.157	36.570	179.037	35.807
57. Licking	37.841	37.134	39.029	26.819	37.613	178.436	35.687
58. Crawford	35.654	35.049	38.296	29.335	37.309	175.644	35.129
59. Morrow	35.369	35.275	37.695	29.238	37.403	174.980	34.996
60. Fayette	36.863	36.247	38.149	27.732	35.844	174.836	34.967
61. Wayne	38.162	34.827	36.623	29.695	33.892	173.198	34.640
62. Madison	35.654	36.047	37.792	27.855	35.417	172.764	34.553
63. Fulton	37.460	36.013	37.203	23.024	39.009	172.710	34.542
64. Fairfield	36.509	35.244	37.134	27.077	35.846	171.810	34.362
65. Knox	36.310	33.551	37.682	29.268	34.626	171.437	34.287
66. Preble	34.430	35.093	38.586	26.722	36.541	171.372	34.274
67. Miami	34.015	36.376	38.845	24.667	36.534	170.437	34.087
68. Highland	33.516	34.492	39.778	27.349	34.449	169.584	33.917
69. Wyandot	33.578	34.568	38.274	25.707	35.642	167.769	33.554
70. Williams	34.771	34.261	35.415	26.510	35.528	166.485	33.297
71. Allen	33.438	31.958	35.335	28.892	34.768	164.391	32.878
72. Ashland	34.333	31.447	33.242	30.638	33.702	163.362	32.672
73. Darke	29.818	33.270	38.516	24.152	36.085	161.841	32.368
74. Henry	33.836	32.954	37.247	22.597	34.639	161.273	32.255
75. Butler	33.715	33.926	35.695	24.112	33.129	160.577	32.115
76. Shelby	28.593	33.518	36.646	25.776	35.968	160.501	32.100
77. Logan	31.896	32.213	37.311	22.977	31.848	156.246	31.249
78. Clinton	29.418	31.792	36.520	23.978	31.574	153.281	30.656
79. Delaware	33.618	30.926	32.508	23.536	29.613	150.201	30.040
80. Van Wert	27.619	31.841	34.146	23.046	30.916	147.567	29.513
81. Union	29.451	29.605	33.253	22.471	31.141	145.921	29.184
82. Mercer	24.500	28.490	35.688	21.821	33.843	144.343	28.869
83. Clermont	29.061	29.948	33.236	21.378	29.358	142.982	28.596
84. Auglaize	25.627	27.971	33.883	22.944	31.269	141.695	28.339
85. Hancock	29.063	28.736	31.209	20.157	30.301	139.466	27.893
86. Putnam	23.301	23.426	30.771	25.237	31.713	134.448	26.890
87. Warren	27.583	27.711	30.842	19.999	28.297	134.431	26.886
88. Holmes	24.037	22.592	27.862	23.078	26.710	124.279	24.856

Republican Vote Strength

Strongest to weakest by percentage, 1996–2004

	COUNTY	BUSH 04	BUSH 00	DOLE 96	TAFT 02	TAFT 98	TOTAL	AVERAGE
1.	Holmes	75.472 %	73.855 %	57.387 %	73.514 %	67.552 %	347.780 %	69.556 %
2.	Warren	72.056	69.947	59.936	76.041	67.346	345.327	69.065
3.	Putnam	76.237	74.014	57.519	69.723	63.433	340.928	68.186
4.	Hancock	70.482	68.540	57.684	76.516	64.979	338.201	67.640
5.	Clermont	70.666	67.446	56.810	74.748	66.352	336.022	67.204
6.	Van Wert	72.017	65.655	53.669	72.521	65.425	329.288	65.858
7.	Auglaize	73.873	69.224	51.798	70.839	62.719	328.454	65.691
8.	Mercer	74.916	68.246	50.031	74.161	60.320	327.674	65.535
9.	Delaware	66.052	66.132	58.247	71.941	63.072	325.443	65.089
10.	Union	70.125	67.563	55.256	71.225	60.631	324.800	64.960
11.	Clinton	70.262	65.189	51.677	71.271	63.719	322.118	64.424
12.	Butler	65.863	63.324	54.758	71.629	61.864	317.439	63.488
13.	Henry	65.554	64.368	49.941	74.421	59.114	313.398	62.680
14.	Allen	66.144	65.412	55.350	64.734	61.246	312.885	62.577
15.	Logan	67.628	64.205	48.556	71.499	59.898	311.786	62.357
16.	Darke	69.570	63.682	46.883	70.520	56.941	307.597	61.519
17.	Ashland	64.891	63.661	52.607	65.798	60.445	307.401	61.480
18.	Shelby	70.899	63.427	47.778	68.903	54.866	305.872	61.174
19.	Highland	66.073	62.977	48.399	67.879	60.386	305.714	61.143
20.	Williams	64.596	62.447	49.667	69.076	58.047	303.833	60.767
21.	Fairfield	62.925	61.972	52.975	67.508	57.784	303.165	60.633
22.	Miami	65.672	60.776	48.766	70.120	56.315	301.650	60.330
23.	Wyandot	65.689	62.206	46.560	69.638	57.053	301.145	60.229
24.	Fulton	62.130	61.103	48.601	73.801	55.236	300.871	60.174
25.	Knox	63.110	62.996	50.623	65.273	58.207	300.209	60.042
26.	Fayette	62.737	61.274	50.286	67.296	58.043	299.636	59.927
27.	Madison	63.898	60.626	51.196	65.998	57.323	299.041	59.808
28.	Wayne	61.485	61.035	48.407	66.658	61.010	298.596	59.719
29.	Preble	65.007	61.522	47.505	67.251	54.362	295.645	59.129
30.	Licking	61.717	59.520	48.779	68.077	55.537	293.631	58.721
31.	Adams	63.775	62.335	45.882	63.410	58.097	293.499	58.700
32.	Geauga	60.208	59.664	50.301	61.410	61.231	292.814	58.563
33.	Brown	63.578	61.032	45.360	68.234	54.464	292.669	58.534
34.	Greene	61.033	58.196	49.654	67.224	55.968	292.074	58.415
35.	Crawford	63.690	60.836	44.882	65.952	55.088	290.449	58.090
36.	Pickaway	61.968	60.411	49.517	62.543	55.369	289.809	57.962
37.	Defiance	61.552	58.737	46.996	66.213	55.224	288.721	57.744
38.	Morrow	64.147	61.080	46.069	63.648	53.444	288.388	57.678
39.	Champaign	62.409	58.801	44.101	66.638	55.396	287.346	57.469
40.	Washington	58.022	57.862	46.060	62.925	62.069	286.938	57.388
41.	Paulding	62.820	58.238	43.741	64.407	55.707	284.914	56.983
42.	Hardin	63.030	59.032	46.362	61.440	53.284	283.149	56.630
43.	Gallia	61.288	58.790	41.192	65.538	55.301	282.109	56.422
44.	Hamilton	52.501	54.029	50.123	65.842	59.194	281.689	56.338

Republican Vote Strength (continued from page 102)

Strongest to weakest by percentage, 1996–2004

COUNTY	BUSH 04	BUSH 00	DOLE 96	TAFT 02	TAFT 98	TOTAL	AVERAGE
45. Coshocton	56.863 %	57.773 %	41.996 %	66.567 %	57.370 %	280.568 %	56.114 %
46. Morgan	56.064	57.584	42.974	64.199	58.627	279.449	55.890
47. Huron	57.974	57.519	41.350	65.769	55.052	277.664	55.533
48. Meigs	58.230	58.703	38.267	65.559	56.434	277.194	55.439
49. Seneca	58.857	56.930	41.313	66.809	53.255	277.163	55.433
50. Muskingum	57.258	55.159	42.039	66.821	55.512	276.789	55.358
51. Richland	59.625	57.102	46.057	59.664	53.588	276.037	55.207
52. Medina	56.783	55.842	44.207	58.315	56.851	271.998	54.400
53. Jackson	59.893	55.709	40.695	62.286	52.836	271.417	54.283
54. Marion	58.688	54.874	45.035	61.196	49.286	269.079	53.816
55. Noble	58.731	57.365	39.590	56.923	55.465	268.073	53.615
56. Wood	53.029	52.696	41.582	66.440	49.581	263.328	52.666
57. Sandusky	55.913	53.212	39.480	64.034	50.250	262.889	52.578
58. Carroll	54.528	54.906	37.735	60.025	53.522	260.717	52.143
59. Guernsey	55.841	53.020	39.515	58.528	53.554	260.459	52.092
60. Lawrence	55.775	51.247	36.914	61.075	52.158	257.168	51.434
61. Lake	51.052	50.453	41.923	56.600	53.734	253.762	50.752
62. Ross	54.406	52.683	39.873	59.372	47.243	253.577	50.715
63. Ottawa	51.907	49.664	37.013	62.975	47.320	248.879	49.776
64. Vinton	54.808	54.994	34.774	56.288	46.471	247.335	49.467
65. Clark	50.781	48.055	38.575	60.887	48.783	247.081	49.416
66. Hocking	52.549	53.012	38.789	55.142	47.197	246.689	49.338
67. Tuscarawas	55.538	52.667	38.521	53.635	45.077	245.438	49.088
68. Montgomery	48.966	47.532	41.302	59.455	47.297	244.552	48.910
69. Columbiana	52.063	49.078	35.266	59.013	48.216	243.636	48.727
70. Franklin	45.120	47.784	44.546	56.574	49.363	243.388	48.678
71. Stark	48.931	48.893	38.026	56.718	50.454	243.022	48.604
72. Perry	51.722	50.203	37.005	56.289	45.701	240.918	48.184
73. Scioto	51.868	50.165	37.280	55.669	45.205	240.187	48.037
74. Pike	51.845	50.502	34.848	52.498	42.423	232.115	46.423
75. Erie	46.394	45.995	36.485	54.701	47.671	231.246	46.249
76. Harrison	52.707	47.717	31.208	54.853	43.417	229.901	45.980
77. Ashtabula	46.332	45.450	34.314	54.116	49.576	229.788	45.958
78. Portage	46.425	44.947	32.520	47.886	45.593	217.370	43.474
79. Jefferson	47.248	43.417	29.495	56.194	40.587	216.940	43.388
80. Summit	42.906	43.018	34.181	47.310	45.785	213.200	42.640
81. Lorain	43.486	42.750	32.822	47.693	43.549	210.300	42.060
82. Lucas	39.541	39.147	31.979	59.135	36.328	206.130	41.226
83. Belmont	46.783	41.886	26.806	49.891	37.192	202.558	40.512
84. Monroe	44.301	44.202	26.640	48.810	38.445	202.398	40.480
85. Athens	36.103	38.130	29.866	42.905	39.812	186.816	37.363
86. Trumbull	37.891	36.008	26.187	47.030	36.219	183.335	36.667
87. Mahoning	36.689	35.454	26.568	46.148	37.725	182.584	36.517
88. Cuyahoga	32.889	33.421	29.146	37.702	37.927	171.086	34.217

Population by County
2000

Total Population

▦ 500,000 and greater

■ 200,000–499,000

▨ 100,000–199,000

☐ Less than 100,000

Source: U.S. Bureau of the Census
Prepared by: Ohio Department of
Development, Office of Strategic Research.
(March 2001)

Fastest Declining Counties

1990–2000

COUNTY	COUNTY SEAT	REGION	2000	1990	%
Jefferson	Steubenville	Northeast	73,894	80,298	-8.0
Mahoning	Youngstown	Northeast	257,555	264,806	-2.7
Montgomery	Dayton	West	559,062	573,809	-2.6
Van Wert	Van Wert	Northwest	29,659	30,464	-2.6
Hamilton	Cincinnati	Southwest	845,303	866,228	-2.4
Monroe	Woodsfield	Southeast	15,180	15,497	-2.0
Crawford	Bucyrus	Central	46,966	47,870	-1.9
Seneca	Tiffin	Northwest	58,683	59,733	-1.8
Lucas	Toledo	Northwest	455,054	462,361	-1.5
Harrison	Cadiz	Northeast	15,856	16,085	-1.4

Population Change
1990–2002

State change: +5.3%

Gained 10% or more

Gained less than 10%

Lost less than 10%

Lost 10% or more

Source: U.S. Bureau of the Census,
Ohio Dept. of Development, Office of
Strategic Research

Ten Largest Counties/Population Changes

1990–2000

COUNTY	COUNTY SEAT	REGION	2000	1990	%
Cuyahoga	Cleveland	Northeast	1,393,978	1,412,140	-1.2
Franklin	Columbus	Central	1,068,978	961,437	11.2
Hamilton	Cincinnati	Southwest	845,303	866,228	-2.4
Montgomery	Dayton	West	559,062	573,809	-2.6
Summit	Akron	Northeast	542,899	514,990	5.4
Lucas	Toledo	Northwest	455,054	462,361	-1.5
Stark	Canton	Northeast	378,098	367,585	2.9
Butler	Hamilton	Southwest	332,807	291,479	14.2
Lorain	Elyria	Northeast	284,664	271,126	5.0
Mahoning	Youngstown	Northeast	257,555	264,806	-2.7

Population Projections 2020

Projected state population: 12,005,733

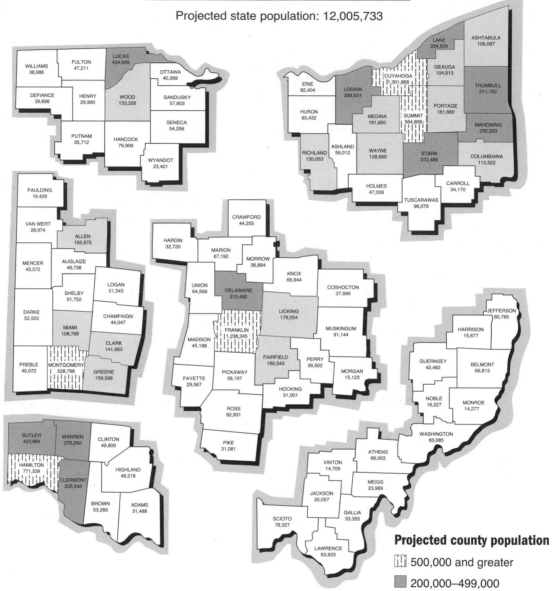

Projected county population

- 500,000 and greater
- 200,000–499,000
- 100,000–199,000
- Less than 100,000

Source: Ohio Dept. of Development,
Office of Strategic Research (July 2004)

Fastest Growing Counties

1990–2000

COUNTY	COUNTYSEAT	REGION	2000	1990	%
Delaware	Delaware	Central	109,989	66,929	64.3
Warren	Lebanon	Southwest	158,383	113,909	39.0
Union	Marysville	Central	40,909	31,969	28.0
Noble	Caldwell	Southeast	14,058	11,336	24.0
Medina	Medina	Northeast	151,095	122,354	23.5
Brown	Georgetown	Southwest	42,285	34,966	20.9
Fairfield	Lancaster	Central	122,759	103,461	18.7
Holmes	Millersburg	Northeast	38,943	32,849	18.6
Clermont	Batavia	Southwest	177,977	150,187	18.5
Vinton	McArthur	Southeast	12,806	11,098	15.4

Employment by Sector *

	2000	1990	1980	1970	1960	1950
Manufacturing ■	19.6%	23.7%	30.7%	48.0%	51.8%	54.7%
Wholesale and □ Retail Trade	24.3%	25.0%	23.4%	25.3%	23.7%	22.9%
Services ▱	28.7%	23.9%	18.0%	9.4%	7.4%	6.8%
Transportation ▤ and Utilities	4.5%	4.4%	4.7%	6.3%	6.3%	5.9%
Finance, Insurance, ▨ and Real Estate	5.6%	5.3%	4.8%	4.9%	4.3%	3.3%
Construction ■	4.4%	4.2%	4.2%	5.2%	5.5%	5.1%
State and ▨ Local Government **	12.6%	12.3%	12.9%	NA	NA	NA
All Other □	0.3%	1.2%	1.3%	0.9%	1.0%	1.3%

* Employment covered by Ohio's unemployment compensation law.

** Beginning January 1, 1972, coverage under the unemployment compensation law was extended to employees of state and local government.

Source: Ohio Department of Job and Family Services, Labor Market Information Division

Unemployment Rates, United States and Ohio
1960–2004

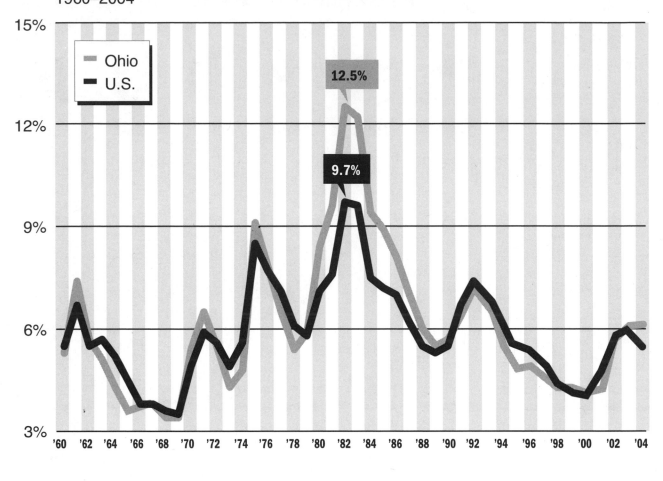

YEAR	U.S.	OHIO	YEAR	U.S.	OHIO	YEAR	U.S.	OHIO
1960	5.5 %	5.3 %	1975	8.5 %	9.1 %	1990	5.5 %	5.7 %
1961	6.7	7.4	1976	7.7	7.8	1991	6.7	6.4
1962	5.5	5.7	1977	7.1	6.5	1992	7.4	7.2
1963	5.7	5.1	1978	6.1	5.4	1993	6.8	6.5
1964	5.2	4.3	1979	5.8	5.9	1994	6.1	5.5
1965	4.5	3.6	1980	7.1	8.4	1995	5.6	4.8
1966	3.8	3.0	1981	7.6	9.6	1996	5.4	4.9
1967	3.8	3.8	1982	9.7	12.5	1997	4.9	4.6
1968	3.6	3.4	1983	9.6	12.2	1998	4.5	4.3
1969	3.5	3.4	1984	7.5	9.4	1999	4.2	4.3
1970	4.9	5.4	1985	7.2	8.9	2000	4.0	4.1
1971	5.9	6.5	1986	7.0	8.1	2001	4.8	4.3
1972	5.6	5.5	1987	6.2	7.0	2002	5.8	5.7
1973	4.9	4.3	1988	5.5	6.0	2003	6.0	6.1
1974	5.6	4.8	1989	5.3	5.5	2004	5.5	6.1

Source: Ohio Department of Job and Family Services, Labor Market Information Division

Land Area by County

Largest to smallest in square miles

1. Ashtabula	709.64	31. Putnam	484.01	61. Vinton	415.04
2. Ross	693.05	32. Mercer	472.77	62. Sandusky	414.52
3. Licking	687.82	33. Gallia	471.58	63. Defiance	413.56
4. Muskingum	673.28	34. Butler	469.83	64. Clinton	412.84
5. Washington	642.15	35. Hardin	469.36	65. Perry	412.58
6. Trumbull	635.56	36. Logan	466.83	66. Hamilton	412.36
7. Wood	620.28	37. Madison	466.49	67. Harrison	411.02
8. Scioto	615.60	38. Montgomery	463.57	68. Miami	410.60
9. Darke	599.88	39. Clermont	459.46	69. Jefferson	410.11
10. Adams	586.14	40. Monroe	457.82	70. Van Wert	409.86
11. Stark	579.40	41. Delaware	457.78	71. Shelby	409.46
12. Tuscarawas	572.05	42. Lawrence	457.37	72. Geauga	409.43
13. Coshocton	567.46	43. Cuyahoga	457.24	73. Wyandot	408.54
14. Highland	558.64	44. Pike	443.88	74. Warren	407.60
15. Wayne	556.58	45. Union	436.54	75. Allen	407.43
16. Seneca	552.32	46. Meigs	433.31	76. Fayette	407.20
17. Franklin	548.24	47. Champaign	430.01	77. Fulton	407.20
18. Belmont	541.48	48. Preble	426.64	78. Morrow	406.83
19. Columbiana	535.48	49. Ashland	426.16	79. Noble	404.82
20. Hancock	534.09	50. Mahoning	425.53	80. Marion	404.14
21. Knox	530.12	51. Medina	424.79	81. Crawford	402.54
22. Guernsey	527.68	52. Hocking	424.39	82. Auglaize	402.28
23. Fairfield	508.34	53. Williams	424.21	83. Clark	400.94
24. Pickaway	507.68	54. Holmes	423.18	84. Carroll	398.47
25. Athens	507.16	55. Jackson	421.99	85. Lucas	348.06
26. Portage	505.07	56. Morgan	420.79	86. Ottawa	266.54
27. Richland	498.68	57. Summit	419.38	87. Erie	258.81
28. Lorain	494.49	58. Henry	419.00	88. Lake	232.38
29. Huron	494.37	59. Paulding	418.09		
30. Brown	493.76	60. Greene	415.52		

Total land area of the 88 counties equals 41,268.03 square miles.

Ohio Farmland

COUNTY	NUMBER OF FARMS		AVERAGE SIZE IN ACRES		ACRES OF LAND IN FARMS	
	2002	2003	2002	2003	2002	2003
State Total:	77,800	77,600	188	188	14,610,000	14,600,000
1. Darke	1,780	1,770	192	192	341,000	340,000
2. Wood	1,070	1,060	293	294	313,000	312,000
3. Putnam	1,360	1,350	226	227	308,000	307,000
4. Seneca	1,200	1,190	241	240	289,000	286,000
5. Hancock	990	980	279	281	276,000	275,000
6. Pickaway	790	790	342	344	270,000	272,000
7. Mercer	1,280	1,270	211	213	270,000	270,000
8. Highland	1,380	1,380	185	189	255,000	261,000
9. Wayne	1,890	1,890	135	137	255,000	259,000
10. Hardin	850	840	298	299	253,000	251,000
11. Ross	950	950	266	264	253,000	251,000
12. Madison	730	730	345	342	252,000	250,000
13. Van Wert	690	680	361	366	249,000	249,000
14. Union	1,010	1,020	236	239	238,000	244,000
15. Henry	850	840	284	287	241,000	241,000
16. Licking	1,480	1,480	163	161	241,000	239,000
17. Clinton	810	810	283	286	229,000	232,000
18. Paulding	650	650	352	357	229,000	232,000
19. Crawford	700	690	326	333	228,000	230,000
20. Huron	870	860	262	265	228,000	228,000
21. Logan	1,040	1,040	215	215	224,000	224,000
22. Fayette	490	480	459	452	225,000	217,000
23. Auglaize	1,030	1,020	208	211	214,000	215,000
24. Brown	1,420	1,400	149	154	212,000	215,000
25. Williams	1,090	1,090	194	194	211,000	212,000
26. Knox	1,260	1,250	170	170	214,000	212,000
27. Champaign	940	940	227	224	213,000	211,000
28. Marion	530	520	402	404	213,000	210,000
29. Shelby	1,030	1,020	203	205	209,000	209,000
30. Wyandot	610	610	343	339	209,000	207,000
31. Defiance	980	980	208	210	204,000	206,000
32. Fulton	800	790	256	258	205,000	204,000
33. Preble	1,070	1,060	192	192	205,000	203,000
34. Adams	1,330	1,320	150	151	200,000	199,000
35. Sandusky	810	800	248	249	201,000	199,000
36. Fairfield	1,170	1,170	171	170	200,000	199,000
37. Holmes	1,790	1,800	106	108	189,000	195,000
38. Miami	1,070	1,070	185	180	198,000	193,000
39. Allen	970	960	199	200	193,000	192,000
40. Muskingum	1,220	1,220	156	157	190,000	191,000
41. Greene	820	820	222	216	182,000	177,000
42. Morrow	860	860	202	205	174,000	176,000
43. Coshocton	1,040	1,040	165	168	172,000	175,000

	COUNTY	NUMBER OF FARMS		AVERAGE SIZE IN ACRES		ACRES OF LAND IN FARMS	
		2002	2003	2002	2003	2002	2003
44.	Clark	760	760	233	228	177,000	173,000
45.	Ashtabula	1,280	1,280	131	132	168,000	169,000
46.	Delaware	780	780	217	214	169,000	167,000
47.	Ashland	1,090	1,090	156	153	170,000	167,000
48.	Richland	1,080	1,080	150	149	162,000	161,000
49.	Tuscarawas	1,070	1,070	144	146	154,000	156,000
50.	Lorain	970	970	152	157	147,000	152,000
51.	Stark	1,330	1,330	109	109	145,000	145,000
52.	Belmont	750	750	192	191	144,000	143,000
53.	Columbiana	1,180	1,180	123	120	145,000	142,000
54.	Washington	960	950	148	149	142,000	142,000
55.	Butler	1,050	1,050	134	133	141,000	140,000
56.	Guernsey	910	910	151	151	137,000	137,000
57.	Harrison	460	450	267	284	123,000	128,000
58.	Warren	1,020	1,030	125	123	128,000	127,000
59.	Trumbull	1,010	1,010	122	123	123,000	124,000
60.	Carroll	750	750	163	164	122,000	123,000
61.	Medina	1,170	1,180	98	100	115,000	118,000
62.	Gallia	930	930	124	125	115,000	116,000
63.	Ottawa	520	520	210	213	109,000	111,000
64.	Clermont	960	970	111	113	107,000	110,000
65.	Monroe	660	650	167	168	110,000	109,000
66.	Montgomery	840	830	130	129	109,000	107,000
67.	Noble	600	600	175	177	105,000	106,000
68.	Morgan	510	510	206	202	105,000	103,000
69.	Scioto	710	710	142	139	101,000	99,000
70.	Athens	660	660	141	147	93,000	97,000
71.	Perry	640	640	155	152	99,000	97,000
72.	Portage	950	960	99	99	94,000	95,000
73.	Erie	390	390	233	236	91,000	92,000
74.	Franklin	560	560	166	159	93,000	89,000
75.	Meigs	550	550	158	160	87,000	88,000
76.	Pike	500	500	174	172	87,000	86,000
77.	Jackson	460	460	178	174	82,000	80,000
78.	Mahoning	650	650	122	120	79,000	78,000
79.	Lucas	410	410	188	188	77,000	77,000
80.	Jefferson	460	460	161	157	74,000	72,000
81.	Geauga	950	960	66	67	63,000	64,000
82.	Lawrence	640	640	98	100	63,000	64,000
83.	Hocking	430	430	133	126	57,000	54,000
84.	Vinton	240	240	196	192	47,000	46,000
85.	Hamilton	400	400	83	80	33,000	32,000
86.	Summit	370	370	51	54	19,000	20,000
87.	Lake	330	330	55	58	18,000	19,000
88.	Cuyahoga	160	160	38	31	6,000	5,000

111

Ohio Congressional Districts
2002–2012

Ohio House Districts
2002-2012

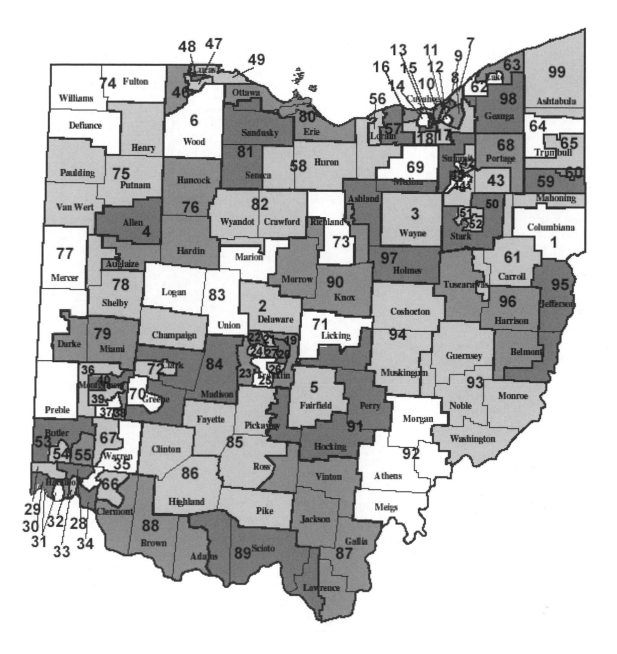

Ohio Senate Districts
2002–2012

CHAPTER 10

Ohio's Counties

ADAMS COUNTY

Established: July 10, 1797
Named for: John Adams
Land area: 586 square miles
Locale: on the Ohio River, about 50 miles east of Cincinnati
2000 Population: 27,330
 White: 97.9%
 Black: 0.0%
County seat: West Union
Largest city: none
Largest village: West Union (2,903)
Second-largest village: Manchester (2,043)
Per-capita income (2002) / ranking among Ohio counties: $19,660/84
Number of school districts (2005): 1

Employment base (2001):
Private sector: 76%
Public sector: 24%

Electoral history:
President (2004): Bush (R) 64%; Kerry (D) 36%
Governor (2002): Taft (R) 63%; Hagan (D) 32%
President (2000): Bush (R) 62%; Gore (D) 35%
Governor (1998): Taft (R) 58%; Fisher (D) 37%
President (1996): Dole (R) 46%; Clinton (D) 42%; Perot 12%
Governor (1994): Voinovich (R) 71%; Burch (D) 26%
President (1992): Bush (R) 44%; Clinton (D) 37%; Perot 19%
Governor (1990): Voinovich (R) 57%; Celebrezze (D) 43%
President (1988): Bush (R) 61%; Dukakis (D) 39%

Party affiliations of county administrative officeholders (2004):
8 Republicans; 2 Democrats; 1 Independent

History:

Adams County—created by the territorial governor's proclamation of July 10, 1797—is one of Ohio's original counties. It was part of the Virginia Military District, and many of its early settlers were Virginians who had purchased land warrants. The county's first settlement was Manchester, founded in 1791 by Nathaniel Massie. The village became a change station for stagecoaches and a point for boarding and unboarding of steamboat passengers. The county's most significant physical feature is the Serpent Mound, a 1,254-foot earthwork created by the Hopewell Indians to the north near the Highland County line. The serpent-effigy mounds are among the largest in the world. Archaeologists believe the Hopewells lived in the area between 300 B.C. and A.D. 600. The Ohio Historical Society maintains Serpent Mound State Park.

ALLEN COUNTY

Established: March 1, 1820
Named for: Col. John Allen (War of 1812)
Land area: 407 square miles
Locale: about 70 miles southwest of Toledo
2000 Population: 108,473
 White: 84.7%
 Black: 12.1%
County seat: Lima
Largest city: Lima (40,081)
Second-largest city: Delphos (6,944)
Per-capita income (2002) / ranking among Ohio counties: $25,237/41
Number of school districts (2005): 9

Employment base (2001):
Private sector: 88%
Public sector: 12%

President (2004): Bush (R) 66%; Kerry (D) 33%
Governor (2002): Taft (R) 65%; Hagan (D) 29%
President (2000): Bush (R) 65%; Gore (D) 32%
Governor (1998): Taft (R) 61%; Fisher (D) 35%
President (1996): Dole (R) 55%; Clinton (D) 35%; Perot 9%
Governor (1994): Voinovich (R) 76%; Burch (D) 20%
President (1992): Bush (R) 54%; Clinton (D) 29%; Perot 17%
Governor (1990): Voinovich (R) 65%; Celebrezze (D) 35%
President (1988): Bush (R) 69%; Dukakis (D) 31%

Party affiliations of county administrative officeholders (2004):
9 Republicans; 2 Independents

History:

Allen County was one of 14 counties formed from lands acquired by the federal government (Congress Lands) from the Wyandot and Shawnee tribes in northwestern Ohio. Fort Amanda, on the west bank of the Auglaize River, was built in October 1812 on the order of Gen. William Henry Harrison. The county was on the edge of the Black Swamp region, where German settlers used large quantities of quinine for medicinal purposes. Because the quinine came from Lima, Peru, the name *Lima* was adopted for the town that became the county seat. Delphos, in the northwestern corner of the county, blossomed from construction of the Miami-Erie Canal, which followed the Auglaize River. The first canal boat passed through Delphos on July 4, 1845. In 1854, the Ohio & Indiana Railroad was built across the county. The discovery of oil in 1885 sparked a speculation boom, but it tapered off by 1900. Swiss Mennonites, who settled Bluffton in the 1830s, founded Bluffton College in 1900.

ASHLAND COUNTY

Established: February 24, 1846
Named for: Henry Clay's Kentucky estate
Land area: 426 square miles
Locale: about 60 miles southwest of Cleveland
2000 Population: 52,523
 White: 97.7%
 Black: 0.9%
County seat: Ashland
Largest city: Ashland (21,249)
Second-largest city: none
Largest village: Loudonville (2,906)
Per-capita income (2002) / ranking among Ohio counties: $22,744/68
Number of school districts (2005): 4

Employment base (2001):
Private sector: 85%
Public sector: 15%

Electoral history:
President (2004): Bush (R) 65%; Kerry (D) 34%
Governor (2002): Taft (R) 66%; Hagan (D) 31%
President (2000): Bush (R) 64%; Gore (D) 31%
Governor (1998): Taft (R) 60%; Fisher (D) 34%
President (1996): Dole (R) 53%; Clinton (D) 33%; Perot 13%
Governor (1994): Voinovich (R) 80%; Burch (D) 17%
President (1992): Bush (R) 47%; Clinton (D) 29%; Perot 24%
Governor (1990): Voinovich (R) 66%; Celebrezze (D) 34%
President (1988): Bush (R) 68%; Dukakis (D) 32%

Party affiliations of county administrative officeholders (2004): 11 Republicans

History:

Ashland County was formed in 1846 from lands previously belonging to Huron, Lorain, Richland, and Wayne counties. Most of the new county had been a part of the Congress Lands. The Delaware and Wyandot tribes inhabited the area before white settlers—many of them Pennsylvania Germans—arrived about 1805. In 1816, the settlers founded Uniontown, later renamed Ashland. The county claims the first Ohioan to enlist in the Civil War—Lorin Andrews, who later was president of Kenyon College. In 1878, Germans affiliated with the United Brethren Church founded Ashland Preparatory College, which later became Ashland College. Charles F. Kettering, inventor of the automobile self-starter, was born on a Loudonville farm. The Ohio Memorial Shrine, honoring 17,000 Ohioans killed in World War II, is near Loudonville in the Mohican State Forest.

ASHTABULA COUNTY

Established: June 7, 1807
Named for: Ashtabula River ("fish river")
Land area: 710 square miles
Locale: on Lake Erie, about 50 miles east of Cleveland
2000 Population: 102,728
 White: 94.2%
 Black: 3.0%
County seat: Jefferson
Largest city: Ashtabula (20,962)
Second-largest city: Conneaut (12,485)
Per-capita income (2002) / ranking among Ohio counties: $23,335/60
Number of school districts (2005): 7

Employment base (2001):
Private sector: 85%
Public sector: 15%

Electoral history:
President (2004): Kerry (D) 53%; Bush (R) 46%
Governor (2002): Taft (R) 54%; Hagan (D) 42%

President (2000): Gore (D) 50%; Bush (R) 45%
Governor (1998): Taft (R) 50%; Fisher (D) 45%
President (1996): Clinton (D) 50%; Dole (R) 34%; Perot 15%
Governor (1994): Voinovich (R) 68%; Burch (D) 28%
President (1992): Clinton (D) 44%; Bush (R) 31%; Perot 25%
Governor (1990): Voinovich (R) 52%; Celebrezze (D) 48%
President (1988): Dukakis (D) 54%; Bush (R) 46%

Party affiliations of county administrative officeholders (2004): 6 Democrats; 5 Republicans

History:

On July 4, 1796, Moses Cleaveland and about 50 pioneers reached the mouth of Conneaut Creek and christened it Port Independence, believed to be the first settlement in the Western Reserve of northern Ohio. Other settlers followed from New York state and, in 1798, established Harpersfield, the first permanent village in the county. Ashtabula County was created from parts of Trumbull and Geauga counties. Gideon Granger, a large landowner and postmaster-general under President Thomas Jefferson, offered to build a courthouse and jail if the county seat were located in the township he named for the president. The courthouse was opened in Jefferson in 1811. A Congregational church, opened in 1801 in Austinburg, was the first church organized in the Western Reserve. In 1816, Ohio's first Episcopal parish was established in Ashtabula. The county was a center of antislavery activity, led by Joshua R. Giddings and Benjamin F. Wade, both of whom are buried in Jefferson. Betsy Cowles, a graduate of Oberlin College and a leader of the women's suffrage movement, presided at the National Suffrage Convention in Salem in 1850. Many of the county's early settlers were Connecticut Yankees. Although farming was the chief occupation, Conneaut and Ashtabula became important shipping ports for iron ore and coal. Platt R. Spencer of Geneva developed the Spencerian script style of penmanship, adopted by many of the nation's schools in the mid-1800s.

ATHENS COUNTY

Established: March 1, 1805
Named for: Athens, Greece
Land area: 507 square miles
Locale: about 60 miles southeast of Columbus
2000 Population: 62,223
White: 93.4%
Black: 2.4%
County seat: Athens
Largest city: Athens (21,342)
Second-largest city: Nelsonville (5,230)
Per-capita income (2002) / ranking among Ohio counties: $19,885/82
Number of school districts (2005): 5

Employment base (2001):
Private sector: 63%
Public sector: 37%

Electoral history:
President (2004): Kerry (D) 63%; Bush (R) 36%
Governor (2002): Hagan (D) 51%; Taft (R) 43%
President (2000): Gore (D) 52%; Bush (R) 38%
Governor (1998): Fisher (D) 52%; Taft (R) 40%
President (1996): Clinton (D) 56%; Dole (R) 30%; Perot 12%
Governor (1994): Voinovich (R) 56%; Burch (D) 40%
President (1992): Clinton (D) 52%; Bush (R) 28%; Perot 20%
Governor (1990): Celebrezze (D) 54%; Voinovich (R) 46%
President (1988): Dukakis (D) 54%; Bush (R) 46%

Party affiliations of county administrative officeholders (2004): 10 Democrats; 1 Republican

History:

Athens County, part of the original Ohio Company purchase, was formed from a portion of Washington County. Originally occupied by the Shawnee and Delaware tribes, the county was settled as the American Revolution was ending. Government land surveys began about 1785. In 1804, Manasseh Cutler and Rufus Putnam of Massachusetts—among the founders of the Ohio Company of Associates—led the effort to establish a university west of the Allegheny Mountains. American Western University, later named Ohio University, was the first university incorporated in Ohio. Two townships were set aside for the campus, and Athens grew up around the university. William Holmes McGuffey, one of the university's early presidents, wrote the McGuffey Reader books for children. Nelsonville, originally called English Town, was settled in 1814 by Daniel Nelson. It became a center of coal mining, especially after the Hocking Canal was completed to Nelsonville in 1840. The county was a center of antislavery activity and part of the Underground Railroad.

AUGLAIZE COUNTY

Established: February 14, 1848
Named for: Auglaize River ("fallen timbers")
Land area: 402 square miles
Locale: about 80 miles southwest of Toledo
2000 Population: 46,611
White: 97.9%
Black: 0.2%
County seat: Wapakoneta
Largest city: Wapakoneta (9,474)
Second-largest city: St. Marys (8,342)
Per-capita income (2002) / ranking among Ohio counties: $27,652/21
Number of school districts (2005): 6
Employment base (2001):
Private sector: 85%
Public sector: 15%

Electoral history:
President (2004): Bush (R) 74%; Kerry (D) 26%

Governor (2002): Taft (R) 71%; Hagan (D) 23%
President (2000): Bush (R) 69%; Gore (D) 28%
Governor (1998): Taft (R) 63%; Fisher (D) 31%
President (1996): Dole (R) 52%; Clinton (D) 34% Perot 13%
Governor (1994): Voinovich (R) 77%; Burch (D) 19%
President (1992): Bush (R) 52%; Clinton (D) 25%; Perot 24%
Governor (1990): Voinovich (R) 67%; Celebrezze (D) 33%
President (1988): Bush (R) 74%; Dukakis (D) 26%

Party affiliations of county administrative officeholders (2004):
9 Republicans; 2 Democrats

History:
The Miami and Shawnee tribes once occupied the land that became Auglaize County. About 1794, Gen. Anthony Wayne ordered the construction of Fort St. Marys as a supply depot. The fort and nearby Fort Amanda attracted settlers. In 1817, the area's tribes agreed to cede much of the region, except certain reservations. In 1831, the Shawnees were persuaded to sell their Wapakoneta reservation. Most of Auglaize County was formed from Mercer County. Residents of the new county chose Wapakoneta over St. Marys as the county seat. Most of the early pioneers were German Protestants; they were followed by German Catholics. Construction of the Miami & Erie Canal attracted many settlers, although there was much protest over the flooding of farmland during the 1843 construction of Grand Lake St. Marys as a reservoir for the canal. The county always has been primarily agricultural, although oil and natural-gas fields were developed in the 1880s and 1890s. Wapakoneta is the home of Neil Armstrong, the first man to walk on the moon (1969). The city is the home of the Neil Armstrong Air and Space Museum.

BELMONT COUNTY

Established: September 7, 1801
Named for: French for "beautiful mountain"
Land area: 541 square miles
Locale: on the Ohio River, about 100 miles east of Columbus
2000 Population: 70,226
 White: 94.8%
 Black: 3.5%
County seat: St. Clairsville
Largest city: Martins Ferry (7,226)
Second-largest city: St. Clairsville (5,057)
Per-capita income (2002) / ranking among Ohio counties: $23,390/59
Number of school districts (2005): 7
Employment base (2001):
Private sector: 83%
Public sector: 17%
Electoral history:
President (2004): Kerry (D) 53%; Bush (R) 47%
Governor (2002): Taft (R) 50%; Hagan (D) 46%

President (2000): Gore (D) 53%; Bush (R) 42%
Governor (1998): Fisher (D) 56%; Taft (R) 37%
President (1996): Clinton (D) 58%; Dole (R) 27%; Perot 15%
Governor (1994): Voinovich (R) 51%; Burch (D) 46%
President (1992): Clinton (D) 52%; Bush (R) 28%; Perot 20%
Governor (1990): Celebrezze (D) 61%; Voinovich (R) 39%
President (1988): Dukakis (D) 62%; Bush 38%

Party affiliations of county administrative officeholders (2004):
10 Democrats; 1 Republican

History:
The Delaware and Shawnee tribes inhabited the area that became Belmont County, one of Ohio's original counties formed September 7, 1801, by a proclamation from territorial governor Arthur St. Clair. During the Revolutionary War, Indians joined the British in the area to attack Fort Henry across the Ohio River at Wheeling, W.Va. The federal government, by the Ordinance of 1785, arranged for the survey of the Seven Ranges, which included Belmont County. In 1806, Ebenezer Zane platted a village and named it Canton; after the construction of a bridge over the river to Wheeling Island, the village was renamed Bridgeport. Many of Belmont County's first settlers were Pennsylvania Quakers, who had strong antislavery sentiments. One of them, Benjamin Lundy, formed the first abolitionist group in Ohio and published a newspaper, *The Genius for Universal Emancipation*. The first county courthouse was at Putney (now Shadyside), just south of Bellaire. Martins Ferry was named for a father and son who operated a ferry business on the river; it was the birthplace of novelist William Dean Howells. In 1804, the first state legislature decided that the county seat should be St. Clairsville, a central location named after St. Clair. Zane's Trace, the first important thoroughfare across Ohio, passed through Belmont County. On July 4, 1825, the construction of the first section of the National Road in Ohio began in St. Clairsville. The county became Ohio's leading coal-mining area, producing 10 million tons annually by 1913.

BROWN COUNTY

Established: March 1, 1818
Named for: Gen. Jacob Brown (War of 1812)
Land area: 494 square miles
Locale: on the Ohio River, about 35 miles east of Cincinnati
2000 Population: 42,285
 White: 98.0%
 Black: 0.8%
County seat: Georgetown
Largest city: none
Largest village: Georgetown (3,691)
Second-Largest village: Mount Orab (2,307)
Per-capita income (2002) / ranking among Ohio counties: $22,815/66

Number of school districts (2005): 5

Employment base (2001):
Private sector: 70%
Public sector: 30%

Electoral history:
President (2004): Bush (R) 64%; Kerry (D) 36%
Governor (2002): Taft (R) 68%; Hagan (D) 28%
President (2000): Bush (R) 61%; Gore (D) 36%
Governor (1998): Taft (R) 54%; Fisher (D) 40%
President (1996): Dole (R) 45%; Clinton (D) 41%; Perot 13%
Governor (1994): Voinovich (R) 72%; Burch (D) 24%
President (1992): Bush (R) 39%; Clinton (D) 37%; Perot 24%
Governor (1990): Voinovich (R) 53%; Celebrezze (D) 47%
President (1988): Bush (R) 60%; Dukakis (D) 40%

Party affiliations of county administrative officeholders (2004):
6 Republicans; 5 Democrats

History:

In 1792, Simon Kenton led a party of Kentuckians in battle against Indians, including Tecumseh, in what today is northern Brown County. Within three years, soldiers led by Gen. Anthony Wayne had driven out the Indians, and settlers began moving to this portion of the Virginia Military Tract. Many of the early settlers were Virginians and Irish. Aberdeen and Ripley, both on the Ohio River, were early settlements. Ripley became the first county seat and was the western terminus of Zane's Trace. Ripley became a commercial center, known for pork packing. In 1821, Georgetown was established as the permanent county seat. In the years preceding the Civil War, Ripley became an important stop on the Underground Railroad, chiefly because of the work of John Rankin, pastor of the local Presbyterian church. Harriet Beecher Stowe, author of *Uncle Tom's Cabin*, visited the Rankin house on the Ohio River and presumably gathered material there for the book. Ulysses S. Grant, the first Ohio-born president, moved with his family to Georgetown in 1823 and lived there until he entered West Point in 1839. After the Civil War, Brown County became an important tobacco-growing center.

BUTLER COUNTY

Established: May 1, 1803
Named for: Gen. Richard Butler (Revolutionary War)
Land area: 470 square miles
Locale: About 20 miles north of Cincinnati
2000 Population: 332,807
 White: 90.9%
 Black: 5.4%
County seat: Hamilton
Largest city: Hamilton (60,690)
Second-largest city: Middletown (49,574)
Per-capita income (2002) / ranking among Ohio counties: $29,415/16

Number of school districts (2005): 10

Employment base (2001):
Private sector: 85%
Public sector: 15%

Electoral history:
President (2004): Bush (R) 66%; Kerry (D) 34%
Governor (2002): Taft (R) 72%; Hagan (D) 24%
President (2000): Bush (R) 63%; Gore (D) 34%
Governor (1998): Taft (R) 62%; Fisher (D) 33%
President (1996): Dole (R) 55%; Clinton (D) 36%; Perot 9%
Governor (1994): Voinovich (R) 78%; Burch (D) 19%
President (1992): Bush (R) 49%; Clinton (D) 30%; Perot 21%
Governor (1990): Voinovich (R) 64%; Celebrezze (D) 36%
President (1988): Bush (R) 69%; Dukakis (D) 31%

Party affiliations of county administrative officeholders (2004):
11 Republicans

History:

In 1791, Gen. Arthur St. Clair supervised the construction of Fort Hamilton near the center of the area that became Butler County. Three years later, Gen. Anthony Wayne led his army to victory over Indians in the Battle of Fallen Timbers, and much of southwestern Ohio was opened for settlement. The lands east of the Great Miami River were part of the Symmes Purchase; those west of the river were part of the Congress Lands. In 1803, the state legislature created eight new counties, including Butler, out of Hamilton County. The first communities developed along the river and many of the early settlers were German and Welsh. In 1809, the state legislature authorized the establishment of Miami University at Oxford, a village named after the English university. In 1853, the Western College for Women—the first women's college in Ohio—was chartered. Hamilton and Middletown developed as important commercial centers along the Miami and Erie Canal. Middletown later became the home of American Rolling Mills (Armco), founded by George M. Verity.

CARROLL COUNTY

Established: January 1, 1833
Named for: Charles Carroll (a signer of the Declaration of Independence)
Land area: 398 square miles
Locale: about 40 miles southwest of Youngstown
2000 Population: 28,836
 White: 98.5%
 Black: 0.5%
County seat: Carrollton
Largest city: none
Largest village: Minerva (3,934)
Second-Largest village: Carrollton (3,190)
Per-capita income (2002) / ranking among Ohio counties:

$22,878/65
Number of school districts (2005): 2

Employment base (2001):
Private sector: 86%
Public sector: 14%

Electoral history:
President (2004): Bush (R) 55%; Kerry (D) 45%
Governor (2002): Taft (R) 60%; Hagan (D) 35%
President (2000): Bush (R) 55%; Gore (D) 40%
Governor (1998): Taft (R) 54%; Fisher (D) 41%
President (1996): Clinton (D) 41%; Dole (R) 38%; Perot 21%
Governor (1994): Voinovich (R) 62%; Burch (D) 35%
President (1992): Clinton (D) 38%; Bush (R) 34%; Perot 28%
Governor (1990): Voinovich (R) 54%; Celebrezze (D) 46%
President (1988): Bush (R) 57%; Dukakis (D) 43%

Party affiliations of county administrative officeholders (2004):
9 Republicans; 2 Democrats

History:

About 1810, German and Scotch-Irish settlers from Pennsylvania, Maryland, and Virginia began locating in the village that later became Carrollton. The area was part of the Seven Ranges, in which the federal government sold lots of 320 acres and larger. In 1832, the state legislature created Carroll County from portions of Columbiana, Harrison, Jefferson, Stark, and Tuscarawas counties. Carrollton, originally called Centreville, became the county seat and was incorporated in 1834. Agriculture and, later, mining became the county's chief industries. The county was home of one branch of the "Fighting McCooks," the families of brothers Daniel and John McCook, which together volunteered 16 men to the Union cause during the Civil War. Leesville, in the southwestern corner of the county, was an important stop on the Underground Railroad.

CHAMPAIGN COUNTY

Established: March 1, 1805
Named for: French for "a plain"
Land area: 430 square miles
Locale: about 40 miles northwest of Columbus
2000 Population: 38,890
 White: 96.0%
 Black: 1.9%
County seat: Urbana
Largest city: Urbana (11,613)
Second-largest city: none
Largest village: St. Paris (1,998)
Per-capita income (2002) / ranking among Ohio counties: $25,743/37
Number of school districts (2005): 5
Employment base (2001):
Private sector: 83%

Public sector: 17%

Electoral history:
President (2004): Bush (R) 62%; Kerry (D) 37%
Governor (2002): Taft (R) 67%; Hagan (D) 27%
President (2000): Bush (R) 59%; Gore (D) 38%
Governor (1998): Taft (R) 55%; Fisher (D) 37%
President (1996): Dole (R) 44%; Clinton (D) 40%; Perot 15%
Governor (1994): Voinovich (R) 76%; Burch (D) 21%
President (1992): Bush (R) 43%; Clinton (D) 32%; Perot 25%
Governor (1990): Voinovich (R) 67%; Celebrezze (D) 33%
President (1988): Bush (R) 68%; Dukakis (D) 32%

Party affiliations of county administrative officeholders (2004):
11 Republicans

History:

The area that is now Champaign County originally was occupied by Shawnee and Wyandot Indians. White settlement began after an army led by Gen. George Rogers Clark defeated the Indians in the Battle of Piqua in 1780. In 1805, the village of Urbana was laid out by Col. William Ward, a Virginian. The same year, the state legislature created Champaign County from Franklin and Greene counties. The eastern third of the county had been part of the Virginia Military District; the western two-thirds was in the Congress Lands. During the War of 1812, Urbana was a base of operations for the Ohio militia led by Gen. William Hull before its march to Detroit. One of the first settlers in Champaign County was Joseph C. Vance, whose son Joseph Vance became Ohio's 13th governor (from 1836 to 1838). Urbana's John Quincy Adams Ward, grandson of William Ward, became one of the nation's greatest sculptors. The Church of the New Jerusalem (followers of Emanuel Swedenborg) made Urbana its Midwest center and, in 1850, founded Urbana College. Champaign County became one of Ohio's leading grain- and livestock-producing counties. The county is the burial place of Indian scout and frontiersman Simon Kenton and of Richard Stanhope, the valet of George Washington.

CLARK COUNTY

Established: March 1, 1818
Named for: Gen. George Rogers Clark
Land area: 401 square miles
Locale: about 45 miles west of Columbus
2000 Population: 144,742
 White: 88.2%
 Black: 8.8%
County seat: Springfield
Largest city: Springfield (65,358)
Second-largest city: New Carlisle (5,735)
Per-capita income (2002) / ranking among Ohio counties: $26,159/33
Number of school districts (2005): 7

Employment base (2001):
Private sector: 87%
Public sector: 13%

Electoral history:
President (2004): Bush (R) 51%; Kerry (D) 49%
Governor (2002): Taft (R) 61%; Hagan (D) 33%
President (2000): Gore (D) 49%; Bush (R) 48%
Governor (1998): Taft (R) 49%; Fisher (D) 44%
President (1996): Clinton (D) 48%; Dole (R) 39%; Perot 12%
Governor (1994): Voinovich (R) 71%; Burch (D) 25%
President (1992): Clinton (D) 42%; Bush (R) 38%; Perot 20%
Governor (1990): Voinovich (R) 59%; Celebrezze (D) 41%
President (1988): Bush (R) 58%; Dukakis (D) 42%

Party affiliations of county administrative officeholders (2004):
8 Democrats; 3 Republicans

History:

The area that became Clark County was inhabited by pre-Columbian people who left behind many burial mounds, stone weapons, pottery, pipes, and other implements. Pioneers of the 1770s and 1780s found the area occupied by the Shawnee, Delaware, Mingo, and Wyandot tribes. Tecumseh, the great Shawnee chief, is believed to have been born in what is now Clark County. After the Battle of Piqua (1780) removed the Indian threat, pioneers from Kentucky settled Springfield at the confluence of Mad River and Buck Creek; it was platted in 1801. In 1818, Clark County was formed from Greene and Madison counties. When the National Road was completed through Ohio in 1840, Springfield—on a direct line between Columbus and Indian-apolis —blossomed as an important commercial and agricultural center. In 1845, the Lutheran Church chartered Wittenberg College in Springfield as a theological seminary for training ministers. Several area inventors obtained patents for threshing machinery, including William N. Whitely, creator of Champion mowers and reapers. Champion Binder Co. was later acquired by International Harvester Co., based in Springfield. Ohio's 40th governor, Asa S. Bushnell (1896–1900), was a resident of Springfield. In 1902, Springfield schoolteacher A.B. Graham founded the 4-H (head, heart, hand, and health) Clubs to teach youngsters sound farming practices and home management.

CLERMONT COUNTY

Established: December 6, 1800
Named for: Province of Clermont, France
Land area: 459 square miles
Locale: about 20 miles east of Cincinnati
2000 Population: 177,977
 White: 97.2%
 Black: 0.9%
County seat: Batavia
Largest city: Loveland (11,677)
Second-largest city: Milford (6,284)
Per-capita income (2002) / ranking among Ohio counties: $29,638/14
Number of school districts (2005): 9

Employment base (2001):
Private sector: 87%
Public sector: 13%

Electoral history:
President (2004): Bush (R) 71%; Kerry (D) 29%
Governor (2002): Taft (R) 75%; Hagan (D) 21%
President (2000): Bush (R) 67%; Gore (D) 30%
Governor (1998): Taft (R) 66%; Fisher (D) 29%
President (1996): Dole (R) 57%; Clinton (D) 33%; Perot 9%
Governor (1994): Voinovich (R) 80%; Burch (D) 16%
President (1992): Bush (R) 50%; Clinton (D) 28%; Perot 22%
Governor (1990): Voinovich (R) 64%; Celebrezze (D) 36%
President (1988): Bush (R) 71%; Dukakis (D) 29%

Party affiliations of county administrative officeholders (2004):
11 Republicans

History:

All of today's Clermont County was part of the Virginia Military District, created to reward Virginians for their service in the Revolutionary War. Other early settlers came from Kentucky, Maryland, and Pennsylvania. Bethel and Williamsburg—occupied before Clermont County was carved from Hamilton County in 1800—were among the earliest settlements. Williamsburg was the first county seat but, in 1824, was replaced by Batavia. Prosperity in the primarily agricultural county was tied to boat traffic along the Ohio River. Antislavery sentiment was strong. Moscow and New Richmond, both on the river, were points of entry into the Ohio net-work of the Underground Railroad. Ulysses S. Grant, the 18th pres-ident, was born April 27, 1822, in Point Pleasant. In 1844, a Fourierite association was formed in the village of Utopia. Fourierism was a short-lived movement based on the doctrines of François Marie Charles Fourier, a French socialist-reformer who espoused organizing society by small, cooperative agricultural com-munities. John M. Pattison, Ohio's 43rd governor, was born near Owensville in 1847.

CLINTON COUNTY

Established: March 1, 1810
Named for: George Clinton (vice president when county was formed)
Land area: 413 square miles
Locale: about 40 miles northeast of Cincinnati
2000 Population: 40,543
 White: 95.8%
 Black: 2.1%
County seat: Wilmington
Largest city: Wilmington (11,921)
Second-largest city: none
Largest village: Blanchester (4,220)
Per-capita income (2002) / ranking among Ohio counties: $25,441/38
Number of school districts (2005): 4

Employment base (2001):
Private sector: 87%
Public sector: 13%

Electoral history:
President (2004): Bush (R) 70%; Kerry (D) 29%
Governor (2002): Taft (R) 71%; Hagan (D) 24%
President (2000): Bush (R) 65%; Gore (D) 32%
Governor (1998): Taft (R) 64%; Fisher (D) 32%
President (1996): Dole (R) 52%; Clinton (D) 37%; Perot 11%
Governor (1994): Voinovich (R) 79%; Burch (D) 18%
President (1992): Bush (R) 48%; Clinton (D) 30%; Perot 22%
Governor (1990): Voinovich (R) 67%; Celebrezze (D) 33%
President (1988): Bush (R) 70%; Dukakis (D) 30%

Party affiliations of county administrative officeholders (2004):
11 Republicans

History:

The area that became Clinton County originally was part of the Virginia Military District. Besides Virginia, pioneers arrived from Pennsylvania, Kentucky, and North Carolina. The county was formed from portions of Ross and Warren counties. Many of the early settlers were Quakers—members of the Religious Society of Friends. The Quakers established the county's first church in 1806. Wilmington, the county seat, was named after the seaport city in North Carolina. The Quakers were fierce opponents of slavery, and Wilmington became a station along the Underground Railroad. In 1870, the Religious Society of Friends purchased Franklin College and reorganized it into Wilmington College. In the 1890s, Sabina became a center of Methodist activity with establishment of the Methodist State Conference Grounds. Clinton County always has been a prime agricultural county, with significant production of grains and livestock.

COLUMBIANA COUNTY

Established: May 1, 1803
Named for: Christopher Columbus and Queen Anna
Land area: 535 square miles
Locale: borders Pennsylvania about 20 miles south of Youngstown
2000 Population: 112,075
 White: 96.0%
 Black: 2.1%
County seat: Lisbon
Largest city: East Liverpool (13,089)
Second-largest city: Salem (12,197)
Per-capita income (2002) / ranking among Ohio counties: $22,771/67
Number of school districts (2005): 11

Employment base (2001):
Private sector: 86%
Public sector: 14%

Electoral history:
President (2004): Bush (R) 52%; Kerry (D) 47%
Governor (2002): Taft (R) 59% Hagan (D) 37%
President (2000): Bush (R) 49%; Gore (D) 47%
Governor (1998): Taft (R) 48%; Fisher (D) 45%
President (1996): Clinton (D) 47%; Dole (R) 35%; Perot 16%
Governor (1994): Voinovich (R) 61%; Burch (D) 35%
President (1992): Clinton (D) 42%; Bush (R) 32%; Perot 27%
Governor (1990): Voinovich (R) 52%; Celebrezze (D) 48%
President (1988): Bush (R) 50%; Dukakis (D) 50%

Party affiliations of county administrative officeholders (2004):
6 Republicans; 5 Democrats

History:

The southern edge of what now is Columbiana County was part of the Seven Ranges, the first Congress Lands to be surveyed and sold. The federal government had a public sale of Seven Ranges land in 1788. In 1797, William Wells of Pennsylvania, the first permanent settler, established Wellsville; other Pennsylvanians soon followed. In 1802, Lewis Kinney settled New Lisbon, which became the county seat and later was renamed Lisbon. In 1803, the state legislature formed Columbiana County from a portion of Jefferson County. In 1808, the *Ohio Patriot* first was published as a German-language newspaper. East Liverpool, originally called Fawcettstown, was settled by Thomas Fawcett and laid out in 1816. Many of the county's early pioneers were Germans, Scotch-Irish, and Quakers. The latter group settled Salem, which became a center of antislavery activity. In 1840, Englishman James Bennett arrived and became East Liverpool's first potter. The city, with rich clay deposits, later became a national center of the pottery industry. The Sandy-Beaver Canal was completed through the county in

1848 but was unsuccessful. In April 1850, the state's first Women's Rights Convention was held in the Second Baptist Church in Salem. In July 1863, Confederate general John Morgan and about 360 men under his command were captured just south of Lisbon. Columbiana County was the birthplace of Harvey S. Firestone, founder of Firestone Tire and Rubber; Marcus A. Hanna, millionaire industrialist, Republican political boss, and U.S. senator; and Clement L. Vallandigham, leader of Ohio's Peace Democrats during the Civil War era.

COSHOCTON COUNTY

Established: January 31, 1810
Named for: Delaware Indian word "union of waters"
Land area: 567 square miles
Locale: about 70 miles northeast of Columbus
2000 Population: 36,665
 White: 97.2%
 Black: 0.9%
County seat: Coshocton
Largest city: Coshocton (11,682)
Second-largest city: none
Largest village: West Lafayette (2,313)
Per-capita income (2002) / ranking among Ohio counties: $23,206/61
Number of school districts (2005): 3

Employment base (2001):
Private sector: 87%
Public sector: 13%

Electoral history:
President (2004): Bush (R) 57%; Kerry (D) 43%
Governor (2002): Taft (R) 67%; Hagan (D) 29%
President (2000): Bush (R) 58%; Gore (D) 39%
Governor (1998): Taft (R) 57%; Fisher (D) 37%
President (1996): Dole (R) 42%; Clinton (D) 42%; Perot 15%
Governor (1994): Voinovich (R) 67%; Burch (D) 27%
President (1992): Clinton (D) 39%; Bush (R) 36%; Perot 26%
Governor (1990): Voinovich (R) 53%; Celebrezze (D) 47%
President (1988): Bush (R) 58%; Dukakis (D) 42%

Party affiliations of county administrative officeholders (2004):
8 Republicans; 3 Democrats

History:
In the early 1700s, the lands that became Coshocton County were occupied by Delaware Indians. In the 1730s, a white child named Mary Harris was carried off by the Indians and later became the wife of a chief. This and other tales were recorded in 1750 in the diary of Christopher Gist, a representative of the Ohio Land Company of Virginia who encountered the Delawares at Coshocton. The area was part of the U.S. Military Tract, reserved by Congress to reward

Revolutionary War veterans. The Walhonding River is said to be named for the "white woman." In 1781, the Delawares were driven off and their villages destroyed by an expedition led by Col. Andrew Brodhead. The Indians ceded the territory in 1785, when a treaty was arranged with several tribes at Fort McIntosh in western Pennsylvania. Permanent settlements were made in the 1790s. Two decades later, the state legislature, meeting in Zanesville, formed Coshocton County out of Muskingum County. Coshocton County did not flourish until the Ohio & Erie Canal was completed in the 1830s; Coshocton, Roscoe, and many other villages then became busy trade centers.

CRAWFORD COUNTY

Established: April 1, 1820
Named for: Col. William Crawford
Land area: 403 square miles
Locale: about 60 miles north of Columbus
2000 Population: 46,966
 White: 97.7%
 Black: 0.7%
County seat: Bucyrus
Largest city: Bucyrus (13,224)
Second-largest city: Galion (11,341)
Per-capita income (2002) / ranking among Ohio counties: $23,721/57
Number of school districts (2005): 6

Employment base (2001):
Private sector: 87%
Public sector: 13%

Electoral history:
President (2004): Bush (R) 64%; Kerry (D) 36%
Governor (2002): Taft (R) 66%; Hagan (D) 29%
President (2000): Bush (R) 61%; Gore (D) 35%
Governor (1998): Taft (R) 55%; Fisher (D) 37%
President (1996): Dole (R) 44%; Clinton (D) 38%; Perot 16%
Governor (1994): Voinovich (R) 76%; Burch (D) 20%
President (1992): Bush (R) 42%; Clinton (D) 31%; Perot 28%
Governor (1990): Voinovich (R) 62%; Celebrezze (D) 38%
President (1988): Bush (R) 67%; Dukakis (D) 33%

Party affiliations of county administrative officeholders (2004):
6 Republicans; 4 Democrats; 1 Independent

History:
In June 1782, Col. William Crawford led an unsuccessful expedition against Indians in the Sandusky Valley area. In retreat, he is said to have broken his sword and dropped it in a creek that since has been called Broken Sword Creek. Sword pieces, unearthed in 1889 and believed to be Crawford's, are on display in an Upper Sandusky museum in Wyandot County. The Indians began ceding lands to the federal government in the early 1800s. In 1820, Crawford County

was one of 14 counties created by the state legislature. Early settlement occurred primarily in the eastern portion of the county because Wyandot and Delaware reservations were in the western section, known for cranberry bogs and marshes. The Wyandots were the last Indians to leave the county—about 1843. Many early settlers were Pennsylvania Germans. Bucyrus was platted in 1822 and Galion in 1831. The Galion name became known worldwide for the brand of heavy road machinery produced in that city. Crestline, platted in 1851 as Livingston, acquired the later name from its location on the crest of the watershed that divides the waters flowing north to Lake Erie from those flowing south to the Ohio River.

CUYAHOGA COUNTY

Established: June 7, 1807
Named for: Cuyahoga River (Indian word "crooked")
Land area: 457 square miles
Locale: on Lake Erie, encompassing Cleveland
2000 Population: 1,393,978
 White: 67.4%
 Black: 27.3%
County seat: Cleveland
Largest city: Cleveland (478,403)
Second-largest city: Parma (85,655)
Per-capita income (2002) / ranking among Ohio counties: $33,382/4
Number of school districts (2005): 31

Employment base (2001):
Private sector: 89%
Public sector: 11%

Electoral history:
President (2004): Kerry (D) 67%; Bush (R) 33%
Governor (2002): Hagan (D) 60%; Taft (R) 38%
President (2000): Gore (D) 63%; Bush (R) 33%
Governor (1998): Fisher (D) 58%; Taft (R) 38%
President (1996): Clinton (D) 61%; Dole (R) 29%; Perot 9%
Governor (1994): Voinovich (R) 71%; Burch (D) 27%
President (1992): Clinton (D) 53%; Bush (R) 29%; Perot 18%
Governor (1990): Voinovich (R) 51%; Celebrezze (D) 49%
President (1988): Dukakis (D) 59%; Bush (R) 41%

Party affiliations of county administrative officeholders (2004):
11 Democrats

History:

In 1796, Moses Cleaveland, an agent for the Connecticut Land Company, led the first group of surveyors to the Western Reserve. They reached the mouth of the Cuyahoga River on July 22, 1796, and soon began surveying the land into lots. Cleaveland Township (the name later was shortened to Cleveland) was the first township established, followed by Euclid Township. The land east of the Cuyahoga River was settled first, after arrangements had been made with the Iroquois Indians. Settlement was slow until after the War of 1812

because the British had control of the Great Lakes and trade with the Indians. Even after American victory, development was hampered by a lack of easy transportation. A major breakthrough occurred when the state legislature chose Cleveland as the northern terminus of the Ohio & Erie Canal, completed from Portsmouth to Cleveland in 1833. Coupled with the opening of New York's Erie Canal in 1825, completion of Ohio's canal system provided the stimulus for Cleveland to grow into one of the world's leading lakeports and industrial centers. In 1834, the Cuyahoga Steam Furnace Company—the county's first foundry—was chartered. In 1843, the legislature set Cuyahoga County's boundaries in their present form. Combining to propel the county were Cleveland's position on the waterways, the city's location between the iron ores of the Lake Superior region and the blast furnaces of the Ohio Valley, and the development of railroads. By 1900, Cuyahoga surpassed Hamilton County to become Ohio's most populous county; it also was the most ethnically diverse. John D. Rockefeller had incorporated Standard Oil in 1870 in Cleveland; by 1890, the company monopolized American oil production. Cleveland became a center for oil refining, steelmaking, shipbuilding, automobile manufacturing, paint production, and many other basic industries. Although noted for its many cultural and educational attributes, Cuyahoga County through the 20th century was known chiefly as an industrial dynamo.

DARKE COUNTY

Established: January 3, 1809
Named for: Gen. William Darke (Revolutionary War)
Land area: 600 square miles
Locale: borders Indiana, 30 miles northwest of Dayton
2000 Population: 53,309
 White: 98.1%
 Black: 0.3%
County seat: Greenville
Largest city: Greenville (13,294)
Second Largest city: none
Largest village: Versailles (2,589)
Per-capita income (2002) / ranking among Ohio counties: $26,042/34
Number of school districts (2005): 7

Employment base (2001):
Private sector: 89%
Public sector: 11%

Electoral history:
President (2004): Bush (R) 70%; Kerry (D) 30%
Governor (2002): Taft (R) 71%; Hagan (D) 24%
President (2000): Bush (R) 64%; Gore (D) 33%
Governor (1998): Taft (R) 57%; Fisher (D) 36%
President (1996): Dole (R) 47%; Clinton (D) 39%; Perot 14%
Governor (1994): Voinovich (R) 76%; Burch (D) 21%
President (1992): Bush (R) 46%; Clinton (D) 29%; Perot 26%
Governor (1990): Voinovich (R) 63%; Celebrezze (D) 37%
President (1988): Bush (R) 69%; Dukakis (D) 31%

Party affiliations of county administrative officeholders (2004):
9 Republicans; 2 Democrats

History:

In 1793, Gen. Anthony Wayne supervised the construction of Fort Greene Ville, a 50-acre stockade, on the present site of Greenville. The fort was among a string of fortifications built in the heart of Ohio's Indian country to provide the U.S. Army with bases of operations and supplies during the Indian wars. Greenville was named for Gen. Nathaniel Greene, under whom Wayne had served in the Revolutionary War. In August 1795, the fort was the site of the signing of the Treaty of Greene Ville, which established a barrier to separate the Indian tribes from the white settlers. The boundary ran from the Cuyahoga and Tuscarawas rivers in northeastern Ohio to a point near Fort Recovery in what now is Mercer County, reserving a large section of northwestern Ohio for the Indians. The treaty opened for settlement the area that today is Darke County. Townships were laid out after 1800. In 1809, the legislature divided Miami County to provide for the creation of Darke County, although it was not organized until 1817. The county contained much swampland, which was cleared to provide some of Ohio's richest agricultural soils. Among the county's most famous natives was Annie Moses, who became known as Annie Oakley, the world's best sharpshooter. She died in 1926 at age 66.

DEFIANCE COUNTY

Established: April 7, 1845
Named for: Fort Defiance
Land area: 414 square miles
Locale: borders Indiana, about 50 miles southwest of Toledo
2000 Population: 39,500
 White: 92.3%
 Black: 1.6%
County seat: Defiance
Largest city: Defiance (16,465)
Second-largest city: none
Largest village: Hicksville (3,649)
Per-capita income (2002) / ranking among Ohio counties: $26,259/32
Number of school districts (2005): 5

Employment base (2001):
Private sector: 89%
Public sector: 11%

Electoral history:
President (2004): Bush (R) 62%; Kerry (D) 38%
Governor (2002): Taft (R) 66%; Hagan (D) 30%
President (2000): Bush (R) 59%; Gore (D) 38%
Governor (1998): Taft (R) 55%; Fisher (D) 39%
President (1996): Dole (R) 47%; Clinton (D) 40%; Perot 12%
Governor (1994): Voinovich (R) 74%; Burch (D) 22%
President (1992): Bush (R) 42%; Clinton (D) 34%; Perot 24%

Governor (1990): Voinovich (R) 60%; Celebrezze (D) 40%
President (1988): Bush (R) 64%; Dukakis (D) 36%

Party affiliations of county administrative officeholders (2004):
11 Republicans

History:

In August 1794, the army of Gen. Anthony Wayne constructed Fort Defiance near the confluence of the Auglaize and Maumee rivers. Wayne is said to have named the fort in defiance of Indian and British threats against it. The next year, the Treaty of Greene Ville stated that Fort Defiance would remain a government preserve within territory otherwise granted to the Indians. The fort eventually was abandoned, but the village of Fort Defiance was laid out near the site in 1822—five years after the Indians ceded the territory to the government. When Williams County was organized in the 1820s, Fort Defiance became the county seat, remaining so until 1840, when Bryan was selected. In 1836, the village was renamed Defiance. In 1845, the legislature created Defiance County from Williams, Paulding, and Henry counties; Defiance was chosen the county seat. Originally part of Ohio's Black Swamp region, the county is known for its rich black loam soils. Among the county's early settlers were many Germans and some Irish. The 1840s brought completion of the Miami & Erie Canal, which passed through Defiance, spurring its development. In 1850, Defiance Female Seminary was founded; it was reorganized in 1903 as Defiance College.

DELAWARE COUNTY

Established: April 1, 1808
Named for: Delaware Indians
Land area: 458 square miles
Locale: about 20 miles north of Columbus
2000 Population: 109,989
 White: 94.2%
 Black: 2.5%
County seat: Delaware
Largest city: Delaware (25,243)
Second-largest city: none
Largest village: Powell (6,247)
Per-capita income (2002) / ranking among Ohio counties: $42,419/1
Number of school districts (2005): 4

Employment base (2001):
Private sector: 87%
Public sector: 13%

Electoral history:
President (2004): Bush (R) 66%; Kerry (D) 34%
Governor (2002): Taft (R) 72%; Hagan (D) 24%
President (2000): Bush (R) 66%; Gore (D) 31%
Governor (1998): Taft (R) 63%; Fisher (D) 30%
President (1996): Dole (R) 58%; Clinton (D) 33%; Perot 8%
Governor (1994): Voinovich (R) 78%; Burch (D) 17%

President (1992): Bush (R) 50%; Clinton (D) 25%; Perot 25%
Governor (1990): Voinovich (R) 58%; Celebrezze (D) 42%
President (1988): Bush (R) 73%; Dukakis (D) 27%

Party affiliations of county administrative officeholders (2004):
11 Republicans

History:

Delaware and Wyandot Indians lived in the area that became Delaware County. About 1800, white pioneers came up the Scioto River to enter the area, most of which was part of the U.S. Military District; a western slice, west of the Scioto River, was in the Virginia Military District. The Scioto Trail, an old Indian path between the Scioto and Olentangy rivers, was followed by some of the pioneers. Liberty Township, in southernmost Delaware County, was laid out in 1801. Many of the early settlers were from Connecticut, Pennsylvania, and New York. Radnor, in the northwestern part of the county, was a Welsh settlement. The village of Delaware was platted on May 9, 1808, and became the county seat; it was incorporated in 1816. Chief Leatherlips, the legendary Wyandot chief, is said to have lived in the Olentangy Caverns. Rutherford B. Hayes, the 19th president, was born in Delaware on October 4, 1822. In the 1830s, Delaware was known as a resort town because of its mineral springs. In 1842, Methodists founded Ohio Wesleyan University, which became coed in 1877 when it merged with Ohio Wesleyan Female College (founded in 1853). Mansion House, one of the resorts, was the first building on the Ohio Wesleyan campus. Since 1980, the county's population has been the fastest-growing in the state; the southern part of Delaware County has become part of suburban Columbus.

ERIE COUNTY

Established: March 15, 1838
Named for: Erie Indians
Land area: 259 square miles
Locale: on Lake Erie, about 40 miles west of Cleveland
2000 Population: 79,551
  White: 88.5%
  Black: 8.6%
County seat: Sandusky
Largest city: Sandusky (27,844)
Second-largest city: Huron (7,958)
Per-capita income (2002) / ranking among Ohio counties:
$30,155/11
Number of school districts (2005): 6

Employment base:
Private sector: 86%
Public sector: 14%

Electoral history:
President (2004): Kerry (D) 53%; Bush (R) 46%
Governor (2002): Taft (R) 55%; Hagan (D) 43%
President (2000): Gore (D) 51%; Bush (R) 46%

Governor: (1998): Fisher (D) 49%; Taft (R) 48%
President (1996): Clinton (D) 50%; Dole (R) 36%; Perot 13%
Governor (1994): Voinovich (R) 70%; Burch (D) 28%
President (1992): Clinton (D) 41%; Bush (R) 35%; Perot 24%
Governor (1990): Voinovich (R) 56%; Celebrezze (D) 44%
President (1988): Bush (R) 52%; Dukakis (D) 48%

Party affiliations of county administrative officeholders (2004):
8 Democrats; 3 Republicans

History:

The Erie, Wyandot, and Iroquois Indians occupied the natural harbors of Sandusky Bay and the mouth of the Huron River—where, in the 1760s, the French established a trading post. The Indians ceded their lands in 1805, and settlements soon dotted the lakeshore and riverbanks. In 1792, the Connecticut legislature had set aside 500,000 acres of the Western Reserve—the Firelands—to compensate people whose property was destroyed by fire from British raids on Connecticut towns during the Revolutionary War. The village of Sandusky was founded in 1818; it became the county seat after Erie County was formed in 1838 from Huron and Sandusky counties. Sandusky became an important shipping and fishing center but—in the 1830s—lost out to Cleveland and Toledo when the legislature chose lakefront sites as canal-system termination points. In the 1850s, Sandusky was a station on the Underground Railroad. During the Civil War, Johnson's Island (formerly Bull's Island) was a prison site for Confederate officers. Jay Cooke, the Civil War financier, was born in Sandusky in 1821. Inventor Thomas A. Edison was born in Milan in 1847. In the mid-1800s, German immigrants developed breweries and wineries in the county; Kelleys Island became known for its vineyards. In 1888, the state opened the Ohio Soldiers and Sailors Home in Sandusky.

FAIRFIELD COUNTY

Established: December 9, 1800
Named for: the area's "fair fields"
Land area: 508 square miles
Locale: about 15 miles southeast of Columbus
2000 Population: 122,759
  White: 95.1%
  Black: 2.6%
County seat: Lancaster
Largest city: Lancaster (35,355)
Second-largest city: Pickerington (9,792)
Per-capita income (2002) / ranking among Ohio counties:
$28,786/18
Number of school districts (2005): 8

Employment base:
Private sector: 79%
Public sector: 21%

Electoral history:
President (2004): Bush (R) 63%; Kerry (D) 37%

Governor (2002): Taft (R) 68%; Hagan (D) 27%
President (2000): Bush (R) 62%; Gore (D) 35%
Governor (1998): Taft (R) 58%; Fisher (D) 36%
President (1996): Dole (R) 53%; Clinton (D) 37%; Perot 9%
Governor (1994): Voinovich (R) 75%; Burch (D) 21%
President (1992): Bush (R) 48%; Clinton (D) 28%; Perot 24%
Governor (1990): Voinovich (R) 58%; Celebrezze (D) 42%
President (1988): Bush (R) 70%; Dukakis (D) 30%

Party affiliations of county administrative officeholders (2004):
11 Republicans

History:

Road-builder Ebenezer Zane laid out the village of New Lancaster in 1800 at the place where his pathway crossed the Hockhocking (later Hocking) River. The area formerly was occupied by Wyandot Indians. Later that year, territorial governor Arthur St. Clair issued a proclamation authorizing the creation of Fairfield County, most of which was within the Congress Lands. Because of the heavy traffic on Zane's Trace, New Lancaster (later Lancaster) developed rapidly and became the county seat. In the early years of statehood, Fairfield County supplied a large number of Ohio's political leaders. Many of the area's early residents were Germans from Pennsylvania, and German was taught in some schools. In 1820, the creation of adjacent counties reduced Fairfield to its current size. In the 1830s, Fairfield County flourished with the completion of the Ohio & Erie Canal, which made the Lancaster area an important transportation link between Lake Erie and the Ohio River. Buckeye Lake, in the northeastern part of the county, was built to furnish water for the canal. Gen. William Tecumseh Sherman, the Civil War hero, was born in Lancaster.

FAYETTE COUNTY

Established: March 1, 1810
Named for: Marquis de LaFayette
Land area: 407 square miles
Locale: about 40 miles southwest of Columbus
2000 Population: 28,433
  White: 95.7%
  Black: 2.1%
County seat: Washington Court House
Largest city: Washington Court House (13,524)
Second-largest city: none
Largest village: Jeffersonville (1,288)
Per-capita income (2002) / ranking among Ohio counties:
$24,964/46
Number of school districts (2005): 2

Employment base (2001):
Private sector: 86%
Public sector: 14%

Electoral history:

President (2004): Bush (R) 63%; Kerry (D) 37%
Governor (2002): Taft (R) 67%; Hagan (D) 28%
President (2000): Bush (R) 61%; Gore (D) 36%
Governor (1998): Taft (R) 58%; Fisher (D) 36%
President (1996): Dole (R) 50%; Clinton (D) 38%; Perot 11%
Governor (1994): Voinovich (R) 77%; Burch (D) 19%
President (1992): Bush (R) 49%; Clinton (D) 30%; Perot 21%
Governor (1990): Voinovich (R) 65%; Celebrezze (D) 35%
President (1988): Bush (R) 70%; Dukakis (D) 30%

Party affiliations of county administrative officeholders (2004):
11 Republicans

History:

Fayette County is within the old Virginia Military District, reserved by Virginia for land grants to the commonwealth's Revolutionary War veterans. The Virginia influence has been evident since the county was formed from Ross and Highland counties. Many of the early settlers were of Scotch-Irish descent. Bloomingburg was the first county seat in 1810; two years later, the designation went to Washington Court House. It was Virginian custom to add "court house" to the name of county seats. Washington Court House is the only county seat in Ohio with such a title. Without a major waterway, Fayette County was slow to develop; the area always has been primarily agricultural, known for horse breeding, Hereford cattle, and other livestock. Its courthouse—opened May 1, 1885,—is one of the most distinctive in the state. The corridor walls contain murals painted by Archibald M. Willard, creator of *The Spirit of '76*; the murals are *The Spirit of the U.S. Mail*, *The Spirit of Electricity*, and *The Spirit of the Telegraph*. Fayette County was the home of Harry Daugherty, U.S. attorney general under President Warren G. Harding.

FRANKLIN COUNTY

Established: April 30, 1803
Named for: Benjamin Franklin
Land area: 543 square miles
Locale: near the center of the state, encompassing Columbus
2000 Population: 1,068,978
  White: 75.5%
  Black: 17.6%
County seat: Columbus
Largest city: Columbus (711,470)
Second-largest city: Westerville (35,318)
Per-capita income (2002) / ranking among Ohio counties:
$32,947/5
Number of school districts (2005): 16

Employment base:
Private sector: 86%
Public sector: 14%

Electoral history:

President (2004): Kerry (D) 54%; Bush (R) 45%
Governor (2002): Taft (R) 57%; Hagan (D) 39%
President (2000): Gore (D) 49%; Bush (R) 48%
Governor (1998): Taft (R) 49%; Fisher (D) 45%
President (1996): Clinton (D) 48%; Dole (R) 45%; Perot 6%
Governor (1994): Voinovich (R) 70%; Burch (D) 26%
President (1992): Bush (R) 42%; Clinton (D) 40%; Perot 18%
Governor (1990): Voinovich (R) 54%; Celebrezze (D) 46%
President (1988): Bush (R) 61%; Dukakis (D) 39%

Party affiliations of county administrative officeholders (2004):
7 Republicans; 4 Democrats

History:

In August 1797, Lucas Sullivant, a Kentuckian who surveyed lands for the Virginia Military District, laid out the town of Franklinton on the west bank of the Scioto River. Until then, the area had been occupied mostly by Wyandot Indians, along with some Delawares and Mingoes. In 1803, the first state legislature created Franklin County with Franklinton as the county seat. The county also included lands that were part of the U.S. Military District and the Congress Lands. In 1804, Col. James Kilbourne founded the town of Worthington. In 1812, the legislature chose Columbus as the state capital. A four-man syndicate had offered to build a statehouse and a penitentiary, each on ten-acre lots, for $50,000—and to have them ready by December 1, 1817. The new capitol building was on the southwest corner of State and High streets. State offices were relocated from Chillicothe to Columbus on October 1, 1816. Earlier that year, the legislature had authorized the creation of the borough of Columbus. In 1824, Columbus was chosen the county seat and, ten years later, incorporated as a city. The selection of Columbus as the state capital—with its location near the center of Ohio, on the National Road, and at the confluence of the Olentangy and Scioto rivers—assured that Franklin would become one of the state's major counties. In 1838, the legislature approved the construction of a new statehouse. A commission adopted a plan for a Greek Revival style of architecture with Doric columns. Construction began in 1839 and was completed in 1861. A Judiciary Annex was added between 1899 to 1901. Beginning in the Civil War era, Franklin County became the site of several military camps. In 1861, on the western edge of Columbus, Camp Chase was established as a training ground for recruits; it was used as a prison for captured Confederates. In 1863, the development of Fort Hayes—as a national armory and arsenal—began on an 80-acre section of northeastern Columbus. In 1873, the Ohio Agricultural and Mechanical College—the forerunner of Ohio State University—was established on the Neil farm north of the city. In 1909, Westerville became the "dry capital" of America when the Anti-Saloon League set up its headquarters. Battelle Memorial Institute, the largest private research organization in the world, was established in Columbus in 1929. In the 1930s, the Pontifical College Josephinum, a seminary for Catholic priests under direct control of the pope, was moved to Worthington; it had originated in 1870 as an orphanage in Pomeroy.

FULTON COUNTY

Established: April 1, 1850
Named for: Robert Fulton, steamboat inventor
Land area: 407 square miles
Locale: borders Michigan, about 15 miles west of Toledo
2000 Population: 42,084
 White: 95.6%
 Black: 0.3%
County seat: Wauseon
Largest city: Wauseon (7,091)
Second-largest city: none
Largest village: Archbold (4,290)
Per-capita income (2002) / ranking among Ohio counties: $27,097/25
Number of school districts (2005): 7

Employment base:
Private sector: 89%
Public sector: 11%

Electoral history:
President (2004): Bush (R) 62%; Kerry (D) 37%
Governor (2002): Taft (R) 74%; Hagan (D) 28%
President (2000): Bush (R) 61%; Gore (D) 36%
Governor (1998): Taft (R) 55%; Fisher (D) 39%
President (1996): Dole (R) 49%; Clinton (D) 37%; Perot 13%
Governor (1994): Voinovich (R) 81%; Burch (D) 17%
President (1992): Bush (R) 45%; Clinton (D) 30%; Perot 26%
Governor (1990): Voinovich (R) 64%; Celebrezze (D) 36%
President (1988): Bush (R) 67%; Dukakis (D) 33%

Party affiliations of county administrative officeholders (2004):
11 Republicans

History:

Formed 87th among Ohio's 88 counties, Fulton County was created in 1850 from Lucas, Henry, and Williams counties. Originally part of Ohio's Black Swamp region, the area was home to Ottawa Indians until the 1830s. At the county's formation, Col. Dresden W. H. Howard, a pioneer and Indian trader, selected Ottokee—a village near the center of the county and named for an Ottawa chief—as the first county seat. Wauseon, named for Ottokee's brother, was laid out in 1854, incorporated in 1859, and chosen the county seat in 1869. A northern section of Fulton County had been claimed by the Territory of Michigan in a boundary dispute with Ohio. In 1836, Congress settled the border war in Ohio's favor. Since its formation, the county has been predominantly agricultural; it has been a major producer of grains and dairy products.

GALLIA COUNTY

Established: April 30, 1803
Named for: Gaul (Latin for France)
Land area: 472 square miles
Locale: on the Ohio River, about 80 miles southeast of Columbus
2000 Population: 31,069
 White: 94.9%
 Black: 2.6%
County seat: Gallipolis
Largest city: Gallipolis (4,180)
Second Largest city: none
Largest village: Rio Grande (915)
Per-capita income (2002) / ranking among Ohio counties: $23,973/52
Number of school districts (2005): 2

Employment base (2001):
Private sector: 84%
Public sector: 16%

Electoral history:
President (2004): Bush (R) 61%; Kerry (D) 38%
Governor (2002): Taft (R) 66%; Hagan (D) 30%
President (2000): Bush (R) 59%; Gore (D) 38%
Governor (1998): Taft (R) 55%; Fisher (D) 39%
President (1996): Clinton (D) 43%; Dole (R) 41%; Perot 14%
Governor (1994): Voinovich (R) 68%; Burch (D) 28%
President (1992): Bush (R) 42%; Clinton (D) 39%; Perot 19%
Governor (1990): Voinovich (R) 56%; Celebrezze (D) 44%
President (1988): Bush (R) 60%; Dukakis (D) 40%

Party affiliations of county administrative officeholders (2004):
8 Republicans; 3 Democrats

History:

In 1789, at the beginning of the French Revolution, some residents of Paris who had been loyal to the ruling Bourbons were eager to flee the mobs for the promise of a safer existence in America. New York speculator William Duer and his associates, doing business as the Scioto Company, made plans to purchase a large tract of land in southern Ohio, west of the Ohio Company's lands. In Paris, the company began selling lots on the promise that the lands at Gallipolis ("city of the French") were a paradise of no taxes, gigantic catfish, superior tobacco, and no inclement weather. The Scioto Company never acquired title to the land; hundreds of unwary French purchasers had been swindled. They arrived at Marietta in late 1790 and learned that they again would have to buy land. Rufus Putnam, an officer of the Ohio Company, arranged to clear a site, build cabins near the mouth of the Kanawha River, and sell the lots to the French at a bargain. In 1791, Gallipolis thus became a settlement of French stonecutters, small farmers, goldsmiths, watchmakers, and other craftsmen. In 1803, Gallia County was formed from the western part of Washington County; it also attracted settlers of Welsh origin,

many of whom occupied upland territory that became part of Jackson and Vinton counties. During the Civil War, Gallipolis was an important supply station for the Union army. In 1875, Rio Grande College was founded by the Free Baptist Church. On December 15, 1967, the Silver Bridge connecting Kanaugua (just upriver from Gallipolis) to Point Pleasant, W.Va., collapsed, killing 46 people.

GEAUGA COUNTY

Established: March 1, 1806
Named for: Indian word "raccoon"
Land area: 409 square miles
Locale: about 15 miles east of Cleveland
2000 Population: 90,895
 White: 97.5%
 Black: 1.2%
County seat: Chardon
Largest city: none
Largest village: Chardon (5,156)
Second-Largest village: South Russell (4,022)
Per-capita income (2002) / ranking among Ohio counties: $37,868/2
Number of school districts (2005): 7

Employment base (2001):
Private sector: 89%
Public sector: 11%

Electoral history:
President (2004): Bush (R) 60%; Kerry (D) 39%
Governor (2002): Taft (R) 61%; Hagan (R) 36%
President (2000): Bush (R) 60%; Gore (D) 36%
Governor (1998): Taft (R) 61%; Fisher (D) 34%
President (1996): Dole (R) 50%; Clinton (D) 36%; Perot 12%
Governor (1994): Voinovich (R) 84%; Burch (D) 14%
President (1992): Bush (R) 45%; Clinton (D) 29%; Perot 26%
Governor (1990): Voinovich (R) 70%; Celebrezze (D) 30%
President (1988): Bush (R) 65%; Dukakis (D) 35%

Party affiliations of county administrative officeholders (2004):
9 Republicans; 2 Democrats

History:

The Connecticut Land Company completed survey work in the area in 1797, and three Connecticut families settled in Burton Township the next year. In 1806, Geauga County was the second county organized in the Western Reserve. The same year, the Burton Academy—the first institution of higher learning on the Western Reserve—was established. The academy was the forerunner of Western Reserve College. The first county seat was New Market (now in Lake County) but soon was moved to Chardon. The county was known for its heavy forests; roads and settlements were slow to develop. Since the pioneer days, agriculture has dominated Geauga

County. It achieved distinction for the production of wool, dairy products, and maple sugar and maple syrup. In 1885, nearly a third of the maple sugar produced in the United States reportedly came from the hard maples of Geauga County. In 1856, county residents built Newbury's Chapel on Rt. 44 after a young James A. Garfield was forbidden to speak in the local church because he was a member of a new denomination, the Disciples of Christ.

GREENE COUNTY

Established: May 1, 1803
Named for: Gen. Nathaniel Greene (Revolutionary War)
Land area: 416 square miles
Locale: about 10 miles east of Dayton
2000 Population: 147,886
 White: 89.0%
 Black: 6.2%
County seat: Xenia
Largest city: Beavercreek (37,984)
Second-largest city: Fairborn (32,052)
Per-capita income (2002) / ranking among Ohio counties: $29,951/12
Number of school districts (2005): 7

Employment base (2001):
Private sector: 82%
Public sector: 18%

Electoral history:
President (2004): Bush (R) 61%; Kerry (D) 39%
Governor (2002): Taft (R) 67%; Hagan (D) 27%
President (2000): Bush (R) 58%; Gore (D) 38%
Governor (1998): Taft (R) 56%; Fisher (D) 37%
President (1996): Dole (R) 50%; Clinton (D) 41%; Perot 8%
Governor (1994): Voinovich (R) 78%; Burch (D) 20%
President (1992): Bush (R) 47%; Clinton (D) 34%; Perot 19%
Governor (1990): Voinovich (R) 67%; Celebrezze (D) 33%
President (1988): Bush (R) 66%; Dukakis (D) 34%

Party affiliations of county administrative officeholders (2004):
11 Republicans

History:

In 1803, Greene County was created by the first state legislature from Hamilton and Ross counties. It previously had been Shawnee territory. The village called Old Town by early settlers—about three miles north of Xenia—had been a Shawnee community. Xenia, from a Greek word meaning "hospitable," was selected as county seat. U.S. Rt. 42, which runs southwest to northeast through the county, generally follows the trail blazed in 1780 by Gen. George Rogers Clark's army in the campaign against the Indians. The English, Irish, Scotch, and Pennsylvania Dutch were among the county's early set-

tlers. They included the Reid family, on whose farm near Cedarville was born Whitelaw Reid, the Civil War correspondent who succeeded Horace Greeley as owner/editor of the *New York Tribune*. Greene County has a rich educational heritage. In 1853, Antioch College opened in Yellow Springs as a nonsectarian institution for men and women, whites and blacks. Its first president was Horace Mann, a pioneer in American education and reformer of Massachusetts's public schools. In 1856, Wilberforce University was established as one of the nation's first permanent institutions of higher education for blacks. Located at the former Tawawa Springs resort, the university was named for English abolitionist William Wilberforce. In an 1887 reorganization, Central State University was created on an adjoining campus. In 1869, the Ohio Soldiers' and Sailors' Orphans Home was established near Xenia. On April 3, 1974, tornadoes plagued southwestern Ohio; the worst hit Xenia, killing 33 people, injuring more than 150 others, and destroying half the city.

GUERNSEY COUNTY

Established: March 1, 1810
Named for: Isle of Guernsey (Great Britain)
Land area: 528 square miles
Locale: about 70 miles east of Columbus
2000 Population: 40,792
 White: 95.9%
 Black: 1.6%
County seat: Cambridge
Largest city: Cambridge (11,520)
Second-largest city: none
Largest village: Byesville (2,574)
Per-capita income (2002) / ranking among Ohio counties: $21,705/72
Number of school districts (2005): 3

Employment base (2001):
Private sector: 82%
Public sector: 18%

Electoral history:
President (2004): Bush (R) 56%; Kerry (D) 44%
Governor (2002): Taft (R) 59%; Hagan (D) 37%
President (2000): Bush (R) 53%; Gore (D) 43%
Governor (1998): Taft (R) 54%; Fisher (D) 41%
President (1996): Clinton (D) 45%; Dole (R) 40%; Perot 15%
Governor (1994): Voinovich (R) 64%; Burch (D) 31%
President (1992): Clinton (D) 40%; Bush (R) 35%; Perot 25%
Governor (1990): Voinovich (R) 56%; Celebrezze (D) 44%
President (1988): Bush (R) 59%; Dukakis (D) 41%

Party affiliations of county administrative officeholders (2004):
7 Republicans; 4 Democrats

History:

In 1796, the opening of Zane's Trace drew travelers into the area that became Guernsey County—previously the province of Delaware and Shawnee Indians. In 1805, Old Washington was laid out along the road; in June 1806, Cambridge was laid out where the road crossed Wills Creek. The first buyers of government lands included 15 to 20 families from the Isle of Guernsey in the English Channel; they named the county, formed in 1810, after their homeland. Among the early settlers, the English and Scotch-Irish predominated. Senecaville was founded in 1815. In 1828, the National Road—laid out along much of the old trace—reached Cambridge. In 1835, a group of Quakers founded Quaker City. In July 1863, Confederate general John Morgan's Raiders rode through the village of Cumberland, plundering and looting. They were captured later that month in Columbiana County. In 1837, Muskingum College was chartered in New Concord—the birthplace of John H. Glenn, the first American to orbit Earth.

HAMILTON COUNTY

Established: January 2, 1790
Named for: Alexander Hamilton
Land area: 412 square miles
Locale: southwestern corner of the state, encompassing Cincinnati
2000 Population: 845,303
 White: 72.9%
 Black: 23.4%
County seat: Cincinnati
Largest city: Cincinnati (331,285)
Second-largest city: Norwood (21,675)
Per-capita income (2002) / ranking among Ohio counties: $35,883/3
Number of school districts (2005): 22

Employment base (2001):
Private sector: 91%
Public sector: 9%

Electoral history:
President (2004): Bush (R) 53%; Kerry (D) 47%
Governor (2002): Taft (R) 66%; Hagan (D) 30%
President (2000): Bush (R) 54%; Gore (D) 43%
Governor (1998): Taft (R) 59%; Fisher (D) 37%
President (1996): Dole (R) 50%; Clinton (D) 43%; Perot 5%
Governor (1994): Voinovich (R) 76%; Burch (D) 21%
President (1992): Bush (R) 48%; Clinton (D) 37%; Perot 15%
Governor (1990): Voinovich (R) 60%; Celebrezze (D) 40%
President (1988): Bush (R) 62%; Dukakis (D) 38%

Party affiliations of county administrative officeholders (2004):
9 Republicans; 2 Democrats

History:

In November 1788, Benjamin Stites laid out the village of Columbia, the first permanent settlement in Hamilton County. In January 1789, about five miles downriver, some Kentucky surveyors settled a village they named Losantiville, which quickly overshadowed Columbia. At Losantiville, Fort Washington was erected to provide security and supplies for the campaign against the Indians of the Northwest Territory. In January 1790, territorial governor Arthur St. Clair arrived at Fort Washington, where he proclaimed the establishment of Hamilton County and changed the name of Losantiville to Cincinnati—after the Order of Cincinnati, the post-Revolutionary society named for the Roman soldier Cincinnatus. With its strategic location on the Ohio River, the close of the Indian wars in 1795, and the opening of the Mississippi River to navigation, Cincinnati was positioned to become the commercial capital of the Midwest. By the early 1800s, Cincinnati was a focal point for the trading, transferring, and shipping of goods; warehousing; and pork packing. As the largest city west of Philadelphia, Cincinnati soon acquired many social and cultural amenities—libraries, museums, music halls, publishing houses, and universities. In 1819, Cincinnati College was chartered; it soon added a law school and medical school and evolved into the University of Cincinnati. The city offered the first Jewish religious service in the Northwest Territory and became the site of Hebrew Union College, the nation's first Jewish theological school. In 1821, Cincinnati became the see for Ohio's first Roman Catholic diocese. In 1831, the forerunner of Xavier University was organized. In 1837, William Procter and James Gamble established Procter & Gamble Co., which became the world's biggest soap maker. In 1839, Alphonso Taft arrived in Cincinnati from Vermont. His son, William Howard Taft, became president and chief justice of the United States. About 1840, a wave of German immigration began to transform Cincinnati. On the boundary between the free North and slaveholding South, Hamilton County was divided by the Civil War. Although the county generally was considered antiwar Copperhead territory, abolitionist sentiment also was apparent; the city was a headquarters for the Anti-Slavery Society. The Red Stockings, the nation's first professional baseball team, was founded in 1869. Cincinnati remained the state's most populous city until after 1890.

HANCOCK COUNTY

Established: April 1, 1820
Named for: John Hancock
Land area: 534 square miles
Locale: about 40 miles south of Toledo
2000 Population: 71,295
 White: 95.0%
 Black: 1.0%
County seat: Findlay
Largest city: Findlay (38,967)
Second-largest city: Fostoria (13,931)
Per-capita income (2002) / ranking among Ohio counties:

$29,425/15
Number of school districts (2005): 8

Employment base (2001):
Private sector: 92%
Public sector: 8%

Electoral history:
President (2004): Bush (R) 70%; Kerry (D) 29%
Governor (2002): Taft (R) 77%; Hagan (D) 20%
President (2000): Bush (R) 69%; Gore (D) 29%
Governor (1998): Taft (R) 65%; Fisher (D) 30%
President (1996): Dole (R) 58%; Clinton (D) 31%; Perot 10%
Governor (1994): Voinovich (R) 77%; Burch (D) 17%
President (1992): Bush (R) 53%; Clinton (D) 25%; Perot 22%
Governor (1990): Voinovich (R) 68%; Celebrezze (D) 32%
President (1988): Bush (R) 73%; Dukakis (D) 27%

Party affiliations of county administrative officeholders (2004):
11 Republicans

History:

Wyandot Indians inhabited the area until 1817. During the War of 1812, Gen. William Hull's army marched through the area on its way to Detroit, forging a trail that became the county's first road. Fort Findlay was named for Col. James Findlay, one of Hull's regiment commanders. The village of Findlay was platted in 1821 on the site of Fort Findlay. Settlement was slow; the county government was not organized until 1828. Although well diggers noticed the presence of natural gas in the 1830s, the county remained predominantly agricultural until the 1880s. On January 20, 1886, drillers hit the massive Karg well; the find made Findlay a natural-gas boom town. Between 1880 and 1890, its population more than quadrupled—to 18,553 from 4,633. The area's natural-gas wells were considered the largest in the world, but production rapidly declined after a few years. The related discovery of oil had more long-lasting effects, as Findlay became the home of the Ohio Oil Co. (later Marathon Oil), incorporated in 1887 and a major employer for more than a century.

HARDIN COUNTY

Established: April 1, 1820
Named for: Gen. John H. Hardin (Revolutionary War)
Land area: 469 square miles
Locale: about 60 miles south of Toledo
2000 Population: 31,945
White: 97.6%
Black: 0.7%
County seat: Kenton
Largest city: Kenton (8,336)
Second-largest city: none
Largest village: Ada (5,582)
Per-capita income (2002) / ranking among Ohio counties:

$21,134/75
Number of school districts (2005): 6

Employment base (2001):
Private sector: 81%
Public sector: 19%

Electoral history:
President (2004): Bush (R) 63%; Kerry (D) 37%
Governor (2002): Taft (R) 61%; Hagan (D) 34%
President (2000): Bush (R) 59%; Gore (D) 38%
Governor (1998): Taft (R) 53%; Fisher (D) 39%
President (1996): Dole (R) 46%; Clinton (D) 41%; Perot 11%
Governor (1994): Voinovich (R) 75%; Burch (D) 21%
President (1992): Bush (R) 45%; Clinton (D) 33%; Perot 22%
Governor (1990): Voinovich (R) 58%; Celebrezze (D) 42%
President (1988): Bush (R) 64%; Dukakis (D) 36%

Party affiliations of county administrative officeholders (2004):
10 Republicans; 1 Democrat

History:

During the war of 1812, Gen. William Hull's army built Fort McArthur—named for Duncan McArthur, a commander and future governor. Until 1817, the area was Wyandot and Shawnee Indian territory. In 1833, settlers established a small community near the fort and named it Kenton, after Indian scout Simon Kenton. Without major waterways or roads, the county was slow to develop. It has remained a lightly populated, primarily agricultural county. In 1871, Dr. Henry S. Lehr founded the Ada Normal Academy, the forerunner of Ohio Northern University. Frank S. Monnett, a native of Kenton, was Ohio attorney general in the late 1890s; he prosecuted the Standard Oil Co. under the state's antitrust laws.

HARRISON COUNTY

Established: February 1, 1813
Named for: Gen. William Henry Harrison
Land area: 411 square miles
Locale: about 80 miles southeast of Cleveland
2000 Population: 15,856
White: 96.6%
Black: 2.0%
County seat: Cadiz
Largest city: none
Largest village: Cadiz (3,308)
Second-Largest village: Hopedale (984)
Per-capita income (2002) / ranking among Ohio counties:
$22,312/71
Number of school districts (2005): 2

Employment base (2001):
Private sector: 78%
Public sector: 22%

Electoral history:
President (2004): Bush (R) 53%; Kerry (D) 47%
Governor (2002): Taft (R) 55%; Hagan (D) 41%
President (2000): Bush (R) 48%; Gore (R) 47%
Governor (1998): Fisher (D) 51%; Taft (R) 43%
President (1996): Clinton (D) 50%; Dole (R) 31%; Perot 18%
Governor (1994): Burch (D) 53%; Voinovich (R) 45%
President (1992): Clinton (D) 49%; Bush (R) 29%; Perot 22%
Governor (1990): Celebrezze (D) 56%; Voinovich (R) 44%
President (1988): Dukakis (D) 54%; Bush (R) 46%

Party affiliations of county administrative officeholders (2004):
7 Democrats; 4 Republicans

History:

In 1804, Cadiz was founded at the junction of two old Indian trails. The area formerly was occupied by Delaware Indians. In 1813, Harrison County was formed from Jefferson and Tuscarawas counties. It was part of the Seven Ranges—the first Congress Lands to be surveyed and sold. Many of the best tracts soon were purchased. Among the early settlers were Scotch-Irish and Quakers from Pennsylvania. For a century, farming was the predominant occupation; the county became known for its sheep and wool. After the turn of the century, coal operators began to exploit the county's rich deposits of shallow coal; strip mining became the dominant enterprise. The county was the birthplace of Gen. George Armstrong Custer and Clark Gable, the motion-picture star.

HENRY COUNTY

Established: April 1, 1820
Named for: Patrick Henry
Land area: 419 square miles
Locale: about 40 miles southwest of Toledo
2000 Population: 29,210
 White: 95.0%
 Black: 0.4%
County seat: Napoleon
Largest city: Napoleon (9,318)
Second-largest city: none
Largest village: Deshler (1,831)
Per-capita income (2002) / ranking among Ohio counties:
$25,343/39
Number of school districts (2005): 4

Employment base (2001):
Private sector: 82%
Public sector: 18%

Electoral history:
President (2004): Bush (R) 66%; Kerry (D) 34%
Governor (2002): Taft (R) 74%; Hagan (D) 23%
President (2000): Bush (R) 64%; Gore (D) 33%
Governor (1998): Taft (R) 59%; Fisher (D) 35%

President (1996): Dole (R) 50%; Clinton (D) 37%; Perot 12%
Governor (1994): Voinovich (R) 81%; Burch (D) 16%
President (1992): Bush (R) 47%; Clinton (D) 30%; Perot 24%
Governor (1990): Voinovich (R) 65%; Celebrezze (D) 35%
President (1988): Bush (R) 70%; Dukakis (D) 30%

Party affiliations of county administrative officeholders (2004):
7 Republicans; 4 Democrats

History:

In 1795, the Treaty of Greene Ville guaranteed the northwestern Ohio lands to the Indians, but they were ceded to the federal government in treaties of 1807 and 1817. Settlement occurred along the Maumee River and the trail blazed in 1794 by Gen. Anthony Wayne's army, part of which today is U.S. Rt. 24. Early pioneers arrived in the area via the Maumee, although settlement was slow even after the War of 1812. The county was established in 1820 but not organized until 1834. The state government's decision to use the Maumee as part of the canal system attracted Germans and Irishmen to help build sections of the Miami-Erie Canal. In 1834, Napoleon was laid out and became the county seat; French settlers won a dispute with Germans over naming it. Part of the former Black Swamp area, the county has rich soils that have supported diversified agriculture. The area has been known for its grains, dairy products, and tomatoes.

HIGHLAND COUNTY

Established: May 1, 1805
Named for: its "high lands"
Land area: 559 square miles
Locale: about 40 miles east of Cincinnati
2000 Population: 40,875
 White: 96.8%
 Black: 1.5%
County seat: Hillsboro
Largest city: Hillsboro (6,368)
Second-largest city: Greenfield (4,906)
Per-capita income (2002) / ranking among Ohio counties:
$21,476/73
Number of school districts (2005): 5

Employment base (2001):
Private sector: 80%
Public sector: 20%

Electoral history:
President (2004): Bush (R) 66%; Kerry (D) 34%
Governor (2002): Taft (R) 68%; Hagan (D) 27%
President (2000): Bush (R) 63%; Gore (D) 34%
Governor (1998): Taft (R) 60%; Fisher (D) 34%
President (1996): Dole (R) 48%; Clinton (D) 40%; Perot 11%
Governor (1994): Voinovich (R) 75%; Burch (D) 22%
President (1992): Bush (R) 46%; Clinton (D) 32%; Perot 22%
Governor (1990): Voinovich (R) 60%; Celebrezze (D) 40%

President (1988): Bush (R) 67%; Dukakis (D) 33%
Party affiliations of county administrative officeholders (2004):
10 Republicans; 1 Democrat

History:

All of what now is Highland County was within the Virginia Military District. After 1800, men with land warrants began building cabins in the "high lands" between the Scioto and Miami valleys. The first settlement was at New Market, where the first court was held in 1805. Two years later, Hillsboro was selected the county seat. Without major waterways or roads, the county did not develop a significant commercial center. The county became known for its limestone deposits and farm crops, including tobacco. In 1865, women in Greenfield raided saloons and smashed the liquor stock with axes and hatchets—putting Highland County on the map for its antiliquor militancy. Between 1873 and 1874, Eliza Jane Thompson of Hillsboro, the wife of a judge and daughter of former governor Allen Trimble, led a group of women who visited area saloons to pray and sing hymns; their tactics succeeded in briefly closing saloons. In 1874, the Woman's Christian Temperance Union was founded in Cleveland.

HOCKING COUNTY

Established: March 1, 1818
Named for: Hocking River
Land area: 424 square miles
Locale: about 40 miles southeast of Columbus
2000 Population: 28,241
White: 97.7%
Black: 1.1%
County seat: Logan
Largest city: Logan (6,704)
Second-largest city: none
Largest village: Laurelville (533)
Per-capita income (2002) / ranking among Ohio counties:
$21,376/74
Number of school districts (2005): 1

Employment base (2001):
Private sector: 76%
Public sector: 24%

Electoral history:
President (2004): Bush (R) 53%; Kerry (D) 47%
Governor (2002): Taft (R) 55%; Hagan (D) 38%
President (2000): Bush (R) 53%; Gore (D) 42%
Governor (1998): Taft (R) 47%; Fisher (D) 45%
President (1996): Clinton (D) 45%; Dole (R) 39%; Perot 15%
Governor (1994): Voinovich (R) 63%; Burch (D) 33%
President (1992): Clinton (D) 37%; Bush (R) 36%; Perot 27%
Governor (1990): Celebrezze (D) 51%; Voinovich (R) 49%
President (1988): Bush (R) 59%; Dukakis (D) 41%

Party affiliations of county administrative officeholders (2004):
8 Democrats; 3 Republicans

History:

Once the hill country of Wyandot Indians, most of what today is Hocking County was included in the Congress Lands. In the 1790s, English and German settlers arrived in the area from Pennsylvania and Virginia. The Hocking River, known as the Hockhocking until about 1818, was the primary means of transport. The same year, the county was formed from Athens, Ross, and Fairfield counties. Gov. Thomas Worthington laid out the town of Logan, naming it for a Mingo Indian chief. In the 1830s and 1840s, construction of the Hocking Canal encouraged the development of the area's mineral resources, especially coal and iron ore. In the 1850s, iron was manufactured in Union Furnace. Coal mining was the county's major industry in the second half of the 19th century and the early 20th century. The county always has been known for its rock caves, now part of the Hocking State Forest.

HOLMES COUNTY

Established: January 20, 1824
Named for: Maj. Andrew H. Holmes (War of 1812)
Land area: 423 square miles
Locale: About 60 miles south of Cleveland
2000 Population: 38,943
White: 98.8%
Black: 0.2%
County seat: Millersburg
Largest city: none
Largest village: Millersburg (3,326)
Second-Largest village: Loudonville (2,906)
Per-capita income (2002) / ranking among Ohio counties:
$19,647/85
Number of school districts (2005): 2

Employment base (2001):
Private sector: 91%
Public sector: 9%

Electoral history:
President (2004): Bush (R) 75%; Kerry (D) 24%
Governor (2002): Taft (R) 74%; Hagan (D) 23%
President (2000): Bush (R) 74%; Gore (D) 23%
Governor (1998): Taft (R) 68%; Fisher (D) 27%
President (1996): Dole (R) 57%; Clinton (D) 28%; Perot 14%
Governor (1994): Voinovich (R) 79%; Burch (D) 17%
President (1992): Bush (R) 57%; Clinton (D) 22%; Perot 22%
Governor (1990): Voinovich (R) 67%; Celebrezze (D) 33%
President (1988): Bush (R) 70%; Dukakis (D) 30%

Party affiliations of county administrative officeholders (2004):
8 Republicans; 1 Democrat; 1 Independent; 1 vacancy

History:

Settlers began arriving about 1809 from Maryland, Virginia, and Pennsylvania. Among them were Amish immigrants from Germany and Switzerland who previously had settled in

Pennsylvania. They settled around Millersburg, which became the county seat. Created mainly from Wayne and Coshocton counties, Holmes County became one of the nation's largest Amish communities. The Amish reject modern conveniences—automobiles, electricity, telephones—and live on their farms in much the same manner of their predecessors generations ago. In June 1863, as the Civil War dragged on, Holmes County was the site of a brief antidraft uprising. More than 900 armed men defied a draft enrollment, prompting the Union army to send a 450-soldier detachment from Camp Chase to suppress the resistance. After a brief skirmish, which left two men wounded, the rebellion fizzled.

HURON COUNTY

Established: March 7, 1809
Named for: Huron Indians
Land area: 494 square miles
Locale: About 50 miles southwest of Cleveland
2000 Population: 59,487
 White: 95.4%
 Black: 1.0%
County seat: Norwalk
Largest city: Norwalk (16,238)
Second-largest city: Bellevue (8,193)
Per-capita income (2002) / ranking among Ohio counties: $24,234/51
Number of school districts (2005): 7

Employment base (2001):
Private sector: 89%
Public sector: 11%

Electoral history:
President (2004): Bush (R) 58%; Kerry (D) 41%
Governor (2002): Taft (R) 66%; Hagan (D) 31%
President (2000): Bush (R) 58%; Gore (D) 38%
Governor (1998): Taft (R) 55%; Fisher (D) 39%
President (1996): Clinton (D) 42%; Dole (R) 41%; Perot 16%
Governor (1994): Voinovich (R) 70%; Burch (D) 22%
President (1992): Bush (R) 39%; Clinton (D) 33%; Perot 28%
Governor (1990): Voinovich (R) 63%; Celebrezze (D) 37%
President (1988): Bush (R) 62%; Dukakis (D) 38%

Party affiliations of county administrative officeholders (2004):
5 Democrats; 5 Republicans; 1 Independent

History:
In 1792, the Connecticut legislature set aside 500,000 acres—what today is Huron and Erie counties—at the western edge of the Western Reserve to compensate people whose property was destroyed by fire from British raids. The settlers from Connecticut named several villages—New London, Greenwich, Fairfield, Norwalk—after villages in their old state. In 1805, Indians ceded the

land, and, in 1809, Huron County was created. In 1815, the county was organized with the first court in Camp Avery, and, in 1818, the county seat was moved to Norwalk. In 1826, the Norwalk Academy—the forerunner of the Norwalk Institute—was organized. Among its students was Rutherford B. Hayes, the 19th U.S. president. In 1838, Erie County was created from the northern part of Huron County. In the second half of the 19th century, Bellevue, Norwalk, and Willard became railroad towns when various lines chose them as terminal points. The county also became known for agriculture, packing plants, and agricultural machinery.

JACKSON COUNTY

Established: March 1, 1816
Named for: Gen. Andrew Jackson
Land area: 422 square miles
Locale: about 60 miles southeast of Columbus
2000 Population: 32,641
 White: 97.3%
 Black: 1.0%
County seat: Jackson
Largest city: Jackson (6,184)
Second-largest city: Wellston (6,078)
Per-capita income (2002) / ranking among Ohio counties: $20,449/80
Number of school districts (2005): 3

Employment base (2001):
Private sector: 87%
Public sector: 13%

Electoral history:
President (2004): Bush (R) 60%; Kerry (D) 40%
Governor (2002): Taft (R) 62%; Hagan (D) 33%
President (2000): Bush (R) 56%; Gore (D) 41%
Governor (1998): Taft (R) 53%; Fisher (D) 42%
President (1996): Clinton (D) 46%; Dole (R) 41%; Perot 13%
Governor (1994): Voinovich (R) 72%; Burch (D) 24%
President (1992): Bush (R) 42%; Clinton (D) 39%; Perot 19%
Governor (1990): Voinovich (R) 53%; Celebrezze (D) 47%
President (1988): Bush (R) 60%; Dukakis (D) 40%

Party affiliations of county administrative officeholders (2004):
9 Republicans; 2 Democrats

History:
Before the arrival of white pioneers, the Shawnee Indians treasured this area for its salt springs and good hunting. In the 1790s, before the land was surveyed and subdivided, squatters were attracted to the salt springs about two miles northwest of Jackson. The settlement of squatters was named Poplar Row. In 1804, a post office named Salt Lick was established. In 1805, after the creation of townships and sections, the Scioto Salt Works were reserved from sale in a

separate township and were operated by the state. In 1815, residents petitioned for a new county, which was established the next year. About 1818, a group of Welsh families moved into the area from Gallipolis. The discovery of coal attracted more Welsh, who settled around Jackson, Wellston, and Oak Hill. The discovery of stronger brine sources along the Muskingum River contributed to the decline of the Scioto Salt Works, but Jackson County prospered from coal mining and iron making. Several charcoal-burning furnaces were established for the production of an off-grade, gray iron called silvery iron. Iron making peaked during the Civil War. Coal mining peaked in the 1890s, exhausting many of the county's mines by the early 1900s. James A. Rhodes, who served as Ohio's governor longer than anyone in the state's history, was born in Coalton on September 13, 1909.

JEFFERSON COUNTY

Established: July 29, 1797
Named for: Thomas Jefferson
Land area: 410 square miles
Locale: on the Ohio River, about 80 miles southeast of Akron
2000 Population: 73,894
 White: 92.6%
 Black: 5.7%
County seat: Steubenville
Largest city: Steubenville (19,015)
Second-largest city: Toronto (5,676)
Per-capita income (2002) / ranking among Ohio counties: $23,622/58
Number of school districts (2005): 5

Employment base (2001):
Private sector: 85%
Public sector: 15%

Electoral history:
President (2004): Kerry (D) 52%; Bush (R) 47%
Governor (2002): Taft (R) 56%; Hagan (R) 40%
President (2000): Gore (D) 50%; Bush (R) 43%
Governor (1998): Fisher (D) 52%; Taft (R) 41%
President (1996): Clinton (D) 56%; Dole (R) 29%; Perot 14%
Governor (1994): Burch (D) 58%; Voinovich (R) 39%
President (1992): Clinton (D) 54%; Bush (R) 28%; Perot 18%
Governor (1990): Celebrezze (D) 58%; Voinovich (R) 42%
President (1988): Dukakis (D) 61%; Bush (R) 39%

Party affiliations of county administrative officeholders (2004):
9 Democrats; 2 Republicans

History:
Delaware Indians occupied this land before the close of the Revolutionary War, when squatters began building cabins along the Ohio River -- some of Ohio's first settlements. Many of the early settlers were Scotch-Irish from Pennsylvania and Virginia and Quakers from North Carolina. In 1786, Fort Steuben -- named for

Prussian nobleman Wilhelm von Steuben -- was built for the protection of surveyors under the direction of U.S. geographer Thomas Hutchins, who laid out the Seven Ranges. The federal government sold the land in squares. The first purchasers included Bezaleel Wells and James Ross of Pennsylvania, who founded Steubenville (incorporated in 1805) on the site of the old fort. In the early 1800s, the area became known for its fruit trees and wool. Later, the county became a center of coal mining, steel making, and glass making. Jefferson County was an early center of Methodism. Steubenville was the birthplace of Edwin M. Stanton, secretary of war for President Abraham Lincoln.

KNOX COUNTY

Established: March 1, 1808
Named for: Gen. Henry Knox (secretary of war under President Washington)
Land area: 530 square miles
Locale: about 45 miles northeast of Columbus
2000 Population: 54,500
 White: 97.4%
 Black: 0.8%
County seat: Mount Vernon
Largest city: Mount Vernon (14,375)
Second-largest city: none
Largest village: Fredericktown (2,428)
Per-capita income (2002) / ranking among Ohio counties: $23,925/53
Number of school districts (2005): 5

Employment base (2001):
Private sector: 84%
Public sector: 16%

Electoral history:
President (2004): Bush (R) 63%; Kerry (D) 36%
Governor (2002): Taft (R) 65%; Hagan (D) 29%
President (2000): Bush (R) 63%; Gore (D) 34%
Governor (1998): Taft (R) 58%; Fisher (D) 35%
President (1996): Dole (R) 51%; Clinton (D) 38%; Perot 11%
Governor (1994): Voinovich (R) 74%; Burch (D) 22%
President (1992): Bush (R) 42%; Clinton (D) 34%; Perot 25%
Governor (1990): Voinovich (R) 54%; Celebrezze (D) 46%
President (1988): Bush (R) 64%; Dukakis (D) 36%

Party affiliations of county administrative officeholders (2004):
10 Republicans; 1 Democrat

History:
This area was Wyandot and Delaware Indian territory before pioneers arrived from Virginia, Maryland, and New Jersey. It was included in the U.S. Military District, reserved for Revolutionary War veterans, and was surveyed into townships five miles square. Many of the first settlers were Quakers. In 1805, Mount Vernon was

laid out; in 1808, with the creation of Knox County, it was chosen county seat. Farming always has been the county's chief business. In 1826, about five miles east of Mount Vernon in Gambier, missionary Episcopal Bishop Philander Chase founded Kenyon College as a theological school. Because funds were obtained from English donors, Gambier was named for Lord Gambier; the college was named for Lord Kenyon. An early student was Salmon P. Chase, an Ohio governor, secretary of the Treasury for President Abraham Lincoln, and a chief justice of the United States.

LAKE COUNTY

Established: March 6, 1840
Named for: Lake Erie
Land area: 232 square miles
Locale: on Lake Erie, about 30 miles northeast of Cleveland
2000 Population: 227,511
　White: 95.5%
　Black: 1.7%
County seat: Painesville
Largest city: Mentor (50,278)
Second-largest city: Willoughby (22,621)
Per-capita income (2002) / ranking among Ohio counties: $30,860/8
Number of school districts (2005): 9

Employment base (2001):
Private sector: 88%
Public sector: 12%

Electoral history:
President (2004): Bush (R) 51%; Kerry (D) 48%
Governor (2002): Taft (R) 57%; Hagan (D) 41%
President (2000): Bush (R) 50%; Gore (D) 45%
Governor (1998): Taft (R) 54%; Fisher (D) 41%
President (1996): Clinton (D) 44%; Dole (R) 42%; Perot 13%
Governor (1994): Voinovich (R) 79%; Burch (D) 18%
President (1992): Bush (R) 39%; Clinton (D) 36%; Perot 26%
Governor (1990): Voinovich (R) 63%; Celebrezze (D) 37%
President (1988): Bush (R) 57%; Dukakis (D) 43%

Party affiliations of county administrative officeholders (2004):
8 Republicans; 3 Democrats

History:

One of Ohio's earliest pathways followed the Erie lakeshore, allowing frontiersmen to travel the territory throughout the 18th century. Part of the Connecticut Western Reserve, the area was surveyed between 1796 to 1797 and settled by New Englanders. Gen. Edward Paine, a Revolutionary War veteran, purchased 1,000 acres and was a chief organizer of the area. Painesville, the county seat, is named for him. Fairport Harbor, a protected natural harbor, provided

the county with an excellent shipping point. In 1825, a lighthouse was built there. In 1833, the Church of Jesus Christ of Latter-day Saints (Mormon Church) built a house of worship in Kirtland Township. Many Mormons settled there but fled in 1837 when a mismanaged Mormon bank failed during a financial panic. The Mormons migrated to Missouri, then to Utah. For most of its history, the county was known for its shipping and agriculture, especially fruit growing. It later became a bedroom community for metropolitan Cleveland. The county was home to James A. Garfield, the 20th president; Frances Jennings Casement, the first president of the Ohio Woman Suffrage Association; and Dan Beard, founder of the Boy Scouts of America.

LAWRENCE COUNTY

Established: December 21, 1815
Named for: Capt. James Lawrence (War of 1812)
Land area: 457 square miles
Locale: on the Ohio River, about 100 miles south of Columbus
2000 Population: 62,319
　White: 96.1%
　Black: 2.4%
County seat: Ironton
Largest city: Ironton (11,211)
Second-largest city: none
Largest village: South Point (3,742)
Per-capita income (2002) / ranking among Ohio counties: $20,472/79
Number of school districts (2005): 7

Employment base (2001):
Private sector: 74%
Public sector: 26%

Electoral history:
President (2004): Bush (R) 56%; Kerry (D) 44%
Governor (2002): Taft (R) 61%; Hagan (D) 35%
President (2000): Bush (R) 51%; Gore (D) 46%
Governor (1998): Taft (R) 52%; Fisher (D) 43%
President (1996): Clinton (D) 48%; Dole (R) 37%; Perot 14%
Governor (1994): Voinovich (R) 79%; Burch (D) 18%
President (1992): Clinton (D) 46%; Bush (R) 37%; Perot 17%
Governor (1990): Voinovich (R) 51%; Celebrezze (D) 49%
President (1988): Bush (R) 53%; Dukakis (D) 47%

Party affiliations of county administrative officeholders (2004):
8 Republicans; 3 Democrats

History:

Some of the early traders on the Ohio River had arrived from Burlington, N.J., and, in 1815, named their riverfront settlement in Lawrence County after their hometown. Burlington remained the county seat until 1851, when voters replaced it with Ironton. Many of the early settlers were Dutch, Irish, German, and Scotch. In 1819, John Means moved to the area from South Carolina and settled in Hanging Rock, named for the high sandstone cliff downriver from Ironton. Iron ore soon was discovered in area rocks, and, in 1826, Means built the first blast furnace north of the Ohio River—Union Furnace. The furnace prospered, and others followed. By the Civil War, Lawrence County had 21 charcoal-burning furnaces for the production of iron, which was used for guns, ordnance, armor, wheels, and heavy machinery. In 1849, ironmaster John Campbell platted the village of Ironton, which flourished for several decades. After 1900, when higher-quality iron ores were developed in the Lake Superior region, iron making declined in the Ironton area.

LICKING COUNTY

Established: March 1, 1808
Named for: the area's salt licks
Land area: 688 square miles
Locale: about 15 miles east of Columbus
2000 Population: 145,491
  White: 95.5%
  Black: 2.2%
County seat: Newark
Largest city: Newark (46,279)
Second-largest city: Pataskala (10,249)
Per-capita income (2002) / ranking among Ohio counties: $27,631/22
Number of school districts (2005): 10

Employment base (2001):
Private sector: 87%
Public sector: 13%

Electoral history:
President (2004): Bush (R) 62%; Kerry (D) 38%
Governor (2002): Taft (R) 68%; Hagan (D) 27%
President (2000): Bush (R) 60%; Gore (D) 37%
Governor (1998): Taft (R) 56%; Fisher (D) 38%
President (1996): Dole (R) 49%; Clinton (D) 39%; Perot 11%
Governor (1994): Voinovich (R) 72%; Burch (D) 22%
President (1992): Bush (R) 45%; Clinton (D) 32%; Perot 23%
Governor (1990): Voinovich (R) 52%; Celebrezze (D) 48%
President (1988): Bush (R) 67%; Dukakis (D) 33%

Party affiliations of county administrative officeholders (2004):
10 Republicans; 1 Democrat

History:

All of Licking County was in the U.S. Military District, established in 1796 for Continental Army veterans, who could buy land for two dollars an acre. Along the southern edge of the district, Congress created a Refugee Tract to compensate Canadian refugees who had aligned with the American cause. The early settlers found many prehistoric mounds as well as other earthworks and implements that were part of the Hopewell Indian culture. The area later provided hunting grounds for the Delaware, Shawnee, and Wyandot tribes, who ceded the land to the federal government in 1785. William C. Schenck and his associates purchased a large tract at the forks of the Licking River and, in 1802, laid out a town they named Newark—after Newark, N.J. About 1806, a group of families from Granville, Mass., established the village of Granville, west of Newark. In 1825, at Licking Summit near Newark, the first shovelful of dirt was turned for the Ohio & Erie Canal. The canal's opening in 1830 stimulated the agriculture and small industries of Newark and other Licking County villages. Buckeye Lake, along the county's southern border, was created from swampy land as a reservoir for the canal. In 1831, Baptists opened the Granville Literary and Theological Institution, which, in 1845, became Granville College. In 1853, it was reorganized as Denison University—named for William Denison of Adamsville, who contributed $10,000 to the college fund.

LOGAN COUNTY

Established: March 1, 1818
Named for: Col. Benjamin Logan, Indian fighter
Land area: 467 square miles
Locale: about 50 miles northwest of Columbus
2000 Population: 46,005
  White: 95.8%
  Black: 1.7%
County seat: Bellefontaine
Largest city: Bellefontaine (13,069)
Second-largest city: none
Largest village: West Liberty (1,813)
Per-capita income (2002) / ranking among Ohio counties: $26,293/31
Number of school districts (2005): 4

Employment base (2001):
Private sector: 89%
Public sector: 11%

Electoral history:
President (2004): Bush (R) 68%; Kerry (D) 32%
Governor (2002): Taft (R) 71%; Hagan (D) 23%
President (2000): Bush (R) 64%; Gore (D) 32%
Governor (1998): Taft (R) 60%; Fisher (D) 32%
President (1996): Dole (R) 49%; Clinton (D) 37%; Perot 13%
Governor (1994): Voinovich (R) 77%; Burch (D) 19%
President (1992): Bush (R) 50%; Clinton (D) 26%; Perot 24%

Governor (1990): Voinovich (R) 69%; Celebrezze (D) 31%
President (1988): Bush (R) 71%; Dukakis (D) 29%

Party affiliations of county administrative officeholders (2004):
11 Republicans

History:

This once was Shawnee and Wyandot Indian territory. Between 1795 (the Treaty of Greene Ville) and 1831, the tribes retained much of what today is northern Logan County, named for the colonel who led raids against Indian villages in the Mad River Valley. The first permanent settlers arrived about 1806. Zanesfield—named for Isaac Zane, a frontiersman who married the daughter of an Indian chief—was laid out in 1819. The next year, Bellefontaine (French for "beautiful fountain") was laid out and chosen the county seat. It became a shipping point for grain, livestock, and other agricultural products. Much of Logan County was within the Virginia Military District, and the Piatt family acquired extensive holdings in the county. After the Civil War, the family (of French Huguenot origin) built two castles near West Liberty—Mac-o-chee Castle and Mac-a-cheek Chateau. At 1,550 feet above sea level, Campbell Hill (Hogue's Hill) outside Bellefontaine is the highest point in Ohio. Indian Lake, in the northwestern part of the county, was a natural marsh that was expanded into a reservoir in the 1840s during construction of the Miami & Erie Canal.

LORAIN COUNTY

Established: December 26, 1822
Named for: Province of Lorraine, France
Land area: 494 square miles
Locale: on Lake Erie, about 25 miles west of Cleveland
2000 Population: 284,664
 White: 85.5%
 Black: 8.3%
County seat: Elyria
Largest city: Lorain (68,652)
Second-largest city: Elyria (55,953)
Per-capita income (2002) / ranking among Ohio counties:
$26,964/26
Number of school districts (2005): 14

Employment base (2001):
Private sector: 86%
Public sector: 14%

Electoral history:
President (2004): Kerry (D) 56%; Bush (R) 43%
Governor (2002): Hagan (D) 49%; Taft (R) 48%
President (2000): Gore (D) 53%; Bush (R) 43%
Governor (1998): Fisher (D) 51%; Taft (R) 44%
President (1996): Clinton (D) 52%; Dole (R) 33%; Perot 14%
Governor (1994): Voinovich (R) 69%; Burch (D) 28%

President (1992): Clinton (D) 43%; Bush (R) 31%; Perot 26%
Governor (1990): Voinovich (R) 53%; Celebrezze (D) 47%
President (1988): Dukakis (D) 52%; Bush (R) 48%

Party affiliations of county administrative officeholders (2004):
7 Democrats; 4 Republicans

History:

In the second half of the 18th century, Wyandot Indians occupied the lands near the mouth of the Black River. Near the close of the War of 1812, pioneers from Connecticut and other New England states began to settle the area—part of the Connecticut Western Reserve. The village first was named Mouth of Black River, then Charleston (1836), then Lorain (1874). In 1817, Herman Ely, who had bought about 12,000 acres near the falls of the Black River, laid out the village of Elyria. Throughout the county's history, Lorain and Elyria have been the dominant communities. The lakeside county was not included in the state's canal system, so it did not develop as quickly as it might otherwise have. Though the first sailing ship was built in Lorain (then Mouth of Black River) in 1819, the area remained primarily agricultural until after 1850. Oberlin College, founded in 1833 in Oberlin, claimed to be the first coeducational college in the United States. It was named for Jean Frederic Oberlin, a French pastor who led a movement to return to plain and simple living. In 1872, the arrival of the Cleveland, Lorain and Wheeling Railroad signaled the industrialization of the region. In 1894, Tom L. Johnson, a future mayor of Cleveland, moved a steel plant to Lorain from Johnstown, Pa.; it opened in 1895 and later was sold to U.S. Steel. Lorain soon became a center of the production of iron and steel, ships and auto parts. Elyria developed a more diversified economy—but one dominated by industrial production. Wellington was the home of artist Archibald M. Willard (*The Spirit of '76*). In June 1924, a tornado ripped through Lorain, killing nearly 100, injuring 1,000, and leaving $25 million in property losses.

LUCAS COUNTY

Established: June 20, 1835
Named for: Gov. Robert Lucas
Land area: 348 square miles
Locale: on the western edge of Lake Erie
2000 Population: 455,054
 White: 77.4%
 Black: 16.9%
County seat: Toledo
Largest city: Toledo (313,619)
Second-largest city: Oregon (19,355)
Per-capita income (2002) / ranking among Ohio counties:
$28,799/17
Number of school districts (2005): 8

Employment base (2001):
Private sector: 88%
Public sector: 12%

Electoral history:

President (2004): Kerry (D) 60%; Bush (R) 40%
Governor (2002): Taft (R) 59%; Hagan (D) 38%
President (2000): Gore (D) 58%; Bush (R) 39%
Governor (1998): Fisher (D) 59%; Taft (R) 36%
President (1996): Clinton (D) 58%; Dole (R) 32%; Perot 10%
Governor (1994): Voinovich (R) 69%; Burch (D) 28%
President (1992): Clinton (D) 50%; Bush (R) 31%; Perot 19%
Governor (1990): Celebrezze (D) 51%; Voinovich (R) 49%
President (1988): Dukakis (D) 54%; Bush (R) 46%

Party affiliations of county administrative officeholders (2004):
9 Democrats; 2 Republicans

History:

In the early 1700s, the French gained influence over the Indians and established trading posts in the Maumee Valley. During the latter part of the century, the British took control of the region. At the end of the Revolutionary War, the territory was surrendered to the Americans—although Indian tribes occupied it until 1794, when Gen. Anthony Wayne defeated them in the Battle of Fallen Timbers, near the present city of Maumee. In 1795, the Treaty of Greene Ville gave Indian tribes occupancy rights in much of the Maumee Valley but reserved for the federal government a 12-square-mile area centered around a British fort at the rapids of the Maumee River. White settlement increased after the War of 1812, and, by 1833, the Indian reservations were ceded. The same year, Toledo was organized from two settlements along the Maumee River—Fort Lawrence and Vistula. Leaders of Ohio and the territory of Michigan were divided over which surveyor's line should be the boundary. In February 1835, the Ohio legislature claimed the disputed strip of land by extending the northern boundaries of Henry, Williams, and Wood counties. Ohio and Michigan militias gathered for battle before Congress intervened and settled the border war in Ohio's favor. On June 20, 1835, Lucas County was established. Toledo was selected the county seat, lost the designation to Maumee from 1841 to 1853, then regained it. By the 1840s, Toledo was the chief port on Lake Erie for the shipment of wheat to the Atlantic coast. The completion of the Miami & Erie Canal in 1845, the development of the railroads in the 1850s, and the discovery of oil and natural gas in northwestern Ohio in the 1880s combined to transform the Toledo region into one of the nation's leading transportation and industrial centers. Immigrants, especially Germans, flocked to the area for jobs. In the 1880s, Edward D. Libbey, a New England glass manufacturer, built a factory in Toledo; an associate, Michael J. Owens, perfected glass-blowing technology. Toledo soon became the world's leader in production of plate glass and sheet glass for the auto industry. The region also became known for automotive parts, Champion spark plugs, the Jeeps of Willys-Overland Co., and oil pipelines and refineries.

MADISON COUNTY

Established: March 1, 1810
Named for: James Madison
Land area: 466 square miles
Locale: about 20 miles west of Columbus
2000 Population: 40,213
 White: 91.5%
 Black: 6.0%
County seat: London
Largest city: London (8,771)
Second-largest city: None
Largest village: West Jefferson (4,331)
Per-capita income (2002) / ranking among Ohio counties:
$26,313/61
Number of school districts (2005): 4

Employment base (2001):
Private sector: 77%
Public sector: 23%

Electoral history:

President (2004): Bush (R) 64%; Kerry (D) 36%
Governor (2002): Taft (R) 66%; Hagan (D) 28%
President (2000): Bush (R) 61%; Gore (D) 36%
Governor (1998): Taft (R) 57%; Fisher (D) 35%
President (1996): Dole (R) 51%; Clinton (D) 38%; Perot 10%
Governor (1994): Voinovich (R) 75%; Burch (D) 21%
President (1992): Bush (R) 49%; Clinton (D) 29%; Perot 23%
Governor (1990): Voinovich (R) 63%; Celebrezze (D) 37%
President (1988): Bush (R) 71%; Dukakis (D) 29%

Party affiliations of county administrative officeholders (2004):
10 Republicans; 1 Independent

History:

This was Shawnee Indian territory before being made part of the Virginia Military District, used to reward Revolutionary War veterans. In 1810, Madison County was created from Ross County; the next year, London was selected the county seat. The pioneers were mostly from Virginia and Kentucky. The county always has been largely agricultural. London became a market town for cattle and sheep, which were driven to the stockyards over the National Road. The thoroughfare was completed through London by 1837, when the Red Brick Tavern was established in Lafayette, just east of London. The tavern was a favorite stagecoach stop; noted visitors included William Henry Harrison and Henry Clay. Besides livestock and stockyards, Madison County became known for its production of corn and wheat. In 1912, the state legislature authorized establishment of the State Prison Farm near London.

MAHONING COUNTY

Established: March 1, 1846
Named for: Indian for "at the licks"
Land area: 426 square miles
Locale: borders Pennsylvania, about 50 miles southeast of Cleveland
2000 Population: 257,555
　White: 81.1%
　Black: 15.0%
County seat: Youngstown
Largest city: Youngstown (82,026)
Second-largest city: Struthers (11,756)
Per-capita income (2002) / ranking among Ohio counties: $25,924/35
Number of school districts (2005): 14

Employment base (2001):
Private sector: 88%
Public sector: 12%

Electoral history:
President (2004): Kerry (D) 63%; Bush (R) 37%
Governor (2002): Hagan (D) 50%; Taft (R) 46%
President (2000): Gore (D) 61%; Bush (R) 35%
Governor (1998): Fisher (D) 56%; Taft (R) 38%
President (1996): Clinton (D) 62%; Dole (R) 27%; Perot 11%
Governor (1994): Voinovich (R) 66%; Burch (D) 32%
President (1992): Clinton (D) 52%; Bush (R) 25%; Perot 24%
Governor (1990): Celebrezze (D) 57%; Voinovich (R) 43%
President (1988): Dukakis (D) 63%; Bush (R) 37%

Party affiliations of county administrative officeholders (2004):
11 Democrats

History:

The Mahoning Valley was the territory of Iroquois Indians when New Englanders began arriving in the late 1700s. James Hillman, an agent for a Pittsburgh trading company, and John Young of New York state—for whom Youngstown was named—were among the first to promote permanent settlement. The land that became Mahoning County was split between the Connecticut Western Reserve to the north and Congress Lands to the south. In 1798, Canfield was settled and Youngstown was platted with 100 lots. Struthers, a settlement at the mouth of Yellow Creek, was named for landowner John Struthers and quickly developed as a mill town. In 1803, the first blast furnace in the Mahoning Valley was built at Struthers to make iron from local ores. Other crude, charcoal-burning furnaces soon followed. By the 1820s, Ohio-mined coal replaced charcoal as fuel for the furnaces, which dotted the valley. David Tod, who became Ohio's 25th governor, was among the founders of Youngstown's iron industry. From 1845 to 1875, 21 blast furnaces were constructed in the valley. During the Civil War, the Youngstown area provided much of the iron for Union army weapons and ammu-

nition. In 1846, the state legislature selected Canfield as Mahoning County's county seat. In 1876, the legislature reversed itself and moved the county seat to Youngstown, prompting a legal battle eventually settled by the U.S. Supreme Court, which upheld the move. At the turn of the century, steel began to replace iron as the chief product of the Mahoning Valley—after the adoption of the Bessemer process of producing steel. The new century also brought a wave of consolidations: small steel companies were merged into giants—United States Steel, Republic Steel, Carnegie Steel, Youngstown Sheet & Tube. By World War I, Youngstown's blast furnaces and rolling mills rivaled Pittsburgh's in iron and steel production. The steel boom attracted waves of immigrant job-seekers, making Mahoning one of Ohio's most ethnically diverse counties. The county prospered for decades but, in the 1970s, fell victim to a series of devastating plant closings. Under the weight of high wages and old technology, steel companies relocated to new and lower-cost plants outside Ohio or outside the United States. From 1973 to 1983, the Mahoning Valley lost 40,000 manufacturing jobs.

MARION COUNTY

Established: April 1, 1820
Named for: Gen. Francis Marion (Revolutionary War)
Land area: 404 square miles
Locale: about 40 miles north of Columbus
2000 Population: 66,217
　White: 92.4%
　Black: 5.4%
County seat: Marion
Largest city: Marion (35,318)
Second-largest city: none
Largest village: Prospect (1,191)
Per-capita income (2002) / ranking among Ohio counties: $23,759/55
Number of school districts (2005): 5

Employment base (2001):
Private sector: 79%
Public sector: 21%

Electoral history:
President (2004): Bush (R) 59%; Kerry (D) 41%
Governor (2002): Taft (R) 61%; Hagan (D) 33%
President (2000): Bush (R) 55%; Gore (D) 42%
Governor (1998): Taft (R) 49%; Fisher (D) 43%
President (1996): Dole (R) 45%; Clinton (D) 42%; Perot 12%
Governor (1994): Voinovich (R) 71%; Burch (D) 24%
President (1992): Bush (R) 42%; Clinton (D) 34%; Perot 24%
Governor (1990): Voinovich (R) 59%; Celebrezze (D) 41%
President (1988): Bush (R) 61%; Dukakis (D) 39%

Party affiliations of county administrative officeholders (2004):
8 Republicans; 2 Democrats; 1 Independent

History:

Before the War of 1812, Wyandot Indians dominated the area that became Marion County. In the early 1800s, white settlers moved into the southern part of the area, although settlement was slow until 1817, when the Wyandots ceded the rest of the land. According to legend, Marion first was called Jacob's Well, named for pioneer surveyor Jacob Foos and his successful search for water there. In 1821, Eber Baker laid out the village of Marion, which was selected the county seat. Claridon, east of Marion, had been laid out earlier that year—the county's first village. In the 1850s, when railroads arrived in the county, Marion became a center for grain mills and elevators. Marion housed one of the Erie Railroad's largest terminals. Pennsylvania Germans were the largest immigrant group. In 1884, Warren G. Harding and two friends purchased the bankrupt *Marion Star* for $300 and quickly turned it into a successful newspaper. The same year, the Marion Steam Shovel Co. was organized; it grew into the largest manufacturing company in the county, and its equipment became known worldwide. The company's giant shovels, earth movers, and other equipment were used in building the Panama Canal, the Boulder Dam, and many railroads and highways. The Harding Memorial, on Marion's south side, contains the bodies of the 29th president and his wife..

MEDINA COUNTY

Established: February 18, 1812
Named for: Medina, Arabia (burial site of Mohammed)
Land area: 425 square miles
Locale: about 25 miles southwest of Cleveland
2000 Population: 151,095
 White: 97.1%
 Black: 0.7%
County seat: Medina
Largest city: Brunswick (33,388)
Second-largest city: Medina (25,139)
Per-capita income (2002) / ranking among Ohio counties: $30,685/9
Number of school districts (2005): 7

Employment base (2001):
Private sector: 88%
Public sector: 12%

Electoral history:
President (2004): Bush (R) 57%; Kerry (D) 43%
Governor (2002): Taft (R) 58%; Hagan (D) 38%
President (2000): Bush (R) 56%; Gore (D) 40%
Governor (1998): Taft (R) 57%; Fisher (D) 38%
President (1996): Dole (R) 44%; Clinton (D) 40%; Perot 15%
Governor (1994): Voinovich (R) 80%; Burch (D) 18%
President (1992): Bush (R) 40%; Clinton (D) 32%; Perot 29%
Governor (1990): Voinovich (R) 64%; Celebrezze (D) 36%

President (1988): Bush (R) 61%; Dukakis (D) 39%

Party affiliations of county administrative officeholders (2004):
9 Republicans; 2 Democrats

History:

This area was the land of Wyandot Indians before 1805, when it was ceded to the federal government. Most was within the Connecticut Western Reserve. The Connecticut Land Co. surveyed, subdivided, and sold it to settlers, most from New England. The first permanent settlements took place between 1811 and 1812; Lodi, originally called Harrisville, was one of the first. In 1818, the village of Medina—originally called Mecca—was platted. Slow to develop, the primarily agricultural county became known for its potatoes, corn, wheat, and oats. Before the Civil War, Lodi was a station on the Underground Railroad. In the late 1860s, retired jeweler Amos I. Root of Medina began studying bees and manufacturing hives, honey extractors, and other beekeeping equipment. His research and products won worldwide recognition. Wadsworth became known for the development of sulphur matches and the Ohio Match Co. For most of its history, the county was mostly agricultural. Since the 1970s, it has been a fast-growing, suburban area from which many residents commute to work in Cuyahoga and Summit counties.

MEIGS COUNTY

Established: April 1, 1819
Named for: Gov. Return Jonathan Meigs
Land area: 433 square miles
Locale: on the Ohio River, about 80 miles southeast of Columbus
2000 Population: 23,072
 White: 97.3%
 Black: 0.6%
County seat: Pomeroy
Largest city: none
Largest village: Middleport (2,525)
Second-Largest village: Pomeroy (1,966)
Per-capita income (2002) / ranking among Ohio counties: $19,760/83
Number of school districts (2005): 3

Employment base (2001):
Private sector: 76%
Public sector: 24%

Electoral history:
President (2004): Bush (R) 58%; Kerry (D) 41%
Governor (2002): Taft (R) 66%; Hagan (D) 29%
President (2000): Bush (R) 59%; Gore (D) 38%
Governor (1998): Taft (R) 56%; Fisher (D) 38%
President (1996): Clinton (D) 45%; Dole (R) 38%; Perot 15%
Governor (1994): Voinovich (R) 67%; Burch (D) 29%
President (1992): Clinton (D) 41%; Bush (R) 38%; Perot 21%

Governor (1990): Voinovich (R) 56%; Celebrezze (D) 44%
President (1988): Bush (R) 60%; Dukakis (D) 40%

Party affiliations of county administrative officeholders (2004):
9 Republicans; 2 Democrats

History:

Meigs County is known for its rock cliffs, some of which rise several hundred feet above the Ohio River. Pioneers found many mounds, rock pictures (depicting humans, animals, and birds), and other signs of prehistoric people. George Washington, who explored the Ohio River region, wrote about walking across the neck of the county's boot-shaped peninsula. Formed mostly from Athens and Gallia counties, Meigs was part of the Ohio Company lands. Permanent settlement began about 1800. Middleport was the first county seat (1819), followed by Chester (1822) and Pomeroy (1841). Samuel W. Pomeroy, originally from Boston, was an area landowner and coal developer. Virtually all the early settlements were along the river. New Englanders arrived first, followed by the Irish, Welsh, and Germans. Chief industries were coal, salt, and agriculture. In July 1863, Union forces led by Maj. Daniel McCook confronted Confederate general John Hunt Morgan at Buffington's Island and temporarily prevented the raiders from crossing the Ohio.

MERCER COUNTY

Established: April 1, 1820
Named for: Gen. Hugh Mercer
(Revolutionary War)
Land area: 473 square miles
Locale: borders Indiana, about 50 miles northwest of Dayton
2000 Population: 40,924
  White: 98.3%
  Black: 0.1%
County seat: Celina
Largest city: Celina (10,303)
Second-largest city: none
Largest village: Coldwater (4,482)
Per-capita income (2002) / ranking among Ohio counties:
$25,760/36
Number of school districts (2005): 6

Employment base (2001):
Private sector: 83%
Public sector: 17%

Electoral history:
President (2004): Bush (R) 75%; Kerry (D) 25%
Governor (2002): Taft (R) 74%; Hagan (D) 22%
President (2000): Bush (R) 68%; Gore (D) 28%
Governor (1998): Taft (R) 60%; Fisher (D) 34%
President (1996): Dole (R) 50%; Clinton (D) 36%; Perot 13%
Governor (1994): Voinovich (R) 70%; Burch (D) 26%

President (1992): Bush (R) 47%; Clinton (D) 26%; Perot 27%
Governor (1990): Voinovich (R) 66%; Celebrezze (D) 34%
President (1988): Bush (R) 69%; Dukakis (D) 31%

Party affiliations of county administrative officeholders (2004):
6 Democrats; 5 Republicans

History:

The area that became Mercer County was the site of some of the fiercest fighting of the Indian wars (1790–1795). On November 4, 1791, on the banks of the Wabash River, a poorly equipped army led by Gen. Arthur St. Clair was routed by the Indian forces of Little Turtle (Miami) and Blue Jacket (Shawnee). Hundreds of American soldiers were killed. In 1794, on the site of the defeat, Gen. Anthony Wayne supervised construction of Fort Recovery as a signal of the nation's determination to make the Ohio territory safe for settlement. On July 30, 1794, Wayne began moving northward from the fort; his campaign against the Indians ended in August 1795 with the signing of the Treaty of Greene Ville. By 1820, the entire area was open for purchase and settlement. That year, Shanesville (later Rockford) was surveyed and platted along the St. Marys River. Although established in 1820, the county was not organized until 1824, when St. Marys was made the county seat. In the 1830s, many Germans moved to the county and established farms and small industries. In 1835, several hundred blacks located near Carthagena, in the southern part of the county, as part of resettlement efforts for former slaves. Upon learning that more were coming, white residents stopped the resettlement project. Between 1837 and 1845, Grand Lake Saint Marys was constructed as a reservoir for the Miami & Erie Canal. In 1840, the county seat was moved to Celina. On July 1, 1913, the Fort Recovery Monument was dedicated.

MIAMI COUNTY

Established: March 1, 1807
Named for: Miami Indians
Land area: 410 square miles
Locale: about 15 miles north of Dayton
2000 Population: 98,868
  White: 95.8%
  Black: 1.8%
County seat: Troy
Largest city: Troy (21,999)
Second-largest city: Piqua (20,738)
Per-capita income (2002) / ranking among Ohio counties:
$28,086/19
Number of school districts (2005): 9

Employment base (2001):
Private sector: 89%
Public sector: 11%

Electoral history:
President (2004): Bush (R) 66%; Kerry (D) 34%

Governor (2002): Taft (R) 70%; Hagan (D) 24%
President (2000): Bush (R) 61%; Gore (D) 36%
Governor (1998): Taft (R) 56%; Fisher (D) 36%
President (1996): Dole (R) 49%; Clinton (D) 39%; Perot 11%
Governor (1994): Voinovich (R) 76%; Burch (D) 20%
President (1992): Bush (R) 46%; Clinton (D) 29%; Perot 25%
Governor (1990): Voinovich (R) 64%; Celebrezze (D) 36%
President (1988): Bush (R) 69%; Dukakis (D) 31%

Party affiliations of county administrative officeholders (2004):
11 Republicans

History:

Pickawillany, at the present site of Piqua on the Great Miami River, was a principal village of the Miami tribes. The name piqua is said to be Shawnee for "a man risen from ashes." John Knoop, a German from Pennsylvania, usually is credited with establishing the county's first permanent settlement—Staunton—in 1798. In 1807, the state legislature created Miami County from Montgomery County; the first court sessions were held in Staunton, which soon was absorbed by Troy. Many of the early settlers were from Kentucky and Virginia. At the start of the War of 1812, Fort Piqua was established. The village that grew up around the fort initially was named Washington but soon was changed to Piqua. In the 1840s, the completion of the Miami & Erie Canal brought prosperity to Troy and Piqua, which were centers for shipping the county's agricultural bounty.

MONROE COUNTY

Established: January 29, 1813
Named for: James Monroe
Land area: 457 square miles
Locale: on the Ohio River, about 100 miles southeast of Columbus
2000 Population: 15,180
  White: 98.5%
  Black: 0.1%
County seat: Woodsfield
Largest city: none
Largest village: Woodsfield (2,598)
Second-Largest village: Clarington (444)
Per-capita income (2002) / ranking among Ohio counties: $20,615/78
Number of school districts (2005): 1

Employment base (2001):
Private sector: 80%
Public sector: 20%

Electoral history:
President (2004): Kerry (D) 55%; Bush (R) 44%
Governor (2002): Taft (R) 49%; Hagan (D) 48%
President (2000): Gore (R) 51%; Bush (R) 44%
Governor (1998): Fisher (D) 55%; Taft (R) 38%
President (1996): Clinton (D) 56%; Dole (R) 27%; Perot 16%

Governor (1994): Voinovich (R) 50%; Burch (D) 47%
President (1992): Clinton (D) 56%; Bush (R) 24%; Perot 20%
Governor (1990): Celebrezze (D) 62%; Voinovich (R) 38%
President (1988): Dukakis (D) 63%; Bush (R) 37%
Party affiliations of county administrative officeholders (2004):
9 Democrats; 1 Republican; 1 Independent

History:

Monroe County was part of the Seven Ranges, the first Congress Lands surveyed and sold by the federal government. Unlike other counties within the Ranges, Monroe was off the primary migration routes and thus attracted few settlers. Throughout its history, Monroe has been among Ohio's least-populous counties. In the late 1700s, Lewis Wetzel, a notorious Indian hunter, spent much time in the area. In the 1790s, a small settlement was made near the mouth of Sunfish Creek, which empties into the Ohio River. Before 1805, the interior of the county went largely unexplored. In 1814, Archibald Wood laid out Woodsfield, which became the county seat. Most of the early settlers were from Pennsylvania and Virginia, although, in 1819, a group of German-Swiss families settled in the hills and produced Swiss cheese and watches. The area became known as "little Switzerland." The 1890s brought a short-lived boom in oil and gas production. In the early 1900s, the county was known for its production of tobacco, sheep, and wool.

MONTGOMERY COUNTY

Established: May 1, 1803
Named for: Gen. Richard Montgomery (Revolutionary War)
Land area: 464 square miles
Locale: about 40 miles north of Cincinnati
2000 Population: 559,062
  White: 76.5%
  Black: 19.9%
County seat: Dayton
Largest city: Dayton (166,179)
Second-largest city: Kettering (57,502)
Per-capita income (2002) / ranking among Ohio counties: $30,528/10
Number of school districts (2005): 16

Employment base (2001):
Private sector: 90%
Public sector: 10%

Electoral history:
President (2004): Kerry (D) 51%; Bush (R) 49%
Governor (2002): Taft (R) 59%; Hagan (D) 37%
President (2000): Gore (D) 50%: Bush (R) 48%
Governor (1998): Fisher (D) 47%; Taft (R) 47%
President (1996): Clinton (D) 50%; Dole (R) 41%; Perot 8%
Governor (1994): Voinovich (R) 72%; Burch (D) 25%
President (1992): Clinton (D) 41%; Bush (R) 40%; Perot 18%
Governor (1990): Voinovich (R) 55%; Celebrezze (D) 45%

President (1988): Bush (R) 58%; Dukakis (D) 42%

Party affiliations of county administrative officeholders (2004):
6 Democrats; 5 Republicans

History:

S ettlement of this area began after 1795, when the Treaty of Greene Ville was signed. Some early settlers traveled up the Great Miami River from Cincinnati. John Cleves Symmes, a New Jersey judge, attempted to purchase a million acres in the area, but Congress granted him only about one-third of that. Many settlers who thought they had bought land from the Symmes Co. discovered that the company did not have a valid title to the land, which had to be purchased from the government at two dollars an acre. Friction over land titles stalled development for some time. In 1803, Montgomery County was formed from Hamilton County. Dayton—named for Jonathan Dayton, a Revolutionary War officer and associate of Symmes—was selected the county seat. Many early settlers were Pennsylvanians of German descent. By 1840, with the National Road completed through Ohio and the canal system nearly built, Dayton became one of the state's largest population centers. An agricultural county until then, Montgomery began developing a diversified manufacturing base. In the Civil War era, the area became known for iron and brass works, paper, boxcars and coaches, and woodworking. In 1850, the Roman Catholic Church opened St. Mary's Institute as a school for boys; in 1913, it became St. Mary's College and, in 1920, the University of Dayton. In 1872, Paul Laurence Dunbar, a son of emancipated slaves, was born in Dayton; he gained worldwide recognition for his poems and short stories. In 1884, Dayton manufacturer John H. Patterson bought the "mechanical money drawer" invented by James Ritty, perfected it, and later founded the National Cash Register Co. Before long, Dayton was known for inventions ranging from fare boxes to ignition systems. In 1909, Col. Edward A. Deeds and Charles F. Kettering formed the Dayton Engineering Laboratories Co.—Delco—which later was acquired by General Motors. On December 17, 1903, Wilbur and Orville Wright, Dayton bicycle repairmen, stayed aloft for almost a minute in a homemade airplane—the first motor-powered flight—in Kitty Hawk, N.C. As a result, Dayton became "the birthplace of aviation." The Wright brothers continued their experiments on Huffman Plains outside Dayton; the area later was expanded into Wright Field, where World War I aviators were trained, and still later into Wright-Patterson Air Force Base (named after Dayton's Lt. Frank S. Patterson, a flier killed on maneuvers). In March 1913, five days of rain produced floods that killed nearly 400 people and destroyed $100 million in property. The disaster sparked development of the Miami Conservancy District, the nation's first comprehensive flood-control project. James M. Cox, a three-term governor and the 1920 Democratic nominee for president, was born on a farm near Dayton.

MORGAN COUNTY

Established: December 29, 1817
Named for: Gen. Daniel Morgan (Revolutionary War)
Land area: 421 square miles

Locale: about 60 miles southeast of Columbus
2000 Population: 14,897
White: 94.0%
Black: 3.2%
County seat: McConnelsville
Largest city: none
Largest village: McConnelsville (1,676)
Second-Largest village: Malta (696)
Per-capita income (2002) / ranking among Ohio counties: $20,052/81
Number of school districts (2005): 1

Employment base (2001):
Private sector: 79%
Public sector: 21%

Electoral history:
President (2004): Bush (R) 56%; Kerry (D) 43%
Governor (2002): Taft (R) 64%; Hagan (D) 30%
President (2000): Bush (R) 58%; Gore (D) 38%
Governor (1998): Taft (R) 59%; Fisher (D) 35%
President (1996): Dole (R) 43%; Clinton (D) 40%; Perot 15%
Governor (1994): Voinovich (R) 71%; Burch (D) 24%
President (1992): Bush (R) 41%; Clinton (D) 36%; Perot 23%
Governor (1990): Voinovich (R) 57%; Celebrezze (D) 43%
President (1988): Bush (R) 64%; Dukakis (D) 36%

Party affiliations of county administrative officeholders (2004):
11 Republicans

History:

P ioneers discovered dozens of mounds with remains of prehistoric people in this area. In the late 1700s, the Delaware Indians occupied the region. On January 2, 1791, an Indian war party came upon settlers in an area known as Big Bottom, below the present site of Stockport. The Indians killed nine men, a woman, and two children; today, the area is a state memorial. After the massacre, settlement of the county was delayed until 1795, when the Treaty of Greene Ville was signed. The early settlers mostly arrived from Pennsylvania and Virginia; they congregated along the Muskingum River, the county's primary transportation route. Malta, on the west side of the river, was platted in 1816; McConnelsville, on the east side, was laid out the next year and became the county seat. The county was formed from Guernsey, Muskingum, and Washington counties. In the 1830s, the area prospered from canal development. In the 1840s, it was the state's leading producer of salt; about the same time, oil and gas wells were developed. Throughout its history, Morgan has been a mostly rural, sparsely populated county.

MORROW COUNTY

Established: March 1, 1848
Named for: Gov. Jeremiah Morrow

Land area: 407 square miles
Locale: about 40 miles north of Columbus
2000 Population: 31,628
 White: 98.8%
 Black: 0.2%
County seat: Mount Gilead
Largest city: none
Largest village: Mount Gilead (3,290)
Second-Largest village: Cardington (1,849)
Per-capita income (2002) / ranking among Ohio counties: $22,484/70
Number of school districts (2005): 4

Employment base (2001):
Private sector: 75%
Public sector: 25%

Electoral history:
President (2004): Bush (R) 64%; Kerry (D) 35%
Governor (2002): Taft (R) 64%; Hagan (D) 29%
President (2000): Bush (R) 61%; Gore (D) 35%
Governor (1998): Taft (R) 59%; Fisher (D) 35%
President (1996): Dole (R) 46%; Clinton (D) 38%; Perot 14%
Governor (1994): Voinovich (R) 71%; Burch (D) 24%
President (1992): Bush (R) 41%; Clinton (D) 31%; Perot 28%
Governor (1990): Voinovich (R) 58%; Celebrezze (D) 42%
President (1988): Bush (R) 67%; Dukakis (D) 33%

Party affiliations of county administrative officeholders (2004):
10 Republicans; 1 Democrat

History:

One of the last counties organized in Ohio, Morrow was created from Delaware, Knox, Marion, and Richland counties. Pioneers of the area found many prehistoric mounds and enclosures. In the late 1700s, Wyandot Indians occupied the land. The area was split, north and south, by the Greenville treaty line of 1795. The first permanent settlements, in 1807 to 1808, were near Chesterville, in the southeastern part of the county. The pioneers were from Connecticut, Maryland, Pennsylvania, and Virginia. Quakers settled in the southwestern part of the county near Whetstone and Alum creeks. Mount Gilead, named for the biblical mountain, was platted in 1824 and became the county seat in 1848. Cardington, southwest of Mount Gilead, was platted in 1836 and named for the county's first carding mill on the banks of Whetstone Creek. Farmers took wool to the mill, where it was rolled and prepared for spinning. Before the Civil War, the county was strongly antislavery and was an important link in the Underground Railroad. Warren G. Harding attended Ohio Central College, an academy chartered in 1854 as Iberia College, which has been defunct for decades. Throughout its history, Morrow has been primarily an agricultural

county.

MUSKINGUM COUNTY

Established: March 1, 1803
Named for: Muskingum River
Land area: 673 square miles
Locale: about 50 miles east of Columbus
2000 Population: 84,585
 White: 93.8%
 Black: 4.0%
County seat: Zanesville
Largest city: Zanesville (25,586)
Second-largest city: none
Largest village: New Concord (2,651)
Per-capita income (2002) / ranking among Ohio counties: $24,540/48
Number of school districts (2005): 6

Employment base (2001):
Private sector: 88%
Public sector: 12%

Electoral history:
President (2004): Bush (R) 57%; Kerry (D) 42%
Governor (2002): Taft (R) 67%; Hagan (D) 28%
President (2000): Bush (R) 55%; Gore (D) 41%
Governor (1998): Taft (R) 56%; Fisher (D) 39%
President (1996): Dole (R) 42%; Clinton (D) 42%; Perot 15%
Governor (1994): Voinovich (R) 73%; Burch (D) 22%
President (1992): Bush (R) 41%; Clinton (D) 34%; Perot 25%
Governor (1990): Voinovich (R) 52%; Celebrezze (D) 48%
President (1988): Bush (R) 63%; Dukakis (D) 37%

Party affiliations of county administrative officeholders (2004):
11 Republicans

History:

Before the 1790s, the Delaware, Shawnee, and Wyandot Indians inhabited this area. In 1796, Ebenezer Zane was authorized by Congress to lay out a road from Wheeling to Limestone (Maysville), Ky.—the first road through the Ohio territory. As compensation, Zane was to receive 640 acres at each of the main river crossings along his route—the future sites of Zanesville, Lancaster, and Chillicothe, where ferries would be established. In 1797, Zane's Trace was opened. In 1799, the village of Zanesville was established on the east side of the Muskingum River where the Licking River joins it. Rufus Putnam of Marietta surveyed the area and laid out Springfield (Putnam) on the west bank; it later was absorbed by Zanesville. From Zanesville east to Wheeling, Zane's Trace became part of the National Road. In the early days of statehood, Zanesville was one of Ohio's best-known communities. From 1810 to 1812, it served as the state capital. In 1814, the first Y-bridge was built over the Muskingum and Licking rivers; the bridge and its successors have been among the nation's most distinctive bridges. The county thrived economically on agriculture, coal, salt, blown glass, sand, clay, and pottery. In the late 1800s, Zanesville was known nationally as a center for the clay industries. In 1837, Muskingum College was chartered in New Concord. Zane Grey, a great-grandson of Ebenezer Zane and the author of popular western novels, lived in Zanesville. In 1927, *Literary Digest* magazine named Zanesville the "typical American city."

NOBLE COUNTY

Established: April 1, 1851
Named for: James Noble
(early settler)
Land area: 405 square miles
Locale: about 80 miles east of
Columbus
2000 Population: 14,058
White: 92.6%
Black: 5.6%
County seat: Caldwell
Largest city: none
Largest village: Caldwell (1,956)
Second-largest village: Summerfield (296)
Per-capita income (2002) / ranking among Ohio counties:
$17,055/88
Number of school districts (2005): 2

Employment base (2001):
Private sector: 67%
Public sector: 33%

Electoral history:
President (2004): Bush (R) 59%; Kerry (D) 41%
Governor (2002): Taft (R) 57%; Hagan (D) 38%
President (2000): Bush (R) 57%; Gore (D) 38%
Governor (1998): Taft (R) 55%; Fisher (D) 40%
President (1996): Clinton (D) 43%; Dole (R) 40%; Perot 16%
Governor (1994): Voinovich (R) 65%; Burch (D) 31%
President (1992): Bush (R) 38%; Clinton (D) 38%; Perot 24%
Governor (1990): Voinovich (R) 54%; Celebrezze (D) 46%
President (1988): Bush (R) 60%; Dukakis (D) 40%

Party affiliations of county administrative officeholders (2004):
7 Republicans; 4 Democrats

History:

Noble County was the last county established in Ohio. After area residents petitioned the state legislature, it was formed from parts of Guernsey, Monroe, Morgan, and Washington counties. The first county seat was Sarahsville, which had been laid out in 1829. In 1854, voters decided to move the county seat to a more central location—a site along Duck Creek that became Caldwell. In the

early 1800s, the pioneers who settled the hilly, forested area discovered oil while drilling for salt. In the 1860s, the county experienced a brief oil boom, although small-scale agriculture always has predominated in the area. The early pioneers mostly were New Englanders. Germans settled Sharon; Irish settled Summerfield, which was a stop on the Underground Railroad. Between 1880 and World War II, coal was a significant industry. In September 1925, a storm brought down the dirigible Shenandoah near the village of Ava; 14 people died.

OTTAWA COUNTY

Established: March 6, 1840
Named for: Indian word for "trader"
Land area: 267 square miles
Locale: about 15 miles southeast
of Toledo
2000 Population: 40,985
White: 96.5%
Black: 0.7%
County seat: Port Clinton
Largest city: Port Clinton (6,391)
Second-largest city: none
Largest village: Oak Harbor (2,841)
Per-capita income (2002) / ranking among Ohio counties:
$29,768/13
Number of school districts (2005): 4

Employment base (2001):
Private sector: 86%
Public sector: 14%

Electoral history:
President (2004): Bush (R) 52%; Kerry (D) 48%
Governor (2002): Taft (R) 63%; Hagan (D) 34%
President (2000): Bush (R) 50%; Gore (D) 48%
Governor (1998): Taft (R) 47%; Fisher (D) 47%
President (1996): Clinton (D) 49%; Dole (R) 37%; Perot 13%
Governor (1994): Voinovich (R) 72%; Burch (D) 26%
President (1992): Clinton (D) 41%; Bush (R) 34%; Perot 25%
Governor (1990): Voinovich (R) 55%; Celebrezze (D) 45%
President (1988): Bush (R) 54%; Dukakis (D) 46%

Party affiliations of county administrative officeholders (2004):
10 Democrats; 1 Republican

History:

This lakefront area was occupied by Wyandot Indians before Detroit-based French settlers established a presence in the mid-1700s. The British soon arrived, built forts, and wrested control from the French. With the British controlling the Sandusky Bay and Indians located to the west, few Americans settled in the area before the War of 1812. On September 10, 1813, Commodore Oliver H. Perry led an American naval fleet to victory over the British—at Put-in-Bay—in the Battle of Lake Erie. Perry's banner – "Don't Give Up the Ship"—later was enshrined at Annapolis. In 1817, the Indians ceded their lands. By 1820, the lands had been surveyed and were made available for purchase. The earliest settlers were New Englanders. Chief occupations were fur trapping, hunting and fishing, and boat building. Port Clinton was founded in 1828 and later became the county seat. Germans settled Middle Bass and North Bass islands, which became known for grape growing and wine making. Middle Bass Island was a retreat for Presidents Rutherford B. Hayes, Grover Cleveland, Benjamin Harrison, and William Howard Taft. The county long has been a vacation spot. In 1906, Camp Perry was founded as a training camp for the Ohio National Guard; it became widely known for national rifle and pistol competitions. In 1913, on the 100th anniversary of Perry's victory, the 350-foot Peace Monument was dedicated at Put-in-Bay.

PAULDING COUNTY

Established: April 1, 1820
Named for: John Paulding (Revolutionary War)
Land area: 418 square miles
Locale: borders Indiana, about 65 miles southwest of Toledo
2000 Population: 20,293
  White: 95.9%
  Black: 1.0%
County seat: Paulding
Largest city: none
Largest village: Paulding (3,595)
Second-Largest village: Antwerp (1,740)
Per-capita income (2002) / ranking among Ohio counties: $22,613/69
Number of school districts (2005): 3

Employment base (2001):
Private sector: 77%
Public sector: 23%

Electoral history:
President (2004): Bush (R) 63%; Kerry (D) 37%
Governor (2002): Taft (R) 64%; Hagan (D) 31%
President (2000): Bush (R) 58%; Gore (D) 38%
Governor (1998): Taft (R) 56%; Fisher (D) 39%
President (1996): Dole (R) 44%; Clinton (D) 40%; Perot 15%
Governor (1994): Voinovich (R) 67%; Burch (D) 28%
President (1992): Bush (R) 39%; Clinton (D) 35%; Perot 26%
Governor (1990): Voinovich (R) 58%; Celebrezze (D) 42%
President (1988): Bush (R) 63%; Dukakis (D) 37%

Party affiliations of county administrative officeholders (2004):
8 Republicans; 3 Democrats

History:

Much of northwestern Ohio once was lake. The western edge of these Lake Plains became known as the Black Swamp—an area of dense forest and marshlands that delayed settlement until

the land was drained. All of what became Paulding County, the slowest developing county in northwestern Ohio, was within the Black Swamp area. Although pioneers arrived about 1820 in the northeastern part of the county, along the Auglaize River, settlement was negligible until the 1830s, when work began on the canals. In 1839, New Rochester was named the county seat. In 1842, the village of Junction was laid out at the point where two canal branches were joined—the Miami & Erie Canal and the Wabash-Erie Canal. Further south on the Auglaize River—near the confluence with the Little Auglaize—was Charloe, an old Ottawa Indian village that, in 1841, became the county seat. It remained the seat until 1851, when Paulding was chosen for its more central location. Large-scale drainage began in the 1870s, which opened up the county to timbering and agriculture. Since the forests were cleared, the county has been one of Ohio's richest agricultural areas.

PERRY COUNTY

Established: March 1, 1818
Named for: Comdr. Oliver H. Perry
Land area: 413 square miles
Locale: about 40 miles east of Columbus
2000 Population: 34,078
  White: 98.7%
  Black: 0.3%
County seat: New Lexington
Largest city: New Lexington (4,689)
Second-largest city: none
Largest village: Crooksville (2,483)
Per-capita income (2002) / ranking among Ohio counties: $19,277/86
Number of school districts (2005): 4

Employment base (2001):
Private sector: 74%
Public sector: 26%

Electoral history:
President (2004): Bush (R) 52%; Kerry (D) 48%
Governor (2002): Taft (R) 56%; Hagan (D) 38%
President (2000): Bush (R) 50%; Gore (D) 46%
Governor (1998): Fisher (D) 47%; Taft (R) 46%
President (1996): Clinton (D) 47%; Dole (R) 37%; Perot 15%
Governor (1994): Voinovich (R) 61%; Burch (D) 32%
President (1992): Clinton (D) 37%; Bush (R) 35%; Perot 28%
Governor (1990): Celebrezze (D) 52%; Voinovich (R) 48%
President (1988): Bush (R) 57%; Dukakis (D) 43%

Party affiliations of county administrative officeholders (2004):
6 Republicans; 5 Democrats

History:

Much evidence suggests that prehistoric people lived in Perry County—especially the northern half, which borders Ohio's agricultural plains. The southern part belongs to the state's

Appalachian hill country. Zane's Trace cut through the north, where settlements began about 1800. Many of the early settlers were Pennsylvania Germans. Somerset, on Zane's Trace midway between Zanesville and Lancaster, was platted in 1810 and was the first county seat. The community—most of the settlers were German Catholics—was the site of some of the earliest Catholic worship in Ohio. Near Somerset, in 1808, the Rev. Edward Fenwick built St. Joseph's Catholic Church and Priory, the first Catholic church in the state. Fenwick became Ohio's first Roman Catholic bishop. In 1818, St. Joseph's Convent, headquarters of the Dominican order, originated as a log chapel near Somerset. After a lengthy court battle, New Lexington, laid out in 1817, became the county seat. Gen. Philip Sheridan, a Civil War hero, grew up in Somerset. In the 1830s, coal mines were opened in the county; after the railroads arrived in the 1850s, Perry became one of the state's chief coal-producing counties. From 1878 to 1890, the county led the state in production. In 1884, disgruntled miners started a fire in the mines near New Straitsville; it burned for about 80 years, causing cave-ins and property damage. In the 1890s, the county had many productive oil wells. In modern times, the county has been known for small-scale farming and small industry.

PICKAWAY COUNTY

Established: March 1, 1810
Named for: the Indian word "piqua"
Land area: 508 square miles
Locale: about 15 miles south of Columbus
2000 Population: 52,727
 White: 92.2%
 Black: 5.7%
County seat: Circleville
Largest city: Circleville (13,485)
Second Largest city: none
Largest village: Ashville (3,174)
Per-capita income (2002) / ranking among Ohio counties: $23,110/63
Number of school districts (2005): 4

Employment base (2001):
Private sector: 73%
Public sector: 27%

Electoral history:
President (2004): Bush (R) 62%; Kerry (D) 38%
Governor (2002): Taft (R) 63%; Hagan (D) 32%
President (2000): Bush (R) 60%; Gore (D) 37%
Governor (1998): Taft (R) 55%; Fisher (D) 38%
President (1996): Dole (R) Clinton (D) 40%; Perot 10%
Governor (1994): Voinovich (R) 72%; Burch (D) 24%
President (1992): Bush (R) 46%; Clinton (D) 31%; Perot 23%
Governor (1990): Voinovich (R) 59%; Celebrezze (D) 41%
President (1988): Bush (R) 69%; Dukakis (D) 31%
Party affiliations of county administrative officeholders (2004):
6 Republicans; 5 Democrats

History:

Along the Scioto River, pioneers in this area found many prehistoric earthworks, including a large circular enclosure (the reason for the naming of Circleville). From about 1750, the territory belonged to the Shawnees. In the 1770s, it was a stronghold of the Indian confederacy that attempted to resist the advance of white settlers. A few miles south of Circleville is a famous tree stump—Logan Elm—where the Mingo chief Logan is said to have composed his famous lament after the Indians' defeat, in 1774, by the Virginia militia. Opened in 1797, Zane's Trace crossed southeastern Pickaway County. In 1803, South Bloomfield was laid out as a stagecoach station on the road from Columbus to Chillicothe. In 1810, the county was formed from Fairfield, Franklin, and Ross counties. Throughout its history, Pickaway County has been a major agricultural producer; it also became known for a wide range of small industries. Caleb Atwater, a longtime resident of Circleville, is credited with writing the state's first history.

PIKE COUNTY

Established: February 1, 1815
Named for: Gen. Zebulon M. Pike (Revolutionary War)
Land area: 444 square miles
Locale: about 60 miles south of Columbus
2000 Population: 27,695
 White: 96.3%
 Black: 0.8%
County seat: Waverly
Largest city: Waverly (4,433)
Second-largest city: none
Largest village: Piketon (1,907)
Per-capita income (2002) / ranking among Ohio counties: $20,845/77
Number of school districts (2005): 4

Employment base (2001):
Private sector: 85%
Public sector: 15%

Electoral history:
President (2004): Bush (R) 52%; Kerry (D) 48%
Governor (2002): Taft (R) 52%; Hagan (D) 44%
President (2000): Bush (R) 51%; Gore (D) 47%
Governor (1998): Fisher (D) 53%; Taft (R) 42%
President (1996): Clinton (D) 51%; Dole (R) 35%; Perot 13%
Governor (1994): Voinovich (R) 58%; Burch (D) 38%
President (1992): Clinton (D) 45%; Bush (R) 36%; Perot 19%
Governor (1990): Celebrezze (D) 56%; Voinovich (R) 44%
President (1988): Bush (R) 52%; Dukakis (D) 48%

Party affiliations of county administrative officeholders (2004):
9 Democrats; 2 Republicans

History:

In 1815, Pike County was formed from Adams, Ross, and Scioto counties. The land east of the Scioto River was part of the Congress Lands; that west of the river belonged to the Virginia Military District. Virginians with military warrants were among the first settlers, followed by Pennsylvanians. Piketon was selected the county seat. Zane's Trace cut through the northwestern corner of the county. In 1832, the Ohio & Erie Canal was completed through Waverly, which had beaten out Piketon for inclusion in the canal system. Robert Lucas, Ohio's 12th governor (1832–1836), was a resident of Piketon when elected to the office. Between 1840 and 1860, many Germans settled in the county. James Emmitt, a Waverly landowner, merchant, and postmaster, led an effort to move the county seat to Waverly; in 1861, a majority of county voters approved the change. Railroads did not reach the county until 1877. For most of its history, Pike has been among the state's least-populous counties. After World War II, the federal government chose Piketon as a site for a uranium-enrichment plant—one of two in the country. The plant produced enriched uranium for nuclear weapons and nuclear submarines.

PORTAGE COUNTY

Established: June 7, 1807
Named for: Indian trail between Cuyahoga and Tuscarawas rivers
Land area: 505 square miles
Locale: about 30 miles southeast of Cleveland
2000 Population: 152,061
 White: 94.6%
 Black: 3.1%
County seat: Ravenna
Largest city: Kent (27,906)
Second-largest city: Aurora (13,556)
Per-capita income (2002) / ranking among Ohio counties:
$26,834/27
Number of school districts (2005): 11

Employment base (2001):
Private sector: 78%
Public sector: 22%

Electoral history:
President (2004): Kerry (D) 53%; Bush (R) 46%
Governor (2002): Taft (R) 48%; Hagan (D) 47%
President (2000): Gore (D) 50%; Bush (R) 45%
Governor (1998): Fisher (D) 47%; Taft (R) 46%
President (1996): Clinton (D) 51%; Dole (R) 33%; Perot 16%
Governor (1994): Voinovich (R) 70%; Burch (D) 26%
President (1992): Clinton (D) 43%; Bush (R) 30%; Perot 28%
Governor (1990): Voinovich (R) 55%; Celebrezze (D) 45%
President (1988): Bush (R) 51%; Dukakis (D) 49%

Party affiliations of county administrative officeholders (2004):
9 Democrats; 1 Republican; 1 Independent
History:

Portage County was part of the Connecticut Western Reserve. Settlers began arriving in the 1790s—via the Cuyahoga River—to the northeastern section of the county. The early settlers were mostly New Englanders. Noah Grant, a tanner and grandfather of Ulysses S. Grant, was an early settler in Deerfield Township. Ravenna, named for an Italian city, was established in 1799 and, in 1807, became the county seat. From its early days, the county had a reputation as a producer of butter, cheese, and other dairy products. From the county's founding until the Civil War era, the city of Kent was known as Franklin Mills; it then adopted the name of Marvin Kent, a prominent businessman and president of the Franklin & Warren Railroad. Being on the route of the Ohio & Erie Canal helped both Ravenna and Kent prosper. In 1850, the Western Reserve Eclectic Institute (later Hiram College) was incorporated by the Disciples of Christ, which had a large following in the county. The next year, James A. Garfield enrolled. Garfield lived much of his adult life in Portage County and for a time headed the institute. In 1910, Kent State University was founded as Kent State Normal College, a two-year school; it became a state university in 1935. The Ravenna Arsenal, encompassing about 21,000 acres, was used extensively during World War II for development of munitions and ordnance. On May 4, 1970, four Kent State students were killed when Ohio National Guardsmen opened fire on Vietnam War protesters.

PREBLE COUNTY

Established: March 1, 1808
Named for: Capt. Edward Preble (Revolutionary War)
Land area: 427 square miles
Locale: borders Indiana, about 20 miles west of Dayton
2000 Population: 42,337
 White: 98.5%
 Black: 0.2%
County seat: Eaton
Largest city: Eaton (8,133)
Largest village: Camden (2,302)
Per-capita income (2002) / ranking among Ohio counties:
$23,751/56
Number of school districts (2005): 5

Employment base (2001):
Private sector: 82%
Public sector: 18%

Electoral history:
President (2004): Bush (R) 65%; Kerry (D) 34%
Governor (2002): Taft (R) 67%; Hagan (D) 27%
President (2000): Bush (R) 62%; Gore (D) 35%
Governor (1998): Taft (R) 54%; Fisher (D) 37%
President (1996): Dole (R) 48%; Clinton (D) 39%; Perot 13%
Governor (1994): Voinovich (R) 74%; Burch (D) 22%

President (1992): Bush (R) 45%; Clinton (D) 31%; Perot 25%
Governor (1990): Voinovich (R) 61%; Celebrezze (D) 39%
President (1988): Bush (R) 68%; Dukakis (D) 32%

Party affiliations of county administrative officeholders (2004):
10 Republicans; 1 Democrat

History:

U.S. Route 127, which bisects Preble County, mainly follows the course that Gen. Arthur St. Clair took in 1791 as he headed north on his disastrous march against the Indians. In 1792, Fort St. Clair was built just west of the present site of Eaton, the county seat. Gen. Anthony Wayne followed the same route in marching toward his victory at Fallen Timbers. In 1806, Eaton was laid out by William Bruce of Kentucky. In 1808, Preble County was created from a western section of Montgomery County. By 1840, the National Road was completed through the county and into Indiana. The county always has been primarily agricultural.

PUTNAM COUNTY

Established: April 1, 1820
Named for: Gen. Israel Putnam
(Revolutionary War)
Land area: 484 square miles
Locale: about 50 miles southwest of
Toledo
2000 Population: 34,726
 White: 96.1%
 Black: 0.1%
County seat: Ottawa
Largest city: none
Largest village: Ottawa (4,367)
Second-largest village: Leipsic (2,236)
Per-capita income (2002) / ranking among Ohio counties:
$26,547/29
Number of school districts (2005): 9

Employment base (2001):
Private sector: 85%
Public sector: 15%

Electoral history:
President (2004): Bush (R) 76%; Kerry (D) 23%
Governor (2002): Taft (R) 70%; Hagan (D) 25%
President (2000): Bush (R) 74%; Gore (D) 23%
Governor (1998): Taft (R) 63%; Fisher (D) 32%
President (1996): Dole (R) 58%; Clinton (D) 31%; Perot 11%
Governor (1994): Voinovich (R) 79%; Burch (D) 17%
President (1992): Bush (R) 55%; Clinton (D) 23%; Perot 22%
Governor (1990): Voinovich (R) 69%; Celebrezze (D) 31%
President (1988): Bush (R) 74%; Dukakis (D) 26%
Party affiliations of county administrative officeholders (2004):
7 Democrats; 4 Republicans

History:

Ottawa took its name from Tawa Town, an Indian village on the Blanchard River. When French traders and missionaries arrived in the 1750s, the territory was occupied by Wyandot and Ottawa Indians. Fort Jennings, on the Auglaize River in the southwestern part of the county, took its name from the fort built during the War of 1812 and commanded by Col. William Jennings. The county was created in 1820 but not organized until 1834, when Kalida was chosen the county seat. In 1817, the Indians ceded most of their territory but remained on the Tawa Town reservation until 1831. The early white settlers included many German and Swiss families; many were Mennonites. In 1834, Ottawa was surveyed and, in 1861, incorporated. The Miami & Erie Canal ran through the west side of the county along the Auglaize River. German Catholics settled Leipsic, which had been laid out in 1857. In 1866, residents voted to move the county seat to Ottawa. The county, always an agricultural area, depends on migrant workers to harvest its vegetable and fruit crops—especially sugar beets and tomatoes.

RICHLAND COUNTY

Established: March 1, 1808
Named for: fertile lands
Land area: 499 square miles
Locale: about 65 miles southwest of
Cleveland
2000 Population: 126,137
 White: 88.3%
 Black: 8.8%
County seat: Mansfield
Largest city: Mansfield (49,346)
Second-largest city: Shelby (9,821)
Per-capita income (2002) / ranking among Ohio counties:
$25,098/44
Number of school districts (2005): 9

Employment base (2001):
Private sector: 86%
Public sector: 14%

Electoral history:
President (2004): Bush (R) 60%; Kerry (D) 40%
Governor (2002): Taft (R) 60%; Hagan (D) 37%
President (2000): Bush (R) 57%; Gore (D) 39%
Governor (1998): Taft (R) 54%; Fisher (D) 42%
President (1996): Dole (R) 46%; Clinton (D) 41%; Perot 13%
Governor (1994): Voinovich (R) 73%; Burch (D) 24%
President (1992): Bush (R) 42%; Clinton (D) 35%; Perot 24%
Governor (1990): Voinovich (R) 61%; Celebrezze (D) 39%
President (1988): Bush (R) 61%; Dukakis (D) 39%

Party affiliations of county administrative officeholders (2004):
6 Republicans; 5 Democrats

History:

Wyandot and affiliated tribes occupied this area until 1805, when the land was ceded to the federal government. In 1807, Jacob Newman established the county's first settlement, three miles southeast of Mansfield. In 1808, the village of Mansfield—named for Col. Jared Mansfield, a federal surveyor—was laid out by Gen. James Hedges. The colonel once described Ohio as a place of wolves and Indians. During the War of 1812, blockhouses were built at Mansfield and became refuges for settlers. Although established in 1808, the county was not organized until 1813. Early settlers included many Pennsylvanians of German and Scotch-Irish origin. Settlement increased rapidly after the War of 1812. Plymouth, laid out in 1825, had been a camping ground during the war for the Pennsylvania militia. The county always has been agriculturally rich, although in the 1880s it developed a diversified industrial base. The Ohio Brass Co., founded in 1888 in Mansfield, made a fortune for Charles K. King. His 47-acre estate, Kingwood Center, was left to the village of Mansfield as a horticultural and nature center. In 1896, the state opened an "intermediate penitentiary" at Mansfield; later called the Mansfield Reformatory, it closed in 1991. Mansfield was home to John Sherman, brother of Gen. William T. Sherman, cabinet member under President Rutherford B. Hayes, and father of the Sherman Antitrust Act. In 1939, Louis Bromfield, a Pulitzer Prize-winning novelist, established Malabar Farm—a 1,000-acre research farm—near the village of Lucas.

ROSS COUNTY

Established: August 20, 1798
Named for: James Ross (friend of Gen. Arthur St. Clair)
Land area: 693 square miles
Locale: about 40 miles south of Columbus
2000 Population: 73,345
 White: 92.0%
 Black: 5.7%
County seat: Chillicothe
Largest city: Chillicothe (21,796)
Second-largest city: none
Largest village: Kingston (1,032)
Per-capita income (2002) / ranking among Ohio counties: $23,123/62
Number of school districts (2005): 7

Employment base (2001):
Private sector: 80%
Public sector: 20%

Electoral history:
President (2004): Bush (R) 54%; Kerry (D) 44%
Governor (2002): Taft (R) 59%; Hagan (D) 37%
President (2000): Bush (R) 53%; Gore (D) 45%
Governor (1998): Fisher (D) 48%; Taft (R) 47%
President (1996): Clinton (D) 49%; Dole (R) 40%; Perot 10%
Governor (1994): Voinovich (R) 68%; Burch (D) 28%
President (1992): Bush (R) 40%; Clinton (D) 39%; Perot 21%
Governor (1990): Voinovich (R) 53%; Celebrezze (D) 47%
President (1988): Bush (R) 61%; Dukakis (D) 39%

Party affiliations of county administrative officeholders (2004):
8 Republicans; 3 Democrats

History:

Ross County contains hundreds of mounds and other traces of the prehistoric Fort Ancient and Hopewell cultures. When the pioneer settlers arrived, the area was inhabited by Shawnees. Many Shawnee villages were called Chillicothe, the name adopted for the settlement founded in 1796 at the falls of Paint Creek by surveyor Nathaniel Massie. The land east of the Scioto River was part of the Congress Lands; that west of the river belonged to the Virginia Military District. Many early settlers were Virginians. In 1798, Ross was the sixth county created in the Northwest Territory; in 1800, the capital of the territory was moved from Cincinnati to Chillicothe. When Ohio became a state in 1803, Chillicothe was made the capital. The capital was moved to Zanesville from 1810 to 1812, returned to Chillicothe, then moved to Columbus in 1816. In 1831, the Ohio Canal was completed from Cleveland to Chillicothe. The canal era boosted the county's agricultural economy. In 1847, paper manufacturing began in Chillicothe; by the mid-1900s, the community claimed to be the white-paper capital of the world. The Mead Corp. operated a major pulp plant in Chillicothe. Mount Logan, about three miles from Chillicothe, provided the inspiration for the design of the state seal.

SANDUSKY COUNTY

Established: April 1, 1820
Named for: Wyandot Indian word "cold water"
Land area: 415 square miles
Locale: about 25 miles southeast of Toledo
2000 Population: 61,792
 White: 91.9%
 Black: 2.8%
County seat: Fremont
Largest city: Fremont (17,375)
Second-largest city: Clyde (6,064)
Per-capita income (2002) / ranking among Ohio counties: $24,831/47
Number of school districts (2005): 5
Employment base (2001):
Private sector: 87%
Public sector: 13%

Electoral history:
President (2004): Bush (R) 56%; Kerry (D) 44%
Governor (2002): Taft (R) 64%; Hagan (D) 32%
President (2000): Bush (R) 53%; Gore (D) 43%
Governor (1998): Taft (R) 50%; Fisher (D) 42%
President (1996): Clinton (D) 45%; Dole (R) 39%; Perot 14%
Governor (1994): Voinovich (R) 76%; Burch (D) 20%
President (1992): Bush (R) 39%; Clinton (D) 36%; Perot 24%
Governor (1990): Voinovich (R) 58%; Celebrezze (D) 42%
President (1988): Bush (R) 59%; Dukakis (D) 41%

Party affiliations of county administrative officeholders (2004):
8 Republicans; 3 Democrats

History:

Before the War of 1812, the territory belonged to Wyandot Indians. During the war, the troops of Gen. William Henry Harrison built a string of forts in the Sandusky Valley, including Fort Stephenson near the lower rapids of the Sandusky River. The site of the old fort became the center of the first permanent settlements. The village of Croghansville was named for Maj. George Croghan, who in August 1813 defended Fort Stephenson against a much larger force of British and Indians. In 1820, Croghansville was named the temporary county seat; the permanent seat was established at Sandusky in 1822. In 1829, Sandusky and Croghansville were merged and named Lower Sandusky. In 1849, to avoid confusion with Upper Sandusky and Sandusky, the name was changed to Fremont—for pioneer John C. Frémont. Many of the early settlers were Pennsylvania Germans. In 1850, Sardis Birchard, an uncle of Rutherford B. Hayes, founded the estate of Spiegel Grove. After serving as president, Hayes and his family lived in Spiegel Grove. Hayes died and is buried in Fremont. The county has had an economic base of diversified agriculture and small manufacturing.

SCIOTO COUNTY

Established: May 1, 1803
Named for: Scioto River
Land area: 616 square miles
Locale: about 75 miles south of Columbus
2000 Population: 79,195
White: 94.7%
Black: 2.6%
County seat: Portsmouth
Largest city: Portsmouth (20,909)
Largest village: New Boston (2,340)
Per-capita income (2002) / ranking among Ohio counties: $20,914/76
Number of school districts (2005): 10

Employment base (2001):
Private sector: 79%
Public sector: 21%
Electoral history:
President (2004): Bush (R) 52%; Kerry (D) 48%
Governor (2002): Taft (R) 56%; Hagan (D) 41%

President (2000): Bush (R) 50%; Gore (D) 47%
Governor (1998): Fisher (D) 51%; Taft (R) 45%
President (1996): Clinton (D) 48%; Dole (R) 37%; Perot 14%
Governor (1994): Voinovich (R) 64%; Burch (D) 33%
President (1992): Clinton (D) 44%; Bush (R) 36%; Perot 20%
Governor (1990): Celebrezze (D) 52%; Voinovich (R) 48%
President (1988): Bush (R) 53%; Dukakis (D) 47%

Party affiliations of county administrative officeholders (2004):
7 Democrats; 4 Republicans

History:

During the summer of 1749, French explorer Celoron de Blainville (Bienville) arrived at the mouth of the Scioto River, where he found an old Shawnee settlement. He sank a lead plate, proclaiming French possession of the Ohio territory. In 1795, Congress set aside 24,000 acres in the southeastern part of the county to compensate French settlers who had been swindled out of land they thought they had purchased at Gallipolis. Most of the French, however, sold their land rights to New Englanders. The land east of the Scioto was part of the Congress Lands; that west of the Scioto was the Virginia Military District. In 1803, Henry Massie, brother of Nathaniel Massie, laid out Portsmouth, named for Portsmouth, Va. Scioto County was created during the first session of the state legislature. In 1797, opposite the mouth of the Little Sandy River, Burrsburg—named for Aaron Burr, the former vice president—was platted; its name later was changed to Haverhill. In 1827, Portsmouth was designated the terminus of the Ohio & Erie Canal; the canal was opened to Portsmouth at the end of 1832. Portsmouth became an important commercial center, developing a diversified industrial base of coal, iron, steel, shoes, stone and brick, railroad operations, and more. Lucasville, named for the Lucas family, was the early home of Robert Lucas, Ohio's 12th governor. In 1972, the Southern Ohio Correctional Facility, the state's maximum-security prison, opened near Lucasville.

SENECA COUNTY

Established: April 1, 1820
Named for: Seneca Indians
Land area: 552 square miles
Locale: About 40 miles southeast of Toledo
2000 Population: 58,683
White: 95.2%
Black: 1.7%
County seat: Tiffin
Largest city: Tiffin (18,135)
Second-largest city: Fostoria (13,931)
Per-capita income (2002) / ranking among Ohio counties: $23,822/54
Number of school districts (2005): 7
Employment base (2001):
Private sector: 86%
Public sector: 14%
Electoral history:
President (2004): Bush (R) 59%; Kerry (D) 41%
Governor (2002): Taft (R) 67%; Hagan (D) 29%

President (2000): Bush (R) 57%; Gore (D) 39%
Governor (1998): Taft (R) 53%; Fisher (D) 40%
President (1996): Clinton (D) 43%; Dole (R) 41%; Perot 15%
Governor (1994): Voinovich (R) 76%; Burch (D) 20%
President (1992): Bush (R) 37%; Clinton (D) 36%; Perot 27%
Governor (1990): Voinovich (R) 60%; Celebrezze (D) 40%
President (1988): Bush (R) 59%; Dukakis (D) 41%

Party affiliations of county administrative officeholders (2004):
8 Republicans; 3 Democrats

History:

Before 1800, the Seneca Indians, also known as Mingoes, inhabited this area. During the War of 1812, the army of Gen. William Henry Harrison marched northward along the Sandusky River on its way to Detroit. In 1812, Fort Ball was established at the present site of Tiffin. In 1813, Fort Seneca was established near the county's northern boundary. In 1817, the Indians ceded most of their lands; in 1831, they ceded the remainder. On the site of Fort Ball, Erastus Bowe established a tavern; the settlement of Oakley developed around it on the west side of the river. Oakley, the county's first village, housed the county's first post office. East of the river, Josiah Hedges laid out Tiffin—named for Edward Tiffin, Ohio's first governor. In 1822, Tiffin was chosen the county seat. About 1849, Tiffin grew across the river, absorbing Oakley. In 1832, the rival villages of Rome and Risdon were platted on the west side of the county; in 1854, they merged into Fostoria—named for storekeeper Charles W. Foster. Many early settlers were English and Southerners; they were followed by Germans. In 1850, the Ohio Synod of the Reformed Church founded Heidelberg College in Tiffin. In 1879, Charles Foster, son of the storekeeper, was elected governor. In 1888, the discovery of natural gas spurred industrial development in the Tiffin area. The county developed a diversified economy of agriculture, manufacturing, and trade.

SHELBY COUNTY
Established: April 1, 1819
Named for: Gen. Isaac Shelby
(Revolutionary War)
Land area: 409 square miles
Locale: about 40 miles north of Dayton
2000 Population: 47,910
White: 95.8%
Black: 1.9%
County seat: Sidney
Largest city: Sidney (20,211)
Second-largest city: none
Largest village: Jackson Center (1,369)
Per-capita income (2002) / ranking among Ohio counties:
$26,801/28
Number of school districts (2005): 8
Employment base (2001):
Private sector: 91%
Public sector: 9%

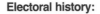

Electoral history:
President (2004): Bush (R) 71%; Kerry (D) 29%
Governor (2002): Taft (R) 69%; Hagan (D) 26%
President (2000): Bush (R) 63%; Gore (D) 34%
Governor (1998): Taft (R) 55%; Fisher (D) 36%
President (1996): Dole (R) 48%; Clinton (D) 37%; Perot 15%
Governor (1994): Voinovich (R) 75%; Burch (D) 21%
President (1992): Bush (R) 44%; Clinton (D) 26%; Perot 29%
Governor (1990): Voinovich (R) 65%; Celebrezze (D) 35%
President (1988): Bush (R) 71%; Dukakis (D) 29%

Party affiliations of county administrative officeholders (2004):
6 Democrats; 5 Republicans

History:

Miami, Wyandot, and Shawnee Indians occupied this area, in which French trader Pierre Loramie established a store and supply post along a creek that bears his name. In 1782, the store was burned. In 1794, Fort Loramie was built nearby under the direction of Gen. Anthony Wayne. In 1795, the site of the old store became part of the boundary established by the Treaty of Greene Ville to separate whites and Indians. In 1817, Indians ceded their lands. In 1819, the county's first post office opened in the temporary county seat of Hardin. In 1820, landowner Charles Starrett offered commissioners 50 acres to locate the county seat at Sidney, named for Sir Philip Sidney, a 16th-century British poet. In the 1830s, construction of the Miami & Erie Canal attracted German settlers, particularly to the northwestern section of the county. The county always has been agricultural but has developed a significant manufacturing base, too.

STARK COUNTY
Established: February 13, 1808
Named for: Gen. John Stark
(Revolutionary War)
Land area: 579 square miles
Locale: about 50 miles southeast of Cleveland
2000 Population: 378,098
White: 90.3%
Black: 7.2%
County seat: Canton
Largest city: Canton (80,806)
Second-largest city: Massillon (31,325)
Per-capita income (2002) / ranking among Ohio counties:
$27,519/23
Number of school districts (2005): 17

Employment base (2001):
Private sector: 89%
Public sector: 11%

Electoral history:
President (2004): Kerry (D) 51%; Bush (R) 49%
Governor (2002): Taft (R) 57%; Hagan (D) 39%
President (2000): Bush (R) 49%; Gore (D) 47%

Governor (1998): Taft (R) 50%; Fisher (D) 44%
President (1996): Clinton (D) 46%; Dole (R) 38%; Perot 15%
Governor (1994): Voinovich (R) 73%; Burch (D) 24%
President (1992): Clinton (D) 40%; Bush (R) 36%; Perot 24%
Governor (1990): Voinovich (R) 58%; Celebrezze (D) 42%
President (1988): Bush (R) 56%; Dukakis (D) 44%

Party affiliations of county administrative officeholders (2004):
8 Democrats; 3 Republicans

History:

In 1785, the Delaware Indians began ceding lands in the area to the federal government, although some Indians remained until after the War of 1812. White settlement began about 1805. In the fall of 1805, Bezaleel Wells laid out Canton; in 1808, it was selected county seat. Early settlers largely were Pennsylvania Germans. In 1811, Kendal was founded as a Quaker settlement; it later was absorbed by Massillon, laid out in 1825, and named for Jean-Baptiste Massillon, a French Catholic bishop during the reign of Louis XIV. In the 1830s, the Ohio & Erie Canal stimulated the development of Massillon and several other Stark County towns. Alliance, laid out in 1838 under the name Freedom, took its present name in 1850 after consolidating with the villages of Williamsport and Mount Union. In 1858, Mount Union College was chartered by the Methodist Episcopal Church. In the 1850s, with the coming of the railroads, Canton and Massillon led the transformation of Stark County from a primarily agricultural area to an industrial one known for iron, steel, coal, bricks, and machinery. In 1872, the Diebold Safe and Lock Co. was founded in Canton. In 1899, in Canton, Henry Timken founded Timken Roller Bearings. In 1908, the Hoover Co., maker of world-famous sweepers, was founded in North Canton. William McKinley, the 25th president, lived in Canton and is buried there. The McKinley Memorial was dedicated September 30, 1907.

SUMMIT COUNTY

Established: March 3, 1840
Named for: the high point along the Ohio & Erie Canal
Land area: 419 square miles
Locale: about 25 miles south of Cleveland
2000 Population: 542,899
 White: 83.4%
 Black: 13.1%
County seat: Akron
Largest city: Akron (217,074)
Second-largest city: Cuyahoga Falls (49,374)
Per-capita income (2002) / ranking among Ohio counties:
$31,155/6
Number of school districts (2005): 17

Employment base (2001):
Private sector: 89%
Public sector: 11%

Electoral history:
President (2004): Kerry (D) 57%; Bush (R) 43%
Governor (2002): Hagan (D) 49%; Taft (R) 47%
President (2000): Gore (D) 53%; Bush (R) 43%
Governor (1998): Fisher (D) 49%; Taft (R) 46%
President (1996): Clinton (D) 52%; Dole (R) 34%; Perot 13%
Governor (1994): Voinovich (R) 72%; Burch (D) 26%
President (1992): Clinton (D) 45%; Bush (R) 32%; Perot 23%
Governor (1990): Voinovich (R) 55%; Celebrezze (D) 45%
President (1988): Dukakis (D) 53%; Bush (R) 47%

Party affiliations of county administrative officeholders (2004):
County executive—Democrat
County council—7 Democrats; 4 Republicans
Other administrative—3 Democrats; 2 Republicans

History:

Nearly all of Summit County was part of the Connecticut Western Reserve. In 1800, the first settlement—Hudson—was formed in the northeastern part of the county. It was named for David Hudson, who led pioneers from Connecticut. The area was agricultural until about 1825, when construction began on the Ohio & Erie Canal. The same year, Gen. Simon Perkins laid out Akron, whose Greek name describes its location on high ground. Many of the canal workers were Irish immigrants. The canal's completion spurred rapid commercial development. By the 1830s, Akron-area plants produced carriages, stoneware, brick and clay products, iron products, and machinery. In 1826, Western Reserve College opened at Hudson to train young men for the ministry; it was moved to Cleveland in 1882. Cuyahoga Falls was laid out in 1828. In 1842, Akron was chosen the county seat. Before the Civil War, Hudson was a center of abolitionist activity; John Brown lived there for 21 years. In 1867, the Universalists built Buchtel College in Akron; in 1913, it became the Municipal University of Akron. In the 1870s, Ferdinand Schumacher established Cascade Mills, making Akron a center for grain and cereal production. After a series of mergers, the Quaker Oats Co. was organized in Akron in 1901. In 1881, George Barber founded Diamond Match Co. in Akron. His son, O. C. Barber, led the development of Barberton, just south of Akron. In 1869, Benjamin Franklin Goodrich was one of three founders of the Akron Rubber Works. A group of leading Akron citizens pledged $13,600 to get Goodrich to move a small rubber business from Melrose, N.Y., to Akron. In 1881, the B. F. Goodrich Rubber Co. was established. In 1898, Frank A. Seiberling established Goodyear Tire & Rubber in Akron. Two years later, Harvey S. Firestone began his tire business. With the beginning of the automobile age, and for most of the 20th century, the "Big Four" tire makers—Goodrich, Goodyear, Firestone, and General Tire—made Akron the rubber capital of the world. Before World War II, the surplus of rubber jobs attracted many Appalachians from West Virginia and Kentucky. In the 1970s and 1980s, many of Akron's rubber-industry jobs were lost to plants outside Ohio and the United States that offered lower wages and newer technology. In 1979, Summit County voters adopted a county charter to establish an executive-legislative form of county government—the first in

Ohio. It took effect January 1, 1981. Summit County is Ohio's only charter county. Under the charter, there is no board of county commissioners. In its place is a county-elected executive and a county council. In 1993, the seven-member council was increased to 11 members.

TRUMBULL COUNTY

Established: July 10, 1800
Named for: Jonathan Trumbull, governor of Connecticut
Land area: 636 square miles
Locale: about 40 miles southeast of Cleveland
2000 Population: 225,116
 White: 90.1%
 Black: 7.6%
County seat: Warren
Largest city: Warren (46,832)
Second-largest city: Niles (20,932)
Per-capita income (2002) / ranking among Ohio counties: $25,156/43
Number of school districts (2005): 20

Employment base (2001):
Private sector: 88%
Public sector: 12%

Electoral history:
President (2004): Kerry (D) 62%; Bush (R) 38%
Governor (2002): Hagan (D) 49%; Taft (R) 47%
President (2000): Gore (D) 60%; Bush (R) 36%
Governor (1998): Fisher (D) 57%; Taft (R) 36%
President (1996): Clinton (D) 59%; Dole (R) 26%; Perot 14%
Governor (1994): Voinovich (R) 64%; Burch (D) 33%
President (1992): Clinton (D) 51%; Perot 25%; Bush (R) 24%
Governor (1990): Celebrezze (D) 58%; Voinovich (R) 42%
President (1988): Dukakis (D) 60%; Bush (R) 40%

Party affiliations of county administrative officeholders (2004):
11 Democrats

History:
Trumbull, the original county of the Connecticut Western Reserve, was the land of Iroquois Indians before white settlement began in the 1790s. Warren, named for surveyor Moses Warren, was founded in 1799. The next year, territorial governor Arthur St. Clair named it the seat of the Western Reserve. Early settlers, mostly from Pennsylvania, located primarily in the southeastern part of the county. Niles, laid out in 1834 by James Heaton, was first known as Heaton's Furnace, named for a small, iron-producing furnace founded by Heaton. U.S. Route 422 basically followed an old Indian trail that led to a salt springs in the area. During the first half of the 19th century, the county was mainly agricultural, noted especially for dairy products; during the second half of the century, it was transformed into a manufacturing center, like its southern neighbor,

Mahoning County. The county became known for coal and iron. The coal-mining jobs attracted many Welsh. In 1843, William McKinley, the 25th president, was born in Niles; he was the son of a blast-furnace operator. In 1857, criminal lawyer Clarence Darrow was born in Farmdale. In the early 1900s, J. W. and W. D. Packard of Warren became automobile pioneers. Republic Steel and Carnegie Steel operated major mills in the county. Throughout the 20th century, the county has developed a diversified industrial base.

TUSCARAWAS COUNTY

Established: March 15, 1808
Named for: Tuscarawas River ("open mouth")
Land area: 572 square miles
Locale: about 60 miles south of Cleveland
2000 Population: 90,914
 White: 97.7%
 Black: 0.7%
County seat: New Philadelphia
Largest city: New Philadelphia (17,056)
Second-largest city: Dover (12,210)
Per-capita income (2002) / ranking among Ohio counties: $23,029/64
Number of school districts (2005): 8

Employment base (2001):
Private sector: 87%
Public sector: 13%

Electoral history:
President (2004): Bush (R) 56%; Kerry (D) 44%
Governor (2002): Taft (R) 54%; Hagan (D) 42%
President (2000): Bush (R) 53%; Gore (D) 43%
Governor (1998): Fisher (D) 50%; Taft (R) 45%
President (1996): Clinton (D) 44%; Dole (R) 39%; Perot 16%
Governor (1994): Voinovich (R) 53%; Burch (D) 44%
President (1992): Clinton (D) 40%; Bush (R) 36%; Perot 24%
Governor (1990): Voinovich (R) 52%; Celebrezze (D) 48%
President (1988): Bush (R) 55%; Dukakis (D) 45%

Party affiliations of county administrative officeholders (2004):
8 Democrats; 3 Republicans

History:
Tuscarawas County produced evidence of preglacial man. In historic times, it was the land of Delaware Indians, whose main village was Gekelemukpechunck, just east of the present-day Newcomerstown. In the 1760s, German-speaking Moravian missionaries arrived from Pennsylvania to spread Christianity among the Indians. The first were John Heckewelder and Frederick Christian Post. Heckewelder laid out the village of Gnadenhutten, which became the site of Ohio's largest Moravian church. In 1772, Moravian David Zeisberger laid out Schoenbrunn (German for *beautiful spring*) near New Philadelphia. The pacifist Moravians attempt-

ed to remain neutral during the Revolutionary War but were situated between the British (based in Detroit) and their Indian allies and Americans at Fort Pitt. In 1777, the Moravians were forced to abandon Schoenbrunn; they later left the Tuscarawas Valley but returned in 1782. On March 8, 1782, Pennsylvania militiamen murdered 90 Christian Indians at Gnadenhutten. In 1785, as compensation for the massacre, the Continental Congress awarded the Indians 12,000 acres in the Tuscarawas Valley under the trusteeship of the Moravians. In 1778, Fort Laurens—the only fort built in Ohio during the Revolutionary War—was constructed in northern Tuscarawas County. Most of the county was part of the U.S. Military District; much of the land was awarded to Revolutionary War veterans; many of the pioneers were Pennsylvanians with German roots. In 1804, John Knisely laid out New Philadelphia; in 1808, it was chosen the county seat. In 1823, the Indians ceded the remainder of their land. Between 1825 and 1830, construction of the Ohio & Erie Canal boosted the fortunes of Canal Dover (now Dover), Port Washington, Newcomerstown, and Bolivar. After the Civil War, the county was known for coal and clay products. The county's economy has been based primarily on agriculture and small industries.

UNION COUNTY

Established: April 1, 1820
Named for: its formation from parts of four counties
Land area: 437 square miles
Locale: about 25 miles northwest of Columbus
2000 Population: 40,909
 White: 95.5%
 Black: 2.4%
County seat: Marysville
Largest city: Marysville (15,942)
Second-largest city: none
Largest village: Plain City (2,832)
Per-capita income (2002) / ranking among Ohio counties: $27,349/24
Number of school districts (2005): 3

Employment base (2001):
Private sector: 88%
Public sector: 12%

Electoral history:
President (2004): Bush (R) 70%; Kerry (D) 29%
Governor (2002): Taft (R) 71%; Hagan (D) 22%
President (2000): Bush (R) 68%; Gore (D) 30%
Governor (1998): Taft (R) 61%; Fisher (D) 31%
President (1996): Dole (R) 55%; Clinton (D) 33%; Perot 11%
Governor (1994): Voinovich (R) 76%; Burch (D) 20%
President (1992): Bush (R) 53%; Clinton (D) 24%; Perot 23%
Governor (1990): Voinovich (R) 66%; Celebrezze (D) 34%
President (1988): Bush (R) 74%; Dukakis (D) 26%

Party affiliations of county administrative officeholders (2004):
11 Republicans

History:

This area was part of the hunting grounds of Shawnee Indians and later part of the Virginia Military District. In the 1790s, pioneers from Pennsylvania and Virginia advanced up the Scioto Valley and settled in Jerome Township, in the southeastern part of the county. North Liberty, along the Darby Creek, was one of the earliest settlements. In 1816, Milford Center was laid out. In 1820, Marysville was established by Samuel W. Cuthbertson; it was named for his daughter, Mary. Amish families settled in a southern part of the county. During the 1840 presidential campaign of William Henry Harrison, Union County supporters built a log cabin for display; the county claims it was the first such display of Harrison's campaign symbol. Sen. Charles W. Fairbanks of Indiana, vice president from 1905 to 1909 during the second administration of Theodore Roosevelt, was born near Unionville Center. In the 1880s, Magnetic Springs—with its mineral springs—became a busy health resort. In 1911, the state legislature approved construction of a women's reformatory at Marysville; it opened in 1916. For most of its history, Union County has been primarily agricultural. In 1979, Honda of America began producing motorcycles at Marysville; three years later, the company began producing automobiles in an adjacent plant. The Honda complex became the county's largest employer.

VAN WERT COUNTY

Established: April 1, 1820
Named for: Isaac Van Wert (Revolutionary War)
Land area: 410 square miles
Locale: borders Indiana, about 70 miles southwest of Toledo
2000 Population: 29,659
 White: 97.1%
 Black: 0.8%
County seat: Van Wert
Largest city: Van Wert (10,690)
Second-largest city: Delphos (6,944)
Largest village: Convoy (1,110)
Per-capita income (2002) / ranking among Ohio counties: $24,277/50
Number of school districts (2005): 3

Employment base (2001):
Private sector: 88%
Public sector: 12%

Electoral history:
President (2004): Bush (R) 72%; Kerry (D) 28%
Governor (2002): Taft (R) 73%; Hagan (D) 23%
President (2000): Bush (R) 66%; Gore (D) 32%
Governor (1998): Taft (R) 65%; Fisher (D) 31%
President (1996): Dole (R) 54%; Clinton (D) 34%; Perot 11%
Governor (1994): Voinovich (R) 76%; Burch (D) 21%
President (1992): Bush (R) 51%; Clinton (D) 27%; Perot 22%
Governor (1990): Voinovich (R) 67%; Celebrezze (D) 33%

President (1988): Bush (R) 71%; Dukakis (D) 29%

Party affiliations of county administrative officeholders (2004):
10 Republicans; 1 Democrat

History:
In 1817, the Miami Indians ceded these lands, which became part of the Congress Lands. In 1820, the area was open for purchase and settlement. That year, Capt. James Riley established the village of Willshire in the southwestern section of the county. Settlement was slow because the land, covered with forests and bogs, had to be cleared and drained before it could be cultivated. In 1835, the county was organized; Willshire was the temporary county seat. The same year, Van Wert was laid out in the center of the county; in 1838, it became the permanent county seat. The first settlers were mostly from New England, Pennsylvania, and Virginia. Later arrivals included many Germans and Welsh. Delphos, mostly in Allen County, edged into the eastern side of Van Wert County; in the 1840s, it became a port on the Miami & Erie Canal, providing a shipping and market point for Van Wert County's agricultural bounty. The county became known for the philanthropy of its leading citizens. John S. Brumback, a merchant and manufacturer, provided for the establishment of a county library. Dedicated January 1, 1901, it claimed to be the first free countywide library in the United States. In 1923, George H. Marsh provided a $5 million endowment for the Marsh Foundation School for orphaned and dependent children. The county also became known for its commercial horticulture and as the home of the American Peony Growers Association.

VINTON COUNTY

Established: March 23, 1850
Named for: Samuel F. Vinton (congressman, 1851 Whig candidate for governor)
Land area: 415 square miles
Locale: about 50 miles southeast of Columbus
2000 Population: 12,806
　White: 97.9%
　Black: 0.1%
County seat: McArthur
Largest city: none
Largest village: McArthur (1,888)
Second-Largest village: Hamden (871)
Per-capita income (2002) / ranking among Ohio counties:
$18,677/87
Number of school districts (2005): 1

Employment base (2001):
Private sector: 64%
Public sector: 36%

Electoral history:
President (2004): Bush (R) 55%; Kerry (D) 45%
Governor (2002): Taft (R) 56%; Hagan (D) 38%
President (2000): Bush (R) 55%; Gore (D) 41%
Governor (1998): Fisher (D) 47%; Taft (R) 46%
President (1996): Clinton (D) 49%; Dole (R) 35%; Perot 15%
Governor (1994): Voinovich (R) 61%; Burch (D) 34%

President (1992): Clinton (D) 43%; Bush (R) 37%; Perot 20%
Governor (1990): Celebrezze (D) 52%; Voinovich (R) 48%
President (1988): Bush (R) 53%; Dukakis (D) 47%

Party affiliations of county administrative officeholders (2004):
6 Republicans; 4 Democrats; 1 Independent

History:
Settlers arrived in this hilly, broken land in the early 1800s in the vicinity of McArthur. Laid out in 1815, it originally was named McArthurtown—after Duncan McArthur, Ohio's 11th governor (1830–1832). The county was considered part of the state's Hanging Rock iron region, offering iron deposits, coal, and clay. In 1850, McArthur was chosen the county seat. The county was exceptionally slow to develop, largely because the early state roads and canals bypassed it and its terrain was unsuitable for extensive farming. The area's chief industry was mineral extraction. In 1856, Polish financier Peter Zaleski, operating from Paris, formed the Zaleski Mining Co.; the village of Zaleski, laid out along Raccoon Creek, was named for him. The county reached its peak in coal production about 1920. The county's population peaked at 17,223 in 1880. Its 2000 census population—12,806—was the lowest among the state's 88 counties.

WARREN COUNTY

Established: May 1, 1803
Named for: Gen. Joseph Warren (Revolutionary War)
Land area: 408 square miles
Locale: about 15 miles north of Cincinnati
2000 Population: 158,383
　White: 94.4%
　Black: 2.7%
County seat: Lebanon
Largest city: Mason (22,016)
Second-largest city: Lebanon (16,962)
Per-capita income (2002) / ranking among Ohio counties:
$30,955/7
Number of school districts (2005): 8

Employment base (2001):
Private sector: 87%
Public sector: 13%

Electoral history:
President (2004): Bush (R) 72%; Kerry (D) 28%
Governor (2002): Taft (R) 76%; Hagan (D) 20%
President (2000): Bush (R) 70%; Gore (D) 28%
Governor (1998): Taft (R) 67%; Fisher (D) 28%
President (1996): Dole (R) 60%; Clinton (D) 31%; Perot 8%
Governor (1994): Voinovich (R) 82%; Burch (D) 15%
President (1992): Bush (R) 53%; Clinton (D) 26%; Perot 21%
Governor (1990): Voinovich (R) 68%; Celebrezze (D) 32%
President (1988): Bush (R) 74%; Dukakis (D) 26%

Party affiliations of county administrative officeholders (2004):
11 Republicans

History:

Fort Ancient, overlooking the Little Miami River, is among the state's grandest prehistoric earthworks and remnants of the Hopewell culture. In historic times, Miami and Shawnee tribes occupied the land that became Warren County. The county contains area from the Virginia Military District, the Symmes Purchase, and the Congress Lands. Settlement began after Gen. Anthony Wayne's campaign against the Indians from 1794–1795. In 1796, Waynesville was named for him; it attracted many Quakers. Many of the county's early settlers were from Kentucky, Virginia, and New Jersey. Lebanon was laid out in 1802 and, in 1805, became the permanent county seat. The Golden Lamb, Ohio's oldest hotel, opened in 1803. Just outside Lebanon, members of the United Society of Believers in Christ's Second Coming (Shakers) established Union Village. By 1913, the community had disappeared. National Normal University, begun in the 1850s, exemplified the efforts of teachers to organize schools as teacher-training institutions. In 1917, the university merged with Wilmington College. For most of its history, Warren County was largely agricultural. Since the 1970s, it has been among the state's fastest-growing counties and has become part of suburban Cincinnati.

WASHINGTON COUNTY

Established: July 27, 1788
Named for: President George Washington
Land area: 642 square miles
Locale: on Ohio River, about 80 miles southeast of Columbus
2000 Population: 63,251
 White: 97.1%
 Black: 0.8%
County seat: Marietta
Largest city: Marietta (14,515)
Second-largest city: Belpre (6,660)
Per-capita income (2002) / ranking among Ohio counties: $25,230/42
Number of school districts (2005): 6

Employment base (2001):
Private sector: 87%
Public sector: 13%

Electoral history:
President (2004): Bush (R) 58%; Kerry (D) 41%
Governor (2002): Taft (R) 63%; Hagan (D) 33%
President (2000): Bush (R) 58%; Gore (D) 39%
Governor (1998): Taft (R) 62%; Fisher (D) 34%
President (1996): Dole (R) 46%; Clinton (D) 42%; Perot 11%
Governor (1994): Voinovich (R) 73%; Burch (D) 24%
President (1992): Bush (R) 44%; Clinton (D) 37%; Perot 19%
Governor (1990): Voinovich (R) 56%; Celebrezze (D) 44%
President (1988): Bush (R) 60%; Dukakis (D) 40%

Party affiliations of county administrative officeholders (2004):
10 Republicans; 1 Democrat

History:

On April 17, 1788, under the auspices of the Ohio Company of Associates, 48 men who had been traveling down the Ohio River arrived at the mouth of the Muskingum River across from Fort HarMarch They were the advance party for those coming to claim land that was part of the Ohio Company Purchase—the first large land sale made directly by the Continental Congress. They named the settlement Marietta, for Queen Marie Antoinette of France. Led by Gen. Rufus Putnam, they established the first permanent settlement in the Northwest Territory. Washington County was the first created in the territory; Marietta, chosen the county seat, is Ohio's oldest continuing city. A large stockade, called Campus Martius, was built to protect the pioneers from Indian attack. On July 9, 1788, Gen. Arthur St. Clair arrived to assume his duties as governor of the Northwest Territory. For several years, the Delaware and other tribes conducted raids that slowed settlement in the outlying Ohio Company lands. Gen. Anthony Wayne's campaign against Ohio's Indians—concluded with the Treaty of Greene Ville on August 3, 1795—ended the resistance. Muskingum Academy, opened in 1800, was the forerunner of Marietta College. In 1805, former vice president Aaron Burr arrived at Blennerhassett's Island, below Marietta, to enlist the help of wealthy Irishman Harman Blennerhassett in plans to influence the western states to secede from the Union. Burr was arrested and charged with treason but was acquitted in 1807 for lack of evidence. Ohio militiamen burned the Blennerhassett mansion. In the late 1800s and early 1900s, Washington County was known for its oil, gas, and mineral resources.

WAYNE COUNTY

Established: August 15, 1796
Named for: Gen. Anthony Wayne
Land area: 557 square miles
Locale: about 45 miles southwest of Cleveland
2000 Population: 111,564
 White: 96.6%
 Black: 1.2%
County seat: Wooster
Largest city: Wooster (24,811)
Second-largest city: Orrville (8,551)
Per-capita income (2002) / ranking among Ohio counties: $25,002/45
Number of school districts (2005): 10

Employment base (2001):
Private sector: 86%
Public sector: 14%

Electoral history:
President (2004): Bush (R) 61%; Kerry (D) 38%
Governor (2002): Taft (R) 67%; Hagan (D) 30%
President (2000): Bush (R) 61%; Gore (D) 35%
Governor (1998): Taft (R) 61%; Fisher (D) 34%
President (1996): Dole (R) 48%; Clinton (D) 37%; Perot 14%
Governor (1994): Voinovich (R) 78%; Burch (D) 18%
President (1992): Bush (R) 44%; Clinton (D) 33%; Perot 23%
Governor (1990): Voinovich (R) 65%; Celebrezze (D) 35%
President (1988): Bush (R) 62%; Dukakis (D) 38%

History:

In 1796, the territorial governor proclaimed the formation of Wayne County, the third county of the Northwest Territory. It extended from the Cuyahoga and Tuscarawas rivers westward and included northwest Ohio, western Indiana, and the lower peninsula of Michigan, with Detroit as its administrative capital. Wayne County, Mich., is the descendant of the original Wayne County. In 1808, the Ohio legislature created a new Wayne County at the same time it created Stark County. Also that year, Wooster was laid out and named for David Wooster, a Revolutionary War soldier. In 1812, a blockhouse was built at Wooster and the county was formally organized. The area had been occupied by Wyandot and Delaware Indians. The early pioneers, including many Germans, primarily arrived from Pennsylvania, Maryland, Virginia, and New Jersey. From its beginning, Wayne has been a leading agricultural county—part of Ohio's grain belt. In 1870, Presbyterian minister James Reed opened the College of Wooster. In 1881, the legislature established the Ohio Agricultural Experiment Station, originally located in Columbus but moved to Wooster in 1892. The name of the agency, which conducts research to benefit agriculture, was changed in 1965 to the Ohio Agricultural Research and Development Center. In 1982, the center was merged with the Ohio State University.

WILLIAMS COUNTY

Established: April 1, 1820
Named for: David Williams (Revolutionary War)
Land area: 424 square miles
Locale: borders Indiana and Michigan, about 50 miles west of Toledo
2000 Population: 39,188
 White: 96.4%
 Black: 0.8%
County seat: Bryan
Largest city: Bryan (8,333)
Second-largest city: none
Largest village: Montpelier (4,320)
Per-capita income (2002) / ranking among Ohio counties:
$25,288/40
Number of school districts (2005): 7

Employment base (2001):
Private sector: 88%
Public sector: 12%

Electoral history:
President (2004): Bush (R) 65%; Kerry (D) 35%
Governor (2002): Taft (R) 69%; Hagan (D) 27%
President (2000): Bush (R) 62%; Gore (D) 34%
Governor (1998): Taft (R) 58%; Fisher (D) 36%
President (1996): Dole (R) 50%; Clinton (D) 35%; Perot 14%
Governor (1994): Voinovich (R) 76%; Burch (D) 20%
President (1992): Bush (R) 44%; Clinton (D) 28%; Perot 28%
Governor (1990): Voinovich (R) 65%; Celebrezze (D) 35%
President (1988): Bush (R) 70%; Dukakis (D) 30%

History:

The most northwestern of Ohio's counties, Williams was among the last sections of the state to be settled. In 1820, the county was created from Indian lands ceded three years earlier; in 1824, the county was organized, with Defiance as the county seat. In June 1836, when Congress settled Ohio's border war with Michigan, Williams County obtained 150 square miles along its northern end – "the Michigan strip." In the 1830s, pioneers settled Montpelier and Pulaski. In 1840, the county seat was moved to Bryan—named for Columbus's John A. Bryan, state auditor from 1833 to 1839, who donated the land. In 1845, unhappy residents of Defiance succeeded in securing the establishment of Defiance County, with Defiance as the county seat. The canal system bypassed Williams County, but, in the 1870s and 1880s, railroads arrived, speeding the area's development. The heavily wooded land supported many sawmills and woodworking industries. Since the timber was cleared, the county has been chiefly agricultural.

WOOD COUNTY

Established: April 1, 1820
Named for: Col. Eleazer D. Wood (War of 1812)
Land area: 620 square miles
Locale: about 20 miles south of Toledo
2000 Population: 121,065
 White: 94.7%
 Black: 1.4%
County seat: Bowling Green
Largest city: Bowling Green (29,636)
Second-largest city: Perrysburg (16,945)
Per-capita income (2002) / ranking among Ohio counties:
$28,055/20
Number of school districts (2005): 9

Employment base (2001):
Private sector: 83%
Public sector: 17%

Electoral history:
President (2004): Bush (R) 53%; Kerry (D) 46%
Governor (2002): Taft (R) 66%; Hagan (D) 30%
President (2000): Bush (R) 53%; Gore (D) 43%
Governor (1998): Taft (R) 50%; Fisher (D) 45%
President (1996): Clinton (D) 47%; Dole (R) 42%; Perot 10%
Governor (1994): Voinovich (R) 74%; Burch (D) 23%
President (1992): Bush (R) 39%; Clinton (D) 39%; Perot 22%
Governor (1990): Voinovich (R) 58%; Celebrezze (D) 42%
President (1988): Bush (R) 58%; Dukakis (D) 42%

Party affiliations of county administrative officeholders (2004):
9 Republicans; 2 Democrats

History:

During the War of 1812, the army of Gen. William Henry Harrison built Fort Meigs in this area; it was named for then-governor Return

Jonathan Meigs Jr. The fort withstood attacks by the British and their Indian allies. Laid out there in 1816 was Perrysburg—named for Oliver H. Perry, the American naval hero in the 1813 Battle of Lake Erie. Four years later, the Indians relinquished their lands. In 1820, Wood was among 14 counties created by the state legislature; it was named for Harrison's chief engineer in the construction of Fort Meigs. Perrysburg was chosen the county seat. Few other settlements occurred until the 1830s, when the Miami & Erie Canal was under construction along the Maumee River, the county's northwestern boundary. Bowling Green, founded in 1834, was incorporated in 1855. During the Civil War, the family of Gen. George A. Custer lived on a farm near Tontogany. In 1866, residents voted to move the county seat to Bowling Green, although county records were not transferred from Perrysburg until January 1870. In 1914, a state normal school opened at Bowling Green. In 1929, it became a college and, in 1935, Bowling Green State University. The Fort Meigs Monument, on the banks of the Maumee, was dedicated September 1, 1908.

WYANDOT COUNTY

Established: February 3, 1845
Named for: Wyandot Indians
Land area: 409 square miles
Locale: about 60 miles south of Toledo
2000 Population: 22,908
 White: 97.8%
 Black: 0.0%
County seat: Upper Sandusky
Largest city: Upper Sandusky (6,533)
Second-largest city: none
Largest village: Carey (3,901)
Per-capita income (2002) / ranking among Ohio counties:
$24,419/49
Number of school districts (2005): 3

Employment base (2001):
Private sector: 88%
Public sector: 12%

Electoral history:
President (2004): Bush (R) 66%; Kerry (D) 34%
Governor (2002): Taft (R) 70%; Hagan (D) 26%
President (2000): Bush (R) 62%; Gore (D) 35%
Governor (1998): Taft (R) 57%; Fisher (D) 36%
President (1996): Dole (R) 47%; Clinton (D) 38%; Perot 14%
Governor (1994): Voinovich (R) 80%; Burch (D) 17%
President (1992): Bush (R) 43%; Clinton (D) 29%; Perot 28%
Governor (1990): Voinovich (R) 63%; Celebrezze (D) 37%
President (1988): Bush (R) 68%; Dukakis (D) 32%

Party affiliations of county administrative officeholders (2004):
9 Republicans; 2 Democrats

History:

This land once was occupied by Wyandot and Delaware Indians. In 1782, an expedition into the Sandusky River Valley, led by Col. William Crawford, attempted to quell Indian uprisings prompted by the massacre of 90 Indians at Gnadenhutten. North of present-day Upper Sandusky, Crawford was captured by the Indians and, on June 11, 1782, burned at the stake. In 1795, the Treaty of Greene Ville left most of these lands to the Indians. In 1812, Gen. William Henry Harrison erected a fort at Upper Sandusky. In 1821, the Rev. James B. Finley built the first Methodist Indian mission in Ohio. In 1829, the Delawares surrendered their reservation. In 1842, the Wyandots, the last of the Indian tribes to leave Ohio, relinquished their land. Carey, laid out in 1843, was named for one of the county's pioneer families. In 1874, St. Mary's Shrine (Our Lady of Consolation) was established by Roman Catholics; it became an attraction for those seeking religious cures. The county always has been chiefly agricultural.

Sources for county data:
Employment base: Ohio Department of Development; Office of Strategic Research; Ohio County Profiles.
Dates of county establishment: Official Roster of Federal, State, and County officers and Departmental Information, 2003-2004. Ohio Secretary of State J. Kenneth Blackwell.
Origin of county names: Official Roster of Federal, State, and County officers and Departmental Information, 2003-2004. Ohio Secretary of State J. Kenneth Blackwell.
Population statistics: Decennial Census of Population, 1900 to 2000, by Place. Ohio Department of Development; Office of Strategic Research.
Per capita income: Ohio County Indicators, August 2004. Ohio Department of Development; Office of Strategic Research.
Number of school districts: Ohio Department of Education.
Electoral history: Ohio secretary of state, official reports.
Land area: Ohio Cooperative Topographic Survey, 1933.

CHAPTER 11

Ohio's Cities

EIGHT CITIES HAVE ACHIEVED RENOWN FOR THEIR
PRODUCTS, LEADING CITIZENS, INSTITUTIONS, AND
PROMINENT ROLES IN THE STATE'S HISTORY: AKRON,
CANTON, CINCINNATI, CLEVELAND, COLUMBUS,
DAYTON, TOLEDO, AND YOUNGSTOWN

AKRON

Incorporated as a city: 1865
Land area: 62.4 square miles
Form of government: mayor, 13-member council

Population:	2000	1990
Total	217,074	223,019
White	145,924 (67%)	164,493 (74%)
Black	61,827 (29%)	54,656 (24%)
Other	9,323 (4%)	3,870 (2%)

The earliest, widely known feature of the area that became Akron was the Portage Path, an eight-mile trail between the Cuyahoga and Tuscarawas rivers used by generations of Indians for transporting canoes over land. From 1785 to 1805, the path designated the boundary between the United States and Indian lands. In 1825—not far from the trail—Gen. Simon Perkins of Warren, a land agent for the Erie Land Co., laid out the village of Akron, named after the Greek word *akros*, meaning "high." Perkins had purchased 1,000 acres for $4.01—the amount of delinquent taxes due on the land; he platted the village on 150 acres along the planned route of the Ohio & Erie Canal. In 1827, the canal opened for traffic between Portage Summit and Cleveland; Akron's population was about 250. Another canal, the Pennsylvania & Ohio, was completed in 1841, linking Akron with Pittsburgh and Beaver, Pa. Both canals spawned business and industry—mills, machine shops, and plants for producing carriages and clay products.

In March 1842, Akron won the battle among several contenders to become the seat of Summit County; Perkins donated the land for a courthouse and jail. During the 1850s and 1860s, the Akron area increasingly became known for its flour mills, clay products, and production of farm machinery. In May 1851, the city hosted the Ohio Women's Rights Convention in the Stone Church on N. High St.—where Sojourner Truth, a former slave, would deliver her momentous "And ain't I a woman?" speech.

Akron's first railroad was built in 1852. During the Civil War era, the German influence became evident in the city's leadership: John R. Buchtel, John F. Seiberling, and Ferdinand Schumacher all changed the face of Akron. between 1862 to 1863, Schumacher, a German immigrant, built the Empire Barley Mill—Akron's first great cereal mill and the forerunner of Quaker Oats. Seiberling developed the Empire and Excelsior mowers and reapers. Buchtel, another farm machinery entrepreneur, was the largest donor to the construction of a college built by the Western Reserve Association of the Universalists; Buchtel College, whose cornerstone was laid in 1871, was the forerunner of the University of Akron.

In 1869, Benjamin Franklin Goodrich, who had graduated in 1861 from Western Reserve Medical College, accepted an offer from the Akron Board of Trade to move his small rubber plant from Melrose, N.Y., to Akron. Local businessmen pledged $13,600 to finance its start. Completed in 1871, the rubber factory produced fire hoses, belting, billiard cushions, and beer tubing. The factory faced many difficulties and nearly perished during the Panic of 1873.

Reorganized as B.F. Goodrich & Co. in 1874, the business prospered—largely because of a growing demand for bicycle tires.

In time, Goodrich became Akron's largest employer, and its success attracted competitors: In 1895, John F. Seiberling established the Akron India Rubber Co.; three years later, sons Frank and Charles Seiberling established Goodyear Tire and Rubber Co. As the horseless carriage grew in popularity, businessmen saw great opportunities in rubber tires. In 1900, Harvey S. Firestone, who had been a tire salesman in Chicago, arrived in Akron and founded the Firestone Tire and Rubber Co. Five years later, Firestone struck a deal with Henry Ford to produce tires for the automaker. In 1909, the University of Akron offered the world's first course in rubber chemistry. By then, Akron was the nation's largest tire-manufacturing center. In 1915, William O'Neil and Winfred E. Fouse founded General Tire and Rubber. Nationwide, Akron was known as the home of the Big Four tire makers: Firestone, Goodrich, Goodyear, and General Tire. Many other tire companies—including Faultless, Kelly-Springfield, Motz, and Union—located here as well. By the 1920s, about 90 percent of the country's tires were manufactured in Akron, whose rubber factories employed 73,000 workers.

Akron was rubber. World War I fueled demand for tires and other rubber products. The jobs attracted thousands of Southerners, especially from West Virginia, Kentucky, and Tennessee. Between 1910 and 1920, Akron's population mushroomed from 69,067 to 208,435. So many West Virginians moved to Akron that the city jokingly was referred to as the capital of West Virginia; the city's annual West Virginia Day picnic became a big event. The rubber companies hired many Southern blacks, increasing Akron's minority population by several thousand before 1920. With the addition of job-seeking Germans, Hungarians, Italians, and Russians, the city's ethnic base also expanded.

Also during World War I, Akron became associated with the production of observation balloons and blimps. Goodrich and Goodyear both had military contracts for such lighter-than-air craft, and Goodyear stayed in the business after the war; in 1924, it formed the Goodyear Zeppelin Co. After the war, Akron experimented with the city-manager form of government; it was established January 1, 1920, but discarded three years later by voters who deemed it no less political than the strong-mayor form of government.

Although not widely noticed, the 1920s also marked the beginning of the tire companies' expansion into the South and West—a sign of things to come. The 1930s brought a wave of labor activism, spurred by the National Labor Relations Act of 1935, which established the right of collective bargaining. The United Rubber Workers became a major economic and political force. The first major rubber strike took place February 14, 1936, at Goodyear; the company shut down for five weeks, idling about 14,000 employees. Other strikes followed at Firestone and Goodrich. By 1941, employees at all the major rubber companies had organized. Increased union activity, higher wages, and poor labor-management relations prompted the big tire makers to shift production elsewhere. In 1930, the rubber industry employed more than three-fourths of Akron's wage earners; a decade later, it employed just more than half.

The heightened demand for rubber during World War II temporarily masked the industry's decline in Akron. By war's end, the city remained the nation's largest rubber producer, but the decline would not be reversed: Between 1950 and 1970, employment in Akron by the Big Four tire producers dropped from 51,000 to 37,000. In the 1960 census, Akron's population peaked at 290,351; it has declined in each subsequent census. Akron produced its last tire for a passenger car in 1977. In 1982, the city's rubber companies combined employed fewer than 10,000. By the mid-1980s, Akron no longer produced tires for trucks and airplanes.

In a 1985 merger, the B.F. Goodrich Tire Division became Uniroyal-Goodrich Tire Co. Two years later, Firestone moved to Chicago. Also in 1987, Continental AG of West Germany acquired the General Tire Division of GenCorp. In May 1988, Japanese-owned Bridgestone Corp. bought Firestone for $2.6 billion. The next year, Bridgestone/Firestone returned its corporate headquarters to Akron. Tire production was gone, but a major share of the American rubber industry's corporate headquarters and research-and-development laboratories remained in Akron.

However, the early 1990s brought an exodus. In 1992, Bridgestone/Firestone moved its corporate headquarters to Nashville, Tenn. In 1994, Michelin moved its Uniroyal-Goodrich headquarters to Greenville, S.C. The same year, General Tire's headquarters was moved to Charlotte, N.C. Those three moves left Goodyear as the sole remaining Akron-based tire producer.

Adapting to this decline, Akron-area leaders since the 1980s have attempted to develop white-collar and high-tech employment. No longer the world's rubber capital, Akron began striving to become the center of polymer (plastics and other synthetics) research. In 1983, the state established the Edison Polymer Innovation Corp., combining the research capabilities of the University of Akron and Case Western Reserve University in Cleveland. In 1988, the University of Akron opened the College of Polymer Science and Polymer Engineering—the first college in the United States devoted exclusively to polymer education and research.

By 1993, the Akron Regional Development Board boasted that the city housed 400 companies specializing in plastics and polymers, and that four-fifths of all polymer research was being conducted in northeast Ohio. The same year, Goodyear—with a payroll of 5,100—still was the city's largest employer. However, Goodyear continued to struggle with heavy debt, inefficient plants, and huge pension obligations. By 2004, the company employed fewer than 3,000 workers in Akron and was continuing efforts to slash payroll and other costs.

In the heart of downtown Akron, a redevelopment project of the 1970s transformed 36 old Quaker Oats grain silos into Quaker Square, a hotel and adjacent shopping mall. The hotel is among the most distinctive in Ohio.

In 1995, the city dedicated the National Inventors Hall of Fame, promoting the history and spirit of innovation and entrepreneurship. In 1997, residents celebrated Opening Day in the new, $31 million Canal Park stadium, home to the Akron Aeros, a minor-league affiliate of the Cleveland Indians.

In May 2003, Akron voters approved a 0.25 percent increase in the city's income tax, raising it to 2.25 percent for 30 years, to provide $400 million to rebuild Akron's public schools. The money will be matched by the state to fund an innovative, $800 million program that will convert each school into a community learning center, open to the public year-round.

AKRON MAYORS	YEARS
Seth Iredell	1836
John C. Singletary Jr.	1837–1838
Lucius V. Bierce	1839
Arad Kent	1840
Lucius V. Bierce	1841
Harvey H. Johnson	1842–43
Lucius V. Bierce	1844
Philo Chamberlin	1845–1846
Levi Rawson	1847
Israel E. Carter	1848
Lucius V. Bierce	1849
George Bliss	1850
Charles G. Ladd	1851
Frederick Wedsworth	1852
Philip Schuyler	1853
William T. Allen	1854
Nathaniel Finch	1855–1856
Frederick A. Nash	1857–1858
George W. McNeil	1859
Henry Purdy	1860–61
Charles A. Collins	1862
Henry A. Collins	1863
George D. Bates	1864
James Mathews	1865–1866
Lucius V. Bierce	1867–1868
John L. Robertson	1869–1872
Henry Purdy	1873–1874
Levi S. Herrold	1875–1876
James F. Scott	1877–1878
John M. Fraze	1879–1880
Samuel A. Lane	1881–1882
Lorenzo D. Watters	1883–1886
Louis D. Seward	1887–1888
William H. Miller	1889–1892
Lorenzo D. Watters	1893–1894
E.R. Harper	1895–1896
W.E. Young	1897–1900
W.B. Doyle	1901–1902
Charles W. Kemple	1903–1907
William T. Sawyer	1908–1911
Frank W. Rockwell	1912–1915
William J. Laub	1916–1917
I.S. Myers	1918–1919
Carl Beck (mayor)	1920–1921
William J. Laub (admin)	1920–1921
D.C. Rybolt (mayor)	1922–1923
M.P. Tucker (admin)	1922–1923
D.C. Rybolt	1924–1927
G. Lloyd Weil	1928–1931
C. Nelson Sparks	1932–1933
I.S. Myers	1934–1935
Lee D. Schroy	1936–1941
George J. Harter	1942–1943
Charles E. Slusser	1944–1953
Russell M. Bird	1953
Leo A. Berg	1954–1961
Edward O. Erickson	1962–1965
John S. Ballard	1966–1979
Roy Ray	1980–1984
Thomas Sawyer	1984–1986
Don Plusquellic	1987–

Source: Akron–Summit County Public Library

CANTON

Incorporated as a city: 1854
Land area: 22 square miles
Form of government: mayor, 12-member council

Population:	2000	1990
Total	80,806	84,161
White	60,164 (74%)	67,890 (81%)
Black	16,999 (21%)	15,325 (18%)
Other	3,643(5%)	946(1%)

For centuries before the early 1700s—about the time that the Delawares began replacing them—the Erie Indians lived in the area that became Canton. In the second half of the 18th century, the Delawares gradually ceded those lands, and, about 1805, Germans from Pennsylvania began settling the site. That fall, Bezaleel Wells, a surveyor and land promoter from Steubenville, laid out a townsite near the forks of Nimishillen Creek. He named it Canton—after the "Canton estate" of the late Capt. John O'Donnell of Baltimore; O'Donnell, an Irish trader, had chosen the name for his plantation after transporting the first cargo from Canton, China, to Baltimore.

In 1806, the first lots were sold; two years later, Canton was chosen the county seat of Stark County. On March 30, 1815, John

Saxton, grandfather of Mrs. William (Ida) McKinley, published the first edition of *The Ohio Repository*. Later renamed *The Repository*, it is among Ohio's newspapers with the longest continuous history of publication. In 1822, Canton was incorporated as a town. In 1827, Canton's Joshua Gibbs developed an improved metal plow. His and other inventions made Canton a manufacturing center for plows and other agricultural implements. In the 1830s, the construction of the Ohio & Erie Canal bypassed Canton. Massillon, eight miles to the west, was on the canal; for two decades, it threatened to overshadow Canton as the county's major city. Then the center of a rich agricultural area, Canton produced much wheat, vegetables, and fruits; it also was known for mineral deposits: coal, shale, clay, and limestone.

In 1851, Canton native Cornelius Aultman established a company to build agricultural reapers; he later developed the Buckeye brand of farm machinery. By the Civil War—just after it was incorporated as a city—Canton was known as a center for the production of mowers, reapers, and threshers. In 1872, the Diebold Safe and Lock Co. was established. In 1886, John Dueber began manufacturing watch cases in the city. Two years later, the Hampden Watch Manufacturing Co. of Springfield, Mass., relocated there. After a merger, the Dueber-Hampden Co. became one of Canton's largest employers, with many German and Swiss craftsmen. About the same time, a paving brick factory was founded in Canton; by the turn of the century, the city claimed to produce one-tenth of the nation's paving brick.

In 1896, William McKinley, who moved to Canton shortly after being admitted to the bar in 1867, waged the original "front porch campaign" from his residence on North Market Avenue. That November, he was elected the nation's 25th president. He was reelected in 1900 but was assassinated in 1901 in Buffalo, N.Y. His body was returned to Canton for burial; the McKinley National Memorial was dedicated September 30, 1907, on the city's west side.

In 1899, German immigrant Henry Timken, a carriage and buggy maker in St. Louis, developed and patented an improved roller bearing for wagon axles. Timken and his sons recognized the potential of the emerging horseless carriages coming from Detroit. They examined possible sites for relocation between the Pittsburgh steelmakers and the Detroit auto builders. the Canton Board of Trade offered five lots for the construction of a new factory. The Timkens accepted the offer and, in the fall of 1901, broke ground for a building on land still occupied by The Timken Co. By 1910, Timken employed 1,200 workers and produced more than 850,000 bearings a year. Through the decades, as the company became the world's largest producer of roller bearings, the names Timken and Canton became nearly synonymous. In 1994, Timken—with a payroll of nearly 7,200—remained Canton's largest employer.

In the early 1900s, when popular sentiment grew for business and political reforms, Canton was among the Ohio cities showing considerable support for Socialist leaders. The city's boom years, partially driven by World War I's demand for roller bearings and other steel products, were 1900 to 1920—when the city's population almost tripled, from 30,667 to 87,091.

In 1920, the American Professional Football Association—the forerunner of the National Football League—was founded in Canton. That heritage inspired civic leaders in 1959 to launch a campaign for a football hall of fame. In 1961, the NFL selected Canton for the honor; the doors to the shrine opened September 7, 1963.

In the 1920s, the city was widely considered to be riddled with prostitution, gambling, and racketeering. Don R. Mellett, editor of the *Canton Daily News,* directed an editorial campaign against such vices. His slaying in 1926 spurred a campaign to rid the city of its corruption. The exclusive Hills and Dales subdivision, laid out in the 1920s, became an early showplace of choice suburban living.

Between 1930 and 1950, Canton's population expanded slowly, reaching its peak—116,912—in the 1950 census. The city developed a diverse industrial base with hundreds of small manufacturing companies that offered jobs for skilled workers. It has been a working-class city but not nearly as Democratic as Akron, its northern neighbor.

During the 1970s and 1980s, recessions and industrial downsizing stripped the Canton area of thousands of blue-collar jobs. In the early 1980s, Canton lost about one-fourth of its manufacturing base. In 1988, the Maytag Corp. of Newton, Iowa, bought the Hoover Co., founded as a vacuum cleaner manufacturer in 1908 in North Canton. For decades, Hoover had been the city's second-largest employer behind Timken. Through the 1990s, Timken and Hoover invested hundreds of millions of dollars in plant expansions and modernizations. However, they continued to trim manufacturing jobs. In May 2004, Timken announced plans to close three of its Canton bearings plants by 2006 unless negotiations with steelworkers could make the plants competitive.

In 1992, *The Repository* endorsed Bill Clinton for president; it was the first time in its history the newspaper endorsed a Democrat for president. In 2000, the Copley Press, Inc. bought *The Repository* from the Thomson Corp.

In 1995, the National First Ladies' Library was established in the Victorian home that was once the residence of Ida Saxton McKinley and President William McKinley. The library's founder was Mary Regula, wife of long-time U.S. representative Ralph Regula of Canton.

In 2003, Janet Weir Creighton made history as the first woman elected as Canton's mayor. A Republican, Creighton previously served for nearly 13 years as Stark County auditor.

CANTON MAYORS	YEARS
John Myers	1838–1839
Jacob Rex	1839–1840
John Myers	1840–1841
William Bryce	1841–1842
Lewis Vail	1842–1844
George Dunbar	1844–1845
Z. Snow	1845–1846
C.C.A. Witting	1846–1847
Daniel Gotshall	1847–1848
C.C.A. Witting	1848–1849
D.H. Harmann	1849–1850
J.G. Lester	1850–1852

B.F. Leiter	1852–1853
John Lahm	1853–1854
B.F. Leiter	1854–1855
Peter Chance	1855–1859
J.C. Bockius	1859
H.P. Dunbar	1860–1862
S. Meyer	1862
J. Crevoisie	1863–1865
W.W. Clark	1865–1867
Daniel Sayler	1867–1871
R.S. Shields	1871–1875
A.D. Braden	1875–1877
John Shimp	1877–1879
James Vallely	1879–1881
William J. Piero	1881–1885
George Rex	1885–1887
John F. Blake	1887–1893
Robert A. Cassidy	1893–1895
James A. Rice	1895–1899
James H. Robertson	1899–1903
W.H. Smith	1903–1906
A.R. Turnbull	1906–1912
Harry Shilling	1912–1913
A.R. Turnbull	1913–1914
Charles A. Stolberg	1914–1917
Henry A. Schrantz	1917
Charles E. Poorman	1918–1919
Henry A. Schrantz	1919
Herman R. Witter	1920–1922
C.C. Curtis	1922–1924
Charles M. Ball	1924–1926
Stanford M. Swarts	1926–1928
C.C. Curtis	1928–1930
Herman R. Witter	1930–1931
James Seccombe	1932–1933
Arthur Turnbull	1934–1935
James Seccombe	1936–1939
Edward Folk	1939–1943
Albert Fromm	1943
Carl Klein	1944–1949
Thomas H. Nichols	1950–1951
Carl F. Wise	1952–1957
Charles L. Babcock	1958–1961
James H. Lawhun	1962–1963
Stanley A. Cmich	1964–1983
Sam Purses	1984–1992
Richard D. Watkins	1992–2003
Janet Weir Creighton	2004–

Source: Stark County District Library

CINCINNATI

Incorporated as a city: 1819
Land area: 78.1 square miles
Form of government: mayor and city manager; nine-member council. Mayor appoints city manager and council committee chairs; city manager wields executive power.

Population:	2000	1990
Total	331,285	364,040
White	175,492 (53%)	220,285 (60%)
Black	142,176 (43%)	138,132 (38%)
Other	13,617(4%)	5,623(2%)

In January 1789, a group of Kentuckians established a village they named Losantiville, meaning "town opposite the mouth of the Licking." The next year, Fort Washington was built there to provide a secure base for the American army's campaign against the Indians of the Northwest Territory. In January 1790, Gen. Arthur St. Clair, newly appointed governor of the territory, arrived at Fort Washington. He proclaimed the establishment of Hamilton County and changed the name of Losantiville to Cincinnati, in honor of the Revolutionary officers' society, the Order of Cincinnati. St. Clair, Gen. Josiah Harmar, and Gen. Anthony Wayne all led expeditions from Fort Washington.

In 1795, at the close of the Indian wars in Ohio, Cincinnati was positioned to become the state's population and commercial hub. Only about 500 people lived in the village then, but it quickly became a destination for flatboats, paddle-wheelers, and steamboats traveling down the Ohio River, an embarkation point for westward travelers and a distribution point for goods being shipped into the South. By 1820, the village had grown into a city of 9,642; it became the most populous city west of Philadelphia. In 1825, work began on the Miami & Erie Canal to provide a water transportation route to inland Ohio. Within a few years, large volumes of corn, wheat, hogs, and other commodities were being shipped from Ohio's interior farmlands to Cincinnati.

As gateway to the South and West, the Cincinnati of 1830 to 1850 was the preeminent city west of the Allegheny Mountains—the "Queen City of the West"—far surpassing Chicago, Cleveland, Detroit, and St. Louis in population, commerce, and culture. But it also earned another nickname: "Porkopolis." The city was a warehousing and processing center for many products, especially pork. By the mid-1840s, Cincinnati slaughtered and packed half of the hogs marketed in Ohio; in 1850, more than 400,000 hogs were slaughtered in Cincinnati, the world's leader in pork-packing. About this time, before railroads acquired dominance, steamboat traffic reached its peak along the Ohio River.

Alphonso Taft (1810–1891) had arrived in Cincinnati from Vermont in 1839. Taft served as secretary of war (1876) and attorney general (1876-77) in the cabinet of President Ulysses S. Grant; through several generations, his family established itself as Cincinnati's most prominent. His son, William Howard Taft, became the 27th U.S. president and later chief justice of the United States. William Howard Taft's son and grandson—Robert A. Taft and Robert Taft Jr.—both were U.S. senators from Ohio. The great-grandson, Bob Taft, was a two-term Ohio governor, serving from 1999 through 2006. All over Cincinnati, streets, buildings, schools, and libraries bear the Taft name.

Throughout the 19th century, Cincinnati was Ohio's most advanced city—in business, politics, education, culture, and religion. By the 1790s, the Baptists and Presbyterians had opened churches in Cincinnati; the Methodists soon followed. In 1819, Cincinnati College was chartered. The same year, the city offered the first Jewish services in the Northwest Territory. In 1821, Cincinnati became the center of Ohio's first Roman Catholic diocese. In 1830, the city began to provide free public education. A Catholic college, the Athenaeum, was opened in 1831; it later became St. Xavier College. In 1843, an astronomical observatory was dedicated on Mount Adams; it later was moved to Mount Lookout.

In the 1830s and 1840s, many Germans fleeing religious and political persecution in their homeland migrated to Cincinnati. In 1830, Germans made up only about five percent of Cincinnati's population; by 1850, more than one-fourth were German natives. The "Over-the-Rhine" district, north of the canal on the city's west side, became the center of German social life. Cincinnati became known for its many German-run breweries. The Irish, many fleeing from the Irish potato famine of 1846 to 1848, became the city's second-leading ethnic group.

On the river border that separated the free North from the slave-holding South, Cincinnati for decades before the Civil War was torn between competing sentiments. Partly because of its considerable commerce with the South, the city had an antiwar, Copperhead majority. Abolitionist activity was common, though, and the city provided many soldiers for the Union army.

After the war, railroads replaced rivers as the chief mode of transporting freight. Chicago surpassed Cincinnati as a meatpacking center, and other northern and western cities grew to challenge and overtake Cincinnati as population and trade centers. Despite its relative decline, Cincinnati enhanced its reputation for cultural refinement with music halls, art museums, and libraries. In 1869, the Red Stockings were established as the nation's first professional baseball club. In 1871, the city's centerpiece—Fountain Square—was unveiled. In 1890, Cincinnati remained Ohio's most populous city but, by 1900, was supplanted by Cleveland.

The turn-of-the-century period was marked by official corruption and boss politics in Ohio's major cities, especially Cincinnati. From the 1880s to the early 1900s, saloon keeper George B. Cox ruled a corrupt Republican machine in Cincinnati. Cox became a millionaire as he dispensed city contracts, franchises, jobs, and judicial favors. The city acquired a reputation as one of the worst governed in the nation. Although reformers made gains against the Republican machine in the first decade of the 20th century, they did not achieve lasting success until 1925, when voters approved a new charter establishing a city-manager form of government and a small council elected at large. Charles P. Taft, younger brother of Sen. Robert A. Taft, was an original member of the Cincinnati Charter Committee and, for decades, the city's most influential Charterite. For two generations, the Charterites operated as a coalition of reform Republicans and Democrats and served as the chief opposition to Cincinnati's regular Republican organization. Through the 1920s, 1930s, and most of the 1940s, the Charterite slates dominated city council elections. By the 1980s and 1990s, as the Democratic Party gained power in city elections, Charterite influence waned, and its future role was in doubt.

Between 1910 and 1920, large numbers of Southern blacks migrated northward to find jobs, fueling an increase in Cincinnati's black population. The percentage of blacks in Cincinnati has increased steadily each decade, accelerated by the movement of whites to suburbs and adjacent counties. In 1940, the black share of the city's population was 12 percent; in 2000, it was 43 percent.

In 1962, voters approved a downtown revitalization plan to demolish and rebuild a dozen blocks of the central business district. The program included the $46 million Riverfront Stadium (completed in 1970 and later renamed Cinergy Field), a $10 million convention hall, office buildings, and hotels. The city also began several neighborhood revival efforts. In the 1980s, more than $800 million was spent on downtown development—including a new world headquarters for Procter & Gamble, the soap maker founded in 1837 in Cincinnati. Like other major Ohio cities, Cincinnati lost manufacturing jobs in the 1970s, 1980s, and 1990s, but it has broadened what already had been a diversified economic base.

In March 1996, Hamilton County voters approved a half-percent sales tax increase to build two new stadiums to replace the multipurpose Cinergy Field. On September 10, 2000, the football Bengals inaugurated the $453 million Paul Brown Stadium. On March 31, 2003, the baseball Reds held Opening Day in the $325 million Great American Ballpark.

In May 1999, Cincinnati voters amended the city charter to strengthen the powers of the mayor. The amendment enabled the mayor to hire the city manager, appoint city council committee chairs, present the annual city budget, and veto ordinances. In 2001, for the first time since 1923, Cincinnati voters directly elected their mayor—Charles J. Luken—rather than have the top vote-getter on council become mayor. Amendment proponents believed a stronger mayor was needed to deal effectively with growing urban problems, especially population decline, inner-city decay, and race relations.

To continue improving the downtown, Luken and other civic leaders focused on developing a 15-acre site known as the Banks riverfront district between the two stadiums, expanding the convention center, and redeveloping Fountain Square.

Race relations, long a simmering problem in Cincinnati, boiled over into riots in April 2001 following the police shooting of an unarmed black man. Investigations and negotiations resulted in the city signing a police reform agreement with the U.S. Department of Justice.

In May 2003, Cincinnati voters approved a $480 million bond issue to rebuild the city's public schools. Passage qualified the school system for more than $210 million in state matching funds.

On August 23, 2004, the city opened the $110 million National Underground Railroad Freedom Center to teach the history of slavery and the struggle for freedom. Founders expressed hope the center could serve as a focal point for racial healing.

In November 2004, voters repealed a 1993 charter amendment that prohibited city government from passing antidiscrimination laws based on sexual orientation. The 1993 amendment had given Cincinnati a national reputation for intolerance and resulted in convention boycotts.

CINCINNATI MAYORS	YEARS
William Corry	1815–1819
Isaac G. Burnet	1819–1831
Elisha Hotchkiss	1831–1833
Samuel W. Davies	1833–1843
Henry E. Spencer	1843–1851
Mark P. Taylor	1851–1853
David T. Snelbaker	1853–1855
James J. Faran	1855–1857
Nicholas W. Thomas	1857–1859
Richard M. Bishop	1859–1861
George Hatch	1861–1863
Leonard A. Harris	1863–1867
Charles F. Wilstach	1867–1869
John F. Torrence	1869–1871
S.S. Davis	1871–1873
George W.C. Johnson	1873–1877
Robert W. Moore	1877–1879
Charles Jacob	1879–1881
William Means	1881–1883
Thomas J. Stephens	1883–1885
Amor Smith, Jr.	1885–1889
John B. Mosby	1889–1894
John A. Caldwell	1894–1897
Gustav Tafel	1897–1900
Julius Fleischman	1900–1905
Edward J. Dempsey	1906–1907
Leopold Markbreit	1908–1909
John Galvin	1909
Louis Schwab	1910–1911
Henry T. Hunt	1912–1913
Frederick S. Spiegel	1914–1915
George Puchta	1916–1917
John Galvin	1918–1921
George P. Carrel	1922–1925
Murray Seasongood	1926–1929
Russell Wilson	1930–1937
James Garfield Stewart	1938–1947
Carl W. Rich	1947
Albert D. Cash	1948–1951
Carl W. Rich	1951–1953
Edward N. Waldvogel	1953–1954
Dorothy N. Dolbey	1954
Carl W. Rich	1954–1955
Charles P. Taft	1955–1957
Donald D. Clancy	1957–1960
Walton Bachrach	1960–1967
Eugene P. Ruehlmann	1967–1971
Willis D. Gradison	1971
Thomas A. Luken	1971–1972
Theodore M. Berry	1972–1975
Bobbie Sterne	1975–1976
James T. Luken	1976–1977
Gerald N. Springer	1977–1978
Bobbie Sterne	1978–1979
J. Kenneth Blackwell	1979–1980
David S. Mann	1980–1982
Thomas B. Brush	1982–1983
Arn Bortz	1983–1984
Charles J. Luken	1984–1991
David S. Mann	1991
Dwight Tillery	1991–1993
Roxanne Qualls	1993–1999
Charles Luken	1999–2005
Mark Mallory	2005–

Source: Cincinnati City Clerk

CLEVELAND

Incorporated as a city: 1836
Land area: 77.6 square miles
Form of government: mayor, 21-member council

Population	2000	1990
Total	478,403	505,616
Black	243,939 (51%)	235,405 (47%)
White	198,510 (41%)	250,234 (49%)
Other	35,954(8%)	19,977(4%)

In 1796, the Connecticut Land Co. sent a survey party into its Western Reserve—3.3 million acres that began at the Pennsylvania–Ohio line and extended 120 miles westward along Lake Erie. Moses Cleaveland, an agent for the land company, led the surveyors into this wilderness to select a site for settlement. On July 22, 1796, the survey party reached the mouth of the Cuyahoga River, the middle point on the reserve's Lake Erie shoreline. There, near the present intersection of St. Clair Avenue and W. 9th Street, Cleaveland and his assistants began surveying the land into lots of two acres each. Cleaveland and most of his survey party stayed only a few months before returning to Connecticut, but the lead surveyor left a settlement that bore his name.

In 1800, the outpost had only seven residents. Few people were willing to locate there as long as the British and Indians posed a threat. In September 1813, the American naval fleet won victory over the British in the Battle of Lake Erie. With the British presence removed, the Great Lakes were opened for trade, the Indians were in retreat, and immigration slowly but steadily increased. In 1814, Cleaveland was incorporated as a village. By 1830, through annexations and immigration, Cleaveland had just more than 1,000 inhabitants. The next year, the lands west of the Cuyahoga River were surveyed into lots—the foundation for Ohio City, which was incorporated in March 1836.

Cleveland acquired its altered name after July 1, 1832, when a newborn newspaper, the *Cleveland Gazette and Commercial Register*, dropped the first "a" in Cleaveland to fit its name across the newspaper's nameplate.

Impressed with the success of New York's Erie Canal, which had opened in 1825, the Ohio legislature decided that the state needed a canal system to move products economically from the state's interior to its ports. Alfred Kelley, Cleveland's first practicing lawyer, outmaneuvered lobbyists for other Lake Erie towns and won legislation designating Cleveland the northern terminus for the Ohio & Erie Canal. In 1827, a section was completed from Cleveland to Akron, and, in 1833, the canal was completed from Portsmouth to Cleveland, linking the Ohio River with Lake Erie. The canal system stimulated the development of Cleveland into a transportation center where grain, coal, lumber, and other products were delivered for loading on lake steamboats and sailing vessels. By 1840, four years after incorporation as a city, Cleveland had 6,000 residents.

Cleveland's great manufacturing base is traced to 1834, when the Cuyahoga Steam Furnace Co.—a foundry—was chartered. Soon, foundries, factories, mills, and warehouses lined an area called the Flats along the Cuyahoga River. Iron manufacturing began to join boat-building and shipping as a major industry. In June 1854, Cleveland spread itself west of the Cuyahoga River by annexing Ohio City. The Bessemer process—for making steel from molten pig iron—was perfected about 1856, foreshadowing Cleveland's rise as a steel-producing center. As demand for iron products shot up during the Civil War, Cleveland's factories boomed. Between 1850 and 1870, the city's population grew more than fivefold—to 92,829. Cleveland had three times the population of Columbus and was gaining rapidly on Cincinnati.

In 1843, the Cleveland Medical College was founded; it eventually became affiliated with Western Reserve College, which had been founded in 1826 in Hudson (Summit County). In 1882, Western Reserve College was moved to Cleveland; two years later, it became Western Reserve University. In 1877, Leonard Case Jr. of Cleveland had endowed the Case School of Applied Science, to be devoted to technical education. In 1885, the Case School moved next door to Western Reserve University. In 1967, the Case Institute and Western Reserve University merged into Case Western Reserve University. In 1886, St. Ignatius College was opened by Jesuits on the city's west side; its name was changed in 1923 to John Carroll University.

In 1855, construction had begun on the first of two Sault Sainte Marie Canals on the United States–Canadian border to bypass the rapids of the St. Marys River, which connects Lakes Superior and Huron. The canals were needed to complete a water route through the Great Lakes; in 1856, the first iron ores from the Lake Superior ranges were sent to Cleveland—ideally located between the iron ranges and the blast furnaces of the Ohio Valley. The opening of the "Soo" canals, combined with the development of railroads in Cleveland, helped make the city one of the world's leading shipping and shipbuilding centers.

In 1859, Pennsylvania's first oil well (in Titusville) was developed. The next year, John D. Rockefeller, a young commission merchant in Cleveland, made his first investment in oil. In 1861, Cleveland had its first oil refinery, and, in November 1862, Rockefeller completed his first refinery—Excelsior Works in the

Flats. By 1865, the city had 30 refineries; four years later, Cleveland was the nation's leader in crude-oil refining. In 1870, Rockefeller incorporated the Standard Oil Co. and began acquiring most of the refineries in Cleveland. By the 1880s, his Standard trust practically controlled the nation's oil business. In 1890, Ohio attorney general David K. Watson brought suit against the oil monopoly; in 1911, the U.S. Supreme Court forced the breakup of the trust.

In the 1870s and 1880s, Marcus Alonzo Hanna—a Republican who had made a fortune in coal, iron, and steel—was the dominant force in Cleveland politics. Using his wealth and influence to install, control, and reject state and local politicians, he personified the era of "boss rule." Hanna was opposed by Thomas L. Johnson, who had made a fortune in steel and transportation. In 1901, Johnson was elected mayor on a progressive platform of a three-cent railway fare, civil-service reform, business regulation, public control of utilities, and home rule for cities. Johnson served as mayor until 1910; in 1915, a statue of him was erected in Public Square.

In the early 1900s, Cleveland was at the center of the emerging automobile industry. Among the 80 makes of cars produced in the city were the Chandler, Peerless, Rollin, and Stearns. By the end of World War II, however, Detroit surpassed Cleveland as the nation's leading automaker. Cleveland's last automobile, a Peerless, came off the assembly line in 1931. With both Ford and General Motors maintaining plants in the city, Cleveland remained a manufacturing center for auto parts.

As one of the nation's leading industrial centers, Cleveland naturally became a focal point for labor-union activity. In 1882, the city hosted a national organizing session of the Federation of Organized Trades and Labor Unions. The convention helped give rise to May Day (May 1) strikes of the 1880s—organized to build support for the eight-hour work day. The city experienced bloodshed during the steel strikes of the 1930s but, in later decades, was able to foster labor-management harmony.

In the late-19th and early-20th centuries, the industrialization of Cleveland—the promise of jobs for those willing to work—transformed the city into one of the most ethnically diverse in the nation. Joining the Germans and Irish were Poles, Czechs, Italians, Hungarians, Greeks, Slavs, Russians, and people of many other nationalities. In the 1900 census, Cleveland surpassed Cincinnati to become Ohio's most populous city: Cleveland's 1930 population of 900,429 was nearly ten times that of 1870. In 1940, more than 40 languages were said to be spoken in Cleveland's neighborhoods. Between the world wars, Cleveland was among the northern destinations in the great migration of job-seeking southern blacks. In 1910, less than 2 percent of Cleveland's population was black; by 1940, nearly 10 percent was black. Blacks accounted for 16 percent of Cleveland's population in 1950 and have accounted for a growing share in each subsequent census, reaching 51 percent in 2000.

In the 1920s, Clevelanders had grown concerned over graft and mismanagement in city government and, in 1924, adopted a city manager form of government. The city administration under manager William R. Hopkins, however, proved even more scandalous; in 1930, the city returned to a strong mayor system. From 1931 to 1932, Cleveland safety director Eliot Ness, who as a federal agent helped fight the Capone mob in Chicago, directed a cleanup of the city's police department under Mayor Harold Burton.

In 1930, Cleveland's most familiar landmark—the 52-story Terminal Tower—opened on Public Square. The next year, on July 3, Municipal Stadium was opened for the heavyweight championship fight between Max Schmeling and Young Stribling.

By the late 1930s, Cleveland had virtually stopped growing in population. Suburbs ringed the city, and many Clevelanders were moving to them. The city's 1940 census population of 878,336 represented a decline of 22,093 from a decade earlier—the first drop in the city's history. By 1950, the population had ticked back up to 914,808, largely because of the buildup of factory jobs during World War II. After 1950, though, Cleveland's population and factory jobs decreased steadily.

The turbulent 1960s proved the city's most troubled decade. With most blacks living east of the Cuyahoga River and whites on the west, Cleveland was racially divided—by geography and attitude. Racial disturbances rocked the city, culminating during the summer of 1966 when four black residents were killed and many other people injured during rioting in the Hough Avenue neighborhood on the east side. About 2,200 National Guardsmen were called in to quell the uprising. Black aspirations flourished on November 7, 1967, when Carl B. Stokes became the first black elected mayor of a major American city; he served until 1971. Cleveland's image as a troubled city again received national exposure on June 22, 1969, when a floating oil slick caught fire on the polluted Cuyahoga River, later declared a fire hazard.

The 1970s delivered more difficulties. Mayor Ralph Perk (1971–77) resorted to borrowing money to cover city operating expenses. Perk's image as well as the city's became fodder for talk-show jokes after his hair caught fire from a welding torch when he visited a factory. In 1977, the brash, 31-year-old Dennis J. Kucinich was elected mayor while promising a "new urban populism." Kucinich and the city's business leaders were constantly at odds. The confrontations climaxed in December 1978, when the Cleveland Trust Co., now Ameritrust, called in a $15 million loan. The bank was not paid by midnight December 15, and Cleveland became the first major American city to default on its obligations since the Great Depression. In all, the city was $110 million in debt. To cap off the troublesome decade, court-ordered busing for school desegregation began in 1979, fueling racial tensions.

In November 1979, the city voted for change by ousting Kucinich and electing Republican George V. Voinovich, who had been the state's lieutenant governor for just ten months. Voinovich rebuilt City Hall's relationship with the business sector. In 1981, he persuaded Cleveland voters to increase the city income tax from 1.5 percent to 2 percent. The same year, voters reduced the size of the city council to 21 members from 33 and extended the terms of the mayor and council members to four years from two years. Although it lost 70,000 jobs in the recessionary years between 1980 and 1983, Cleveland stepped up a major downtown rebuilding program begun in the 1970s, continued efforts to clean up the Cuyahoga River and Lake Erie, and invested in rebuilding streets, buildings, and other infrastructure.

In the 1980s, the city proclaimed its comeback. Between 1983 and 1988, employment in Cleveland grew by nearly 60,000 jobs. In 1985, Sohio Oil (now British Petroleum) completed a $200 million headquarters on Public Square—an integral part of the city's downtown building boom. In June 1987, Cleveland paid the final installment on the debt that led to default, emerging from its state of fiscal emergency. The same year, Cleveland was selected as the site for a national Rock and Roll Hall of Fame, for which ground was broken in the summer of 1993. In November 1989, Democrat Michael R. White defeated George L. Forbes to succeed Voinovich in the mayor's office. In 1990, Voinovich was elected governor of Ohio, partly on a platform of having resuscitated Cleveland.

Also during the 1980s, the old Flats industrial area along the Cuyahoga River was transformed into an entertainment and nightlife district. In 1989, the city began plans for a new 42,000-seat stadium for the Cleveland Indians; on the site of the old Central Market, Jacobs Field was completed in time for the 1994 baseball season. The other half of Cleveland's $362 million Gateway sports complex, the 20,593-seat Gund Arena, opened in October 1994.

In November 1995, Clevelanders were stunned when Art Modell, majority owner of the Cleveland Browns, announced he would move the professional football team to Baltimore, beginning with the 1996 season. The Browns had been a fixture in Cleveland since 1946, when the team became a charter member of the All America Football Conference.

Mayor White led a legal fight against Modell and the National Football League; he negotiated a deal requiring the NFL to grant the city an expansion franchise and to leave the team's name, colors and heritage in Cleveland. On November 26, 1996, the wrecking ball began demolishing Municipal Stadium. On May 15, 1997, construction began on a new football stadium. On September 12, 1999, the Browns played their first regular-season game in the $290 million Cleveland Browns Stadium.

On May 8, 1996, a federal judge ended nearly two decades of court-imposed busing in Cleveland's public schools. The ruling closed the books on a 23-year desegregation case that fueled white flight from the city. The troubled school district was under state control from 1995 to 1998 because of massive debts and organizational failures. On September 9, 1998, Mayor White took control of the district by appointing a new, nine-member board of education.

In June 2001, LTV Corp. closed its west side mill after 90 years of steelmaking. LTV's bankruptcy and mill closing were emblematic of the industrial decline of Cleveland and northeastern Ohio.

On January 7, 2002, Jane Campbell was inaugurated as the first woman mayor of Cleveland. She previously had served as a state representative and Cuyahoga County commissioner.

CLEVELAND MAYORS	YEARS
John W. Willey	1836–1837
Joshua Mills	1838–1839
Nicholas Dockstadter	1840
John W. Allen	1841
Joshua Mills	1842
Nelson Hayward	1843
Samuel Starkweather	1844–1845
George Hoadley	1846
Josiah A. Harris	1847
Lorenzo A. Kelsey	1848
Flavel W. Bingham	1849
William Case	1850–1852
Abner C. Brownell	1852–1855
William B. Castle	1855–1857
Samuel Starkweather	1857–1858
George B. Senter	1859–1861
Edward S. Flint	1861–1862
Irvine U. Masters	1863–1864
Herman A. Chapin	1865–1866
Stephen Buhrer	1867–1870
Frederick W. Pelton	1871–1872
Charles A. Otis	1873–1874
Nathan P. Payne	1875–1876
William G. Rose	1877–1878
R.R. Herrick	1879–1882
John H. Farley	1883–1884
George W. Gardner	1885–1886
Brenton D. Babcock	1887–1888
George W. Gardner	1889–1890
William G. Rose	1891–1892
Robert Blee	1893–1894
Robert McKisson	1895–1898
John H. Farley	1899–1900
Tom L. Johnson	1901–1909
Herman C. Baehr	1910–1911
Newton Baker	1912–1915
Harry L. Davis	1915–1920
William S. Fitzgerald	1920–1921
Fred Kohler	1921–1923
William R. Hopkins (mgr.)	1924–1929
Daniel E. Morgan (mgr.)	1930–1931
Harold Burton	1931–1932
Ray T. Miller	1932–1933
Harry L. Davis	1933–1935
Harold R. Burton	1935–1940
Edward Blythin	1940–1941
Frank J. Lausche	1941–1944
Thomas A. Burke	1945–1953
Anthony J. Celebrezze	1953–1962
Ralph S. Locher	1962–1967
Carl B. Stokes	1967–1971
Ralph J. Perk	1971–1977
Dennis J. Kucinich	1977–1979
George V. Voinovich	1979–1990
Michael R. White	1990–2002
Jane Campbell	2002–2005
Frank Johnson	2006–

Source: Cleveland Public Library

COLUMBUS

Incorporated as a city: 1834
Land area: 220 square miles
Form of government: mayor, seven-member council

Population	2000	1990
Total	702,132	632,910
White	475,838 (68%)	471,025 (74%)
Black	172,847 (25%)	142,748 (23%)
Other	53,447(7%)	19,137(3%)

After the Revolutionary War, Kentuckian Lucas Sullivant was among those appointed to survey lands in the Virginia Military District—lands set aside to reward war veterans from Virginia. In August 1797, Sullivant laid out the town of Franklinton on the west bank of the Scioto River, near its confluence with the Olentangy (then Whetstone) River. The area was swampy and heavily wooded, slowing the pace of settlement for several years. By 1800, Franklinton was a small trading center with a population of about 250. In 1803, the first state legislature created Franklin County, with Franklinton as the county seat.

Ohio's first constitution designated Chillicothe the state capital until 1808, when the General Assembly would select a permanent site. In 1809, as wrangling continued over selecting a permanent capital, the legislature chose a temporary capital—Zanesville—where it was located from 1810 to 1812. Meanwhile, communities and land speculators throughout central Ohio worked to attract the capital. In February 1812, a syndicate made up of James Johnson, John Kerr, Alexander McLaughlin, and Lynn Starling offered to lay out a town on the east bank of the Scioto River. Their proposal called for conveying a 10-acre tract for a statehouse and other public buildings and another 10-acre tract for a penitentiary, laying out 4,000 acres of town lots, and finishing the work by December 1, 1817.

On February14, 1812, the legislature accepted the plan to lay out the capital "on the high bank of the Scioto opposite Franklinton." One week later, at the suggestion of Joseph Foos, the legislature determined that the capital would be named Columbus—after explorer Christopher Columbus. The first sale of town lots took place on June 18, 1812, the day President James Madison announced war on Great Britain.

On February10, 1816, the legislature authorized creation of the borough of Columbus. On October 1, state offices were relocated from Chillicothe to Columbus. In December, a brick statehouse was ready for occupancy at the southwest corner of State and High streets. Since then, government and politics have dominated the city's affairs. The same year, about 700 people lived in the borough; its adult white males voted for 22-year-old Jarvis W. Pike as Columbus's first mayor. In 1824, the county seat was moved from Franklinton to Columbus.

In July 1825, the state began construction of the Ohio & Erie Canal, whose main route crossed the southeastern corner of Franklin County. On April 30, 1827, construction began on a feeder canal to link Columbus (the Scioto River) with a canal branch at Lockbourne (Big Walnut Creek). Irish and Germans moved into the borough, joining families of English stock. By 1830, the borough's population had increased to 2,435. Four years later, Columbus was incorporated as a city and spread across the Scioto to absorb Franklinton. About the same time, the National Road was completed through Columbus, drawing many westward travelers to the city. In 1834, the Ohio State Penitentiary was opened on W. Spring Street. It was the state's largest penal institution—total cost: $93,370—designed to hold 700 prisoners behind 24-foot walls.

On January 26, 1838, the legislature approved construction of a new statehouse. A commission adopted a plan for a Greek Revival style of architecture with Doric columns. The first stone was hauled to Capitol Square on May 16, 1838; the cornerstone was laid July 4, 1839. Planners expected construction to take six years and cost $400,000. The legislature began holding sessions in the new Statehouse on January 7, 1857, but it wasn't declared completed until November 15, 1861. The final cost: $1,359,121.

During the Civil War era, the Columbus area was the site of several military camps. On the city's western edge, Camp Chase was established on 160 acres as a training ground for recruits; it became the North's largest prison camp for captured Confederates. In 1863, in northeast Columbus, the Columbus Barracks was developed on 77 acres as a national armory and arsenal; it later was renamed Fort Hayes, for President Rutherford B. Hayes.

On July 2, 1862, Congress approved the Morrill Act, which offered land to each state for the establishment of agricultural colleges. Based on the size of its congressional delegation, Ohio was entitled to 630,000 acres. The state legislature accepted the offer, acquiring farmland from William Neil about four miles north of Columbus. On September 17, 1873, the Ohio Agricultural and Mechanical College was opened to 17 students; five years later, it was renamed the Ohio State University.

In the mid-1800s, Germans concentrated on Columbus's south side, accounting for about one-third of the city's population. The area became distinguished by its story-and-a-half brick houses and its family breweries; Blenkner, Born, and Hoster were among them. The Germans opened grade schools and, in 1858, the first kindergarten in the United States. One hundred years later—in the late

1950s—a movement to preserve and restore the 233-acre German Village area became a national example of urban neighborhood revitalization. In the 1980s and thereafter, the village was one of Columbus's trendiest neighborhoods.

After the Civil War, Columbus's central location spurred the city's development as a center of transportation, manufacturing, and trade. Columbus became one of the nation's leading producers of buggies, carriages, and wagons. With the abolition of slavery, the city's black population began to increase steadily. By 1880, the first black had been elected to city council. In the early 1900s, black migrants streamed into Columbus and began to settle on the city's east side, especially along E. Long Street. In 1897, the city's first skyscraper, the 11-story Wyandot Building, was erected on W. Broad Street. In 1899, construction began on a Statehouse annex. Completed in 1901 at a cost of $450,000, the annex housed the Ohio Supreme Court, the court library, and the attorney general's office.

The city experienced its worst flood in history in March 1913, when the Scioto River overran its banks, inundating the west side. More than 100 people were killed and 20,000 left homeless; property damage was estimated at more than $9 million.

In 1914, voters approved a new city charter, requiring that—beginning in 1916—the council be made up of seven members, all elected at large. Previously, the council had two members from each of 15 city wards. The change made it difficult for blacks to get elected to the council. In 1969, Dr. John H. Rosemond became the first black to win a seat on the at-large council.

Ohio Stadium, a giant horseshoe of a football stadium, was completed in 1922 at a cost of $1.5 million. In September 1927, the American Insurance Union Citadel was completed at Broad and Front streets. The 47-story skyscraper—555.5 feet—cost $7.8 million and became the symbol of Columbus; it later was known as the LeVeque-Lincoln Tower. In 1929, the Battelle Memorial Institute was established as a private research organization, in accordance with the will of Gordon Battelle, who died in 1923. Founded to encourage scientific and industrial research, it grew into the world's largest private research organization. Also in 1929, Port Columbus Airport was opened and became a terminal for Transcontinental Air Transport's pioneering efforts to offer air-rail, transcontinental passenger service. On April 21, 1930, a fire at the Ohio State Penitentiary killed 322 prisoners.

Besides being a center of government, Columbus developed a balanced economy on banking, education, trade, retailing, research, and warehousing and distribution. Because it has not been overly dependent on manufacturing or any other sector of the economy, Columbus generally has weathered recessions more easily than Ohio's other major cities.

In 1943, Republican James A. Rhodes won election as mayor and, from 1944 to 1953, earned a reputation for cleaning up much of the city's vice and corruption. In November 1947, he persuaded Columbus voters to approve the city's first income tax—at 0.5 percent—which helped wipe out a deficit. In the spring of 1949, the Town and Country Shopping Center was opened on E. Broad Street; it was billed as the nation's first regional shopping center.

In 1950, Columbus was barely 40 square miles. As suburban development began, Columbus faced the threat of becoming landlocked—as happened with other major Ohio cities. Democrat M.E. Sensenbrenner, elected mayor in 1953, began an aggressive annexation program, requiring areas to be annexed to Columbus in exchange for water and sewer service. As a result, Columbus grew to 91 square miles by 1960, 143 square miles by 1970, and more than 220 square miles by 2004. In land area, it became the largest city in Ohio and one of the largest in the nation.

In the 1970s, Columbus began substantial restoration efforts downtown and in several neighborhoods, most notably the Victorian Village area just north of the central business district. In August 1974, the state completed construction on the 41-story, 629-foot James A. Rhodes State Office Tower. On July 2, 1979, the U.S. Supreme Court upheld a lower-court order requiring systemwide busing for the desegregation of Columbus schools; the ruling prompted some flight to the suburbs, especially among whites, and tested the city's ability to maintain a strong urban school district. In late 1980, the Ohio Center, a convention center–hotel complex, was opened on the site of the former Union Station. In August 1989, the Columbus City Center was opened; the three-level enclosed mall was the centerpiece of a three-square-block redevelopment project just south of the Statehouse.

In 1993, the Ohio House of Representatives, which had met continuously in the Statehouse since 1857, moved to temporary quarters while the capitol building underwent a $112.7 million restoration, designed to restore its original grandeur. The renovated Statehouse was reopened in July 1996.

In November 1995, the state sold the old Ohio Penitentiary to the city of Columbus for one dollar; the prison had been closed since 1984. On March 26, 1997, the city began demolishing the penitentiary. Following demolition, the city sold the 13.5-acre site to Nationwide Insurance for $11.7 million. Nationwide began development of a 95-acre entertainment district, the centerpiece of which was the $150 million, 20,000-seat Nationwide Arena. The National Hockey League's Columbus Blue Jackets began play in the arena October 7, 2000. The surrounding arena district became the focus of downtown redevelopment.

In November 1999, Columbus voters elected the city's first black mayor—Michael B. Coleman, an attorney who had been president of city council. He became the first Democrat to hold the mayor's office in 28 years. In 2003, Coleman was re-elected without opposition.

In the fall of 2001, the Ohio State University completed a $200 million renovation of Ohio Stadium, with capacity expanded to 101,568. It was the largest and most expensive project in university history.

COLUMBUS MAYORS	YEARS
Jarvis Pike	1816–1817
John Kerr	1818–1819
Eli C. King	1820–1822
John Laughrey	1823
William T. Martin	1824–1826
James Robinson	1827
William Long	1827–1833
Philo H. Olmsted	1833
John Brooks	1834
John Bailhache	1835

Warren Jenkins	1836–1837
Philo H. Olmsted	1838–1839
John G. Miller	1840–1841
Thomas Wood	1841
Abram I. McDowell	1842
Smithson E. Wright	1843–1844
Alexander Patton	1845
Augustus S. Decker	1846
Alexander Patton	1847–1849
Lorenzo English	1850–1861
Wray Thomas	1861–1864
James G. Bull	1865–1868
George W. Meeker	1869–1870
James G. Bull	1871–1875
John H. Heitmann	1875–1878
Gilbert G. Collins	1879–1880
George S. Peters	1881–1882
Charles C. Walcutt	1883–1886
Philip H. Bruck	1887–1890
George J. Karb	1891–1894
Cotton H. Allen	1895–1896
Samuel L. Black	1897–1898
Samuel J. Swartz	1899–1900
John N. Hinkle	1901–1902
Robert H. Jeffrey	1903–1905
DeWitt C. Badger	1906–1907
Charles Anson Bond	1908–1909
George S. Marshall	1910–1911
George J. Karb	1912–1919
James J. Thomas	1920–1931
Henry William Worley	1932–1935
Myron B. Gessaman	1936–1939
Floyd F. Green	1940–1943
James A. Rhodes	1944–1952
Robert T. Oestreicher	1953
M.E. Sensenbrenner	1954–1959
W. Ralston Westlake	1960–1963
M.E. Sensenbrenner	1964–1971
Tom Moody	1972–1983
Dana G. Rinehart	1984–1991
Greg Lashutka	1992–1999
Michael B. Coleman	2000–

Sources: Columbus Citizen-Journal; Columbus Dispatch

DAYTON

Incorporated as a city: 1805
Land area: 55 square miles
Form of government: weak mayor; city manager, five-member city commission

Population:	2000	1990
Total	166,179	182,044
White	88,676 (53%)	106,258 (58%)
Black	71,668 (43%)	73,595 (40%)
Other	5,835(4%)	2,191(1%)

The land at the convergence of the Stillwater, Mad, and Great Miami rivers was part of the hunting grounds of the Miami and Shawnee Indians. In the Treaty of Greene Ville—signed August 3, 1795—the land was surrendered by the Indians and opened for settlement. The same year, Israel Ludlow made the first survey of the town, named for Revolutionary soldier Jonathan Dayton. Soon after the treaty signing, settlers led by Samuel C. Thompson traveled up the Great Miami River from Cincinnati to claim land they thought they had purchased from John Cleves Symmes, a Revolutionary War soldier, New Jersey judge, and land speculator. On April 1, 1796, the first of about 60 settlers set foot on Dayton. They quickly discovered, however, that the Symmes Co. did not have a valid title to the land, which had to be purchased from the government at two dollars an acre. Embittered by the experience, some settlers moved on. Daniel C. Cooper, a surveyor, purchased 3,000 acres and acted as trustee in clearing titles and parceling land to other claimants—process completed in 1801.

Dayton began to grow slowly but steadily—from 383 residents in 1810 to 1,000 in 1820. Many early settlers were English and Scotch-Irish, closely followed by Germans from eastern Pennsylvania; each group was attracted to the rich agricultural lands of the Miami Valley. On January 25, 1829, the first canal boats reached Dayton from Cincinnati via the first completed section of the Miami & Erie Canal; by 1845, the canal would be extended to Toledo. In 1830, Dayton was Ohio's second-largest town, behind Cincinnati—a short stagecoach trip away. The canal spurred the development of paper mills and other industries dependent upon water power. By 1840, the National Road was completed through Ohio; it passed through Vandalia, just north of Dayton, bringing many westward travelers into the area.

In 1846, Daniel Mead, a young bookkeeper, joined a papermaking business and began working his way up the ranks. By 1881, he was the sole owner of the company, which became the Mead Paper Co.—one of the city's largest employers. Between 1850 and 1900, the city also became known for its iron and brass works, agricultural implements, lumber, boxcars and railroad operations, and Huffy bicycles. In 1850, St. Mary's Institute opened as a Roman Catholic school for boys. It became St. Mary's College in 1913 and, in 1920, the University of Dayton. Paul Laurence Dunbar (1872–1906), a son of emancipated slaves, was born in Dayton and educated in city schools; he gained worldwide recognition for his poems and short stories.

In 1879, restaurateur James Ritty developed a mechanical money drawer. Five years later, Dayton manufacturer John H. Patterson bought the rights to it for $6,500. Patterson perfected the device and founded National Cash Register, which grew into Dayton's largest employer. The invention was the first of many that gave Dayton a reputation as a center of innovation. The city's creative minds produced fare boxes for streetcars and taxicabs, precision machinery and measuring devices, ignition systems, and other high-grade products.

The city's most famous inventors captured the world's attention on December 17, 1903. At Kitty Hawk, N.C., bicycle repairmen Wilbur and Orville Wright stayed aloft in their homemade airplane for almost a minute, giving the world its first motor-powered flight. On a prairie outside Dayton, the Wright brothers continued their experiments with heavier-than-air aircraft. In 1917, the Dayton Wright Airplane Co. was organized to make airplanes for war purposes. The same year, the federal government established McCook Field to train aviators. In 1927, when more land was needed for such operations, the government established Wright Field east of Dayton; in 1946, it was expanded and renamed Wright-Patterson Air Force Base. The base became the site of some of the nation's most advanced aeronautical research—the home of the Aeronautical Systems Division, the Air Force Logistics Command, and the Air Force Institute of Technology. In 2005, Wright-Patterson Air Force Base was the largest employer in the Dayton area, with approximately 21,000 civilian and military employees.

Another Dayton innovator was Charles F. Kettering, who developed an electric motor for cash registers. With fellow engineer Edward A. Deeds, Kettering in 1909 perfected an auto ignition system. They formed the Dayton Engineering Laboratories Co. (Delco), which became a branch of General Motors in 1919. In the

early 1900s, Dayton factories produced several makes of motor cars, including the Stoddard, Maxwell, Speedwell, and Big Four. Many residents of Appalachia were attracted to Dayton to work in the auto plants. In 1904, the Dayton Arcade was built on Ludlow Street between Third and Fourth streets. The architecturally splendid markethouse designed by Frank M. Andrews included a variety of shops and boutiques under one roof; it is listed on the National Register of Historic Places.

In September 1912, Ohio voters approved a state constitutional amendment allowing cities to adopt home-rule charters. The next year, Dayton voters adopted a commission—city manager form of government, effective January 1, 1914; Dayton was the first large city in the United States to adopt such a reform. Under the plan, a mayor and four city council members—all elected at large—form the city commission, which appoints a city manager. Henry M. Waite, Dayton's city engineer, was chosen the first city manager.

In March 1913, five days of rain produced floods that killed nearly 400 people and destroyed $100 million in property. The disaster sparked development of the Miami Conservancy District, the nation's first comprehensive flood-control project. The construction of five earthen dams and channel improvements in the Miami Valley began in 1918; the work was completed four years later. The Dayton area has not experienced a disastrous flood since.

James M. Cox, editor and publisher of the *Dayton Daily News*, was a leader of the Progressive movement in Ohio. He was a congressman, a three-term governor (1913–1915, 1917–1921) and the Democratic nominee for president in 1920—a race he lost to fellow Ohioan Warren G. Harding, publisher of the *Marion Star*. In 1928, work was completed on the Dayton Art Institute, which houses one of the finest art collections in Ohio.

In the 1940s, Dayton's black population began to increase significantly. The city began to separate between a mostly black west side and mostly white east side. After World War II, movement to suburban communities—Kettering, Oakwood, Fairborn, Huber Heights, Vandalia—advanced rapidly. In the early 1950s, the city began slum clearance and urban-renewal projects. Like many of the nation's urban areas, Dayton experienced riots in the 1960s. On September 1, 1966, the shooting of a black man by a white motorist triggered a major riot. Several blocks in one of the city's most depressed areas were destroyed, 130 people were arrested, and the National Guard was called in to quell the disturbance.

Dayton's population began to decline from its 1960 peak of 262,332. It has declined in each census since. The decline has been partially attributed to court-ordered busing for school desegregation, which began in 1976. At the time, Dayton's public schools had 40,257 students. In April 2002, a negotiated settlement ended busing for desegregation; the school system returned to neighborhood schools. Enrollment in the district stood at 20,835 students.

On July 15, 1970, James McGee was sworn in as Dayton's first black mayor; he served until 1982. In the 1970s and subsequent decades, Dayton launched efforts to stabilize and reinvigorate its downtown. A convention center opened in 1972, followed four years later by Stouffer's Dayton Plaza Hotel. In April 2000, Dayton celebrated the opening of the $16.7-million, 7,230-seat Fifth Third Field, home of the Dayton Dragons, the Class A affiliate of the Cincinnati Reds. In May 2001, the city opened the $21.1 million RiverScape Park. In March 2003, the $125 million Schuster Center for the Performing Arts opened its doors.

On January 7, 2002, Rhine McLin was sworn in as Dayton's first woman mayor.

DAYTON MAYORS	YEARS
David Reid	1805
Daniel C. Cooper	1806
William McClure	1807–1808
Isaac G. Burnet	1809
Daniel C. Cooper	1810
John Folkereth*	1811
Joseph Pierce	1812–1813
Daniel C. Cooper	1814–1817
Aaron Baker	1818
Horatio Phillips	1818–1820
Matthew Patton	1821
John Compton	1822–1824
Simeon Broadwell	1825
Elisha Brabham	1826
John Steele	1827–1828
John Folkereth	1829
John W. Van Cleve	1830–1832
Job Haines	1833
Henry Stoddard	1834
John Anderson	1835
Daniel W. Wheelock	1836–1838
William J. McKinney	1839–1840
Morris Seely	1841
Charles Anderson	1841
William J. McKinney	1841–1847
George W. Bomberger	1848
John Howard	1848–1854
George M. Young	1854–1856
Daniel W. Iddings	1856–1860
W.H. Gillespie	1860–1864
E.C. Ellis	1864–1866
Jonathan Kenny	1866–1868
C.L. Bauman	1868–1870
James D. Morrison	1870–1872
W.H. Sigman	1872–1874
Lawrence Butz Jr.	1874–1876
W.H. Rouzer	1876–1878
Lawrence Butz Jr.	1878–1880
F.M. Hosier	1880–1882
John L. Miller	1882–1884
John Bettleon	1884–1886
Ira Crawford	1886–1888
J.E.D. Ward	1888–1892
C.G. McMillen	1892–1896
Jacob Linxweiler	1896–1898

J.R. Lindemuth	1898–1902
Charles A. Snyder	1902–1906
Calvin Wright	1906–1907
Edward E. Burkhart	1908–1911
Edward Phillips	1912–1913
George W. Shroyer	1914–1917
J.M. Switzer	1918–1921
Frank B. Hale	1922–1925
Allen C. McDonald	1926–1932
Charles J. Brennan	1933–1940
Frank M. Krebs	1941–1945
Edward Breen	1946–1948
Louis W. Lohrey	1948–1953
Henry S. Stout	1954–1957
William R. Patterson	1958–1961
Frank Somers	1962–1966
Dave Hall	1966–1970
James McGee	1970–1982
Paul R. Leonard	1982–1986
Richard Clay Dixon	1987–1994
Mike Turner	1994–2002
Rhine McLin	2002–

* First to have title of mayor

Source: Dayton & Montgomery County Public Library

TOLEDO

Incorporated as a city: 1837
Land area: 81 square miles
Form of government: mayor, nine-member council

Population	2000	1990
Total	313,619	332,943
White	220,261 (70%)	256,239 (77%)
Black	73,854 (24%)	65,598 (20%)
Other	19,504 (6%)	11,106 (3%)

About 1701, the French extended their influence over the Indian tribes in the Maumee Valley and established trading posts in the region. In 1760, the British supplanted the French. At the end of the Revolutionary War, the British surrendered the territory—although Indians occupied it until 1794, when Gen. Anthony Wayne led American forces against them in the Battle of Fallen Timbers. In 1795, the Treaty of Greene Ville gave the tribes occupancy rights in the Miami Valley but reserved for the federal government a 12-square-mile area centered around a British fort at the rapids of the Maumee River. The reserve was surveyed in December 1805. On November 17, 1807, a treaty ceded to the government all lands north of the Maumee River except three Indian reservations.

After the War of 1812, settlers increasingly moved into the valley. On September 29, 1817, the Indians gave up virtually all rights to Ohio lands. The same year, land was offered for public sale; a Cincinnati group bought 974 acres along the Maumee River at the mouth of Swan Creek, naming the settlement Port Lawrence. The syndicate soon failed, but it was reorganized in 1832 and a new plat filed. The next year, Maj. Benjamin F. Stickney laid out the rival town of Vistula a short distance downriver, and the last of the nearby Indian reservations were ceded.

In the fall of 1833, a majority of property owners in Port Lawrence and Vistula agreed to merge the two towns under the name Toledo. From 1835 to 1836, the state of Ohio and the territory of Michigan disputed the location of their common boundary. When Toledo residents attempted to assume public office under Ohio laws, the Michigan territorial government passed a Pains and Penalties Act (February12, 1835), threatening to fine and imprison anyone attempting to establish unauthorized jurisdiction. The same month, the Ohio legislature claimed the disputed land by extending the northern boundaries of Henry, Williams, and Wood counties. Michigan's acting governor, Stevens T. Mason, called out the militia to enforce the penalties act. Ohio's governor Robert Lucas responded by accompanying 1,000 soldiers to Perrysburg to face the Michigan troops. Before any fighting occurred, though, Congress intervened by granting the disputed territory to Ohio and offering Michigan its Upper Peninsula as a condition of being admitted to the Union. On June 20, 1835, the legislature established Lucas County and designated Toledo the county seat.

On January 7, 1837, Gov. Joseph Vance signed legislation to incorporate Toledo as a city; that year, it had just more than 1,000 residents. On March 6, 1837, Toledo's white males elected Whig John Berdan the city's first mayor. The Irish made up the bulk of early immigrants, arriving to work on construction of the Wabash & Erie and Miami & Erie canals. The first barge arrived in Toledo over the Wabash & Erie in 1843 from Lafayette, Ind.; the entire canal system was completed in 1845, allowing traffic between Toledo and Cincinnati. German immigrants followed, soon outnumbering the Irish in Toledo.

Sawmills, flour mills, and factories sprung up along the Maumee. In 1840, Toledo had 1,222 residents. The next year, the county seat was moved to Maumee, but, in 1852, a majority of county voters decided to return it to Toledo. With the completion of the canal system, Toledo established itself in the 1840s as the chief port on Lake Erie for shipping wheat to the Atlantic coast. By 1850, its population had climbed to 3,829—a figure that almost quadrupled during the next 10 years. The 1850s brought railroads to Toledo; five major lines were completed to the city in the decade, making it one of the nation's leading rail centers—a transfer point for moving wheat, coal, and other cargoes from railroad car to lake freighter. Toledo's growing industries attracted many Polish immigrants in the 1870s, when the city's population passed the 50,000 mark.

In 1872, Jessup W. Scott, a newspaper publisher and real-estate developer, donated 160 acres for a university; the Toledo University of Arts and Trades opened January 14, 1875. The school struggled and closed, but the city levied a tax in 1883 to support it. In 1884, it reopened as Toledo University, a municipal university that in 1967—as the University of Toledo—became part of the state's higher education system.

In the 1880s, oil and natural gas were discovered in Findlay and other areas of northwestern Ohio; Toledo became a major oil-refining and pipeline center. The city became more attractive to industry because of the availability of cheap sources of fuel. One of those industries was the New England Glass Co. of Cambridge, Mass., owned by Edward D. Libbey. In 1888, Libbey relocated his glass factory to Toledo and soon made an association with Michael J. Owens, owner of the Owens Bottle Co. (incorporated in 1907), who perfected glass-blowing technology. A third Toledo glassmaker, Edward Ford, arrived in Toledo in 1896 to establish a plate-glass factory. Toledo soon became the world's leader in production of plate glass and sheet glass for the auto industry.

The 1890s brought Toledo its first skyscraper—the nine-story Nasby Building (1892). Allen DeVilbiss invented the springless computing scale, and the Toledo Scale Co. was founded in 1898. Toledo also was home of the National Supply Co., one of the nation's largest drilling-supply companies. The city also developed a thriving bicycle industry. In 1897, Samuel M. "Golden Rule" Jones was elected mayor, ushering in a period of reform in municipal government. Jones warred against corruption, established a municipally owned utility (the Toledo Municipal Gas Co.), developed public playgrounds, and established an eight-hour day for city employees. He was rewarded with four consecutive terms as mayor. He died in 1904 while still in office. His successor, Brand Whitlock, carried on the reformist movement.

During the early 1900s, Toledo was a major shipbuilding center and also developed a motorcar industry. By 1902, the Pope automobile was being produced. In 1907, the Pope Motor Car Co. went into receivership; two years later, it was purchased by John Willys, who moved from Indianapolis and established the Willys-Overland Co. in Toledo. By 1915, Willys was the nation's second-largest auto builder, behind Ford. Toledo became an auto industry town; it built autos, but it became known more for parts and equipment—ignitions, lighting systems, batteries, spark plugs, and, especially, glass. Major employers included Champion Spark Plug Co., Libbey-Owens, and Willys-Overland.

On November 3, 1914, Toledo voters approved a city charter, effective January 1, 1916, to provide home rule and nonpartisan municipal elections.

During World War I, Toledo's factories were major producers of war supplies. On July 4, 1919, 24-year-old Jack Dempsey claimed boxing's world heavyweight championship in Toledo, with a third-round knockout of Jess Willard in Bay View Park. In the 1920s, the glass industry became so dominant that Toledo was dubbed "the glass capital of the world." In 1929, the Owens Bottle Co. acquired the Illinois Glass Co. of Alton, Ill., to form Owens-Illinois. The next year, Libbey-Owens merged with Ford Plate Glass to form Libbey-Owens-Ford.

In the 1920s and especially the 1930s, Toledo's automotive industries—like those across the Midwest—became unionized. Union-management problems became commonplace. The city's black population increased from 5,691 in 1920 to 13,260 in 1930; Toledo became segregated, as blacks congregated primarily in the southwestern part of the city.

As they struggled to recover from the Great Depression, Toledo residents grew increasingly dissatisfied with the perceived corruption and inefficiency of city government. A Citizens' Charter Commission proposed an amendment to provide for a city manager and nine-member council, with members elected at large. On November 6, 1934, Toledo voters approved the amendment, and, in 1935, John N. Edy became Toledo's first city manager.

During World War II, Toledo again played a leading role in producing war supplies, especially Jeeps. From 1941 to 1945, Willys-Overland manufactured more than 300,000 of the rugged, four-wheel-drive vehicles. After the war, on April 11, 1946, Toledo voters approved a 1 percent payroll tax, the first municipal income tax in Ohio and the second in the nation. (Philadelphia was first in 1939.) In the 1950s, Willys-Overland was the city's largest employer; the company stopped producing passenger cars, concentrating only on utility vehicles.

From 1940 to 1960—because of black migration and white movement to the suburbs—the city's black population increased from 5 percent to 12.5 percent. In 1955, the 241-mile Ohio Turnpike was completed across northern Ohio; Toledo motorists were among the first in the state to enjoy the benefits of a modern, limited-access highway. In 1959, the city began an urban-renewal program. In the 1960s, Toledo initiated housing projects and other programs designed to alleviate blight in old and poor neighborhoods. The city also began annexing territory to the north and west to expand its economic base. The glass, automotive, and oil industries still dominated the city's economy. In 1969, American Motors Corp. bought the Kaiser Jeep Corp. for $70 million. The same year, the state-assisted Medical College of Ohio opened, graduating its first class in 1972.

In November 1983, Toledo elected its first woman mayor, Donna Owens, who was sworn into office December 1. In May 1984, the city opened the Portside Festival Marketplace, an $18 million retail mall on the Maumee River downtown. The two-level, 70-store mall was meant to revive a foundering downtown but never managed to make a principal payment to its creditors. The loans were written off as uncollectible, and the mall closed in 1990. Four years later, efforts were launched to resurrect the mall with a branch of the Columbus-based Center of Science and Industry.

In November 1992, Toledoans voted to eliminate the city manager form of government and return—after 58 years—to a strong-mayor form. The next year, Carty Finkbeiner, a city councilman for 10 years, was elected mayor. The same year, state and local officials put together a rescue plan to keep Libbey-Owens-Ford Co. in Toledo when it appeared the company might move to Detroit. The plan included a state infusion of $4.5 million to enable the city to purchase the company's building for $3 million, lease it back to the company, and make improvements to the building and surrounding area.

In November 2001, Jack Ford was elected mayor—the first black to hold the office. A lawyer, Ford previously had served seven years as a state representative and seven years on Toledo City Council.

On April 9, 2002, the Toledo Mud Hens—Triple-A affiliate of the Detroit Tigers—began play in the new, $39.2 million Fifth Third Field in the downtown's warehouse district.

TOLEDO MAYORS	YEARS
John Berdan	1837–1838
Hezekiah D. Mason	1839
Myron H. Tilden	1840–1843
James Myers	1843
George B. Way	1844
Richard Mott	1845–1846
Emory D. Potter	1846–1848
Daniel O. Morton	1849
Caleb F. Abbott	1850
Charles M. Dorr	1851
Daniel McBain	1852
Egbert B. Brown	1852
Ira L. Clark	1852
Mavor Brigham	1853
Charles M. Dorr	1853–1856
Alexander M. Brownlee	1857–1860
Alexander H. Newcomb	1860–1861
John Manor	1861–1863
Charles M. Dorr	1863–1866
Charles A. King	1867–1868
William Kraus	1869–1870
William W. Jones	1871–1874
Guido Marx	1875–1876
William W. Jones	1877–1878
Jacob Romeis	1879–1885
George Scheets	1885
Samuel F. Forbes	1885–1886
James K. Hamilton	1887–1890
Vincent J. Emmick	1891–1892
Guy G. Major	1893–1896
Samuel M. Jones	1897–1904
Robert H. Finch	1904–1905
Brand Whitlock	1906–1913
Carl H. Keller	1914–1915
Charles Milroy	1916–1917
Cornell Schreiber	1918–1921
Bernard F. Brough	1922–1925
Fred J. Mery	1926–1927
William T. Jackson	1928–1931
Addison Q. Thacher	1932–1933
Solon T. Klotz	1934–1935
Roy C. Start	1936–1939
John Q. Carey	1940–1942
Lloyd E. Roulet	1943–1947

Michael V. DiSalle	1948–1950
Ollie Czelusta	1950–1951
Lloyd E. Roulet	1952–1953
Ollie Czelusta	1954–1957
John W. Yager	1957–1959
Michael J. Damas	1959–1961
John W. Potter	1961–1967
William J. Ensign	1967–1971
Harry W. Kessler	1971–1976
Douglas DeGood	1977–1982
Donna Owens	1983–1989
John McHugh	1990–1993
Carty Finkbeiner	1994–2001
Jack Ford	2002–2005
Carty Finkbeiner	2006–

Source: The (Toledo) Blade

YOUNGSTOWN

Incorporated as a city: 1868
Land area: 34 square miles
Form of government: mayor, seven-member council

Population	2000	1990
Total	313,619	332,943
White	220,261 (70%)	256,239 (77%)
Black	73,854 (24%)	65,598 (20%)
Other	19,504(6%)	11,106(3%)

Iroquois Indians inhabited this region when New England traders began arriving in the late 1700s, following a trail from Pittsburgh to Lake Erie. One of the first was James Hillman, an agent for a Pittsburgh trading company. In 1797, on the advice of Hillman, John Young of Whitestown, N.Y., bought land at the junction of the Mahoning River and Mill Creek from the Connecticut Land Co. and brought a party of settlers to the area. The settlement was named for Young, though he never became a permanent resident. Hillman provided more leadership, assisting the settlement of pioneers, negotiating with the Indians, helping construct Youngstown's

first log cabin, and later serving as sheriff of Trumbull County and a state representative. In August 1798, a 100-lot plat of Youngstown was laid out, with Federal and Market as the main streets.

The pioneers engaged in wheat and corn farming and operated sawmills and grist mills powered by water. In 1803, near the mouth of Yellow Creek, Daniel and James Heaton built a crude, charcoal-fired blast furnace just outside Youngstown and made iron from local ores. Other furnaces soon were built. In 1826, Youngstown's first coal mine opened, and coal quickly replaced charcoal as furnace fuel. In May 1839, the Ohio and Pennsylvania Canal was opened to traffic between Warren, Ohio, and Beaver, Pa., stimulating industrial and agricultural commerce in the area. In 1846, local investors organized the Youngstown Rolling Mill, the area's first finishing mill. From 1845 to 1875, 21 blast furnaces were built in the Mahoning Valley.

The industry's early expansion had been speeded by the availability of black-band ores in nearby hillsides, but by 1856 higher-quality ores were being imported from the Lake Superior region. One of the industry's pioneers was David Tod, son of George Tod, Youngstown's first lawyer. David Tod made a fortune in coal and iron and was a founder of the Cleveland & Mahoning Valley Railroad, which opened in 1856. In 1861, David Tod was elected Ohio's 25th governor on the Union Party ticket. As governor, he supervised the mobilization of Ohio's war effort, and his home city provided much of the iron for Union army weapons.

In 1868, Youngstown was incorporated as a city. Its population nearly tripled between 1860 and 1870, when the city had 8,075 residents—mostly Irish, German, and Welsh. The city had become one of the nation's leading iron-making centers, although its industrial progress was slowed considerably by the depression of 1873. The next year, the state legislature voted to move the county seat from Canfield to Youngstown. The decision prompted a legal battle, settled in Youngstown's favor in 1879 by the U.S. Supreme Court. By the 1880s, Youngstown's iron business had recovered from the depression and its mills were flourishing.

In 1892, as steel was about to replace iron, the Union Iron & Steel Co. began construction of Youngstown's first steel plant, which opened three years later. In 1899, it was among the plants acquired by the National Steel Co. In 1901, the United States Steel Co. took over the plant in a consolidation wave that swept the industry. Through similar mergers, Carnegie Steel, Republic Steel, and Youngstown Sheet & Tube emerged as giants of the industry in Youngstown. The city was perfectly positioned for the industry—midway between the Appalachian coal fields and the Lake Erie docks where iron ore was received from Lake Superior.

Job-seeking immigrants—Poles, Italians, Greeks, Slovaks, and Slovenians—flocked to Youngstown to work in the furnaces and mills that lined the Mahoning River, producing the steel for America's automobiles, bridges, buildings, and military. Between 1900 and 1920, the city's population nearly tripled to more than 132,000. By World War I, Youngstown rivaled Pittsburgh in the production of iron and steel. During and after the war, many blacks from the South migrated to Youngstown to find work. By 1940, the black share of the city's population—less than 3 percent in 1910—approached 10 percent.

Between 1930 and 1960, Youngstown's population held steady at about 170,000. During the latter half of that period, though, steel producers in the South and overseas gained a competitive edge with newer technology and lower wages. By the late 1970s, Youngstown's time was up. In September 1977, Youngstown Sheet & Tube shut down, idling 4,200 workers. One by one, Youngstown's other steel plants closed. From 1973 to 1983, Youngstown lost 40,000 manufacturing jobs. The city's unemployment rate in the early 1980s ranked among the highest in the nation. Youngstown epitomized the nation's industrial decline.

Over several decades, Youngstown established a reputation as a center of organized crime and corrupt politics. The reputation was given national focus in 1983, when Democrat James A. Traficant Jr. the Mahoning County sheriff, was tried on federal charges of taking bribes from mobsters to overlook their activities. Faced with tapes of the transactions, Traficant contended that he was conducting his own sting operation; a jury acquitted him. Traficant had become a local hero as sheriff when he refused to foreclose on the homes of laid-off steelworkers. In 1984, Traficant was elected to Congress; he was re-elected eight times. In April 2002, he was convicted of ten felonies, including bribery and racketeering. In July 2002, Traficant was expelled from Congress. Over a five-year period, the federal strike force that nailed Traficant indicted more than 70 Youngstown-area government and mob figures.

The city's unsavory political image also was punctuated in 1990, when colorful County Democratic Chairman Don Hanni, a former amateur boxer, told interviewers for 60 Minutes that "all politicians in Mahoning County take money from the mob." Hanni ran an old-fashioned Democratic machine in the county from 1978 to 1994, when he was ousted by the reform movement Mahoning Democrats for Change.

Since the closing of the mills, Youngstown has been trying to rebuild its economy with a diversity of small businesses. One success was Sovereign Circuits, Inc., a high-technology company that produced circuit boards. Lured by state-backed loans and other incentives, Sovereign moved in 1987 from Corby, England, to become Youngstown's first high-tech company. In 2004, Sovereign employed 120 people. The state-assisted Technology Development Corp., part of Youngstown State University, is a focal point for the Mahoning Valley's efforts to attract small and medium-size manufacturing companies. Youngstown officials also have been trying to take advantage of so-called brownfield legislation, which eases environmental standards that prevent the redevelopment of old industrial sites.

In 2002, General Motors delivered welcome news by announcing it would invest more than $500 million to modernize the 37-year-old Lordstown Assembly Plant for production of a new compact car, the Chevrolet Cobalt. City and union leaders had feared the plant would be shut down, which would have idled 3,600 workers.

In 2004, city leaders broke ground for the Youngstown Convocation Center, a 5,500-seat arena and multipurpose facility. Opened in 2005, the center was seen as a focal point for downtown redevelopment efforts. The arena enabled Youngstown to be selected for an expansion franchise in the Central Hockey League.

YOUNGSTOWN MAYORS	YEARS
John Heiner	1850–1851
Robert W. Tayler	1851–1852
Stephen F. Burnett	1852–1853
William G. Moore	1853–1855
William Rice	1855–1856
Thomas W. Sanderson	1856–1857
Reuben Carroll	1857–1862
Peter W. Carroll	1862–1863
John Manning	1863
Thomas E. Wells	1863–1864
Brainard S. Higley	1864–1866
George McKee	1866–1871
John D. Raney	1872–1873
William M. Osborn	1874–1875
Mathew Logan	1876–1879
William J. Lawthers	1880–1883
Walter L. Campbell	1884–1885
Samuel A. Steele	1886–1887
Randall Montgomery	1888–1891
I.B. Miller	1892–1895
Edmond H. Moore	1896–1899
Frank L. Brown	1900–1903
W.T. Gibson	1904–1906
Frank L. Baldwin	1906–1908
Alvin W. Craver	1908–1912
F.A. Hartenstein	1912–1916
Carroll Thornton	1916–1918
Alvin W. Craver	1918–1920
Fred J. Warnock	1920–1922
George L. Olds	1922
William W. Reese	1922–1924
Charles F. Scheible	1924–1928
Joseph F. Heffernan	1928–1932
Mark E. Moore	1932–1936
Lionel Evans	1936–1940
William B. Spagnola	1940–1944
Ralph W. O'Neill	1944–1948
Charles P. Henderson	1948–1954
Frank X. Kryzan	1954–1960
Frank R. Franko	1960–1962
Harry N. Savasten	1962–1964
Anthony B. Flask	1964–1970
Jack C. Hunter	1970–1978
J. Phillip Richley	1978–1980
George Vukovich	1980–1984
Patrick J. Ungaro	1984–1998
George McKelvey	1998–2005
Jay Williams	2005–

Source: The Public Library of Youngstown and Mahoning County

CHAPTER 12

Ohio by the Numbers

CENSUS TRENDS, 1800–2000

Ohio Population

CENSUS YEAR	POPULATION	CHANGE	RANK AMONG STATES
2000	11,353,140	4.7	7
1990	10,847,115	0.4	7
1980	10,797,630	1.3	6
1970	10,657,423	9.8	6
1960	9,706,397	22.1	5
1950	7,946,627	15.0	5
1940	6,907,612	3.9	4
1930	6,646,697	15.4	4
1920	5,759,394	20.8	4
1910	4,767,121	14.7	4
1900	4,157,545	13.2	4
1890	3,672,329	14.8	4
1880	3,198,062	20.0	3
1870	2,665,260	13.9	3
1860	2,339,511	18.1	3
1850	1,980,329	30.3	3
1840	1,519,467	62.0	3
1830	937,903	61.3	4
1820	581,434	152.0	5
1810	230,760	408.7	13
1800	45,365	—	18 *

* On February 19, 1803, Ohio was admitted into the Union as the 17th state. Its population in 1800, when it was still a territory, would have ranked it 18th among the states and territories.

Black Population

CENSUS YEAR	POPULATION	% OF TOTAL
2000	1,301,307	11.5
1990	1,152,230	10.6
1980	1,076,734	10.0
1970	970,477	9.1
1960	786,000	8.1
1950	513,072	6.5
1940	339,461	4.9
1930	309,304	4.7
1920	186,187	3.2
1910	111,452	2.3
1900	96,901	2.3
1890	87,113	2.3
1880	80,142	2.5
1870	63,213	2.4
1860	36,673	1.6
1850	25,279	1.3
1840	17,342	1.1
1830	9,586	1.0
1820	4,723	0.8
1810	1,890	0.8
1800	337	0.7

Urban and Rural Population

YEAR	URBAN	%	RURAL	%
2000	8,782,329	77.4	2,570,811	22.6
1990	8,039,037	74.1	2,808,078	25.9
1980	7,918,259	73.3	2,879,371	26.7
1970**	8,025,775	75.3	2,626,242	24.6
1960	7,123,162	73.4	2,583,235	26.6
1950	5,578,274	70.2	2,368,353	29.8
1940	4,612,986	66.8	2,294,626	33.2
1930	4,507,371	67.8	2,139,326	32.2
1920	3,677,136	63.8	2,082,258	36.2
1910	2,663,143	55.9	2,101,978	44.1
1900	1,998,382	48.1	2,159,163	51.9
1890	1,510,153	41.1	2,162,176	58.9
1880	1,030,769	32.2	2,167,293	67.8
1870	682,922	25.6	1,982,338	74.4
1860	400,435	17.1	1,939,076	82.9
1850	242,418	12.2	1,737,911	87.8
1840	83,491	5.5	1,435,976	94.5
1830	36,658	3.9	901,245	96.1
1820	9,642	1.7	571,792	98.3
1810	2,540	1.1	228,220	98.9
1800	—	—	45,365	100.0

** Urban and rural populations for 1970 total less than 10,657,423 because of post-census adjustment of total population.

Population by County

1800–2000

Adams

CENSUS YEAR	POPULATION
2000	27,330
1990	25,371
1980	24,328
1970	18,957
1960	19,982
1950	20,499
1940	21,705
1930	20,381
1920	22,403
1910	24,755
1900	26,328
1890	26,093
1880	24,005
1870	20,750
1860	20,309
1850	18,883
1840	13,183
1830	12,281
1820	10,406
1810	9,434
1800	3,432

Allen

CENSUS YEAR	POPULATION
2000	108,473
1990	109,755
1980	112,241
1970	111,144
1960	103,691
1950	88,183
1940	73,303
1930	69,419
1920	68,223
1910	56,580
1900	47,976
1890	40,644
1880	31,314
1870	23,623
1860	19,185
1850	12,109
1840	9,079

CENSUS YEAR	POPULATION
1830	578
1820	—
1810	—
1800	—

Ashland

CENSUS YEAR	POPULATION
2000	52,523
1990	47,507
1980	46,178
1970	43,303
1960	38,771
1950	33,040
1940	29,785
1930	26,867
1920	24,627
1910	22,975
1900	21,184
1890	22,223
1880	23,883
1870	21,933
1860	22,951
1850	23,813
1840	—
1830	—
1820	—
1810	—
1800	—

Ashtabula

CENSUS YEAR	POPULATION
2000	102,728
1990	99,821
1980	104,215
1970	98,237
1960	93,067
1950	78,695
1940	68,674
1930	68,361
1920	65,545
1910	59,547
1900	51,448
1890	43,655
1880	37,139
1870	32,517
1860	31,814
1850	28,767
1840	23,724
1830	14,584
1820	7,382
1810	—
1800	—

Athens

CENSUS YEAR	POPULATION
2000	62,223

CENSUS YEAR	POPULATION
1990	59,549
1980	56,399
1970	55,747
1960	46,998
1950	45,839
1940	46,166
1930	44,175
1920	50,430
1910	47,798
1900	38,730
1890	35,194
1880	28,411
1870	23,768
1860	21,364
1850	18,215
1840	19,109
1830	9,787
1820	6,338
1810	2,791
1800	—

Auglaize

CENSUS YEAR	POPULATION
2000	46,611
1990	44,585
1980	42,554
1970	38,602
1960	36,147
1950	30,637
1940	28,037
1930	28,034
1920	29,527
1910	31,246
1900	31,192
1890	28,100
1880	25,444
1870	20,041
1860	17,187
1850	11,338
1840	—
1830	—
1820	—
1810	—
1800	—

Belmont

CENSUS YEAR	POPULATION
2000	70,226
1990	71,074
1980	82,569
1970	80,917
1960	83,864
1950	87,740
1940	95,614
1930	94,719
1920	93,193

CENSUS YEAR	POPULATION
1910	76,856
1900	60,875
1890	57,413
1880	49,638
1870	39,714
1860	36,398
1850	34,600
1840	30,901
1830	28,627
1820	20,329
1810	11,097
1800	—

Brown

CENSUS YEAR	POPULATION
2000	42,285
1990	34,966
1980	31,920
1970	26,635
1960	25,178
1950	22,221
1940	21,638
1930	20,148
1920	22,621
1910	24,832
1900	28,237
1890	29,899
1880	32,911
1870	30,802
1860	29,958
1850	27,332
1840	22,715
1830	17,867
1820	13,356
1810	—
1800	—

Butler

CENSUS YEAR	POPULATION
2000	332,807
1990	291,479
1980	258,787
1970	226,207
1960	199,076
1950	147,203
1940	120,249
1930	114,084
1920	87,025
1910	70,271
1900	56,870
1890	48,597
1880	42,579
1870	39,912
1860	35,840
1850	30,789
1840	28,173

CENSUS YEAR	POPULATION
1830	27,142
1820	21,746
1810	11,150
1800	—

Carroll

CENSUS YEAR	POPULATION
2000	28,836
1990	26,521
1980	25,598
1970	21,579
1960	20,857
1950	19,039
1940	17,449
1930	16,057
1920	15,942
1910	15,761
1900	16,811
1890	17,566
1880	16,416
1870	14,491
1860	15,738
1850	17,685
1840	18,108
1830	—
1820	—
1810	—
1800	—

Champaign

CENSUS YEAR	POPULATION
2000	38,890
1990	36,019
1980	33,649
1970	30,491
1960	29,714
1950	26,793
1940	25,258
1930	24,103
1920	25,071
1910	26,351
1900	26,642
1890	26,980
1880	27,817
1870	24,188
1860	22,698
1850	19,782
1840	16,721
1830	12,131
1820	8,479
1810	6,303
1800	—

Clark

CENSUS YEAR	POPULATION
2000	144,742

CENSUS YEAR	POPULATION
1990	147,548
1980	150,236
1970	157,115
1960	131,440
1950	111,661
1940	95,647
1930	90,936
1920	80,728
1910	66,435
1900	58,939
1890	52,277
1880	41,948
1870	32,070
1860	25,300
1850	22,178
1840	16,882
1830	13,114
1820	9,533
1810	—
1800	—

Clermont

CENSUS YEAR	POPULATION
2000	177,977
1990	150,187
1980	128,483
1970	95,372
1960	80,530
1950	42,182
1940	34,109
1930	29,786
1920	28,291
1910	29,551
1900	31,610
1890	33,553
1880	36,713
1870	34,268
1860	33,034
1850	30,455
1840	23,106
1830	20,466
1820	15,820
1810	9,965
1800	—

Clinton

CENSUS YEAR	POPULATION
2000	40,543
1990	35,415
1980	34,603
1970	31,464
1960	30,004
1950	25,572
1940	22,574
1930	21,547

CENSUS YEAR	POPULATION
1920	23,036
1910	23,680
1900	24,202
1890	24,240
1880	24,756
1870	21,914
1860	21,462
1850	18,838
1840	15,719
1830	11,436
1820	8,085
1810	2,674
1800	—

Columbiana

CENSUS YEAR	POPULATION
2000	112,075
1990	108,276
1980	113,572
1970	108,310
1960	107,004
1950	98,920
1940	90,121
1930	86,484
1920	83,131
1910	76,619
1900	68,590
1890	59,029
1880	48,602
1870	38,299
1860	32,836
1850	33,621
1840	40,378
1830	35,592
1820	22,033
1810	10,878
1800	—

Coshocton

CENSUS YEAR	POPULATION
2000	36.655
1990	35,427
1980	36,024
1970	33,486
1960	32,224
1950	31,141
1940	30,594
1930	28,976
1920	29,595
1910	30,121
1900	29,337
1890	26,703
1880	26,642
1870	23,600
1860	25,032

CENSUS YEAR	POPULATION
1850	25,674
1840	21,590
1830	11,161
1820	7,086
1810	—
1800	—

Crawford

CENSUS YEAR	POPULATION
2000	46,966
1990	47,870
1980	50,075
1970	50,364
1960	46,775
1950	38,738
1940	35,571
1930	35,345
1920	36,054
1910	34,036
1900	33,915
1890	31,927
1880	30,583
1870	25,556
1860	23,881
1850	18,177
1840	13,152
1830	4,791
1820	—
1810	—
1800	—

Cuyahoga

CENSUS YEAR	POPULATION
2000	1,393,978
1990	1,412,140
1980	1,498,400
1970	1,720,835
1960	1,647,895
1950	1,389,532
1940	1,217,250
1930	1,201,455
1920	943,495
1910	637,425
1900	439,120
1890	309,970
1880	196,943
1870	132,010
1860	78,033
1850	48,099
1840	26,506
1830	10,373
1820	6,328
1810	1,459
1800	—

Darke

CENSUS YEAR	POPULATION
2000	53,309
1990	53,619
1980	55,096
1970	49,141
1960	45,612
1950	41,799
1940	38,831
1930	38,009
1920	42,911
1910	42,933
1900	42,532
1890	42,961
1880	40,496
1870	32,278
1860	26,009
1850	20,276
1840	13,282
1830	6,204
1820	3,717
1810	—
1800	—

Defiance

CENSUS YEAR	POPULATION
2000	39,500
1990	39,350
1980	39,987
1970	36,949
1960	31,508
1950	25,925
1940	24,367
1930	22,714
1920	24,549
1910	24,498
1900	26,387
1890	25,769
1880	22,515
1870	15,719
1860	11,886
1850	6,966
1840	—
1830	—
1820	—
1810	—
1800	—

Delaware

CENSUS YEAR	POPULATION
2000	109,989
1990	66,929
1980	53,840
1970	42,908

CENSUS YEAR	POPULATION
1960	36,107
1950	30,278
1940	26,780
1930	26,016
1920	26,013
1910	27,182
1900	26,401
1890	27,189
1880	27,381
1870	25,175
1860	23,902
1850	21,817
1840	22,060
1830	11,504
1820	7,639
1810	2,000
1800	—

Erie

CENSUS YEAR	POPULATION
2000	79,551
1990	76,779
1980	79,655
1970	75,909
1960	68,000
1950	52,565
1940	43,201
1930	42,133
1920	39,789
1910	38,327
1900	37,650
1890	35,462
1880	32,640
1870	28,188
1860	24,474
1850	18,568
1840	12,599
1830	—
1820	—
1810	—
1800	—

Fairfield

CENSUS YEAR	POPULATION
2000	122,759
1990	103,461
1980	93,678
1970	73,301
1960	63,912
1950	52,130
1940	48,490
1930	44,010
1920	40,484
1910	39,201
1900	34,259

CENSUS YEAR	POPULATION
1890	33,939
1880	34,284
1870	31,138
1860	30,538
1850	30,264
1840	31,924
1830	24,786
1820	16,633
1810	11,361
1800	—

Fayette

CENSUS YEAR	POPULATION
2000	28,433
1990	27,466
1980	27,467
1970	25,461
1960	24,775
1950	22,554
1940	21,385
1930	20,755
1920	21,518
1910	21,744
1900	21,725
1890	22,309
1880	20,364
1870	17,170
1860	15,935
1850	12,726
1840	10,984
1830	8,182
1820	6,316
1810	1,854
1800	—

Franklin

CENSUS YEAR	POPULATION
2000	1,068,978
1990	961,437
1980	869,126
1970	833,249
1960	682,923
1950	503,410
1940	388,712
1930	361,055
1920	283,951
1910	221,567
1900	164,460
1890	124,087
1880	86,797
1870	63,019
1860	50,361
1850	42,909
1840	25,049
1830	14,741

CENSUS YEAR	POPULATION
1820	10,292
1810	3,486
1800	—

Fulton

CENSUS YEAR	POPULATION
2000	42,084
1990	38,498
1980	37,751
1970	33,071
1960	29,301
1950	25,580
1940	23,626
1930	23,477
1920	23,445
1910	23,914
1900	22,801
1890	22,023
1880	21,053
1870	17,789
1860	14,043
1850	7,781
1840	—
1830	—
1820	—
1810	—
1800	—

Gallia

CENSUS YEAR	POPULATION
2000	31,069
1990	30,954
1980	30,098
1970	25,239
1960	26,120
1950	24,910
1940	24,930
1930	23,050
1920	23,311
1910	25,745
1900	27,918
1890	27,005
1880	28,124
1870	25,545
1860	22,043
1850	17,063
1840	13,444
1830	9,733
1820	7,098
1810	4,181
1800	—

Geauga

CENSUS YEAR	POPULATION
2000	90,895

CENSUS YEAR	POPULATION
1990	81,129
1980	74,474
1970	62,977
1960	47,573
1950	26,646
1940	19,430
1930	15,414
1920	15,036
1910	14,670
1900	14,744
1890	13,489
1880	14,251
1870	14,190
1860	15,817
1850	17,827
1840	16,297
1830	15,813
1820	7,791
1810	2,917
1800	—

Greene

CENSUS YEAR	POPULATION
2000	147,886
1990	136,731
1980	129,769
1970	125,057
1960	94,642
1950	58,892
1940	35,863
1930	33,259
1920	31,221
1910	29,733
1900	31,613
1890	29,820
1880	31,349
1870	28,038
1860	26,197
1850	21,946
1840	17,528
1830	14,801
1820	10,529
1810	5,870
1800	—

Guernsey

CENSUS YEAR	POPULATION
2000	40,792
1990	39,024
1980	42,024
1970	37,665
1960	38,579
1950	38,452
1940	38,822
1930	41,486

CENSUS YEAR	POPULATION
1920	45,352
1910	42,716
1900	34,425
1890	28,645
1880	27,197
1870	23,838
1860	24,474
1850	30,438
1840	27,748
1830	18,036
1820	9,292
1810	3,051
1800	—

Hamilton

CENSUS YEAR	POPULATION
2000	845,303
1990	866,228
1980	873,204
1970	925,944
1960	864,121
1950	723,952
1940	621,987
1930	589,356
1920	493,678
1910	460,732
1900	409,479
1890	374,573
1880	313,374
1870	260,370
1860	216,410
1850	156,844
1840	80,145
1830	52,317
1820	31,764
1810	15,258
1800	14,692

Hancock

CENSUS YEAR	POPULATION
2000	71,295
1990	65,536
1980	64,581
1970	61,217
1960	53,686
1950	44,280
1940	40,793
1930	40,404
1920	38,394
1910	37,860
1900	41,993
1890	42,563
1880	27,784
1870	23,847
1860	22,886

CENSUS YEAR	POPULATION
1850	16,751
1840	9,986
1830	813
1820	—
1810	—
1800	—

Hardin

CENSUS YEAR	POPULATION
2000	31,945
1990	31,111
1980	32,719
1970	30,813
1960	29,633
1950	28,673
1940	27,061
1930	27,635
1920	29,167
1910	30,407
1900	31,187
1890	28,939
1880	27,023
1870	18,714
1860	13,570
1850	8,251
1840	4,598
1830	210
1820	—
1810	—
1800	—

Harrison

CENSUS YEAR	POPULATION
2000	15,856
1990	16,085
1980	18,152
1970	17,013
1960	17,995
1950	19,054
1940	20,313
1930	18,844
1920	19,625
1910	19,076
1900	20,486
1890	20,830
1880	20,456
1870	18,682
1860	19,110
1850	20,157
1840	20,099
1830	20,916
1820	14,345
1810	—
1800	—

Henry

CENSUS YEAR	POPULATION
2000	29,210
1990	29,108
1980	28,383
1970	27,058
1960	25,392
1950	22,423
1940	22,756
1930	22,524
1920	23,362
1910	25,119
1900	27,282
1890	25,080
1880	20,585
1870	14,028
1860	8,901
1850	3,434
1840	2,503
1830	262
1820	—
1810	—
1800	—

Highland

CENSUS YEAR	POPULATION
2000	40,875
1990	35,728
1980	33,477
1970	28,996
1960	29,716
1950	28,188
1940	27,099
1930	25,416
1920	27,610
1910	28,711
1900	30,982
1890	29,048
1880	30,281
1870	29,133
1860	27,773
1850	25,781
1840	22,269
1830	16,345
1820	12,308
1810	5,766
1800	—

Hocking

CENSUS YEAR	POPULATION
2000	28,241
1990	25,533
1980	24,304
1970	20,322
1960	20,168
1950	19,520
1940	21,504
1930	20,407
1920	23,291
1910	23,650
1900	24,398
1890	22,658
1880	21,126
1870	17,925
1860	17,057
1850	14,119
1840	9,741
1830	4,008
1820	2,130
1810	—
1800	—

Holmes

CENSUS YEAR	POPULATION
2000	38,943
1990	32,849
1980	29,416
1970	23,024
1960	21,591
1950	18,760
1940	17,876
1930	16,726
1920	16,965
1910	17,909
1900	19,511
1890	21,139
1880	20,776
1870	18,177
1860	20,589
1850	20,452
1840	18,088
1830	9,135
1820	—
1810	—
1800	—

Huron

CENSUS YEAR	POPULATION
2000	59,487
1990	56,240
1980	54,608
1970	49,587
1960	47,326
1950	39,353
1940	34,800
1930	33,700
1920	32,424
1910	34,206
1900	32,330

CENSUS YEAR	POPULATION
1890	31,949
1880	31,609
1870	28,532
1860	29,616
1850	26,203
1840	23,933
1830	13,341
1820	6,675
1810	—
1800	—

Jackson

CENSUS YEAR	POPULATION
2000	32,641
1990	30,230
1980	30,592
1970	27,174
1960	29,372
1950	27,767
1940	27,004
1930	25,040
1920	27,342
1910	30,791
1900	34,248
1890	28,408
1880	23,686
1870	21,759
1860	17,941
1850	12,719
1840	9,744
1830	5,941
1820	3,746
1810	—
1800	—

Jefferson

CENSUS YEAR	POPULATION
2000	73,894
1990	80,298
1980	91,564
1970	96,193
1960	99,201
1950	96,495
1940	98,129
1930	88,307
1920	77,580
1910	65,423
1900	44,357
1890	39,415
1880	33,018
1870	29,188
1860	26,115
1850	29,133
1840	25,030
1830	22,489
1820	18,531
1810	17,260
1800	8,766

Knox

CENSUS YEAR	POPULATION
2000	54,500
1990	47,473
1980	46,304
1970	41,795
1960	38,808
1950	35,287
1940	31,024
1930	29,338
1920	29,580
1910	30,181
1900	27,768
1890	27,600
1880	27,431
1870	26,333
1860	27,735
1850	28,872
1840	29,579
1830	17,085
1820	8,326
1810	2,149
1800	—

Lake

CENSUS YEAR	POPULATION
2000	227,511
1990	215,499
1980	212,801
1970	197,200
1960	148,700
1950	75,979
1940	50,020
1930	41,674
1920	28,667
1910	22,927
1900	21,680
1890	18,235
1880	16,326
1870	15,935
1860	15,576
1850	14,654
1840	13,719
1830	—
1820	—
1810	—
1800	—

Lawrence

CENSUS YEAR	POPULATION
2000	62,319
1990	61,834
1980	63,849
1970	56,868
1960	55,438
1950	49,115
1940	46,705
1930	44,541
1920	39,540
1910	39,488
1900	39,534
1890	39,556
1880	39,068
1870	31,380
1860	23,249
1850	15,246
1840	9,738
1830	5,376
1820	3,499
1810	—
1800	—

Licking

CENSUS YEAR	POPULATION
2000	145,491
1990	128,300
1980	120,981
1970	107,799
1960	90,242
1950	70,645
1940	62,279
1930	59,962
1920	56,426
1910	55,590
1900	47,070
1890	43,279
1880	40,450
1870	35,756
1860	37,011
1850	38,846
1840	35,096
1830	20,869
1820	11,861
1810	3,852
1800	—

Logan

CENSUS YEAR	POPULATION
2000	46,005
1990	42,310
1980	39,155
1970	35,072
1960	34,803
1950	31,329
1940	29,624
1930	28,981
1920	30,104
1910	30,084
1900	30,420
1890	27,386
1880	26,267
1870	23,028
1860	20,996
1850	19,162
1840	14,015
1830	6,440
1820	3,181
1810	—
1800	—

Lorain

CENSUS YEAR	POPULATION
2000	284,664
1990	271,126
1980	274,909
1970	256,843
1960	217,500
1950	148,162
1940	112,390
1930	109,206
1920	90,612
1910	76,037
1900	54,857
1890	40,295
1880	35,526
1870	30,308
1860	29,744
1850	26,086
1840	18,467
1830	5,696
1820	—
1810	—
1800	—

Lucas

CENSUS YEAR	POPULATION
2000	455,054
1990	462,361
1980	471,741
1970	483,551
1960	456,931
1950	395,551
1940	344,333
1930	347,709
1920	275,721
1910	192,728
1900	153,559
1890	102,296
1880	67,377
1870	46,722
1860	25,831

CENSUS YEAR	POPULATION
1850	12,363
1840	9,382
1830	—
1820	—
1810	—
1800	—

Madison

CENSUS YEAR	POPULATION
2000	40,213
1990	37,068
1980	33,004
1970	28,318
1960	26,454
1950	22,300
1940	21,811
1930	20,253
1920	19,662
1910	19,902
1900	20,590
1890	20,057
1880	20,129
1870	15,633
1860	13,015
1850	10,015
1840	9,025
1830	6,190
1820	4,799
1810	1,603
1800	—

Mahoning

CENSUS YEAR	POPULATION
2000	257,555
1990	264,806
1980	289,487
1970	304,545
1960	300,480
1950	257,629
1940	240,251
1930	236,142
1920	186,310
1910	116,151
1900	70,134
1890	55,979
1880	42,871
1870	31,001
1860	25,894
1850	23,735
1840	—
1830	—
1820	—
1810	—
1800	—

Marion

CENSUS YEAR	POPULATION
2000	66,217
1990	64,274
1980	67,974
1970	64,724
1960	60,221
1950	49,959
1940	44,898
1930	45,420
1920	42,004
1910	33,971
1900	28,678
1890	24,727
1880	20,565
1870	16,184
1860	15,490
1850	12,618
1840	14,765
1830	6,551
1820	—
1810	—
1800	—

Medina

CENSUS YEAR	POPULATION
2000	151,095
1990	122,354
1980	113,150
1970	82,717
1960	65,315
1950	40,417
1940	33,034
1930	29,677
1920	26,067
1910	23,598
1900	21,958
1890	21,742
1880	21,453
1870	20,092
1860	22,517
1850	24,441
1840	18,352
1830	7,560
1820	3,082
1810	—
1800	—

Meigs

CENSUS YEAR	POPULATION
2000	23,072
1990	22,987
1980	23,641
1970	19,799

CENSUS YEAR	POPULATION
1960	22,159
1950	23,227
1940	24,104
1930	23,961
1920	26,189
1910	25,594
1900	28,620
1890	29,813
1880	32,325
1870	31,465
1860	26,534
1850	17,971
1840	11,452
1830	6,158
1820	4,480
1810	—
1800	—

Mercer

CENSUS YEAR	POPULATION
2000	40,924
1990	39,443
1980	38,334
1970	35,558
1960	32,559
1950	28,311
1940	26,256
1930	25,096
1920	26,872
1910	27,536
1900	28,021
1890	27,220
1880	21,808
1870	17,254
1860	14,104
1850	7,712
1840	8,277
1830	1,110
1820	—
1810	—
1800	—

Miami

CENSUS YEAR	POPULATION
2000	98,868
1990	93,182
1980	90,381
1970	84,342
1960	72,901
1950	61,309
1940	52,632
1930	51,301
1920	48,428
1910	45,047

CENSUS YEAR	POPULATION
1900	43,105
1890	39,754
1880	36,158
1870	32,740
1860	29,959
1850	24,999
1840	19,688
1830	12,807
1820	8,851
1810	3,941
1800	—

Monroe

CENSUS YEAR	POPULATION
2000	15,180
1990	15,497
1980	17,382
1970	15,739
1960	15,268
1950	15,362
1940	17,641
1930	18,426
1920	20,660
1910	24,244
1900	27,031
1890	25,175
1880	26,496
1870	25,779
1860	25,741
1850	28,351
1840	18,521
1830	8,768
1820	4,645
1810	—
1800	—

Montgomery

CENSUS YEAR	POPULATION
2000	559,062
1990	573,809
1980	571,697
1970	608,413
1960	527,080
1950	398,441
1940	295,480
1930	273,481
1920	209,532
1910	163,763
1900	130,146
1890	100,852
1880	78,550
1870	64,006

CENSUS YEAR	POPULATION
1860	52,230
1850	38,218
1840	31,938
1830	24,362
1820	15,999
1810	7,722
1800	—

Morgan

CENSUS YEAR	POPULATION
2000	14,897
1990	14,194
1980	14,241
1970	12,375
1960	12,747
1950	12,836
1940	14,227
1930	13,583
1920	14,555
1910	16,097
1900	17,905
1890	19,143
1880	20,074
1870	20,363
1860	22,119
1850	28,585
1840	20,852
1830	11,800
1820	5,297
1810	—
1800	—

Morrow

CENSUS YEAR	POPULATION
2000	31,628
1990	27,749
1980	26,480
1970	21,348
1960	19,405
1950	17,168
1940	15,646
1930	14,489
1920	15,570
1910	16,815
1900	17,879
1890	18,120
1880	19,072
1870	18,583
1860	20,445
1850	20,280
1840	—
1830	—
1820	—
1810	—
1800	—

Muskingum

CENSUS YEAR	POPULATION
2000	84,585
1990	82,068
1980	83,340
1970	77,826
1960	79,159
1950	74,535
1940	69,795
1930	67,398
1920	57,980
1910	57,488
1900	53,185
1890	51,210
1880	49,774
1870	44,886
1860	44,416
1850	45,049
1840	38,749
1830	29,334
1820	17,824
1810	10,036
1800	—

Noble

CENSUS YEAR	POPULATION
2000	14,058
1990	11,336
1980	11,310
1970	10,428
1960	10,982
1950	11,750
1940	14,587
1930	14,961
1920	17,849
1910	18,601
1900	19,466
1890	20,753
1880	21,138
1870	19,949
1860	20,751
1850	—
1840	—
1830	—
1820	—
1810	—
1800	—

Ottawa

CENSUS YEAR	POPULATION
2000	40,985
1990	40,029
1980	40,076
1970	37,099
1960	35,323
1950	29,469
1940	24,360
1930	24,109
1920	22,193
1910	22,360
1900	22,213
1890	21,974
1880	19,762
1870	13,364
1860	7,016
1850	3,308
1840	2,248
1830	—
1820	—
1810	—
1800	—

Paulding

CENSUS YEAR	POPULATION
2000	20,293
1990	20,488
1980	21,302
1970	19,329
1960	16,792
1950	15,047
1940	15,527
1930	15,301
1920	18,736
1910	22,730
1900	27,528
1890	25,932
1880	13,485
1870	8,544
1860	4,945
1850	1,766
1840	1,034
1830	161
1820	—
1810	—
1800	—

Perry

CENSUS YEAR	POPULATION
2000	34,078
1990	31,557
1980	31,032
1970	27,434
1960	27,864
1950	28,999
1940	31,087
1930	31,445
1920	36,098
1910	35,396
1900	31,841

CENSUS YEAR	POPULATION
1890	31,151
1880	28,218
1870	18,453
1860	19,678
1850	20,775
1840	19,344
1830	13,970
1820	8,429
1810	—
1800	—

Pickaway

CENSUS YEAR	POPULATION
2000	52,727
1990	48,255
1980	43,662
1970	40,011
1960	35,855
1950	29,352
1940	27,889
1930	27,238
1920	25,788
1910	26,158
1900	27,016
1890	26,959
1880	27,415
1870	24,875
1860	23,469
1850	21,006
1840	19,725
1830	16,001
1820	13,149
1810	7,124
1800	—

Pike

CENSUS YEAR	POPULATION
2000	27,695
1990	24,249
1980	22,802
1970	19,114
1960	19,380
1950	14,607
1940	16,113
1930	13,876
1920	14,151
1910	15,723
1900	18,172
1890	17,482
1880	17,927
1870	15,447
1860	13,643
1850	10,953
1840	7,626
1830	6,024

CENSUS YEAR	POPULATION
1820	4,253
1810	—
1800	—

Portage

CENSUS YEAR	POPULATION
2000	152,061
1990	142,585
1980	135,856
1970	125,868
1960	91,798
1950	63,954
1940	46,660
1930	42,682
1920	36,269
1910	30,307
1900	29,246
1890	27,868
1880	27,500
1870	24,584
1860	24,208
1850	24,419
1840	22,965
1830	18,826
1820	10,095
1810	2,995
1800	—

Preble

CENSUS YEAR	POPULATION
2000	42,337
1990	40,113
1980	38,223
1970	34,719
1960	32,498
1950	27,081
1940	23,329
1930	22,455
1920	23,238
1910	23,834
1900	23,713
1890	23,421
1880	24,533
1870	21,809
1860	21,820
1850	21,736
1840	19,482
1830	16,291
1820	10,237
1810	3,304
1800	—

Putnam

CENSUS YEAR	POPULATION
2000	34,726
1990	33,819
1980	32,991
1970	31,134
1960	28,331
1950	25,248
1940	25,016
1930	25,074
1920	27,751
1910	29,972
1900	32,525
1890	30,188
1880	23,713
1870	17,081
1860	12,808
1850	7,221
1840	5,189
1830	230
1820	—
1810	—
1800	—

Richland

CENSUS YEAR	POPULATION
2000	128,852
1990	126,137
1980	131,205
1970	129,997
1960	117,761
1950	91,305
1940	73,853
1930	65,902
1920	55,178
1910	47,667
1900	44,289
1890	38,072
1880	36,306
1870	32,516
1860	31,158
1850	30,879
1840	44,532
1830	24,006
1820	9,169
1810	—
1800	—

Ross

CENSUS YEAR	POPULATION
2000	73,345
1990	69,330
1980	65,004

CENSUS YEAR	POPULATION
1970	61,211
1960	61,215
1950	54,424
1940	52,147
1930	45,181
1920	41,556
1910	40,069
1900	40,940
1890	39,454
1880	40,307
1870	37,097
1860	35,071
1850	32,074
1840	27,460
1830	24,069
1820	20,619
1810	15,514
1800	8,540

Sandusky

CENSUS YEAR	POPULATION
2000	61,792
1990	61,963
1980	63,267
1970	60,983
1960	56,486
1950	46,114
1940	41,014
1930	39,731
1920	37,109
1910	35,171
1900	34,311
1890	30,617
1880	32,057
1870	25,503
1860	21,429
1850	14,305
1840	10,182
1830	2,851
1820	852
1810	—
1800	—

Scioto

CENSUS YEAR	POPULATION
2000	79,195
1990	80,327
1980	84,545
1970	76,951
1960	84,216
1950	82,910
1940	86,565
1930	81,221
1920	62,850

CENSUS YEAR	POPULATION
1910	48,463
1900	40,981
1890	35,377
1880	33,511
1870	29,302
1860	24,297
1850	18,428
1840	11,192
1830	8,740
1820	5,750
1810	3,399
1800	—

Seneca

CENSUS YEAR	POPULATION
2000	58,683
1990	59,733
1980	61,901
1970	60,696
1960	59,326
1950	52,978
1940	48,499
1930	47,941
1920	43,176
1910	42,421
1900	41,163
1890	40,869
1880	36,947
1870	30,827
1860	30,868
1850	27,104
1840	18,128
1830	5,159
1820	—
1810	—
1800	—

Shelby

CENSUS YEAR	POPULATION
2000	47,910
1990	44,915
1980	43,089
1970	37,748
1960	33,586
1950	28,488
1940	26,071
1930	24,924
1920	25,923
1910	24,663
1900	24,625
1890	24,707
1880	24,137
1870	20,748
1860	17,493

CENSUS YEAR	POPULATION
1850	13,958
1840	12,154
1830	3,671
1820	2,106
1810	—
1800	—

Stark

CENSUS YEAR	POPULATION
2000	378,098
1990	367,585
1980	378,823
1970	372,210
1960	340,345
1950	283,194
1940	234,887
1930	221,784
1920	177,218
1910	122,987
1900	94,747
1890	84,170
1880	64,031
1870	52,508
1860	42,978
1850	39,878
1840	34,603
1830	26,588
1820	12,406
1810	2,734
1800	—

Summit

CENSUS YEAR	POPULATION
2000	542,899
1990	514,990
1980	524,472
1970	553,371
1960	513,569
1950	410,032
1940	339,405
1930	344,131
1920	286,065
1910	108,253
1900	71,715
1890	54,089
1880	43,788
1870	34,674
1860	27,344
1850	27,485
1840	22,560
1830	—
1820	—
1810	—
1800	—

Trumbull

CENSUS YEAR	POPULATION
2000	225,116
1990	227,813
1980	241,863
1970	232,579
1960	208,256
1950	158,915
1940	132,315
1930	123,063
1920	83,920
1910	52,766
1900	46,591
1890	42,373
1880	44,880
1870	38,659
1860	30,656
1850	30,490
1840	38,107
1830	26,153
1820	15,546
1810	8,671
1800	1,302

Tuscarawas

CENSUS YEAR	POPULATION
2000	90,914
1990	84,090
1980	84,614
1970	77,211
1960	76,789
1950	70,320
1940	68,816
1930	68,193
1920	63,578
1910	57,035
1900	53,751
1890	46,618
1880	40,198
1870	33,840
1860	32,463
1850	31,761
1840	25,631
1830	14,298
1820	8,328
1810	3,045
1800	—

Union

CENSUS YEAR	POPULATION
2000	40,909
1990	31,969
1980	29,536

CENSUS YEAR	POPULATION
1970	23,786
1960	22,853
1950	20,687
1940	20,012
1930	19,192
1920	20,918
1910	21,871
1900	22,342
1890	22,860
1880	22,375
1870	18,730
1860	16,507
1850	12,204
1840	8,422
1830	3,192
1820	1,996
1810	—
1800	—

Van Wert

CENSUS YEAR	POPULATION
2000	29,659
1990	30,464
1980	30,458
1970	29,194
1960	28,840
1950	26,971
1940	26,759
1930	26,273
1920	28,210
1910	29,119
1900	30,394
1890	29,671
1880	23,028
1870	15,823
1860	10,238
1850	4,793
1840	1,577
1830	49
1820	—
1810	—
1800	—

Vinton

CENSUS YEAR	POPULATION
2000	12,806
1990	11,098
1980	11,584
1970	9,420
1960	10,274
1950	10,759
1940	11,573
1930	10,287
1920	12,075

CENSUS YEAR	POPULATION
1910	13,096
1900	15,330
1890	16,045
1880	17,223
1870	15,027
1860	13,631
1850	9,353
1840	—
1830	—
1820	—
1810	—
1800	—

Warren

CENSUS YEAR	POPULATION
2000	158,383
1990	113,909
1980	99,276
1970	85,505
1960	65,711
1950	38,505
1940	29,894
1930	27,348
1920	25,716
1910	24,497
1900	25,584
1890	25,468
1880	28,392
1870	26,689
1860	26,902
1850	25,560
1840	23,141
1830	21,468
1820	17,837
1810	9,925
1800	—

Washington

CENSUS YEAR	POPULATION
2000	63,251
1990	62,254
1980	64,266
1970	57,160
1960	51,689
1950	44,407
1940	43,537
1930	42,437
1920	43,049
1910	45,422
1900	48,245
1890	42,380
1880	43,244
1870	40,609
1860	36,268

CENSUS YEAR	POPULATION
1850	29,540
1840	20,823
1830	11,731
1820	10,425
1810	5,991
1800	5,427

Wayne

CENSUS YEAR	POPULATION
2000	111,564
1990	101,461
1980	97,408
1970	87,123
1960	75,497
1950	58,716
1940	50,520
1930	47,024
1920	41,346
1910	38,058
1900	37,870
1890	39,005
1880	40,076
1870	35,116
1860	32,483
1850	32,981
1840	35,808

CENSUS YEAR	POPULATION
1830	23,333
1820	11,933
1810	—
1800	—

Williams

CENSUS YEAR	POPULATION
2000	39,188
1990	36,956
1980	36,369
1970	33,669
1960	29,968
1950	26,202
1940	25,510
1930	24,316
1920	24,627
1910	25,198
1900	24,953
1890	24,897
1880	23,821
1870	20,991
1860	16,633
1850	8,018
1840	4,465
1830	387
1820	—

CENSUS YEAR	POPULATION
1810	—
1800	—

Wood

CENSUS YEAR	POPULATION
2000	121,065
1990	113,269
1980	107,372
1970	89,772
1960	72,596
1950	59,605
1940	51,796
1930	50,320
1920	44,892
1910	46,330
1900	51,555
1890	44,392
1880	34,022
1870	24,596
1860	17,886
1850	9,157
1840	5,357
1830	1,102
1820	733
1810	—
1800	—

Wyandot

CENSUS YEAR	POPULATION
2000	22,908
1990	22,254
1980	22,651
1970	21,826
1960	21,648
1950	19,785
1940	19,218
1930	19,036
1920	19,481
1910	20,760
1900	21,125
1890	21,722
1880	22,395
1870	18,553
1860	15,596
1850	11,194
1840	—
1830	—
1820	—
1810	—
1800	—

Population of Major Cities

EARLIEST CENSUS TO 2000

Akron

CENSUS YEAR	POPULATION
2000	217,074
1990	223,019
1980	237,590
1970	275,425
1960	290,351
1950	274,605
1940	244,791
1930	255,040
1920	208,435
1910	69,067
1900	42,728
1890	27,601
1880	16,512
1870	10,006
1860	3,477
1850	3,266

Canton

CENSUS YEAR	POPULATION
2000	80,806
1990	84,161
1980	93,077
1970	110,053
1960	113,631
1950	116,912
1940	108,401
1930	104,906
1920	87,091
1910	50,217
1900	30,667
1890	26,189
1880	12,258
1870	8,660
1860	4,041
1850	2,603
1840	N.A.
1830	1,257

Cincinnati

CENSUS YEAR	POPULATION
2000	331,285
1990	364,040
1980	385,410
1970	453,514
1960	502,550
1950	503,998
1940	455,610
1930	451,160
1920	401,247
1910	363,591
1900	325,902
1890	296,908
1880	255,139
1870	216,239
1860	161,044
1850	115,435
1840	46,338
1830	24,831
1820	9,642
1810	2,540

Cleveland

CENSUS YEAR	POPULATION
2000	478,403
1990	505,616
1980	573,822
1970	750,879
1960	876,050
1950	914,808
1940	878,336
1930	900,429
1920	796,841
1910	560,663
1900	381,768
1890	261,353
1880	160,146
1870	92,829
1860	43,417
1850	17,034
1840	6,071
1830	1,076
1820	606

Columbus

CENSUS YEAR	POPULATION
2000	711,470
1990	632,910
1980	565,032
1970	540,025
1960	471,316
1950	375,901
1940	306,087
1930	290,564
1920	237,031
1910	181,511
1900	125,560
1890	88,150
1880	51,647
1870	31,274
1860	18,554
1850	17,882
1840	6,048
1830	2,435

Dayton

CENSUS YEAR	POPULATION
2000	166,179
1990	182,044
1980	193,549
1970	243,023
1960	262,332
1950	243,872
1940	210,718
1930	200,982
1920	152,559
1910	116,577
1900	85,333
1890	61,220
1880	38,678
1870	30,473
1860	20,081
1850	10,977
1840	6,067
1830	2,950
1820	1,000
1810	383

Elyria

CENSUS YEAR	POPULATION
2000	55,953
1990	56,746
1980	57,538
1970	53,427
1960	43,782
1950	30,307
1940	25,120
1930	25,633
1920	20,474
1910	14,825
1900	8,791
1890	5,611
1880	4,777
1870	3,038

1860	1,613
1850	1,482

Hamilton

CENSUS YEAR	POPULATION
2000	60,690
1990	61,368
1980	63,189
1970	67,865
1960	72,354
1950	57,951
1940	50,592
1930	52,176
1920	39,675
1910	35,279
1900	23,914
1890	17,565
1880	12,122
1870	11,081
1860	7,223
1850	3,210
1840	1,409
1830	1,079
1820	660

Kettering

CENSUS YEAR	POPULATION
2000	57,502
1990	60,569
1980	61,186
1970	71,864
1960	54,462

Lakewood

CENSUS YEAR	POPULATION
2000	56,646
1990	59,718
1980	61,963
1970	70,173
1960	66,154
1950	68,071
1940	69,160
1930	70,509
1920	41,732
1910	15,181
1900	3,355

Lorain

CENSUS YEAR	POPULATION
2000	68,652
1990	71,245
1980	75,416
1970	78,185
1960	68,932
1950	51,202
1940	44,125
1930	44,512
1920	37,295
1910	28,883
1900	16,028
1890	4,863
1880	1,595

Parma

CENSUS YEAR	POPULATION
2000	85,655
1990	87,876
1980	92,548
1970	100,216
1960	82,845
1950	28,897
1940	16,365
1930	13,899

Springfield

CENSUS YEAR	POPULATION
2000	65,358
1990	70,487
1980	72,563
1970	81,941
1960	82,723
1950	78,508
1940	70,662
1930	68,743
1920	60,840
1910	46,921
1900	38,253
1890	31,895
1880	20,730
1870	12,652
1860	7,002
1850	5,108
1840	2,062
1830	1,080
1820	1,868

Toledo

CENSUS YEAR	POPULATION
2000	313,619
1990	332,943
1980	354,635
1970	383,062
1960	318,003
1950	303,616
1940	282,349
1930	290,718
1920	243,164
1910	168,497
1900	131,822
1890	81,434
1880	50,137
1870	31,584
1860	13,768
1850	3,829
1840	1,222

Youngstown

CENSUS YEAR	POPULATION
2000	82,026
1990	95,732
1980	115,510
1970	140,909
1960	166,689
1950	168,330
1940	167,720
1930	170,002
1920	132,358
1910	79,066
1900	44,885
1890	33,220
1880	15,435
1870	8,075
1860	2,759

An Ohio Politics Timeline

March 3, 1787—The Ohio Land Company organized.

July 13, 1787—Congress enacts the Northwest Ordinance, establishing a government for the Northwest Territory.

April 17, 1788—Forty-eight men, traveling down the Ohio River under the auspices of the Ohio Company of Associates, arrive at the mouth of the Muskingum River and establish Marietta.

July 26, 1788 — Washington County established as Ohio's first county.

November 9, 1793 — William Maxwell prints first Ohio newspaper, *The Centinel of the Northwestern Territory*, in Cincinnati.

July 22, 1796—Survey party led by Moses Cleaveland, of the Connecticut Land Co., reaches the mouth of the Cuyahoga River.

September 24, 1799—Delegates from nine counties constituting the Northwest Territory assemble in Cincinnati and elect William Henry Harrison as their representative to Congress.

November 24, 1799—The first territorial legislature assembles.

May 7, 1800—Congress approves an act dividing the Northwest Territory into the Territory of Ohio and the Territory of Indiana.

April 30, 1802—Congress passes an act enabling the people of Ohio to form a constitution and state government.

November 1-29, 1802—The Ohio Constitutional Convention meets in Chillicothe and adopts the state's first constitution.

November 22, 1802—President Thomas Jefferson dismisses Arthur St. Clair as governor of the Northwest Territory.

January 2, 1803—Edward Tiffin of Chillicothe is elected Ohio governor.

February 19, 1803—President Thomas Jefferson signs law admitting Ohio into the Union as the 17th state.

March 1, 1803—First state legislature meets in Chillicothe; Edward Tiffin assumes office as Ohio's first governor.

March 24, 1806—Congress gives final approval to construct the National Road from Cumberland, Md., to Ohio.

February 14, 1812—General Assembly accepts plan to lay out a new statehouse "on the high bank of the Scioto opposite Franklinton."

February 26, 1816—General Assembly authorizes counties to build poorhouses.

October 1, 1816—State offices are moved from Chillicothe to Columbus.

September 12, 1817—*The Philanthropist*, America's first antislavery newspaper, is published by Charles Osborn in Mount Pleasant, Jefferson County.

September 29, 1817—Indians give up virtually all remaining rights to Ohio lands.

April 27, 1822—Ulysses S. Grant, the 18th president, is born in Point Pleasant.

October 4, 1822—Rutherford B. Hayes, the 19th president, is born in Delaware.

February 4, 1825—General Assembly authorizes construction of the Ohio & Erie Canal. First shovelful of earth for the canal is turned July 4, 1825, at Licking Summit.

February 5, 1825 — General Assembly sets statewide property tax of a half-mill for support of schools.

July 4, 1825—Construction begins on first section of the National Road in Ohio, in St. Clairsville.

July 12, 1830—The first state convention of the Ohio Democratic Party is held in Columbus.

November 19, 1831—James A. Garfield, the 20th president, is born in Orange Township in Cuyahoga County.

August 20, 1833—Benjamin Harrison, the 23rd president, is born in North Bend near Cincinnati.

1834—The 333-mile Ohio & Erie Canal, including feeders, is completed from Portsmouth to Cleveland.

January 26, 1838—The legislature approves construction of a new statehouse.

July 4, 1839—Cornerstone laid for new statehouse.

December 2, 1840—William Henry Harrison of Hamilton County is first Ohioan elected president.

January 29, 1843—William McKinley, the 25th president, is born in Niles.

March 13, 1845—General Assembly requires voters to register.

1845—The 266-mile Miami & Erie Canal, including feeders, is completed from Cincinnati to Toledo.

October 9, 1849—Ohioans vote to hold a second constitutional convention.

April 19–20, 1850—First Women's Rights Convention in Ohio, and nation's second, is held in Salem, Ohio.

May 6, 1850—The second constitutional convention meets in Columbus.

March 10, 1851—Second constitutional convention completes its work.

June 17, 1851—Ohio voters adopt a new constitution, the state's second.

July 13, 1854—State Republican nominating convention held in Columbus, the party's first in Ohio. Other conventions held in Indiana, Wisconsin, and Vermont.

April 2, 1855 — John Mercer

Langston elected clerk of Brownhelm Township in Lorain County, becoming the first black to win an elected position in the United States.

January 7, 1857—Legislature begins holding sessions in new Statehouse.

September 15, 1857—William Howard Taft, the 27th president, is born in Cincinnati.

November 2, 1865—Warren G. Harding, the 29th president, is born in Blooming Grove.

November 3, 1868—Ulysses S. Grant, native of Ohio and Civil War hero, elected president.

March 30, 1870 — Ohio's black residents cast their first votes.

May 14, 1873—Delegates to third constitutional convention assemble in Columbus.

September 17, 1873—The Ohio Agricultural and Mechanical College is opened to 17 students in Columbus.

November 7, 1876—The presidential election gives Democrat Samuel J. Tilden, the New York governor, a 254,000-vote popular vote plurality over Ohio Republican Rutherford B. Hayes, but Republicans refuse to concede; they challenge the results from Louisiana, Florida, South Carolina, and Oregon.

March 2, 1877—Congress accepts the decision of a special election commission, which awarded 185 electoral votes to Rutherford B. Hayes and 184 electoral votes to Samuel J. Tilden.

March 4, 1877—Rutherford B. Hayes of Delaware County is

sworn in as the 19th president.

November 2, 1880—James A. Garfield of Cuyahoga County is elected as the 20th president.

September 19, 1881 — President James A. Garfield dies, 78 days after being shot by a mentally imbalanced job seeker in Washington D.C.

January 16, 1883 — President Chester A. Arthur signs Civil Service Act, effectively dooming the spoils system in American government.

October 13, 1885—Ohioans approve amendment changing the state's fall elections from October to November.

December 8, 1886 — Representatives of 25 trade unions meet in Columbus to create the American Federation of Labor.

November 6, 1888—Benjamin Harrison of Hamilton County is elected as the 23rd president.

May 1, 1889—First county boards of election are established; vote purchasing is outlawed.

April 30, 1891—Ohio adopts the secret ballot (Australian ballot) to reduce votebuying and election fraud.

January 6, 1896—Law is enacted allowing women to vote for members of school boards.

November 1, 1896—Catherine Hitchcock Tilden is elected to the Cleveland Board of Education, becoming the first woman elected to public office in Ohio.

November 3, 1896—William McKinley, a Republican from Canton, is elected 25th president of the United States.

July 9, 1901—Delegates to the state Democratic convention call for municipal home rule and the nomination of U.S. senators in open convention.

September 30, 1907—The McKinley National Memorial is dedicated in Canton, honoring William McKinley, the nation's 25th president.

November 3, 1908—William Howard Taft of Hamilton County is elected as the 27th president.

January 9, 1912—Delegates to fourth constitutional convention meet in Columbus.

September 3, 1912—Ohio voters adopt 33 of 41 proposed constitutional amendments, including home rule for cities and the initiative and referendum.

1912—A nonpartisan ticket for judges used for the first time.

November 4, 1913—Ohio voters approve amendment to allow women to serve on boards and commissions and in state departments and institutions caring for women and children.

August 11, 1914—Ohio has its first statewide direct primary election.

November 3, 1914—Ohio voters defeat amendment to give women the right to vote.

November 5, 1918—After rejecting state prohibition amendments in 1914, 1915, and 1917, Ohioans approve the prohibition of the sale and manufacture of intoxicating liquors.

June 16, 1919—Ohio becomes the fifth state to ratify the 19th

Amendment, granting women the right to vote.

November 2, 1920—Ohio women are able to exercise the full franchise. Warren G. Harding of Ohio is elected as 29th president.

July 11, 1921 — William Howard Taft named chief justice of the United States by President Warren G. Harding.

November 7, 1922—Florence E. Allen of Cleveland is elected to the Ohio Supreme Court; Ohio becomes the first state supreme court in the nation with a woman judge.

November 6, 1923—Ohioans approve amendment to eliminate the words "white male" from the Ohio Constitution to conform to federal amendments.

November 7, 1933—Ohioans repeal statewide prohibition.

February 14, 1936—The first major rubber strike in Ohio takes place at Goodyear Tire and Rubber Co. in Akron. The company shuts down for five weeks, idling about 14,000 workers.

February 27, 1940—Frances P. Bolton, of the Cleveland area, is elected to the U.S. House of Representatives in a special election to fill the vacancy created by the death of her husband, Chester C. Bolton. Mrs. Bolton is the first woman elected to Congress from Ohio.

April 11, 1946—Toledo voters approve a 1 percent payroll tax, the first municipal income tax in Ohio and the second in the nation.

November 8, 1949—Ohioans approve a state constitutional amendment to eliminate straight-ticket voting, requiring separate votes for each contest.

November 2, 1954—Ohio voters establish four-year terms for governor and limit the governor to two successive terms.

November 4, 1958—Ohio voters crush a proposed right-to-work amendment, which would have outlawed the union shop; Democrats sweep all statewide offices.

October 1, 1959 — Ohio adopts the motto, "With God all things are possible."

November 7, 1967—Carl B. Stokes is elected mayor of Cleveland, becoming the first black to be elected mayor of a major American city.

October 24, 1969 —"Beautiful Ohio" is named official state song.

November 3, 1970—Gertrude W. Donahey is elected state treasurer, she is the first woman elected to a statewide executive office in Ohio.

June 30, 1971 — Ohio becomes the 38th and pivotal state to ratify the 26th Amendment, lowering the voting age from 21 to 18.

December 10, 1971—Final enactment of Ohio's personal income tax.

November 4, 1975—Ohio voters approve amendment to require ballot rotation of candidate names.

November 2, 1976—Katherine Crumbley, elected Belmont County sheriff, is the first woman sheriff in Ohio history.

December 15, 1978—Cleveland becomes the first major American city to default on its obligations since the Great Depression.

November 8, 1983—Toledo elects its first woman mayor, Donna Owens.

November 8, 1994—Nancy P. Hollister is the first woman to be elected lieutenant governor; Betty D. Montgomery is the first woman to be elected attorney general; J. Kenneth Blackwell is the first black to be elected treasurer.

July 5, 1996 — Joint session of the legislature commemorates reopening of the renovated Statehouse.

December 31, 1998 — Nancy Putnam Hollister becomes Ohio's first woman governor, serving the 11 days remaining in the term of George V. Voinovich, who moves to the U.S. Senate.

APPENDIX B

Major Officeholders

GOVERNORS

	GOVERNORS	PARTY	COUNTY	IN OFFICE
1	Edward Tiffin	Democratic-Republican	Ross	1803–1807
2	Thomas Kirker	Democratic-Republican	Adams	1807–1808
3	Samuel Huntington	Democratic-Republican	Trumbull	1808–1810
4	Return J. Meigs Jr.	Democratic-Republican	Washington	1810–1814
5	Othneil Looker	Democratic-Republican	Hamilton	1814
6	Thomas Worthington	Democratic-Republican	Ross	1814–1818
7	Ethan Allen Brown	Democratic-Republican	Hamilton	1818–1822
8	Allen Trimble	Federalist	Highland	1822
9	Jeremiah Morrow	Democratic-Republican	Warren	1822–1826
10	Allen Trimble	National Republican	Highland	1826–1830
11	Duncan McArthur	National Republican	Ross	1830–1832
12	Robert Lucas	Democratic	Pike	1832–1836
13	Joseph Vance	Whig	Champaign	1836–1838
14	Wilson Shannon	Democratic	Belmont	1838–1840
15	Thomas Corwin	Whig	Warren	1840–1842
16	Wilson Shannon	Democratic	Belmont	1842–1844
17	Thomas W. Bartley	Democratic	Richland	1844
18	Mordecai Bartley	Whig	Richland	1844–1846
19	William Bebb	Whig	Butler	1846–1849
20	Seabury Ford	Whig	Geauga	1849–1850
21	Reuben Wood	Democratic	Cuyahoga	1850–1853
22	William Medill	Democratic	Fairfield	1853–1856
23	Salmon P. Chase	Republican	Hamilton	1856–1860

	GOVERNORS	PARTY	COUNTY	IN OFFICE
24	William Dennison, Jr.	Republican	Franklin	1860–1862
25	David Tod	Union	Mahoning	1862–1864
26	John Brough	Union	Cuyahoga	1864–1865
27	Charles Anderson	Union	Montgomery	1865–1866
28	Jacob D. Cox	Union	Trumbull	1866–1868
29	Rutherford B. Hayes	Republican	Hamilton	1868–1872
30	Edward F. Noyes	Republican	Hamilton	1872–1874
31	William Allen	Democratic	Ross	1874–1876
32	Rutherford B. Hayes	Republican	Sandusky	1876–1877
33	Thomas L. Young	Republican	Hamilton	1877–1878
34	Richard M. Bishop	Democratic	Hamilton	1878–1880
35	Charles Foster	Republican	Seneca	1880–1884
36	George Hoadly	Democratic	Hamilton	1884–1886
37	Joseph B. Foraker	Republican	Hamilton	1886–1890
38	James E. Campbell	Democratic	Butler	1890–1892
39	William McKinley	Republican	Stark	1892–1896
40	Asa S. Bushnell	Republican	Clark	1896–1900
41	George K. Nash	Republican	Franklin	1900–1904
42	Myron T. Herrick	Republican	Hamilton	1904–1906
43	John M. Pattison	Democratic	Clermont	1906
44	Andrew L. Harris	Republican	Preble	1906–1909
45	Judson Harmon	Democratic	Hamilton	1909–1913
46	James M. Cox	Democratic	Montgomery	1913–1915
47	Frank B. Willis	Republican	Delaware	1915–1917
48	James M. Cox	Democratic	Montgomery	1917–1921
49	Harry L. Davis	Republican	Cuyahoga	1921–1923
50	A. Victor Donahey	Democratic	Tuscarawas	1923–1929
51	Myers Y. Cooper	Republican	Hamilton	1929–1931
52	George White	Democratic	Washington	1931–1935
53	Martin L. Davey	Democratic	Portage	1935–1939
54	John W. Bricker	Republican	Franklin	1939–1945
55	Frank J. Lausche	Democratic	Cuyahoga	1945–1947
56	Thomas J. Herbert	Republican	Cuyahoga	1947–1949
57	Frank J. Lausche	Democratic	Cuyahoga	1949–1957
58	John W. Brown	Republican	Medina	1957
59	C. William O'Neill	Republican	Washington	1957–1959
60	Michael V. DiSalle	Democratic	Lucas	1959–1963
61	James A. Rhodes	Republican	Franklin	1963–1971
62	John J. Gilligan	Democratic	Hamilton	1971–1975
63	James A. Rhodes	Republican	Franklin	1975–1983
64	Richard F. Celeste	Democratic	Cuyahoga	1983–1991
65	George V. Voinovich	Republican	Cuyahoga	1991–1998
66	Nancy P. Hollister	Republican	Washington	1999
67	Bob Taft	Republican	Hamilton	1999–

LIEUTENANT GOVERNORS

LIEUTENANT GOVERNORS	PARTY	COUNTY	IN OFFICE
William Medill	Democratic	Fairfield	1852–1854
James Myers	Democratic	Lucas	1854–1856
Thomas H. Ford	Whig	Richland	1856–1858
Martin Welker	Whig	Stark	1858–1860
Robert C. Kirk	Republican	Knox	1860–1862
Benjamin Stanton	Republican	Logan	1862–1864
Charles Anderson	Republican	Montgomery	1864–1866

LIEUTENANT GOVERNORS	PARTY	COUNTY	IN OFFICE
Andrew R. McBurney	Republican	Warren	1866–1868
John C. Lee	Republican	Lucas	1868–1872
Jacob Mueller	Republican	Cuyahoga	1872–1874
Alphonso Hart	Democratic	Highland	1874–1876
Thomas L. Young	Republican	Hamilton	1876–1877
H.W. Curtiss	Republican	Cuyahoga	1877–1878
Jabez W. Fitch	Democratic	Cuyahoga	1878–1880
Andrew Hickenlooper	Republican	Hamilton	1880–1882
Reese G. Richards	Republican	Jefferson	1882–1884
John G. Warwick	Democratic	Stark	1884–1886
Robert P. Kennedy	Republican	Logan	1886–1887
Silas A. Conrad	Republican	Stark	1887–1888
William C. Lyon	Republican	Licking	1888–1890
Elbert L. Lampson	Republican	Ashtabula	1890
William V. Marquis	Democratic	Logan	1890–1892
Andrew L. Harris	Republican	Preble	1892–1896
Asa W. Jones	Republican	Mahoning	1896–1900
John A. Caldwell	Republican	Hamilton	1900–1902
Carl L. Nippert	Republican	Hamilton	1902
Harry L. Gordon	Republican	Hamilton	1902–1904
Warren G. Harding	Republican	Marion	1904–1906
Andrew L. Harris	Republican	Preble	1906–1909
Francis W. Treadway	Republican	Cuyahoga	1909–1911
Atlee Pomerene	Democratic	Stark	1911
Hugh L. Nichols	Democratic	Clermont	1911–1913
W.A. Greenlund	Democratic	Cuyahoga	1913–1915
John H. Arnold	Republican	Franklin	1915–1917
Earl D. Bloom	Democratic	Wood	1917–1919
Clarence J. Brown	Republican	Clinton	1919–1923
Earl D. Bloom	Democratic	Wood	1923–1925
Charles H. Lewis	Republican	Wyandot	1925–1927
Earl D. Bloom	Democratic	Wood	1927–1928
William G. Pickrel	Democratic	Montgomery	1928
George C. Braden	Republican	Trumbull	1928–1929
John T. Brown	Republican	Champaign	1929–1931
William G. Pickrel	Democratic	Montgomery	1931–1933
Charles Sawyer	Democratic	Hamilton	1933–1935
Harold G. Mosier	Democratic	Cuyahoga	1935–1937
Paul P. Yoder	Democratic	Preble	1937–1939
Paul M. Herbert	Republican	Franklin	1939–1945
George D. Nye	Democratic	Pike	1945–1947
Paul M. Herbert	Republican	Franklin	1947–1949
George D. Nye	Democratic	Pike	1949–1953
John W. Brown	Republican	Medina	1953–1957
Paul M. Herbert	Republican	Franklin	1957–1959
John W. Donahey	Democratic	Stark	1959–1963
John W. Brown	Republican	Medina	1963–1975
Richard F. Celeste	Democratic	Cuyahoga	1975–1979
George V. Voinovich	Republican	Cuyahoga	1979
Myrl H. Shoemaker	Democratic	Ross	1983–1985
Paul R. Leonard	Democratic	Montgomery	1987–1991
Michael DeWine	Republican	Greene	1991–1994
Nancy P. Hollister	Republican	Washington	1995–1998
Maureen O'Connor	Republican	Summit	1999–2002
Jennette Bradley	Republican	Franklin	2003–2005
Bruce E. Johnson	Republican	Franklin	2005–

ATTORNEYS GENERAL

ATTORNEYS GENERAL	PARTY	COUNTY	IN OFFICE
Harry Stanbery	Whig	Fairfield	1846–1851
Joseph McCormick	Democratic	Adams	1851–1852
George Ellis Pugh*	Democratic	Hamilton	1852–1854
George W. McCook	Democratic	Jefferson	1854–1856
Francis D. Kimball	Whig	Medina	1856
Christopher Wolcott	Republican	Summit	1856–1861
James Murray	Republican	Wood	1861–1863
Lyman R. Critchfield	Democratic	Holmes	1863–1865
William P. Richardson	Unionist	Washington	1865
Chauncey N. Olds	Republican	Pickaway	1865–1866
William H. West	Republican	Logan	1866–1868
Francis Bates Pond	Republican	Morgan	1868–1872
John Little	Republican	Greene	1872–1878
Isaiah Pillars	Democratic	Allen	1878–1880
George K. Nash	Republican	Franklin	1880–1883
David Hollingsworth	Republican	Harrison	1883–1884
James Lawrence	Democratic	Cuyahoga	1884–1886
Jacob A. Kohler	Republican	Summit	1886–1888
David K. Watson	Republican	Franklin	1888–1892
John K. Richards	Republican	Lawrence	1892–1896
Frank S. Monnett	Republican	Crawford	1896–1900
John M. Sheets	Republican	Putnam	1900–1904
Wade H. Ellis	Republican	Hamilton	1904–1908
Ulysses G. Denman	Republican	Lucas	1908–1911
Timothy S. Hogan	Democratic	Jackson	1911–1915
Edward C. Turner	Republican	Franklin	1915–1917
Joseph McGhee	Democratic	Jackson	1917–1919
John G. Price	Republican	Franklin	1919–1923
Charles C. Crabbe	Republican	Madison	1923–1927
Edward C. Turner	Republican	Franklin	1927–1929
Gilbert Bettman	Republican	Franklin	1929–1933
John W. Bricker	Republican	Franklin	1933–1937
Herbert S. Duffy	Democratic	Franklin	1937–1939
Thomas J. Herbert	Republican	Cuyahoga	1939–1945
Hugh S. Jenkins	Republican	Mahoning	1945–1949
Herbert S. Duffy	Democratic	Franklin	1949–1951
C. William O'Neill	Republican	Washington	1951–1957
William B. Saxbe	Republican	Champaign	1957–1959
Mark McElroy	Democratic	Cuyahoga	1959–1963
William B. Saxbe	Republican	Champaign	1963–1969
Paul W. Brown	Republican	Franklin	1969–1971
William J. Brown	Democratic	Mahoning	1971–1983
Anthony J. Celebrezze Jr.	Democratic	Cuyahoga	1983–1991
Lee Fisher	Democratic	Cuyahoga	1991–1995
Betty Montgomery	Republican	Wood	1995–2002
James M. Petro	Republican	Cuyahoga	2003

* Pugh was the first elected attorney general.

AUDITORS

AUDITORS	PARTY	COUNTY	IN OFFICE
Thomas Gibson	Democratic-Republican	Washington	1803–1808
Benjamin Hough	Democratic-Republican	Jefferson	1808–1815
Ralph Osborn	Democratic-Republican	Franklin	1815–1833
John A. Bryan	N.A.	Franklin	1833–1839
John Brough	Democratic	Cuyahoga	1839–1845
John Woods	Whig	Butler	1845–1852
William D. Morgan	Democratic	Muskingum	1852–1856
Francis M. Wright	Whig	Champaign	1856–1860
Robert W. Taylor	Republican	Mahoning	1860–1863
Oviatt Cole	Republican	Medina	1863–1864
James H. Godman	Republican	Marion	1864–1872
James Williams	Republican	Franklin	1872–1880
John F. Oglevee	Republican	Clark	1880–1884
Emil Kieswetter	Democratic	Franklin	1884–1888
Ebenezer W. Poe	Republican	Wood	1888–1896
Walter D. Guilbert	Republican	Noble	1896–1909
Edward M. Fullington	Republican	Union	1909–1913
A. Victor Donahey	Democratic	Tuscarawas	1913–1921
Joseph T. Tracy	Republican	Franklin	1921–1937
Joseph T. Ferguson	Democratic	Franklin	1937–1953
James A. Rhodes	Republican	Franklin	1953–1963
Roger W. Tracy	Republican	Franklin	1963–1964
Chester W. Goble	Republican	Franklin	1964–1965
Roger Cloud	Republican	Logan	1965–1966
Archer E. Reilly	Republican	Franklin	1966–1967
Roger Cloud	Republican	Logan	1967–1971
Joseph T. Ferguson	Democratic	Franklin	1971–7195
Thomas E. Ferguson	Democratic	Franklin	1975–1995
James M. Petro	Republican	Cuyahoga	1995–2002
Betty Montgomery	Republican	Wood	2003–

SECRETARIES OF STATE

SECRETARIES OF STATE*	PARTY	COUNTY	IN OFFICE
William Trevitt	Democratic	Perry	1852–1856
James H. Baker	Republican	Ross	1856–1858
Addison P. Russell	Republican	Clinton	1858–1862
Benjamin R. Cowen	Republican	Hamilton	1862
Wilson S. Kennon	Republican	Belmont	1862–1863
William W. Armstrong	Democratic	Columbiana	1863–1865
William H. Smith	Republican	Hamilton	1865–1868
John Russell	N.A.	N.A.	1868–1869
Isaac R. Sherwood	Republican	Lucas	1869–1873
Allen T. Wikoff	Republican	Adams	1873–1875
William Bell, Jr.	Democratic	Licking	1875–1877
Milton Barnes	Republican	Guernsey	1877–1881
Charles Townsend	Republican	Athens	1881–1883
James W. Newman	Democratic	Scioto	1883–1885
James S. Robinson	Republican	Hardin	1885–1889
Daniel J. Ryan	Republican	Scioto	1889–1891
Christian L. Poorman	Republican	Belmont	1891–1893
Samuel M. Taylor	Republican	Champaign	1893–1897
Charles Kinney	Republican	Scioto	1897–1901

SECRETARIES OF STATE*	PARTY	COUNTY	IN OFFICE
Lewis C. Laylin	Republican	Huron	1901–1907
Carmi Thompson	Republican	Lawrence	1907–1911
Charles H. Graves	Democratic	Ottawa	1911–1915
C.Q. Hildebrant	Republican	Clinton	1915–1917
William D. Fulton	Democratic	Licking	1917–1919
Harvey C. Smith	Republican	Muskingum	1919–1923
Thad H. Brown	Republican	Franklin	1923–1927
Clarence J. Brown	Republican	Clinton	1927–1933
George S. Myers	Democratic	Cuyahoga	1933–1936
William J. Kennedy	Democratic	Cuyahoga	1936–1939
Earl Griffith	Republican	Morrow	1939–1940
George M. Neffiner	Republican	Clinton	1940–1941
John E. Sweeney	Democratic	Cuyahoga	1941–1943
Edward J. Hummel	Republican	Hamilton	1943–1949
Charles F. Sweeney	Democratic	Erie	1949–1951
Ted W. Brown	Republican	Clark	1951–1979
Anthony J. Celebrezze Jr.	Democratic	Cuyahoga	1979–1983
Sherrod Brown	Democratic	Richland	1983–1991
Bob Taft	Republican	Hamilton	1991–1998
Kenneth Blackwell	Republican	Hamilton	1999–

* Under the 1851 Constitution, the office of secretary of state was made elective. Previously, the secretary of state was appointed by the General Assembly.

TREASURERS

TREASURERS	PARTY	COUNTY	IN OFFICE
John Armstrong	N.A.	Washington	1796–1803
William McFarland	N.A.	Jefferson	1803–1816
Hiram M. Curry	N.A.	Champaign	1816–1820
Samuel Sullivan	Democratic-Republican	Muskingum	1820–1823
Henry Brown	N.A.	Franklin	1823–1835
Joseph Whitehill	N.A.	Union	1835–1847
Albert A. Bliss	N.A.	Lorain	1847–1852
John G. Breslin	Democratic	Seneca	1852–1856
William H. Gibson	Republican	Seneca	1856–1857
A.P. Stone	Republican	Franklin	1857–1862
G.V. Dorsey	Democratic	Miami	1862–1865
William Hooper	Republican	Hamilton	1865–1866
S.S. Warner	Republican	Lorain	1866–1872
Isaac Welsh	Republican	Belmont	1872–1875
Leroy Welsh	Republican	Belmont	1875–1876
John M. Millikin	Republican	Butler	1876–1878
Anthony Howells	Democratic	Stark	1878–1880
Joseph Turney	Republican	Cuyahoga	1880–1884
Peter Brady	Democratic	Huron	1884–1886
John C. Brown	Republican	Jefferson	1886–1892
William T. Cope	Republican	Cuyahoga	1892–1896
Samuel B. Campbell	Republican	Jefferson	1896–1900
Isaac B. Cameron	Republican	Columbiana	1900–1904
William S. McKinnon	Republican	Ashtabula	1904–1908
Charles C. Green	Republican	Franklin	1908–1909
David S. Creamer	Democratic	Belmont	1909–1913
John P. Brennan	Democratic	Champaign	1913–1915

TREASURERS	PARTY	COUNTY	IN OFFICE
Rudolph W. Archer	Republican	Belmont	1915–1917
Chester E. Bryan	Democratic	Madison	1917–1919
Rudolph W. Archer	Republican	Belmont	1919–1923
Harry S. Day	Republican	Sandusky	1923–1927
Bert B. Buckley	Republican	Montgomery	1927–1929
H. Ross Ake	Republican	Stark	1929–1930
Edwin A. Todd	Republican	Clark	1930–1931
Harry S. Day	Republican	Sandusky	1931–1937
Clarence H. Knisley	Democratic	Ross	1937–1939
Don H. Ebright	Republican	Summit	1939–1951
Roger W. Tracy	Republican	Franklin	1951–1959
Joseph T. Ferguson	Democratic	Franklin	1959–1963
John D. Herbert	Republican	Franklin	1963–1971
Gertrude W. Donahey	Democratic	Franklin	1971–1983
Mary Ellen Withrow	Democratic	Marion	1983–1994
J. Kenneth Blackwell	Republican	Hamilton	1994–1998
Joseph T. Deters	Republican	Hamilton	1999–2005
Jennette Bradley	Republican	Franklin	2005–

U.S. SENATE (1)

U.S. SENATE (1)	PARTY	COUNTY	IN OFFICE
Thomas Worthington	Democratic-Republican	Ross	1803–1807
Edward Tiffin	Democratic-Republican	Ross	1807–1809
Stanley Griswold	Democratic-Republican	Cuyahoga	1809
Alexander Campbell	Democratic-Republican	Brown	1809–1813
Jeremiah Morrow	Democratic-Republican	Warren	1813–1819
William A. Trimble	Democratic-Republican	Highland	1819–1821
Ethan Allen Brown	Democratic-Republican	Hamilton	1822–1825
William Henry Harrison	Whig	Hamilton	1825–1828
Jacob Burnet	Federalist	Hamilton	1828–1831
Thomas Ewing	Whig	Fairfield	1831–1837
William Allen	Democratic	Ross	1837–1849
Salmon P. Chase	Republican	Hamilton	1849–1855
George E. Pugh	Democratic	Hamilton	1855–1861
Salmon P. Chase	Republican	Hamilton	1861
John Sherman	Republican	Richland	1861–1877
Stanley Matthews	Republican	Hamilton	1877–1879
George H. Pendleton	Democratic	Hamilton	1879–1885
Henry B. Payne	Democratic	Cuyahoga	1885–1891
Calvin S. Brice	Democratic	Allen	1891–1897
Joseph B. Foraker	Republican	Hamilton	1897–1909
Theodore E. Burton	Republican	Cuyahoga	1909–1915
Warren G. Harding	Republican	Marion	1915–1921
Frank B. Willis	Republican	Delaware	1921–1928
Cyrus Locher	Democratic	Cuyahoga	1928
Theodore E. Burton	Republican	Cuyahoga	1928–1929
Roscoe E. McCulloch	Republican	Stark	1929–1930
Robert J. Bulkley	Democratic	Cuyahoga	1930–1939
Robert A. Taft	Republican	Hamilton	1939–1953
Thomas A. Burke	Democratic	Cuyahoga	1953–1954
George H. Bender	Republican	Cuyahoga	1954–1957

U.S. SENATE (1)	PARTY	COUNTY	IN OFFICE
Frank J. Lausche	Democratic	Cuyahoga	1957–1969
William B. Saxbe	Republican	Champaign	1969–1974
Howard M. Metzenbaum	Democratic	Cuyahoga	1974
John Glenn	Democratic	Franklin	1974–1998
George V. Voinovich	Republican	Cuyahoga	1999–

U.S. SENATE (2)

U.S. SENATE (2)	PARTY	COUNTY	IN OFFICE
John Smith	Democratic-Republican	Hamilton	1803–1808
Return J. Meigs	Democratic-Republican	Washington	1809–1810
Thomas Worthington	Democratic-Republican	Ross	1810–1814
Joseph Kerr	Democratic-Republican	Ross	1814–1815
Benjamin Ruggles	Democratic-Republican	Belmont	1815–1833
Thomas Morris	Democratic	Clermont	1833–1839
Benjamin Tappan	Democratic	Jefferson	1839–1845
Thomas Corwin	Whig	Warren	1845–1850
Thomas Ewing	Whig	Fairfield	1850–1851
Benjamin F. Wade	Republican	Ashtabula	1851–1869
Allen G. Thurman	Democratic	Franklin	1869–1881
John Sherman	Republican	Richland	1881–1897
Marcus A. Hanna	Republican	Cuyahoga	1897–1904
Charles Dick	Republican	Summit	1904–1911
Atlee Pomerene	Democratic	Stark	1911–1923
Simeon D. Fess	Republican	Greene	1923–1935
A. Victor Donahey	Democratic	Logan	1935–1941
Harold H. Burton	Republican	Cuyahoga	1941–1945
James W. Huffman	Democratic	Franklin	1945–1946
Kingsley A. Taft	Republican	Cuyahoga	1946–1947
John W. Bricker	Republican	Franklin	1947–1959
Stephen M. Young	Democratic	Cuyahoga	1959–1971
Robert Taft Jr.	Republican	Hamilton	1971–1976
Howard M. Metzenbaum	Democratic	Cuyahoga	1976–1994
Michael DeWine	Republican	Greene	1995–

Note: U.S. senators were elected by the General Assembly from 1803 to 1914, when the direct election
of senators became effective, in accord with the 17th Amendment to the U.S. Constitution.

Ohio Representation in the U.S. House of Representatives

1944–2004

AFTER ELECTION OF:	OHIO		UNITED STATES		AFTER ELECTION OF:	OHIO		UNITED STATES	
	D	R	D	R		D	R	D	R
2004	6	12	200	231	1970	7	17	255	180
2002	6	12	205	229	1968	6	18	243	192
2000	8	11	212	221	1966	5	19	248	187
1998	8	11	211	223	1964	10	14	295	140
1996	8	11	206	228	1962	6	18	259	176
1994	6	13	204	230	1960	7	16	262	175
1992	10	9	258	176	1958	9	14	283	153
1990	11	10	267	167	1956	6	17	234	201
1988	11	10	260	175	1954	6	17	232	203
1986	11	10	258	177	1952	6	16	213	221
1984	11	10	253	182	1950	7	15	234	199
1982	10	11	268	167	1948	12	11	263	171
1980	11	12	243	192	1946	4	19	188	246
1978	10	13	277	158	1944	6	17	243	190
1976	10	13	292	143					
1974	8	15	291	144					
1972	7	16	242	192					

* Excludes "other" and "vacant"

Source: Office of the Clerk, U.S. House of Representatives

Campaign Expenditures for State Executive Offices

1974–2002, BY MAJOR PARTY NOMINEES

(* denotes winning candidate)

Governor

	PRIMARY	GENERAL	TOTAL
2002			
Bob Taft (R)*	604,655	9,729,831	10,334,486
Tim Hagan (D)	240,059	1,142,501	1,382,560
			11,717,046
1998			
Bob Taft (R)*	726,010	9,813,380	10,539,390
Lee Fisher (D)	3,954,023	8,099,764	12,053,787
			22,593,177
1994			
George V. Voinovich (R)*	$903,379	5,625,490	6,528,869
Robert L. Burch, Jr. (D)	$203,309	160,659	363,968
			6,892,837
1990			
George V. Voinovich (R)*	1,280,767	6,969,724	8,250,491
Anthony J. Celebrezze Jr. (D)	1,819,977	5,983,180	7,803,157
			16,053,648
1986			
Richard F. Celeste (D)*	1,841,986	4,214,238	6,056,224
James A. Rhodes (R)	873,039	1,952,589	2,825,628
			8,881,852
1982			
Richard F. Celeste (D)*	1,585,717	3,661,275	5,246,992
Clarence J. Brown Jr. (R)	1,183,062	1,559,441	2,742,503
			7,989,495
1978			
James A. Rhodes (R)*	198,292	2,089,312	2,287,604
Richard F. Celeste (D)	551,207	1,752,244	2,303,451
			4,591,055
1974			
James A. Rhodes (R)*	N.A.	755,861	755,861
John J. Gilligan (D)	N.A.	1,062,143	1,062,143
			1,818,004

Attorney General

	PRIMARY	GENERAL	TOTAL
2002			
Jim Petro (R)*	1,393,166	1,399,106	2,792,272
Leigh Herington (D)	60,234	314,091	374,325
			3,166,597
1998			
Betty Montgomery (R)*	165,760	3,207,212	3,372,972
Richard Cordray (D)	308,235	997,353	1,305,588
			4,678,560
1994			
Betty Montgomery (R)*	107,295	2,138,048	2,245,343
Lee Fisher (D)	439,277	3,726,331	4,165,608
			6,410,951
1990			
Lee Fisher (D)*	1,104,850	2,124,636	3,229,486
Paul E. Pfeifer (R)	87,513	1,429,846	1,517,359
			4,746,845
1986			
Anthony J. Celebrezze Jr. (D)*	229,835	1,545,301	1,775,136
Barry Levey (R)	7,015	318,325	325,340
			2,100,476
1982			
Anthony J. Celebrezze Jr. (D)*	141,557	700,220	841,777
Charles R. Saxbe (R)	136,070	140,211	276,281
			1,118,058
1978			
William J. Brown (D)*	79,589	408,983	488,572
George C. Smith (R)	142,742	232,709	375,451
			864,023
1974			
William J. Brown (D)*	N.A.	133,608	133,608
George C. Smith (R)	N.A.	96,941	96,941
			230,549

Auditor

	PRIMARY	GENERAL	TOTAL
2002			
Betty Montgomery (R)*	256,667	1,635,027	1,891,694
Helen Knipe Smith (D)	2,692	11,278	13,970
			1,905,664
1998			
Jim Petro (R)*	153,331	1,065,690	1,219,021
Louis Strike (D)	159,458	134,488	293,945
			1,512,966
1994			
Jim Petro (R)*	90,252	1,178,030	1,268,282
Randall W. Sweeney (D)	159,807	481,562	641,369
			1,909,651
1990			
Thomas E. Ferguson (D)*	78,072	1,732,862	1,810,934
Jim Petro (R)	58,464	665,378	723,842
			2,534,776
1986			
Thomas E. Ferguson (D)*	79,286	977,490	1,056,776
Ben Rose (R)	38,432	74,104	112,536
			1,169,312
1982			
Thomas E. Ferguson (D)*	88,110	393,686	481,796
Vincent C. Campanella (R)	96,450	304,207	400,657
			882,453
1978			
Thomas E. Ferguson (D)*	105,134	287,909	393,043
Donald E. Lukens (R)	105,189	187,148	292,337
			685,380
1974			
Thomas E. Ferguson (D)*	N.A.	143,151	143,151
Roger W. Tracy Jr. (R)	N.A.	45,463	45,463
			188,614

Secretary of State

	PRIMARY	GENERAL	TOTAL
2002			
J. Kenneth Blackwell (R)*	133,817	117,099	250,916
Bryan Flannery (D)	76,497	247,501	323,998
			574,914
1998			
J. Kenneth Blackwell (R)*	335,962	1,779,034	2,114,996
Charleta Tavares (D)	170,913	326,972	497,885
			2,612,881
1994			
Bob Taft (R)*	129,323	704,789	834,112
Dan Brady (D)	14,846	93,408	108,254
			942,366
1990			
Bob Taft (R)*	332,624	2,357,582	2,690,206
Sherrod Brown (D)	153,041	1,873,441	2,026,482
			4,716,688

1986			
Sherrod Brown (D)*	87,176	754,246	841,422
Vincent C. Campanella (R)	29,525	395,867	425,392
			1,266,814
1982			
Sherrod Brown (D)*	134,133	330,152	464,285
Virgil E. Brown (R)	48,600	141,579	190,179
			654,464
1978			
Anthony J. Celebrezze Jr. (D)*	72,950	279,723	352,673
Ted W. Brown (R)	40,376	168,821	209,197
			561,870
1974			
Ted W. Brown (R)*	N.A.	30,592	30,592
Tony P. Hall (D)	N.A.	143,376	143,376
			173,968

Treasurer

	PRIMARY	GENERAL	TOTAL
2002			
Joseph Deters (R)*	1,596,779	741,590	2,338,369
Mary Boyle (D)	46,290	626,278	672,568
			3,010,937
1998			
Joseph Deters (R)*	59,444	1,580,929	1,640,373
John Donofrio (D)	282,205	696,474	978,679
			2,619,052
1994			
J. Kenneth Blackwell (R)*	119,105	1,153,376	1,272,481
Barbara Sykes (D)	27,998	203,351	231,349
			1,503,830
1990			
Mary Ellen Withrow (D)*	41,606	473,471	515,077
Judith Brachman (R)	611	308,573	309,184
			824,261
1986			
Mary Ellen Withrow (D)*	164,205	605,103	769,308
Jeff Jacobs (R)	299,246	1,172,144	1,471,390
			2,240,698
1982			
Mary Ellen Withrow (D)*	25,540	156,553	182,093
Dana G. Rinehart (R)	225,952	248,262	474,214
			656,307
1978			
Gertrude W. Donahey (D)*	7,642	74,958	82,600
George C. Rogers (R)	16,094	31,953	48,047
			130,647
1974			
Gertrude W. Donahey (D)*	N.A.	74,273	74,273
Richard H. Harris (R)	N.A.	14,909	14,909
			89,182

Source: Campaign finance reports, Ohio secretary of state
Excludes in-kind contributions

BIBLIOGRAPHY

Abbott, John S. C. The History of the State of Ohio. Detroit: R.D.S. Tyler & Co., 1875.

Adams, Willi Paul. The First American Constitutions: Republican Ideology and the Making of the State Constitutions in the Revolutionary Era. Chapel Hill: University of North Carolina Press, 1980.

Aley, Howard C. A Heritage to Share: The Bicentennial History of Youngstown and Mahoning County, Ohio. The Bicentennial Commission of Youngstown and Mahoning County, 1975.

Ambler, Charles Henry. A History of Transportation in the Ohio Valley. Westport, Conn.: Arthur H. Clark Co., 1932.

American Historical Publications, Inc. Ohio Biographical Dictionary: People of All Times and All Places Who Have Been Important to the History and Life of the State. Wilmington, Del.: American Historical Publications, 1986.

Annual Reports, Ohio secretary of state, 1873-2002.

Asher, Herbert B. "The Emergence of the Democratic Party in Ohio." Unpublished paper, 1984.

Baum, Lawrence, and Samuel C. Patterson. "Ohio: Party Change without Realignment." Party Realignment and State Politics, edited by Maureen Moakley. Columbus: Ohio State University Press, 1992.

Brusk, Susan Pam. "The History of the Office of Attorney General in Ohio." Unpublished paper, 1990.

Bureau of the Census. County and City Data Book: 1994. Washington: U.S. Government Printing Office, 1994.

Bureau of the Census. The Statistical History of the United States: From Colonial Times to the Present. New York: Basic Books, Inc., 1976.

Cayton, Andrew R. L. The Frontier Republic: Ideology and Politics in The Ohio Country, 1780-1825. Kent,

Ohio: Kent State University Press, 1986.

Congressional Quarterly, Inc. American Leaders 1789-1987: A Biographical Summary, 1987.

Constitution of the State of Ohio. As adopted Novembe 29, 1802; as adopted March 10, 1851; as amended September 3, 1912; and as amended subsequently.

Croly, Herbert. Marcus Alonzo Hanna: His Life and Work. New York: Macmillan, 1923.

Fess, Simeon D., ed. Ohio: A Four-Volume Reference Library. New York: Lewis Publishing Co., 1937.

Friedman, Lawrence M. A History of American Law, 2nd edition. New York: Simon and Schuster, 1985.

Galbreath, C. B. Constitutional Conventions of Ohio. Columbus: Ohio Journal of Commerce Co., 1911.

Galbreath, Charles B. History of Ohio. Chicago: American Historical Society, Inc., 1925.

Gargan, John J., and James G. Coke, eds. Political Behavior and Public Issues in Ohio. Kent, Ohio: Kent State University Press, 1972.

Garrett, Betty, with Edward R. Lentz. Columbus: America's Crossroads. Tulsa: Continental Heritage Press, Inc., 1980.

Gilkey, Elliot Howard, ed. The Ohio Hundred Year Book. Columbus: Fred J. Heer, state printer, 1901.

Gobetz, Edward, ed. Ohio's Lincoln: Frank J. Lausche. Willoughby Hills, Ohio: Slovenian Research Center, Inc., 1985.

Goulder, Grace. This is Ohio: Ohio's 88 Counties in Words. Cleveland: World Publishing Co., 1965.

Heisel, W. Donald, director. State Government for Our Times. Cincinnati: Stephen H. Wilder Foundation, 1970.

Hess, Stephen. "The Taft Dynasty." America's Political Dynasties: From

Adams to Kennedy. Garden City, N.Y.: Doubleday & Co., 1966.

Hickok, Charles Thomas. "The Negro in Ohio, 1802–1870." Thesis. Western Reserve University. New York: AMS Press, 1896.

Howe, Henry. Historical Collections of Ohio: An Encyclopedia of the State, Vols. I & II. Cincinnati: C.J. Krehbiel & Co., 1902.

Jordan, Philip D. The National Road. Indianapolis: Bobbs-Merrill, 1948.

Kent, Frank R. The Democratic Party: A History. New York: Century Co., 1928.

Knepper, George W. Akron: City at the Summit. Tulsa: Continental Heritage Press, Inc., 1981.

Knepper, George W. Ohio and Its People. Kent, Ohio: Kent State University Press, 2003.

Larson, David R. "Ohio's Fighting Liberal: A Political Biography of John J. Gilligan." Ph.D. diss. The Ohio State University, 1982.

Malone, Dumas, ed. The Dictionary of American Biography. New York: Charles Scribner's Sons, 1934.

Martin, Ralph G. The Bosses. New York: G.P. Putnam's Sons, 1964.

Mayer, George H. The Republican Party, 1854–1964. New York: Oxford University Press, 1964.

Nye, R. B., and J. E. Morpurgo, A History of the United States, Vols. I and II. Baltimore: Penguin Books, 1955.

Ohio Department of Industrial and Economic Development. Statistical Abstract of Ohio, 1960.

Ohio Historical Society. The Governors of Ohio. Columbus: The Stoneman Press, 1954.

Ohio House of Representatives journals; Ohio Senate journals, 1803–2004.

Ohio Legislative Service Commission: Staff Research Report No. 47. The Ohio Court System: Its

Organization and Capacity. Columbus: Ohio Legislative Service Commission, 1961.

Ohio State Archaeological and Historical Society. Ohio Centennial Celebration—1903. Columbus: Ohio State Archaeological and Historical Society, 1903.

Patterson, Isaac Franklin. The Constitutions of Ohio. Cleveland: Arthur H. Clark Co., 1912.

Pauly, Karl B. Bricker of Ohio: The Man and His Record. New York: G.P. Putnam's Sons, 1944.

Pearson, F. B., and J. D.Harlor, Ohio History Sketches. Columbus: Fred J. Heer Publishing, 1903.

Perrin, William Henry, ed. History of Stark County. Chicago: Baskin and Battey, 1881.

Porter, Tana Mosier. Toledo Profile: A Sesquicentennial History. Toledo: Toledo Sesquicentennial Commission, 1987.

Powell, Thomas E., ed. The Democratic Party of Ohio. Columbus: Ohio Publishing Co., 1913.

Proceedings and Debates of the Constitutional Convention of the State of Ohio. 1912. Volumes I and II. Columbus. The F. J. Heer Printing Co.

Queen City Publishing Co. The Book of Ohio: A History of the Development of the State. Cincinnati: Queen City Publishing Co., 1912.

Report of the Debates and Proceedings of the Convention for the Revision of the Constitution of the State of Ohio, 1850-1851, Volumes I and II. J. V. Smith, official reporter to the convention. Columbus. S. Medary, printer to the convention.

Ronald, Bruce W., and Virginia Ronald. Dayton: The Gem City. Tulsa: Continental Heritage Press, Inc., 1981.

Roseboom, Eugene H., and Francis P. Weisenburger. A History of Ohio. Columbus: Ohio Historical

Society, 1953.

Rossiter, Clinton. Parties and Politics in America. Ithaca, N.Y.: Cornell University Press, 1960.

Schlesinger, Arthur M. Paths to the Present. New York: Macmillan, 1949.

Schlesinger, Arthur M., Jr. The Cycles of American History. Boston: Houghton Mifflin Co., 1986.

Shafritz, Jay M., ed. The Dorsey Dictionary of American Government and Politics. Chicago: Dorsey Press, 1988.

Sheridan, Richard G. Governing Ohio: Administration and Judiciary.

Cleveland: Federation for Community Planning, 1990.

Smith, Joseph P., ed. History of the Republican Party in Ohio, Vols. I and II. Columbus: Lewis Publishing Co., 1898.

Stevens, Harry R. The Early Jackson Party in Ohio. Durham, N.C.: Duke University Press, 1957.

Stuckey, James Herbert. "The Formation of Leadership Groups in a Frontier Town: Canton, Ohio, 1805–1855." Ph.D. diss. Case Western Reserve University, 1976.

Supreme Court of Ohio. Ohio Courts Summary 2002.

Swisher, Thomas R., ed. Ohio

Constitution Handbook. Cleveland: Banks-Baldwin Publishing Co., 1990.

Teaford, Jon C. Cities of the Heartland: The Rise and Fall of the Industrial Midwest. Bloomington: Indiana University Press, 1993.

Timken Company. History of the Timken Company. Canton, 1990.

Walker, Harvey, ed. An Analysis and Appraisal of the Ohio State Constitution, 1851–1951. A Report to the Stephen H. Wilder Foundation. Cincinnati, 1951.

Walker, James Edward. "A City Tries to Save Itself: Youngstown, Ohio." Unpublished thesis.

Claremont Graduate School, 1981.

Warner, Hoyt Landon. Progressivism in Ohio, 1897–1917. Columbus: Ohio State University Press, 1964.

Webster, Homer J. History of the Democratic Party Organization in the Northwest, 1824–1840. Columbus: Ohio Archaeological and Historical Society, 1915.

The Writer's Program of the Works Projects Administration. The Ohio Guide. Works Projects Administration, 1940.

Index of Names

Abbott, Caleb F., 179
Adams, Perry M., 68
Aigler, Allan G., 69
Ake, H. Ross, 205
Albaugh, Arla A., 55
Allen, Cotton H., 175
Allen, Florence E., 77, 198
Allen, John W., 115, 172
Allen, Virgil D., 51
Allen, William (governor), 4, 17, 31, 39, 40, 200, 205
Allen, William T. (Akron mayor), 165
Anderson, Byron, 59
Anderson, Charles, 38, 177, 200
Anderson, John, 177
Anderson, Richard Clough, 38
Andrews, Frank M., 176
Andrews, John S., 91, 93, 94
Andrews, Lorin, 116
Anthony, Charles, 67
Archer, Frank B., 69
Archer, Rudolph W., 205
Armstrong, John, 204
Armstrong, Neil, 118
Armstrong, William W., 203
Arnold, John H., 201
Aronoff, Stanley J., 69
Arthur, Chester A., 21, 198
Ashenhurst, John J., 44
Atherton, Gibson, 76
Atkinson, Robert J., 68
Attia, James E., 62
Aultman, Cornelius, 166
Avery, Coleman, 77
Avery, Edward, 76

Babcock, Brenton D., 172
Babcock, Charles L., 167
Bachrach, Walton, 169
Badger, DeWitt C., 175
Baehr, Herman C., 172
Bailhache, John, 174
Baker, Aaron, 177
Baker, Eber, 142
Baker, James H., 203
Baker, Newton, 172
Baldwin, Eli, 31
Baldwin, Frank L., 181

Baldwin, Michael, 67
Ball, Charles M., 167
Ballard, John S., 165
Bandlow, Robert, 46, 48
Barber, George, 155
Barber, O. C., 155
Barnes, Earl T., 91
Barnes, Milton, 203
Barrere, Nelson, 2, 35
Bartley, Mordecai, 32, 33, 37, 199
Bartley, Thomas W., 32–33, 68, 76, 199
Bates, George D., 165
Bauman, C. L., 177
Beard, Dan, 137
Bebb, William, 33, 37, 199
Beck, Carl, 165
Beecher Stowe, Harriet, 119
Beecher, Philemon, 35, 67
Beetham, Rupert R., 67
Bell, Charles S., 77
Bell, James F. (judge), 77
Bell, James M. (House Speaker), 67
Bell, William, Jr., 203
Bender, George H., 55, 205
Bennett, James, 122
Bennett, Robert T., 91, 94, 95
Berdan, John, 178, 179
Berg, Leo A., 165
Berry, Theodore M., 169
Bettleon, John, 177
Bettman, Gilbert, 77, 202
Betts, Jackson E., 67
Bevis, Howard L., 77
Bierce, Lucius V., 165
Bigelow, Herbert, 81
Bigger, John, 28, 67
Bingham, Flavel W., 172
Birchard, Matthew, 76
Birchard, Sardis, 39, 153
Bird, Russell M., 165
Bishop, Richard M., 41, 169, 200
Bittinger, J. Freer, 67
Black, Guy Templeton, 61
Black, Samuel L., 175
Blackwell, J. Kenneth, 95, 169, 199, 204, 205, 209
Blaine, James G., 7, 17, 18, 19, 23
Blainville, Celeron de, 153

Blake, Harrison G., 68
Blake, John F., 167
Blee, Robert, 172
Blennerhassett, Harman, 159
Bliss, Albert A., 204
Bliss, George, 165
Bliss, Ray C., 91, 92, 93
Bloom, Earl D., 201
Blythin, Edward, 172
Bockius, J. C., 167
Bolton, Chester C., 69, 198
Bolton, Frances P., 198
Bomberger, George W., 177
Bond, Charles Anson, 175
Bond, Lewis H., 41
Bookwalter, John W., 42
Bortz, Arn, 169
Bowen, Ozias, 76
Bowles, Chester, 61
Boxwell, Alexander, 67
Boyle, Mary O., 63, 95, 209
Boynton, W. W., 76
Brabham, Elisha, 177
Brachman, Judith, 209
Bracken, Edward J., 44
Bradbury, Joseph P., 76
Braden, A. D., 167
Braden, George C., 201
Bradley, Jennette, 201, 205
Brady, Dan, 209
Brady, Peter, 204
Branstool, Eugene, 91
Breen, Edward, 177
Brennan, Charles J., 177
Brennan, John P., 204
Breslin, John G., 36, 67, 204
Brice, Calvin S., 205
Bricker, John W., 53, 54, 57, 58, 91, 92, 200, 202, 206
Brigham, Mavor, 179
Briley, John Marshall, 55
Brinkerhoff, Jacob, 76
Brinsmade, Allen T., 68
Britton, Nancy, 24
Broadwell, Simeon, 177
Brodhead, Andrew, 123
Bromfield, Louis, 152
Brooks, John, 174

Brough, Bernard F., 179
Brough, Charles, 88
Brough, John, 37–38, 38, 200, 203
Brown, Clarence J., 53, 61, 201, 204
Brown, Clarence J., Jr., 208
Brown, Clifford F., 77
Brown, Egbert B., 179
Brown, Ethan Allen, 27–28, 29, 76, 199, 205
Brown, Frank L., 181
Brown, Henry, 204
Brown, Herbert R., 77
Brown, John (abolitionist), 155
Brown, John C. (treasurer), 204
Brown, John T. (lieutenant governor 1929–31)), 201
Brown, John W. (lieutenant governor, 1953–57), 56–57, 61, 94, 200, 201
Brown, Lloyd O., 77
Brown, Paul W., 77, 202
Brown, Robert B., 49
Brown, Sherrod, 63, 94, 204, 209
Brown, Ted W., 94, 204, 209
Brown, Thad H., 204
Brown, Thomas V., 61
Brown, Virgil E., 209
Brown, William B. (judge), 77
Brown, William J. (attorney general), 61, 94, 202, 208
Brownell, Abner C., 172
Brownlee, Alexander M., 179
Bruce, William, 151
Bruck, Philip H., 175
Brumback, John S., 158
Brunner, Henry, 91
Brush, Henry, 76
Brush, Thomas B., 169
Bryan, Chester E., 205
Bryan, John A., 160, 203
Bryan, William Jennings, 20, 21, 22
Bryce, William, 166
Buchanan, James, 3, 13, 35
Buchanan, Thomas J., 67
Buchtel, John R., 163
Buckley, Bert B., 205
Buhrer, Stephen, 172
Bulkley, Robert J., 91, 205
Bull, James G., 175
Burch, Robert L., Jr., 62, 95, 208
Burke, Thomas A., 172, 205
Burkhart, Edward E., 177
Burnet, Isaac G., 169, 177
Burnet, Jacob (1821), 65, 76, 205
Burnett, Jacob F. (1893), 76

Burnett, Stephen F., 181
Burnside, Ambrose, 88
Burr, Aaron, 25, 153, 159
Burton, Harold H. (U.S. senator), 206
Burton, Harold R. (Cleveland mayor), 171, 172
Burton, Theodore E., 43, 205
Bushnell, Asa S., 44, 45, 121, 200
Butz, Lawrence, Jr., 177

Caldwell, John A., 169, 201
Caldwell, William B., 76
Cameron, Isaac B., 204
Campanella, Vincent C., 209
Campbell, Alexander, 28, 67, 205
Campbell, James E., 20, 43–44, 45, 200
Campbell, Jane, 172
Campbell, John (ironmaster), 138
Campbell, John W. (governor candidate), 28, 86
Campbell, Samuel B., 204
Campbell, Walter L., 181
Cantwell, John F., 67
Carey, John Q., 179
Carrel, George P., 169
Carroll, Peter W., 181
Carroll, Reuben, 181
Carter, Israel E., 165
Case, Leonard, Jr., 170
Case, William, 172
Casement, Frances Jennings, 137
Cash, Albert D., 169
Cassidy, Robert A., 167
Castle, William B., 172
Catlin, Franklin J., 51
Cave, Frank, 67
Celebrezze, Anthony J., Jr., 62, 94, 172, 202, 204, 208, 209
Celebrezze, Frank D., 77
Celebrezze, James P., 77
Celeste, Richard F., 57, 59, 60–62, 63, 94, 200, 201, 208
Chamberlain, G. H., 69
Chamberlin, Philo, 165
Chambers, David, 68
Chance, Peter, 167
Chaney, John, 67
Chapin, Herman A., 172
Chapman, Horace L., 45
Chase, Ithamar, 35
Chase, Philander, 35, 137
Chase, Salmon P., 35–36, 42, 87–88, 137, 199, 205
Clancy, Donald D., 169

Clark, George H., 77
Clark, George Rogers, 120, 130
Clark, Ira L., 179
Clark, Jonas, 34
Clark, Pamela, 27
Clark, W. W., 167
Clay, Henry, 2, 29, 140
Cleaveland, Moses, 117, 124, 170, 197
Cleveland, Grover, 3, 8, 13, 19, 20, 148
Clifford, Tom, 48, 49
Cloud, Roger, 60, 67, 94, 203
Cmich, Stanley A., 167
Cole, Oviatt, 203
Coleman, Michael B., 174, 175
Coleman, William L., 91, 92, 93
Collett, Joshua, 76
Colley, Michael F., 91
Collins, Charles A., 165
Collins, Gilbert G., 175
Collins, Henry A., 165
Collins, Isaac C., 40
Compton, John, 177
Conn, Harry L., 77
Conover, Charles D., 67
Conrad, Silas A., 68, 201
Convers, Charles C., 68, 76
Converse, George L., 67
Cook, Deborah, 77
Cooke, Jay, 126
Coolidge, Calvin, 13, 23
Cooper, Daniel C., 175, 177
Cooper, Myers Y., 51–52, 53, 91, 200
Cope, William T., 204
Cordray, Richard, 208
Corrigan, J. J. P., 77
Corry, William, 169
Corwin, John A., 76
Corwin, Matthias, 32, 67
Corwin, Thomas, 31, 32, 199, 206
Couch, Jessup N., 76
Cowan, Isaac, 46, 47
Cowen, Benjamin R., 203
Cowgill, Thomas A., 67
Cowles, Betsy, 117
Cox, George B. ("Boss Cox"), 46, 89, 90, 168
Cox, Jacob D., 38, 200
Cox, James M., 8, 23, 49–50, 90, 145, 176, 200
Coxey, Jacob S., 45
Crabbe, Charles C., 202
Cramer, Charles F., 24
Craver, Alvin W., 181
Crawford, Ira, 177

Crawford, William, 123, 161
Creamer, David S., 204
Creamer, Nelson D., 46
Creed, John M., 67
Creighton, Janet Weir, 166, 167
Crevoisie, J., 167
Crew, William B., 76
Critchfield, Lyman R., 202
Crites, John A., 60
Croghan, George, 153
Cromley, Thaddeus E., 69
Crumbley, Katherine, 199
Cunningham, A. J., 67
Curry, Hiram M., 204
Curtis, C. C., 167
Curtiss, H. W., 68, 201
Custer, George Armstrong, 133, 161
Cuthbertson, Samuel W., 157
Cutler, Manasseh, 117
Cutler, William P., 67
Czelusta, Ollie, 180
Czolgosz, Leon F., 21

Damas, Michael J., 180
Darrow, Clarence, 156
Daugherty, Harry M., 23, 127
Davey, Martin L., 52, 53–54, 94, 200
Davidson, Jo Ann, 67
Davies, Samuel W., 169
Davis, Evan H., 50
Davis, Harry L., 50–51, 172, 200
Davis, S. S., 169
Davis, Theodore F., 68
Davis, William Z., 76
Dawes, Charles G., 23
Day, Arthur H., 77
Day, Harry S., 205
Day, Luther, 76
Day, Robert H., 77
Dayton, Jonathan, 145, 175
DeArmond, D. H., 69
Decker, Augustus S., 175
Deeds, Edward A., 145, 176
DeGood, Douglas, 180
Dempsey, Edward J., 169
Dempsey, Jack, 178
Denison, William, 138
Denman, Ulysses G., 202
Dennison, William, Jr., 36, 200
Deters, Joseph T., 95, 205, 209
DeVilbiss, Allen, 178
DeWine, Michael, 63, 95, 201, 206
Dexter, Julius, 45
Dick, Charles, 206

Dickason, John H., 49
Dickman, Franklin J., 76
DiSalle, Michael V. ("Tax-Hike Mike"), 57, 58, 59, 92, 93, 180, 200
Disney, David T., 67, 68
Dixon, Richard Clay, 177
Dixon, William C., 77
Dockstadter, Nicholas, 172
Doheny, E. L., 24
Doherty, William, 68
Dolbey, Dorothy N., 169
Donahey, A. Victor, 50, 51, 52, 53, 90, 92, 200, 203, 206
Donahey, Gertrude W., 94, 199, 205, 209
Donahey, John W., 201
Donahue, Maurice H., 76
Donofrio, John, 209
Dorr, Charles M., 179
Dorsey, G. V., 204
Douglas, Andrew, 77
Dowd, David D., 77
Doyle, John H., 76
Doyle, W. B., 165
Drake, Elias F., 67
Dueber, John, 166
Duer, William, 129
Duffy, Herbert S., 202
Dukakis, Michael, 11
Dunbar, George, 166
Dunbar, H. P., 167
Dunbar, Paul Laurence, 145, 176
Duncan, Robert M., 77
Dunlap, James, 27, 28

Eagleson, Freeman T., 67
Eastman, John, 64
Ebright, Don H., 55, 92, 205
Edison, Thomas A., 126
Edy, John N., 179
Ellis, E. C., 177
Ellis, Seth H., 45, 46
Ellis, Wade H., 202
Ely, Herman, 139
Emmick, Vincent J., 179
Emmitt, James, 150
English, Lorenzo, 175
Ensign, William J., 180
Entrekin, John C., 67
Erickson, Edward O., 165
Evans, Lionel, 181
Ewing, Thomas, 42, 205, 206

Fairbanks, Charles W., 157
Fall, Albert B., 23, 24

Faran, James J., 67, 68, 169
Farley, John H., 172
Fawcett, Thomas, 122
Feitler, Zanna, 64
Fenwick, Edward, 149
Ferguson, Joseph T., 58, 59, 94, 203, 205
Ferguson, Thomas E., 203, 209
Fess, Simeon D., 51, 206
Fillmore, Millard, 32
Finan, Richard H., 69
Finch, Nathaniel, 165
Finch, Robert H., 179
Findlay, James, 30, 65, 132
Finkbeiner, Carty, 179, 180
Finley, James B., 161
Firestone, Harvey S., 123, 155, 164
Fisher, Lee, 63, 64, 95, 202, 208
Fitch, Jabez W., 201
Fitzgerald, William S., 172
Flannery, Bryan, 209
Flask, Anthony B., 181
Fleischman, Julius, 169
Flint, Edward S., 172
Folk, Edward, 167
Folkereth, John, 177
Follett, John F., 67
Follett, Martin D., 76
Foos, Jacob, 142
Foos, Joseph, 173
Foote, Earl H., 50
Foraker, Joseph B., 21, 23, 42, 43, 44, 45, 89, 200, 205
Forbes, Charles R., 23, 24
Forbes, George L., 172
Forbes, Samuel F., 179
Ford, Edward, 178
Ford, Gerald, 10
Ford, Henry, 164
Ford, I. O., 53
Ford, Jack, 179, 180
Ford, Seabury, 34, 67, 68, 199
Ford, Thomas H., 200
Foster, Charles (son), 41–42, 154, 200
Foster, Charles W. (father), 41, 154
Fought, Howard E., 77
Fourier, François Marie Charles, 121
Fouse, Winfred E., 164
Franko, Frank R., 181
Fraze, John M., 165
Freeman, Walter, 51
Frémont, John C., 3, 7, 19, 40, 153
Friedman, Allan, 59
Fromm, Albert, 167
Fullington, Edward M., 203

Fulton, William D., 204

Gable, Clark, 133
Gallagher, John M., 67
Galvin, John, 169
Gamble, James, 131
Garber, Harvey C., 89
Gardner, George W., 172
Gardner, Joseph R., 69
Garfield, James Abram (president), 4, 8, 13, 17, 18–19, 36, 130, 137, 150, 197–98
Garfield, James R., 49, 50
Garford, Arthur L., 49
Garver, W. F., 77
Gessaman, Myron B., 175
Gholson, William Y., 76
Gibbs, Joshua, 166
Gibson, Rankin, 77
Gibson, Thomas, 203
Gibson, W. T. (Youngstown mayor), 181
Gibson, William H. (U.S. senator), 36, 204
Giddings, Joshua R., 117
Gillespie, W. H., 177
Gilligan, John J., 55, 56, 57, 59–60, 93, 94, 200, 208
Gillmor, Paul E., 59, 69
Gilmore, William J., 76
Gist, Christopher, 123
Glenn, John (U.S. senator), 6, 63, 94, 95, 206
Glenn, John H. (astronaut), 131
Glidden, Charles E., 20, 44
Goble, Chester W., 203
Goddard, Charles B., 68
Godfrey, Thomas J., 68
Godman, James H., 203
Goerke, John D., 46, 52
Goetz, Phyllis, 61
Goodenow, John Milton, 76
Goodrich, Benjamin Franklin, 155, 163, 164
Gordon, Harry L., 201
Gore, Al, 7, 8, 12
Gorman, Robert N., 77
Gotshall, Daniel, 166
Gould, Jay, 17
Gradison, Willis D., 169
Graham, A. B., 121
Granger, Gideon, 117
Grant, Ulysses S. (Hiram Ulysses), 4, 8, 13, 16–17, 88, 119, 121, 197, 198
Grant, Jesse Root, 16
Grant, Noah, 150
Graves, Charles H., 204

Gray, O. C., 67
Gray, Theodore M., 69
Greeley, Horace, 17
Green, Charles C., 204
Green, Floyd F., 175
Green, William, 69
Greene, Nathaniel, 125
Greenlund, W. A., 201
Gresham, Walter Q., 19
Grey, Zane, 147
Griffith, Earl, 204
Griffith, Lynn B., 77
Grimke, Frederick, 76
Griswold, H. H., 67
Griswold, Stanley, 205
Grosvenor, Charles H., 67
Gruttadauria, Frank, 95
Guilbert, Walter D., 203
Guiteau, Charles J., 18

Hagan, Timothy, 64, 208
Haines, Job, 177
Hale, Frank B., 177
Hall, Dave, 177
Hall, Tony P., 209
Hamer, Thomas L., 67
Hamilton, Alexander, 1, 28
Hamilton, Arthur, 67
Hamilton, Frank B., 50
Hamilton, James K., 179
Hammell, George M., 46
Hammond, Charles, 31
Hancock, Winfield Scott, 8, 18
Hanhart, Eugene H., 91, 92
Hanna, Marcus Alonzo, 20, 21, 23, 44–47, 89, 123, 171, 206
Hanni, Don, 181
Harding, George Tryon, 23
Harding, Warren G., 8, 13, 22–24, 43, 48,49, 50, 88, 90, 142, 176, 198, 201, 205
Harmann, D. H., 166
Harmar, Josiah, 30, 167
Harmon, Judson, 23, 48–49, 90, 200
Harper, E. R., 165
Harris, Andrew L., 47–48, 49, 57, 200, 201
Harris, Bill, 69
Harris, Josiah A., 172
Harris, Leonard A., 169
Harris, Mary, 123
Harris, Richard H., 209
Harrison, Benjamin, 4, 7, 8, 13, 15, 19–20, 21, 148, 197, 198
Harrison, Richard A., 68
Harrison, William Henry, 7, 13, 15–16, 26,

28, 30, 33, 65, 87, 116, 140, 153–54, 157, 160–61, 197, 205
Hart, Alphonso, 201
Hart, William L., 77
Hartenstein, F. A., 181
Harter, George J., 165
Hatch, George, 169
Hawkins, Joseph S., 67
Hawkins, William, 68
Hayes, Rutherford B., 4, 8, 13, 17–18, 20, 39–42, 126, 135, 148, 153, 173, 197, 198, 200
Hayward, Elijah, 76
Hayward, Nelson, 172
Hearst, William Randolph, 21, 43
Heaton, Daniel and James, 156, 180
Heckewelder, John, 156
Hedge, James, 152
Hedges, Josiah, 154
Heffernan, Joseph F., 181
Heiner, John, 181
Heitmann, John H., 175
Helwig, John B., 44
Henderson, Charles P., 181
Herbert, John D., 94, 205
Herbert, Paul M., 77, 201
Herbert, Thomas J. (Cuyahoga County), 55–56, 77, 92, 200, 202
Herbert, Thomas M. (judge), 77
Herington, Leigh, 208
Herrick, Myron T., 46–47, 48, 90, 200
Herrick, R. R., 172
Herrold, Levi S., 165
Hickenlooper, Andrew, 201
Higgins, David, 67
Higley, Brainard S., 181
Hildebrant, C. Q., 204
Hillman, James, 141, 180
Hinkle, John N., 175
Hitchcock, Peter, 68, 76
Hoadley, George (Cleveland mayor), 172
Hoadly, George (governor), 42–43, 48, 200
Hobart, Garret A., 20
Hodge, Orlando J., 67
Hogan, Timothy S., 23, 202
Holiday, John C., 45
Hollingsworth, David, 202
Hollister, Nancy Putnam, 63, 199, 200, 201
Holmes, Robert E., 77
Hood, John, 42
Hooper, William, 204
Hoover, Herbert, 13, 23
Hopkins, Harry L., 53
Hopkins, William R., 171, 172

Hopple, E. J., 67
Horner, John S., 31
Horr, R. A., 68
Horstman, Albert A., 91, 92
Hosier, F. M., 177
Hotchkiss, Elisha, 169
Hough, Benjamin, 203
Hough, Benson W., 77
Householder, Larry, 67
Howard, C. J., 69
Howard, Dresden W. H., 128
Howard, John, 177
Howells, Anthony, 204
Howells, William Dean, 118
Hubbard, William B., 67
Hubbell, James R., 67
Hudson, David, 155
Huffman, James W., 206
Hughes, Charles Evans, 8, 23
Hull, William, 30, 31, 120, 132
Hummel, Edward J., 204
Humphrey, Hubert H., 10
Humphreyville, Samuel, 68
Hunt, Henry T., 169
Hunt, Samuel F., 68
Hunter, Hocking, 76
Hunter, Jack C., 181
Huntington, Samuel, 26, 76, 199
Husted, Jon, 67
Hutchins, John, 37
Hutchins, Thomas, 4, 136
Hutsinpiller, John C., 69
Hyatt, Joel, 95
Hysell, Nial R., 67

Iddings, Daniel W., 177
Ingalls, David S., 52, 53
Inmon, Billy, 62
Iredell, Seth, 165
Irvin, William W., 29, 67, 76

Jackson, Andrew, 2, 13, 15, 28, 29, 30, 31
Jackson, William T., 179
Jacob, Charles, 169
Jacobs, Jeff, 209
Jeffrey, Robert H., 175
Jenkins, Charles, 42
Jenkins, Hugh S., 202
Jenkins, Warren, 175
Jennings, David, 31
Jennings, William, 151
Jewett, Hugh J., 37
Johnson, Andrew, 16, 18, 36
Johnson, Bruce E., 201

Johnson, Frank, 172
Johnson, Fred H., 91, 92
Johnson, George W. C., 169
Johnson, Harvey H., 165
Johnson, Hiram, 23
Johnson, James C. (House speaker), 67
Johnson, James G. (judge), 77
Johnson, James, 173
Johnson, Stephen, 41
Johnson, Thomas L., 46, 47, 49, 63, 89, 90, 139, 171, 172
Johnston, William (Whig), 34
Johnson, William W. (judge), 76
Jones, Asa W., 201
Jones, Samuel M. ("Golden Rule"), 46, 89, 178, 179
Jones, Thomas A., 77
Jones, William W., 179
Juergens, John H. T., 46

Karb, George J., 175
Keith, John H., 67
Keller, Carl H., 179
Kelley, Alfred, 170
Kelsey, Lorenzo A., 172
Kemple, Charles W., 165
Kennedy, John F., 8, 9, 13
Kennedy, Robert P., 201
Kennedy, William J., 204
Kennon, William, 76
Kennon, Wilson S., 203
Kenny, Jonathan, 177
Kent, Arad, 165
Kent, Marvin, 150
Kenton, Simon, 119, 120, 132
Kerr, John, 173, 174
Kerr, Joseph, 206
Kerry, John F., 7, 12
Kessler, Harry W., 180
Kettering, Charles F., 116, 145, 176
Kieswetter, Emil, 203
Kilbourne, James, 46, 128
Kimball, Carl R., 67
Kimball, Francis D., 202
King, Charles A. (Toledo mayor), 179
King, Charles K. (Ohio Brass Co.), 152
King, Edward, 40, 67
King, Eli C., 174
King, Frank W., 69
King, Leiscester, 31, 33
King, Rufus, 27, 38, 81
Kinkade, Reynolds R., 77
Kinney, Charles, 203
Kinney, Lewis, 122

Kircher, John, 48, 49
Kirk, Robert C., 200
Kirker, Thomas, 25–26, 67, 68, 199
Klein, Carl, 167
Kline, Virgil P., 43, 44
Klotz, Solon T., 179
Knisely, Clarence H., 205
Knisely, John, 157
Knoop, John, 144
Kohler, Fred, 172
Kohler, Jacob A., 202
Kraus, William, 179
Krebs, Frank M., 177
Krupansky, Blanche, 77
Kryder, George E., 69
Kryzan, Frank X., 181
Kucinich, Dennis J., 62, 171, 172
Kurfess, Charles F., 67

Ladd, Charles G., 165
Lahm, John, 167
Lamneck, John H., 77
Lampson, Elbert L., 67, 68, 201
Lancione, A. G., 67
Landefeld, Kurt O., 61
Lane, Ebenezer, 76
Lane, Samuel A., 165
Langham, Elias, 67
Langston, John Mercer, 197, 198
Lantz, James A., 67
Lanzinger, Judith, 77
Lashutka, Greg, 175
Laub, William J., 165
Laughrey, John, 174
Lausche, Frank J., 53, 54–56, 57, 58, 59, 60, 61, 91–94, 172, 200, 206
Lavelle, Bill, 91
Lawhun, James H., 167
Lawrence, James, 202
Lawrence, Keith, 69
Lawthers, William J., 181
Lawton, Edwin G., 60
Laylin, Lewis C., 67, 204
Lazar, Nancy Brown, 59
Leach, Robert E., 77
Leatherlips, Chief, 126
LeBlond, Francis C., 67
Lee, John C., 201
Lehr, Henry S., 132
Leiter, Benjamin F., 67, 167
Leland, David J., 91
Leonard, Adna B., 43
Leonard, Paul R., 177, 201
Lesiak, Donald R., 60

Lester, J. G., 166
Levey, Barry, 208
Lewis, Charles H., 201
Lewis, Earl R., 69
Lewis, Samuel J. (Negro protection), 45
Lewis, Samuel (Free Soil), 33, 34, 35
Libbey, Edward D., 140, 178
Limbach, Arthur, 91
Lindbergh, Charles A., 47
Lindemuth, J. R., 177
Linxweiler, Jacob, 177
Little, John, 202
Locher, Cyrus, 55, 205
Locher, Ralph S., 77, 172
Logan, Mathew, 181
Lohrey, Louis W., 177
Long, William, 174
Longworth, Nicholas, 76
Looker, Othniel, 27, 68, 199
Loramie, Pierre, 154
Lowden, Frank O., 23
Lowes, Joseph E., 89
Lucas, Robert, 30–31, 68, 86, 150, 153, 178, 199
Ludlow, Abraham R., 42
Ludlow, Israel, 175
Luken, Charles J., 169
Luken, James T., 169
Luken, Thomas A., 169
Lukens, Donald E., 209
Lundy, Benjamin, 118
Lyman, Darius, 30
Lyon, William C., 201

Macklin, Gideon P., 44
Maddox, Lester G., 10
Mahan, John B., 31
Mahoney, Margaret A., 69
Major, Guy G., 89, 179
Malley, J. R., 48
Mallory, Mark, 169
Mann, David S., 169
Manning, John, 181
Manor, John, 179
Mansfield, Jared, 152
Marie Antoinette, Queen of France, 159
Markbreit, Leopold, 169
Marquis, William V., 201
Marsh, Archeleus D., 67
Marsh, George H., 158
Marshall, Carrington T., 77
Marshall, David, 62
Marshall, George S., 175
Martin, H. S., 68

Marshall, John, 52
Martin, John B., 48
Martin, William T., 174
Marx, Guido, 179
Mason, Harry C., 67
Mason, Hezekiah D., 179
Mason, Samuel, 31
Mason, Stevens T., 31, 178
Massie, Henry, 153
Massie, Nathaniel, 25, 26, 27, 30, 68, 115, 152
Massillon, Jean-Baptiste, 155
Masters, Irvine U., 172
Mather, Nation O., 69
Mathews, James, 165
Matthews, Stanley, 205
Matthias, Edward S., 77
Matthias, John M., 77
Maxwell, William, 197
McArthur, Duncan, 29–30, 40, 67, 68, 86, 132, 158, 199
McBain, Daniel, 179
McBurney, Andrew R., 201
McCarthy, Eugene J., 10
McClellan, George, 36
McClure, William, 177
McConica, Thomas H., 68
McCook, Daniel and John (the "Fighting McCooks"), 120, 143
McCook, George W., 40, 202
McCormick, Joseph, 202
McCulloch, Roscoe E., 205
McCulloch, William M., 67
McDonald, Allen C., 177
McDonald, Nancy, 30
McDowell, Abram I., 175
McElroy, Mark, 202
McFarland, William, 204
McGee, James, 176, 177
McGhee, Joseph, 202
McGough, Kent B., 91
McGovern, George S., 10
McGuffey, William Holmes, 117
McHugh, John, 180
McIlvaine, George W., 76
McKee, George, 181
McKelvey, George, 181
McKinley, Ida Saxton, 20, 44, 166
McKinley, William, 4, 8, 13, 20–21, 22, 23, 44–45, 46, 48, 155, 156, 166, 197, 198, 200
McKinney, William J., 177
McKinnon, William S., 67, 204
McKisson, Robert, 172
McLaughlin, Alexander, 173

McLaughlin, William, 68
McLean, John R. (Boss), 46, 89
McLean, John (judge), 76
McLin, Rhine, 177
McMillen, C. G., 177
McNeil, George W., 165
McSweeney, John, 54
Mead, Daniel, 176
Means, John, 138
Means, William, 169
Mechem, C. Stanley, 69
Medill, William, 35, 36, 67, 199, 200
Meeker, George W., 175
Meigs, Return Jonathan, Jr., 25, 26–27, 76, 161, 199, 206
Mellett, Don R., 166
Mellon, Andrew, 23
Merrill, Stanley W., 77
Mery, Fred J., 179
Meshel, Harry, 69, 91
Metzenbaum, Howard M., 62, 94, 95, 206
Meyer, S., 167
Middletown, Henry A., 77
Mifsud, Paul C., 62
Miller, I. B., 181
Miller, J. H., 69
Miller, John G. (Columbus mayor), 175
Miller, John L. (Dayton mayor), 177
Miller, Ray T., 172
Miller, Samuel R., 68
Miller, William H., 165
Millikin, John M., 204
Mills, Joshua, 172
Milroy, Charles, 179
Minshall, Thaddeus A., 76
Mitchel, John R., 64
Mondale, Walter F., 11
Monnett, Frank S., 132, 202
Monroe, James, 13, 18, 68
Montgomery, Betty D., 95, 199, 202, 203, 208, 209
Montgomery, Randall, 181
Moody, Tom, 175
Mooney, Granville W., 67
Moore, Edmond H., 181
Moore, Mark E., 181
Moore, Robert W., 169
Moore, William G., 181
Morgan, Daniel E., 172
Morgan, George W., 38
Morgan, John Hunt (Confederate general), 37, 123, 131, 143
Morgan, William D., 203
Morris, Thomas, 76, 206

218

Morrison, James D., 177
Morrow, Jeremiah, 28, 29, 199, 205
Morrow, John, 29
Morse, John F., 67
Morton, Daniel O., 179
Morton, Oliver P., 19
Mosby, John B., 169
Mosier, Harold G., 201
Mott, Richard, 179
Moyer, Thomas J., 77
Mueller, Jacob, 201
Murray, James, 202
Myers, George S., 77, 204
Myers, I. S., 165
Myers, James, 179, 200
Myers, John, 166

Nader, Ralph, 12
Nash, Frederick A., 165
Nash, George K., 45–46, 200, 202
Neal, James E., 67
Neal, Lawrence T., 20, 43, 44, 45
Neffiner, George M., 204
Neil, William, 36, 173
Neipp, Morton, 91, 93
Nelson, Daniel, 117
Ness, Eliot, 55, 171
Newcomb, Alexander H., 179
Newman, Jacob, 152
Newman, James W., 203
Newman, Oscar W., 77
Nichols, Hugh L., 77, 201
Nichols, Thomas H., 167
Nippert, Carl L., 201
Noe, Thomas, 64
Northrop, John W., 43
Noyes, Edward F., 39–40, 200
Nye, George D., 201

Oakley, Annie, 125
Oberlin, Jean Frederic, 139
Ocasek, Oliver, 69
O'Connor, Maureen, 77, 201
Odell, Jay, 39
O'Donnell, John, 165
O'Donnell, Terrence, 77
Oestreicher, Robert T., 175
Oglevee, John F., 203
O'Grady, Eugene (Pete), 91, 93
O'Hara, Joseph W., 76
Okey, John W., 76
Olds, Chauncey N., 202
Olds, Edson B., 68
Olds, George L., 181

Oliver, Robert, 65
Olmsted, Philo H., 174, 175
Onda, Andrew R., 53
O'Neil, William (1915), 164
O'Neill, C. William (1957), 57–58, 67, 77, 92, 93, 200, 202
O'Neill, John, 59, 68
O'Neill, Ralph W., 181
Osborn, Charles, 197
Osborn, Ralph, 203
Osborn, William M., 181
Otis, Charles A., 172
Otte, Andrew F., 48
Ottokee (Ottawa chief), 128
Owen, Selwyn N., 76
Owens, Donna, 179, 180, 199
Owens, James W., 68
Owens, Michael J., 140, 178

Packard, J. W. and W. D., 156
Paine, Edward, 137
Parrott, Edwin A., 67
Parsons, Richard C., 67
Parsons, Samuel H., 65
Patterson, Frank S., 145
Patterson, John H., 145, 176
Patterson, William (governor candidate), 52
Patterson, William R. (Dayton mayor), 177
Pattison, John M., 47, 48, 57, 90, 121, 200
Patton, Alexander, 175
Patton, Matthew, 177
Payne, Henry B., 35, 36, 205
Payne, Nathan P., 172
Pease, Calvin, 26, 76
Peck, John W., 77
Peck, William V., 76
Pelton, Frederick W., 172
Pendleton, George H., 39, 205
Pendleton, Nathaniel G., 36
Perk, Ralph J., 62, 171, 172
Perkins, Simon, 155, 163
Perot, Ross, 11, 12
Perry, Oliver H., 147, 148, 161
Peters, George S., 175
Petro, James M., 95, 202, 203, 208, 209
Pfeifer, Paul E., 59, 77, 208
Phelps, Edward M., 68
Phillips, Edward, 177
Phillips, Horatio, 177
Piatt, A. Sanders, 42
Pickrel, William G., 201
Pierce, Franklin, 13, 32
Pierce, Joseph, 177
Piero, William J., 167

Pike, Jarvis W., 173, 174
Pillars, Isaiah, 202
Pinney, E. Jay, 46
Pirincin, Joseph, 59, 60
Plusquelic, Don, 165
Poe, Ebenezer W., 203
Poling, Daniel A., 49
Pollock, John, 67
Pomerene, Atlee, 201, 206
Pomeroy, Samuel W., 143
Pond, Francis Bates, 202
Poorman, Charles E., 167
Poorman, Christian L., 203
Post, Frederick Christian, 156
Potter, Emory D., 68, 179
Potter, John W., 180
Powell, Thomas E., 43, 89
Price, James L., 76
Price, John G., 202
Pritchard, James, 68
Procter, William, 131
Puchta, George, 169
Pugh, George Ellis, 202, 205
Pulitzer, Joseph, 21
Purdy, Henry, 165
Purses, Sam, 167
Putnam, Rufus, 117, 129, 146, 159

Qualls, Roxanne, 169

Randall, Brewster, 68
Raney, John D., 181
Rankin, John, 119
Ranney, Rufus P., 36, 76
Rawson, Levi, 165
Ray, Roy, 165
Reams, Frazier, Jr., 59, 93
Redfern, Chris, 91
Reed, James, 160
Reed, Nathaniel C., 76
Reese, William W., 181
Regula, Mary, 166
Regula, Ralph, 166
Reid, David, 177
Reid, Whitelaw, 130
Reilly, Archer E., 203
Renner, Gordon, 67
Resnick, Alice Robie, 77
Reupert, Erwin J., 61
Rex, George, 68, 76, 167
Rex, Jacob, 166
Reynolds, Arlington G., 67
Rhodes, James A., 55, 57, 58–59, 61, 62, 63, 82, 93–94, 136, 174, 175, 200, 203, 208

Rhodes, John H., 44
Rhodes, Susie, 58
Rice, James A., 167
Rice, William, 181
Rich, Carl W., 169
Richards, John K., 202
Richards, Reese G., 68, 201
Richardson, John, 45, 46
Richardson, Joseph, 67
Richardson, William P., 202
Richley, J. Phillip, 181
Riffe, Vernal G., Jr., 67
Riley, James, 158
Rinehart, Dana G., 175, 209
Ritty, James, 145, 176
Robertson, James H., 167
Robertson, John L., 165
Robinson, James (Columbus mayor), 174
Robinson, James E. (judge), 77
Robinson, James S. (secretary of state), 203
Rockefeller, John D., 124, 170, 171
Rockwell, Frank W., 165
Rogers, George C., 209
Rogers, James E., 61
Romeis, Jacob, 179
Root, Amos I., 142
Root, Elihu, 22
Rose, Ben, 209
Rose, William G., 172
Rosemond, John H., 174
Ross, James, 136
Roulet, Lloyd E., 179, 180
Rouzer, W. H., 177
Ruehlmann, Eugene P., 169
Ruggles, Benjamin, 206
Russell, Addison P., 203
Russell, John, 203
Ruthenberg, C. E., 49
Ruvolo, James M., 91, 94
Ryan, Daniel J., 203
Rybolt, D. C., 165

Sanderson, Thomas W., 181
Savasten, Harry N., 181
Sawyer, Charles, 53, 54, 91, 201
Sawyer, Thomas, 165
Sawyer, William (House Speaker), 67
Sawyer, William T. (Akron mayor), 165
Saxbe, Charles R., 208
Saxbe, William B., 56, 60, 67, 93, 202, 206
Saxton, John, 165, 166
Sayler, Daniel, 167
Scheets, George, 179
Scheible, Charles F., 181

Schenck, William C., 138
Scherr, Roberta L., 61
Schmeling, Max, 171
Schmitz, John G., 10
Schneider, Louis J., Jr., 77
Schorr, Ed. D., 91
Schrantz, Henry A., 167
Schreiber, Cornell, 179
Schroy, Lee D., 165
Schumacher, Ferdinand, 42, 155, 163
Schuyler, Philip, 165
Schwab, Louis, 169
Scott, James F., 165
Scott, Jessup W., 178
Scott, Josiah, 76
Scott, Samuel, 39
Scott, Thomas, 26, 27, 76
Scott, Winfield, 16
Seasongood, Murray, 169
Seccombe, James, 167
Seely, Morris, 177
Seiberling, Charles, 164
Seiberling, Frank A., 155, 164
Seiberling, John F., 163, 164
Seitger, John E., 47
Seitz, John, 42, 43, 44
Sensenbrenner, M. E., 175
Senter, George B., 172
Seward, Louis D., 165
Seymour, Horatio, 16
Shannon, Wilson, 31, 32, 86, 199
Sharman, James S., 22
Sharp, Morris, 43
Sharts, Joseph W., 51, 52
Shauck, John A., 76
Sheets, John M., 202
Shepherd, Abraham, 67, 68
Sheppard, Oscar, 69
Sheridan, Philip, 149
Sherman, Charles R., 76
Sherman, John, 19, 21, 152, 205, 206
Sherman, William Tecumseh, 127
Sherwood, Isaac R., 203
Shields, R. S., 167
Shilling, Harry, 167
Shimp, John, 167
Shoemaker, Myrl H., 201
Shroyer, George W., 177
Sidney, Sir Philip, 154
Sigman, W. H., 177
Silver, Harry D., 67
Sinclair, Harry F., 24
Singletary, John C., Jr., 165
Sleeper, David L., 67

Sloane, John, 67
Slusser, Charles E., 165
Smith, Amor, Jr., 169
Smith, Edward, 34
Smith, George C. (attorney general candidate), 208
Smith, George J. (Senate Speaker), 68
Smith, Harvey C., 204
Smith, Helen Knipe, 209
Smith, Jess W., 24
Smith, John, 27, 206
Smith, W. H. (Akron mayor), 167
Smith, William H. (secretary of state), 203
Snelbaker, David T., 169
Snow, Z., 166
Snyder, Charles A., 177
Snyder, Jack A., 59
Sohngen, Robert M., 77
Somers, Frank, 177
Sorg, Paul, 49
Spagnola, William B., 181
Spalding, Rufus R., 67, 76
Sparks, C. Nelson, 165
Spear, William T., 76
Spencer, Henry E., 169
Spencer, Platt R., 117
Spiegel, Frederick S., 169
Spriggs, William, 76
Springer, Gerald N., 169
Springer, Jerry, 61
St. Clair, Arthur, 1, 25–27, 65, 118, 119, 127, 131, 143, 151, 156, 159, 167, 197
Stanbery, Harry, 202
Stanhope, Richard, 120
Stanton, Benjamin, 200
Stanton, Edwin M., 16, 136
Stanton, Frank W., 52
Starkweather, Samuel, 172
Starling, Lynn, 173
Starrett, Charles, 154
Start, Roy C., 179
Steele, John, 177
Steele, Samuel A., 181
Stephens, Thomas J., 169
Stephenson, Will P., 77
Stern, Leonard J., 77
Sterne, Bobbie, 169
Steuben, Wilhelm von, 136
Stevenson, Adlai E., 9
Stewart, Gideon T., 40, 42
Stewart, James Garfield, 55, 56, 57, 77, 169
Stickney, Benjamin F., 178
Stites, Benjamin, 131
Stoddard, Henry, 177

Stokes, Carl B., 171, 172, 199
Stolberg, Charles A., 167
Stone, A. P., 36, 204
Stone, Walter F., 76
Stout, Henry S., 177
Stratton, Evelyn L., 77
Stribling, Young, 171
Strickland, Ted, 63
Strike, Louis, 209
Struthers, John, 141
Sullivan, Samuel, 204
Sullivant, Lucas, 128, 173
Summers, Augustus N., 76
Sutliff, Milton, 76
Swain, Charles L., 67
Swan, Gustave, 76
Swan, Joseph R., 76
Swarts, Stanford M., 167
Swartz, Samuel J., 175
Sweeney, A. William, 77
Sweeney, Charles F., 204
Sweeney, Francis E., 77
Sweeney, John E., 204
Sweeney, Randall W., 209
Sweetenham, Maria, 60
Switzer, J. M., 177
Sykes, Barbara, 209
Symmes, Daniel, 68, 76
Symmes, John Cleves, 4, 65, 145, 175

Tafel, Gustav, 169
Taft, Alphonso, 21, 22, 63, 131, 168
Taft, Bob (Robert Alphonso II), 62, 63–64, 94, 95, 168, 200, 204, 208, 209
Taft, Charles P., 55, 168, 169
Taft, Kingsley A., 77, 206
Taft, Robert, Jr., 59, 60, 63, 93, 94, 168, 206
Taft, Robert A., 91, 168, 205
Taft, William Howard, 8, 13, 21–22, 23, 63, 90, 131, 148, 168, 198
Taney, Roger B., 36
Tappan, Benjamin, 28, 206
Tavares, Charleta, 209
Tayler, Robert W., 181
Taylor, Mark P., 169
Taylor, Robert W., 68, 203
Taylor, Samuel M., 203
Taylor, Zachary, 13, 16, 31
Tecumseh (Shawnee leader), 15, 121
Thacher, Addison Q., 179
Thomas, George T., 67
Thomas, James J., 175
Thomas, Nicholas W., 169
Thomas, Preston E., 53

Thomas, Wray, 175
Thompson, Carmi A. ("Honest Vic"), 51, 67, 204
Thompson, Eliza Jane, 134
Thompson, Harry C., 46
Thompson, Henry A., 41, 48
Thompson, Samuel C., 175
Thornton, Carroll, 181
Thurman, Allen G., 17, 39, 76, 206
Tiffin, Edward, 2, 25, 65, 67, 79, 154, 197, 199, 205
Tilden, Catherine Hitchcock, 198
Tilden, Myron H., 179
Tilden, Samuel J., 8, 17, 42, 198
Tillery, Dwight, 169
Timken, Henry, 155, 166
Tipps, Paul, 91
Tod, David, 32, 33, 36, 37, 88, 141, 180, 200
Tod, George, 26, 37, 76, 180
Todd, Edwin A., 205
Torrence, John F., 169
Townsend, Charles, 203
Tracy, Joseph T., 203
Tracy, Roger W., 203, 205
Tracy, Roger W., Jr., 94, 209
Traficant, James A., Jr., 181
Treadway, Francis W., 201
Trevitt, William, 203
Trimble, Allen, 28–29, 35, 36, 68, 134, 199
Trimble, James, 28
Trimble, William A., 28, 205
Truman, Harry S., 7, 9, 13
Truth, Sojourner, 163
Tucker, M. P., 165
Turnbull, A. R., 167
Turner, Edward C., 77, 202
Turner, Mike, 177
Turner, Robin T., 94
Turney, Joseph, 204
Tyler, John, 16, 32, 33

Uible, Frank R., 67
Ungaro, Patrick J., 181
Upson, William H., 76

Vail, Lewis, 166
Vallandigham, Clement L., 37, 88, 123
Vallandingham, Robert, 62
Vallely, James, 167
Van Buren, Martin, 13, 15, 16, 31
Van Cleve, John W., 177
Vance, David, 65
Vance, Elijah, 68

Vance, Joseph (governor), 2, 31, 32, 178, 199
Vance, Joseph C. (settler), 120
Vanderburgh, Henry, 65
Van Trump, P., 35
Van Vorhes, Nelson H., 67
Varnum, James M., 65
Verity, George M., 119
Vining, Samuel J., 67
Vinton, Samuel F., 34
Voinovich, George V., 62–63, 94, 95, 171, 172, 199, 200, 201, 206, 208
Vukovich, George, 181

Wade, Benjamin F., 117, 206
Waite, Henry M., 176
Waite, Morrison R., 81
Walcutt, Charles C., 175
Walcutt, Roscoe R., 69
Waldvogel, Edward N., 169
Wallace, George C., 10
Wallace, Jonathan H., 20
Wanamaker, R. M., 77
Ward, J. E. D., 177
Ward, John Quincy Adams, 120
Ward, William, 120
Warden, Robert B., 76
Warner, S. S., 204
Warnock, Fred J., 181
Warren, Moses, 156
Warwick, John G., 201
Washington, George, 1, 143
Watkins, Aaron S., 47, 52
Watkins, Richard D., 167
Watkins, William, 45
Watson, David K., 171, 202
Watters, Lorenzo D., 165
Wauseon (Ottawa), 128
Way, George B., 179
Wayne, Anthony, 118, 119, 125, 133, 140, 143, 151, 154, 159, 167, 178
Weaver, James B., 19
Wedsworth, Frederick, 165
Weil, G. Lloyd, 165
Welch, John, 76
Welker, Martin, 200
Weller, John B., 34
Wells, Bezaleel, 136, 155, 165
Wells, Thomas E., 181
Wells, William, 122
Welsh, Isaac, 204
Welsh, Leroy, 204
West, Charles, 51
West, William H., 41, 76, 202

Westlake, W. Ralston, 175
Wetzel, Lewis, 144
Weygandt, Carl V., 77
Wheeler, Samuel, 68
Wheelock, Daniel W., 177
White, Dennis L., 91, 95
White, Doug, 69
White, Edward D., 22
White, Elmer, 68
White, George, 51, 52–53, 200
White, Hugh L., 15
White, Michael R., 172
White, William, 76
Whitehill, Joseph, 204
Whitely, William N., 121
Whitlock, Brand, 178, 179
Whittemore, Frank E., 69
Wikoff, Allen T., 203
Wilder, Horace, 76
Wilkin, J. Foster, 76
Wilkin, Robert N., 77
Wilkins, Scott, 49
Willard, Archibald M., 127, 139
Willard, Jess, 178
Willey, John W., 172
Williams, James (auditor), 203
Williams, James M. (president pro tem),

69
Williams, Jay, 181
Williams, Marshall J., 76
Williams, Micajah T., 67
Williams, Roy H., 77
Willis, Frank B., 49, 50, 200, 205
Willkie, Wendell L., 53, 91
Willys, John, 178
Wilson, Joel W., 68
Wilson, Russell, 169
Wilson, Shannon, 31–32
Wilson, Woodrow, 3, 8, 13, 22, 23
Wilstach, Charles F., 169
Wise, Carl F., 167
Withrow, Mary Ellen, 205, 209
Witter, Herman R., 167
Witting, C. C. A., 166
Wolcott, Christopher, 202
Wood, Archibald, 144
Wood, Leonard, 23
Wood, Reuben, 34–35, 76, 199
Wood, Richard, 44
Wood, Thomas, 175
Woodhouse, William, 52
Woods, John, 203
Woods, William B., 67
Wooster, David, 160

Worley, Henry William, 175
Worthington, James T., 27
Worthington, Thomas, 1, 25, 26, 27, 134, 199, 205, 206
Wright, Calvin, 177
Wright, Craig, 77
Wright, Francis M., 203
Wright, John C., 76
Wright, Patricia H., 59
Wright, Smithson E., 175
Wright, Wilbur and Orville, 145, 176

Yager, John W., 180
Yates, Richard, 16
Yoder, Paul P., 69, 201
Young, George M., 177
Young, John, 141, 180
Young, Stephen M., 53, 54, 93, 206
Young, Thomas L., 40–41, 200, 201
Young, W. E., 165

Zaleski, Peter, 158
Zane, Ebenezer, 118, 127, 146, 147
Zane, Isaac, 139
Zeisberger, David, 156
Zimmerman, Charles B., 77